THE GEORGE GUND FOUNDATION
IMPRINT IN AFRICAN AMERICAN STUDIES

The George Gund Foundation has endowed
this imprint to advance understanding of
the history, culture, and current issues
of African Americans.

The publisher gratefully acknowledges the generous support of the African American Studies Endowment Fund of the University of California Press Foundation, which was established by a major gift from the George Gund Foundation.

The Black Revolution on Campus

The Black Revolution on Campus

Martha Biondi

UNIVERSITY OF CALIFORNIA PRESS
Berkeley · Los Angeles · London

University of California Press, one of the most distinguished university presses in the United States, enriches lives around the world by advancing scholarship in the humanities, social sciences, and natural sciences. Its activities are supported by the UC Press Foundation and by philanthropic contributions from individuals and institutions. For more information, visit www.ucpress.edu.

University of California Press
Berkeley and Los Angeles, California

University of California Press, Ltd.
London, England

© 2012 by Martha Biondi

Library of Congress Cataloging-in-Publication Data

Biondi, Martha.
  The Black revolution on campus / Martha Biondi.
    p. cm.
  Includes bibliographical references and index.
  ISBN 978-0-520-26922-4 (cloth : alk. paper)
    1. African American student movements.
2. African American college students—Political activity—History—20th century. 3. African Americans—Education (Higher)—History. I. Title.
  LC2781.B38 2012
  378.1'982996073—dc23   2012001211

Manufactured in the United States of America

20 19 18 17 16 15 14 13 12
10 9 8 7 6 5 4 3 2 1

In keeping with a commitment to support environmentally responsible and sustainable printing practices, UC Press has printed this book on Rolland Enviro100, a 100 percent postconsumer fiber paper that is FSC certified, deinked, processed chlorine-free, and manufactured with renewable biogas energy. It is acid-free and EcoLogo certified.

Contents

Illustrations

The Black Revolution on Campus

"Black young people feel they can change society," a minister in San Francisco observed in 1969. "Now that's very important." Black students want "revolutionary change in the basic institutions in this country," echoed a young politician. According to students in San Diego, "Racism runs rampant in the educational system, while America, in a pseudohumanitarian stance, proudly proclaims that it is the key to equal opportunity for all." "This is the hypocrisy," they declared, that "our generation must now destroy."[1] This widespread feeling of power and purpose among Black college students, combined with a sense of urgency and context of crisis, produced an extraordinary chapter in the modern Black freedom struggle. Black students organized protests on nearly two hundred college campuses across the United States in 1968 and 1969, and continued to a lesser extent into the early 1970s. This dramatic explosion of militant activism set in motion a period of conflict, crackdown, negotiation, and reform that profoundly transformed college life. At stake was the very mission of higher education. Who should be permitted entry into universities and colleges? What constituted merit? Who should be the future leaders of the nation in this postsegregation era, and how should this group be determined? What should be taught and who should teach it? Perhaps most controversially, should students have a hand in faculty selection or governance? Moreover, what would happen to public Black colleges in this era of integration? Would they close, as happened to primary and secondary schools after *Brown v. Board of Education?*

With remarkable organization and skill, this generation of Black students challenged fundamental tenets of university life. They insisted that public universities should reflect and serve the people of their communities; that private universities should rethink the mission of elite education; and that historically Black colleges should survive the era of integration and shift their mission to community-based Black empowerment. Most crucially, Black students demanded a role in the definition and production of scholarly knowledge. These students constituted the first critical mass of African Americans to attend historically white universities. Deeply inspired by the *Autobiography of Malcolm X* and the charismatic leadership of Stokely Carmichael, yet shaken by the murder of Martin Luther King Jr., they were engaged in a redefinition of the civil rights struggle at a time when cities were in flames, hundreds of thousands of young Americans were at war in southeast Asia, and political assassination was commonplace. These were "Malcolm's children," and they were inspired by the slain leader's denunciation of American hypocrisy and his call for Black control over Black institutions. In essence, student leaders were turning the slogan "Black Power" into a grassroots social movement. For many of the young people in this book, it was a revolutionary, hopeful time, a time they were determined to shape. Their energy and idealism inspired Latino, Asian American, and progressive white students to launch and intensify their own campus crusades. *The Black Revolution on Campus* shows how students moved to the forefront of the Black freedom struggle and transformed American higher education, sometimes in unexpected ways.[2]

There were two critical moments in the Black freedom struggle when students took the lead: 1960, with the lunch-counter sit-ins and creation of the Student Non-Violent Coordinating Committee (SNCC); and 1968, with the explosion of campus activism. Yet most studies of campus protest in the late 1960s focus on the white New Left's opposition to the war in Vietnam. Black students, so prevalent in representations of the sit-ins, freedom rides, and voter registration drives of the early 1960s, virtually disappear in histories of the late 1960s. While the white student movement of the late 1960s has garnered much more attention, Black student protest produced greater campus change. In contrast to conventional wisdom, the most prevalent demand in the hundreds of campus protests in 1968–1969 was African American inclusion, not opposition to the Vietnam War. The centrality of race to campus uprisings of the late 1960s has been forgotten.

The students often faced harsh reprisals, including criminal prosecution and, particularly at historically Black colleges, violent police invasions. While their confrontational tactics and Black Power rhetoric alienated many, their achievements were impressive. Their efforts pushed colleges to formalize and expand affirmative action policies and provide greater financial aid, leading to a sharp jump in Black college enrollment in the 1970s. In essence, these student activists forced a permanent change in American life, transforming overwhelmingly white campuses into multiracial learning environments. The academic community would never be the same. Reflecting the rights consciousness of the era, Black student activists asserted a right to attend college, especially public ones. Moreover, student protest stimulated demand for Black faculty and sparked the desegregation of college curricula with the creation of hundreds of African American studies departments and programs.

In the style of social movement history, the first five chapters tell the dramatic story of the Black student movement at selected campuses across the country. Every region in the country was part of this story, so every region has a chapter, including the South, with its historically Black colleges. The last three chapters explore the outcomes of the Black student movement, focusing in particular on the early formation of Black studies in traditional academic settings, as well as its influence on community-based initiatives. *The Black Revolution on Campus* combines activist history and intellectual history in order to show the critical linkage between the student movement and changes in university culture in the United States. It is imperative to understand the two in tandem. I chart the rise of an academic discipline that has widely influenced intellectual production in the United States even though, in the eyes of some of its founders, Black studies has failed to realize its radical potential. For many students and scholars, Black studies signified the inclusion of the histories and cultures of African-descended people, taught from the perspective of Black scholars, in the curriculum of higher education. But for many others, Black studies meant more than the creation of a new academic discipline. It "began with the utopian vision of a constant stream of young black people from the colleges and the universities helping ghetto dwellers to achieve Black Power and to transform their neighborhoods."[3]

The thousands of African American students in the United States who engaged in sit-ins, demonstrations, picket lines, and campus strikes in the late 1960s were not the first Black students on these campuses. Small numbers of African Americans had been attending majority white colleges and universities since the nineteenth century. Many of the Black students who began to enter predominantly white northern universities in the early 1960s were athletes, but this early group also included middle-class children of college-educated parents. A jump in Black enrollments came in 1967 and 1968, when new federal policy and the mounting effects of the civil rights movement modestly increased the numbers of Black undergraduates. These students tended to be from working-class, migrant families and were often the first in their families to attend college. They, in turn, engaged in direct action protest to demand greater numbers of Black students. From 1970 to 1974, college enrollments for African Americans shot up 56 percent, compared to a 15 percent increase for whites.[4] In many respects, the broader desegregation of institutions of higher education in the American North and West was won by the children of southern migrants and constitutes another legacy of the twentieth century's massive internal migration.

The Black student movement was part of the Black Power movement, whose rhetoric, political analysis, and tactics broke from the civil rights movement, but whose goals of Black representation and inclusion were shared with civil rights activists. Black Power emphasized the creation of Black-controlled institutions and racial solidarity and entailed a vigorous emphasis on culture—both in celebrating African American culture and in seeing it as a catalyst for political action and the forging of a new Black consciousness. Black Power advocates saw themselves as unmasking U.S. institutions—including liberal ones like universities—and exposing the whiteness disguised as universalism. They were seeking to change the terms of desegregation: it must not be color-blind, but pluralist. Their call for self-determination was not antithetical to the quest for full inclusion and equal rights, but a strategy for achieving it in a nation deeply shaped by a history of white supremacy. Crucially, Black Power encouraged African Americans to see themselves as African descendants, as part of a global majority rather than an American minority. This international consciousness intensified in the 1970s, giving rise to new Pan-African and Third World identities, initiatives, and solidarities.[5]

No single individual or organization directed the activist energies of Black college students in this era, but several leaders and groups played important roles. Founded by Huey Newton and Bobby Seale in 1966, the Black Panther Party initially focused on combating police brutality, but within a few years it was calling for revolution and an end to the war in Vietnam, as well as advocating free health clinics, Black studies in high school and college, and other programs to meet local needs. To a greater extent than has been appreciated, students admired, followed, and sometimes joined the Black Panther Party.[6] For its part, faced with the escalating deindustrialization of Oakland, the Black Panther Party wanted to recruit from the "lumpenproletariat," a Marxist term describing a social stratum outside the formal economy: hustlers, gang members, and ex-convicts. Nevertheless, the party was surprisingly successful in appealing to high school and college students, and as a result, Panther chapters in Oakland, New York, Los Angeles, and Chicago included student leaders. As Black students sought to build new institutions on college campuses, they were deeply inspired by the Panthers' success in creating and running their own programs. Indeed, a nationwide independent Black schooling movement would arise in the 1970s from this ethos of countercultural self-reliance. SNCC was a second critically important source of influence on Black students nationwide. By the late 1960s, many veteran SNCC organizers had shifted their attention away from the rural south toward college campuses. The most famous SNCC leader who inspired and shaped the nationwide Black student movement was the former Howard University student Stokely Carmichael, who by 1968 had become a seasoned organizer and charismatic orator, crisscrossing the country urging Black college students to fight for greater recognition and power.[7] But most important, leadership in the Black student movement was indigenous and local: students formed their own campus organizations and led their own struggles, even as they traveled to other campuses and learned from each other.

A major victory for the students, the achievement of African American studies quickly became its own site of struggle with a new group of protagonists, mainly professors who held competing views of how to build Black studies. The seemingly arcane question of whether Black studies should take the form of a program, college, department, or center became deeply enmeshed in the political struggle for self-determination and the academic struggle for stature and legitimacy. Even after commitments to create Black studies had been won, another round of conflict often ensued over precisely what form it would take and who would be calling the shots. Similarly, an intellectual battle over the character of Black studies developed at the same time. Pressure to show a rationale for Black studies led many scholars to argue for the advantages of and need for a "Black perspective" in teaching and research. While some observers feared lockstep thinking in such an approach, the defense of a Black perspective in academe relatively quickly gave way to a critical search for various ways to understand the multivalent Black experience. Three factors shaped the turbulent emergence of Black studies as a site for innovative and influential scholarship: ideological disputes over what should serve as the intellectual basis for Black studies, which had the effect of establishing multiple streams of intellectual thought within the field; the desire of some scholars to pursue relatively conventional academic careers, which led them into an ambivalent, even contentious relationship with Black studies; and the influence within Black studies of Marxist and feminist critiques of cultural nationalist approaches to the study of the Black experience. Indeed, in contrast to what many might expect, Afrocentricism, with its focus on reclaiming precolonial African achievements, cultures, and value systems, was not the predominant philosophical approach as African American studies entered higher education in the United States.

The first chapter examines the experiences and political outlooks of Black college students in the mid- to late 1960s, with an eye toward capturing their fast-growing impatience with "token integration" and their attraction to a new politics of racial pride and assertion. The students' Black nationalism was controversial, in both Black and white communities. In addition to setting up the shift in Black student consciousness that helped pave the way for new forms of student protest, I identify the beginnings of the Black student movement at historically Black colleges and universities. Student activists met with lethal violence in Orangeburg, South Carolina, and experienced a major police assault on the campus of Texas Southern University in Houston, but they won an important victory at Howard University. By highlighting the activism at historically Black colleges in the opening chapter, I unsettle the usual geography of vanguard student radicalism, which emphasizes the New Left at Berkeley, Ann Arbor, and Columbia. In contrast to their conservative image, Black colleges were important incubators of leadership in the Black student movement throughout the entire decade of the 1960s.

Chapters 2 through 5 narrate student struggles in different regions of the country in the late 1960s and into the early 1970s. The chapters are roughly chronological, but it is crucial to understand that campus upheavals (especially in 1968 and 1969) were happening at virtually the same time across the nation. Chapter 2 provides a close analysis of what is widely understood to be the launching pad of the Black studies movement. Vowing to shut the campus down until their demands were met, the Black Student Union at San Francisco State College launched a five-month strike that convulsed the Bay Area, drew national media attention, and put Governor Ronald Reagan, the striking students, the faculty, college president S.I. Hayakawa, and Black community leaders on a collision course. Deeply influenced by the Panthers, the students adopted militant tactics. The state's conservative leadership, however, was ready for a confrontation, and liberal San Francisco became, ironically, the setting for aggressive police tactics—officers made nearly eight hundred arrests and more or less occupied the campus for months. Remarkably, no historian has written about this enormously significant story.[8]

The third chapter showcases two diverse institutions in the Chicago area where Black student organizing produced sweeping campus reforms and laid the basis for a broader modernization of the university and for Black empowerment in the city of Chicago. In the early morning hours of May 4, 1968, one month after the assassination of Martin Luther King Jr., about one hundred Black students at Northwestern University in Evanston, Illinois, took over the campus building housing the bursar's office. Occurring a few days after New York City police had arrested seven hundred students in a violent confrontation to end a protest at Columbia University, the Northwestern protest was engulfed from the start by the fear of a police raid. It was ultimately hailed as a success, both for its peaceful resolution and a settlement granting several of the students' demands. In many respects, Northwestern typified Black experiences at elite, private historically white universities. There was an emerging liberalism, and many openings for change, side by side with the legacy of a racially exclusionary cultural and institutional history. But in Evanston, as elsewhere, the students forcefully and creatively asserted themselves and offered solutions that would transform many aspects of campus life in the 1970s. They invited the famed historian Lerone Bennett and legendary Caribbean scholar and activist C.L.R. James to Northwestern, but it took several years to establish a Black studies program, a lag between activism and meaningful curricular reform that was common at elite universities.

A major location of the Black student–Black studies movements was urban public colleges and universities, both two- and four-year institutions. Located on the predominantly Black west side of Chicago, Crane Junior College had a largely white faculty, curriculum, and administrators. Black student activists at Crane began by organizing the

Negro History Club, but their struggle grew rapidly, aiming to change the mission and character of the whole campus. They succeeded in changing the college's name to Malcolm X and gaining an African American as college president—the first in the city—but they were unsuccessful in their particular candidate, an African American woman. The movement at Malcolm X College involved the Black Panther Party and a group of activists who would go on to play key roles in political, labor, and civil rights struggles in Chicago. In the students' successful effort to redefine the mission of a community college, Malcolm X typifies struggles in Oakland, New York City, Detroit, San Francisco, Los Angeles, and other large American cities.

Chapter 4 looks at Black student activism at City College and Brooklyn College, elite four-year institutions in New York City. On the eve of the movement, these two colleges—taxpayer financed in the city with the largest Black population in the United States—were overwhelmingly white: Brooklyn College at 96 percent white in 1968, and City at 91 percent. A two-week occupation of City College in Harlem precipitated a political crisis in the city and ushered in a major shift in public policy, but strikingly it has garnered little attention from historians. Similarly, the struggle at Brooklyn College has been virtually forgotten, even though it was crucial in reshaping the admissions policy, the university's relationship to communities of color, and the curriculum. The radical transformation of admissions requirements at the entire City University of New York produced the biggest structural shift in opportunity during the long civil-rights era. This generation of students remade public higher education in New York City, although at Brooklyn College they fell victim to police infiltration and trumped-up criminal charges. In addition to the Black Panther Party, Black student unions were targets of the FBI's Counterintelligence Program, known as COINTELPRO.

Chapter 5 makes clear that the Black student–Black studies movements did not happen only on white campuses. The quest for self-determination inspired Black students to fight to strengthen and preserve historically Black colleges. Many students at historically Black colleges and universities had participated in the southern civil rights movement, but after 1967 they increasingly turned their activist energies to the campuses, demanding Black studies departments, student inclusion in governance, more resources, and the end of compulsory ROTC and in loco parentis. They sought to end the white control associated with the funding, mission, and governance of private Black colleges; and in the public sector their quest was nothing less than the preservation of Black colleges. In this era of integration, "saving Black colleges" was a largely unheralded but critically important struggle. By the early 1970s, unrest was rocking Black colleges throughout the South. Students at Black colleges were more likely to encounter violence and campus invasion from law enforcement during their protests than were Black students at other schools. I explore conflicts that led to police occupations and sometimes arrests and shootings—such as those at Southern University in Baton Rouge—which have been more or less excluded from scholarship on the era and from public memorializing of deaths associated with the civil rights movement. At Southern University in November 1972, law enforcement officers fired at fleeing students, killing two young men. In the long term the violence at historically Black colleges and universities led to a quelling of student activism. Together with assassinations and COINTELPRO, this wave of campus violence contributed to a decline in such open and adversarial Black resistance.

Chapter 6 moves away from the focus on student activism to an examination of the political controversies swirling around the early Black studies movement. The establishment of hundreds of Black studies programs in colleges and universities across the country was a major achievement of the Black student movement, but their birth was marked by contention. I explore various struggles and debates that interrogate the meaning of Black studies; a point of contention arose around the idea that Black studies advocated a "Black perspective," and some expressed concern that this would give rise to an excessively political, narrowly nationalist, anti-intellectual thrust. In contrast, as I argue, most articulations of a Black perspective strove to be international, critical, and expansive.

The battle around the shape of the new Black studies unit at Harvard illustrates how political anxieties could derail an academic unit. A student proposal for a department prevailed over an administration and faculty proposal for a program, leading to years of struggle over the form of Afro-American studies at Harvard, but the department ultimately survived. I conclude with a brief look at a pivotal Ford Foundation conference in Aspen, Colorado, in which this debate over the shape of Black studies came to a head and reinforced a shift in Ford's funding strategy toward promoting diversity in American higher education. In this era of Black self-determination, funding from white philanthropic sources became extremely controversial. Black nationalists sometimes rejected it but, more typically, sought to gain greater control over its use.

Chapter 7 explores how a sizeable segment of scholars and activists in the early Black studies movement imagined Black studies as having a broader social impact, beyond academic life. They viewed the widespread dissemination of Black history written and taught by Black people as a means of instilling pride among African Americans and of furthering the process of Black liberation. I examine several nonacademic initiatives that were deeply related to the Black student–Black studies movements, including a remarkable series of televised Black history lectures, *Black Heritage: A History of Afro-Americans*. Even with its controversial late-night/early-morning screen times, it brought prominent Black scholars like John Henrik Clarke, Vincent Harding, Robert Browne, and St. Clair Drake into American living rooms. The Institute of the Black World, a group of radical scholar-activists in Atlanta, succeeded to some degree in modeling a movement-inspired public intellectualism; but shorn of regular funds, it struggled to fully implement its ambitious vision. The Nairobi Schools in East Palo Alto, California, an example of an independent Black institution, were the locus of an impressive grassroots project that offered instruction from preschool through junior college. Reflecting the influence of the Black Panthers as well as a utopian Pan-Africanism, independent Black institutions saw themselves as building new value systems in Black communities and countering the destructive, profit-seeking ethos of racist America. Relatedly, the Student Organization for Black Unity, formed by radical students from various campus struggles, set up a base in North Carolina and, ultimately, adopted the view that Black people in diaspora should acquire skills useful for building strong postcolonial nations in Africa. Each of these examples illustrates the diverse legacies of Black Power–era student activism, beyond the campus and beyond the creation of African American studies and affirmative action.

In the final chapter, I analyze debates and tensions in the definition of the discipline of African American studies. Should it create and emphasize a single methodology, or does its strength lie in the use of multiple methodologies? Similarly, should the Black studies movement aim for standardized curricula across the nation, or is innovation and difference a hallmark of academic inquiry in the United States? I conclude with attention to scholarly innovations that have helped advance African American studies, focusing on the effort to encompass the African diaspora in Black studies and the rise of Black women's studies. The Black

student and early Black studies movements were part of a broader con-
stellation of social, cultural, and political developments that eventually
gave rise to Black feminism. Whether known as Africana womanism or
Black women's studies, systematic attention to gender and women
would significantly shape scholarship and pedagogy in African American studies. But this development would have been hard to predict
in 1968, and took years of struggle against patriarchal attitudes and a
male-dominated opportunity structure.

In the 1970s, in particular, Black women scholars often found themselves in Black studies units indifferent or hostile to feminist perspectives. But Black feminist scholarship, particularly the concept of inter-
sectionality, would come to exert considerable influence in the discipline
and in the humanities and social sciences more generally.

In contrast to conventional wisdom, which posits that Black studies
was born as a United States–centered, nation-bound enterprise that, only
in more recent years, has discovered the concepts of globalism and diaspora, I argue that the early Black studies movement was internationalist
and always deeply skeptical of the mythology of American exceptionalism. Many Black studies programs and departments struggled from the
beginning—with varying degrees of success—to encompass Africa and
the diaspora in their curricula, nomenclature, personnel, and programming. Not a new departure, the rise of African diaspora studies reflects
a deeply rooted tradition and aspiration.

Finally, why label a few years of campus unrest a "revolution"? Students neither aimed for nor achieved a revolution in the traditional
sense of seizing state power or precipitating a transformation of social
relations. Moreover, with their demands they sought inclusion and were
motivated by a desire to improve the collegiate experience. As one
scholar-activist noted about open admissions: "This was certainly a
militant demand though not revolutionary, since at its core it simply
called for a widening of American democracy, not the institution of a
totally new educational or social order." But, he acknowledged, "by
widening educational democracy, Black studies could pave the way for
the introduction of new and revolutionary ideas into the curriculum,
and this was correctly perceived as a threat by conservative administrators and faculty."[9] The title of this book hopes to capture the sweeping
nature of many of their demands. Indeed, at San Francisco State College, students demanded that all Black applicants be admitted. Moreover,
the audacity of the children of sharecroppers and factory workers in
asserting a right to shape these institutions was in a sense revolutionary.

The Black Revolution illuminates the sense of possibility and expectation among a large cohort of ambitious, dedicated, politically attuned African American students in the late 1960s—a significant demographic who were attending college in unprecedented numbers. *Revolution* reflects the students' sense of their own agency, their sense of their ability to affect the course of history, and the sense among many students that 1968 was indeed a revolutionary moment—even if this turned out to be false. Finally, the title conveys the sense of rapid, traumatic upheaval across society, especially in cities, which had been shaken by violent unrest since 1964. Even the usually celebrity-focused, middle-class *Ebony* magazine titled a special 1969 issue "The Black Revolution."

CHAPTER I

Moving toward Blackness

The Rise of Black Power on Campus

The explosion of Black student activism in 1968 took many observers by surprise. Earlier in the decade, the violence unleashed by whites on nonviolent protesters in the South riveted a national television audience. Now, television news gave daily coverage to African American college students assertively seeking social change, but the images were often unsettling: violent clashes between Black students and the police in San Francisco; militant Black students disrupting classes in Madison; Black students occupying the computer center in Santa Barbara, the president's office at Roosevelt University in Chicago, and the entire south campus of City College in Harlem. This phase of the Black student movement was markedly different from the sit-ins of the early 1960s, which had featured courteous young men and women in dresses and suits and ties. Now students hurled a defiant vocabulary, wore African-inspired or countercultural clothing, and otherwise pushed the line between Black bourgeois ideals and revolutionary aesthetics. They wanted both upward mobility and an affirmation of African American culture and history, inclusion as well as social justice. The students wanted to expand Black access to higher education and make white colleges more responsive to the needs of a diverse student body, but their confrontational tactics and rhetoric dominated news coverage and shaped popular reception and understanding of their struggles.

Where did the new style come from, and how did Black students all over the country, without formal organizational links, express such similar grievances and demands? Why did the call for Black Power become increasingly popular among Black youth in the late 1960s? And why were students at historically Black colleges also up in arms? In fact, this phase of the Black student movement actually began on Black college campuses. Why? The explosion of activism seemed abrupt to some, and many media accounts linked it to the anger and sorrow over the assassination of civil rights leader Dr. Martin Luther King Jr. But the search for a new approach to racial reform had begun to take shape in the early 1960s, and accelerated after 1966, when most Black student organizations were formed. The idea of Black Power spread nationally as a challenge to nonviolence and integration and as urban insurrection became an annual summer event. By 1969 these developments culminated in what many observers were calling "a Black revolution," and universities were on the front lines.

The burgeoning racial liberalism of the early post–World War II years had given rise to an expectation that dismantling formal racial barriers would dramatically reduce racism among whites and usher in rapid and meaningful social change. Even the discerning W.E.B. Du Bois estimated shortly after the *Brown v. Board of Education* decision that it would take about five years to implement integration, and this was likely a generous amount of time, in his view, for states to obey a federal mandate.[1] For a variety of reasons, education emerged as the terrain for this national saga of racial transformation. The GI Bill's expansion of higher education, the long-standing emphasis within the Black community on higher education, and the Supreme Court victories against professional and primary school segregation reinforced the belief that education was the key to both Black progress and the creation of a new nation. At the same time, the combination of cold war anxieties, a rapidly expanding social science literature on "race relations" and the legal liberalism of the 1950s produced a narrative of the underprivileged Negro American's gradual and steady assimilation into the modern (white) nation. As one student said of the relentless pressure to conform to white cultural norms: "We didn't feel we had a choice; the implication was plain that we were being let into the university on the condition that we become white men with dark skins."[2] According to Edgar W. Beckham, a 1958 graduate of Wesleyan University in Middletown, Connecticut, "We believed in what you might call automatic assimilation. We thought the black students would mysteriously merge into the white landscape." This worked because "there were so few of us, and Stokely hadn't shouted 'Black Power' yet."[3] This feeling was widespread. "From 1948, when George McLaurin became the first black student enrolled at the University of Oklahoma, until the late 1960s," writes pioneering Oklahoma professor George Henderson, "black students at the University wished year after year that goodness would prevail and they would be treated as people of equal worth to whites. But it seldom happened."[4]

Southern students hoped that traveling North to college would provide a respite from insult and indignity. The idea that the North and West were more racially liberal and tolerant than the South was deeply ingrained in the national self-image and in many individual expectations. Many Black southerners expected to encounter a liberal racial climate in the North, but found instead a jarring disconnect between image and reality. Frank Monteith came to Northwestern University in Evanston, Illinois, in the late 1950s from South Carolina, where his aunt Modjeska Simkins was a nationally known leader of the state NAACP. From the airport, he shared a taxi to campus with a white freshman from Iowa. She pestered him relentlessly, asking, among other things: "Can I touch your hair?" Monteith worked with the Evanston NAACP to try to remove the racial identification question from the Northwestern application form, a question that was used by many colleges in the pre-affirmative-action era to enforce a limit on minority student admissions. The university pressured Monteith to join the band so that its lone Black musician would have a roommate on the road. "It was ugly traveling with the band," he recalls. In a sign of how widespread Jim Crow exclusions were across the Midwest, the two young men had to stay in private homes because no hotel across Indiana, Illinois, and Ohio would admit them. Madelyn Coar graduated from Northwestern in the early 1960s. She hailed from a neighborhood in Birmingham, Alabama, called "Dynamite Hill" because of the string of Klan bombings of Black homes there. "I chose a Northern school," she says, "so there would be no racism." But Coar said she would not have made it through college were it not for an African American family in Evanston who became a second family to dozens of Black students at Northwestern in the 1950s and 1960s. Another student, Sandra Malone, says she came "not expecting racism." But within minutes of her arrival freshman year, her white roommate requested a transfer.[5] A Wellesley freshman from St. Louis echoes these memories, recalling her arrival on campus in 1965: "This was Massachusetts, the home of the abolitionists. I thought I was escaping segregation." But she soon found herself embroiled in protest against the conservative culture at Wellesley.[6]

The turmoil of the 1960s profoundly altered the liberal and colonialist conception of race and racism that had been forged in cold war America. Notwithstanding the strength of conservative resistance to racial reform in the United States, the civil rights struggle brought the limits of American racial liberalism to the fore, sparking a crisis that pushed many activists to consider more radical strategies and philosophies. Year after year of beatings, shootings, and murders of civil rights workers made growing numbers of African Americans question the morality of the nation and the veracity of its claims to liberal democracy. At the same time, rising unemployment, police violence, and segregation in the North made many Black Americans lose faith in the call for integration and in the sincerity of northern white allies, many of whom continued to counsel patience and gradualism. In 1963 Malcolm X offered a critique of integration: "It took the United States Army to get one Negro into the University of Mississippi; it took troops to get a few Negroes in the white schools at Little Rock and another dozen places in the South. It has been nine years since the Supreme Court decision outlawing segregated schools, yet less than ten per cent of the Negro students in the South are in integrated schools. That isn't integration, that's tokenism!"[7]

This critique of token integration would spread rapidly among late 1960s college students who began to pay close attention to numbers and the actual scale of integration. Malcolm X convinced them of the failure of old modes of change, and they would rise up en masse to demand new ones. "Color blindness has led to blacks coming out on the short end of the academic stick," two campus observers wrote. Universities are "seas of whiteness," and student activism is forcing this out in the open. "What the universities have failed to realize in almost every case," they declared, "is that the American educational experience is a white experience, an experience based on white history, white tradition, white culture, white customs, and white thinking, an education designed primarily to produce a culturally sophisticated, middle class, white American."[8]

Many collegiate activists of the late 1960s were first exposed to Black studies as high school students, especially in large cities like New York, Detroit, Philadelphia, Chicago, and Oakland, where Black nationalist ideas were already in wide circulation and where large-scale school boycotts and demonstrations had begun to move beyond the call for integration and now called for community control of schools, Black history in the curriculum, and more Black teachers. In 1968 in New

York, for one example, community control advocates ran a demonstration district in the Ocean Hill–Brownsville section of Brooklyn and built on a rich local history of alternative education. Keith Baird was the director of its Afro-American and Latin American studies programs. A veteran public school teacher, son of a Garveyite and longtime Black nationalist, Baird taught in the church-based "freedom schools" during the 1964 New York City school boycott. And from 1965 to 1968, he taught alongside legendary Harlem historian John Henrik Clarke in a youth heritage program in Harlem. Baird taught lessons on freedom fighters Denmark Vesey and Sojourner Truth, and institution-builders Carter G. Woodson and Mary McLeod Bethune, as well as one comparing Caribbean calypso, U.S. jazz, and African music. He taught about precolonial African societies and exposed Harlem youth to the writings of W. E. B. Du Bois, J. A. Rogers, Melville Herskovits, and Basil Davidson.[9] These experiences, as well as the introduction of Black history courses in many urban high schools in these years, demonstrated to young people that Black studies programs were imaginable and possible. A handful of colleges in the country offered Black history or literature courses, but the overwhelming majority did not, and none offered a degree-granting program in African American studies.

Notwithstanding gradual gains in mid-decade, Black student enrollment in public or private white universities in the late 1960s was still small. A nationwide survey of major state universities found that "black Americans are grossly underrepresented in higher education," but noted that many state universities in the North and West, but not the South, had launched special admissions programs. In 1969, white universities in the South had an average Black enrollment of 1.76 percent; in the East, the figure was 1.84 percent, in the Midwest it was 2.98 percent, and in the West it was 1.34 percent—a strikingly homogeneous national portrait.[10]

Many students who entered college in the mid-1960s narrate stories of social awakening, budding activism, and transformed racial consciousness. Initially, according to a member of the class of 1969 at Wesleyan, "they wanted us to pretend we were just like them." But then "we began to see that the whites weren't supermen. They were just ordinary cats with ordinary hang-ups. That's when we stopped assimilating." Like many colleges, Wesleyan had dispersed Black students in the dormitories. The "official policy was to keep us apart," one student remembers. "But it didn't take us long to find each other." In contrast, at Wellesley, the six African American students who arrived in 1965 were given separate rooms away from white students: "You began to realize that racism was alive and well," one of the students recalls. According to Francille Rusan Wilson, "We were these nice little Southern girls, who had probably even brought white gloves with us. This was a period where, literally, you started off as a colored girl and ended up four years later a black woman."[11]

Ramona Tascoe entered San Francisco State College in 1967 after twelve years of Catholic school. Born in Baton Rouge, she moved with her family to San Francisco in the early 1950s because her father had gotten a job at the San Francisco Bay Naval Shipyard. Despite the California migration, her cultural roots were firmly in Louisiana. Her father was "a dark-skinned Creole," her was mother was light skinned, and the children were "not raised to be black." Her parents taught her not to speak about race and to "assimilate." She remembers that they were "not permitted to acknowledge our ethnicity, except in the pejorative." Her parents instructed her to "identify white folks who set the standard, and then do all you can to mold yourself in that model." Entering college, she felt like "a dry sponge, ready to absorb all that was missing," and took a Black studies course at the student-run Experimental College, "something I had never been exposed to." A freshman with "long, straightened hair," she "converted to an Afro quickly" and began to question the whole process of assimilation. Tascoe became a leader in the Black Student Union.[12]

Wesley Profit entered Harvard in 1965 right after the Watts rebellion in Los Angeles, his hometown. The son of a Southern University graduate, Profit had attended boarding school and considered himself fairly sheltered. Part of a cohort of forty Black students, the largest group by far to enter Harvard at the same time, Profit says, they "were made to feel insecure in a thousand different ways. . . . We were an experiment of sorts, and a lot of us had experiences that were discomforting and a little bit alienating." Few whites believed they were actually Harvard students. Clerks in campus and town stores would not accept their checks or charges, questioning their affiliation with the school. One night Profit and a group of fellow Black male students were departing a Radcliffe dormitory at the close of visiting hours, and were asked for identification by a Harvard security officer. They were reaching for their wallets, but upon noticing that a group of white males had not been similarly stopped, one student instructed the others: "Put your cards away!" This slightly older Army veteran announced, "I fought for this country and marched at the Tomb of the Unknown Soldier, and I am not going to be treated this way and submit to a discriminatory request." And in a story that shows both the anxiety triggered by the presence of Black students, and the burden placed upon them to perform integration, a Harvard dean called a group of Black students into his office to object that they had been sitting together so often in the cafeteria and urge them to sit with white students. Profit recalls their effort to educate him, explaining that "the kids from Phillips Andover are all sitting together but you don't see it. You notice us."[13]

The small number of Black students at Columbia University in New York in 1966 and 1967 encountered daily acts of suspicion regarding their status as students. "From day one our life on campus was political protest," says Leon Denmark. Every time he entered a building, he was asked for identification. Angered at this selective treatment, he and a classmate confronted the guard at Ferris Booth Hall: "We're gonna stand here for half an hour and see if you ask every white student for an ID." But the harassment faced by Black students was even more explicit. "People actually called us nigger on campus," Denmark recalls, and says that Black students were "naturally politicized by these things." Columbia student Al Dempsey, who was raised in the South and became a judge in Georgia, insists that "the worst racism I have seen is here at Morningside Heights." Coming together as Black students became a critical means of coping in a hostile environment. Denmark describes how important it was to them to form a chapter of the Black fraternity Omega Psi Phi, and to form study groups where they taught themselves the Black history absent in the curriculum.[14]

Increasingly, Black students had to contend with the charge of separatism—that they were undermining progress toward integration, that they were afraid of competing with whites, or that they were practicing reverse racism and unfairly rejecting association with all whites. Students had a range of reactions to this charge, depending upon their social and political perspective. But those who did reject the assumptions underlying integration did not reject equal access to the rights and resources of the society. Rather, most students wanted to redefine integration—as multiculturalism rather than assimilation into white culture. They roundly rejected the notion that they were in retreat. As one observer put it: "They were not running away from whites, but moving toward Blackness."[15] To be sure, some students vigorously critiqued integration as part of a larger critique of the ills of white American society. In a 1969 essay, "Separatism and Black Consciousness," a Black female student wrote, "The perversion of integration is that Black people are expected to give up a strong, healthy lifestyle, for one that is sick, dying and rotten. . . . What can living with white people teach me that is good?" she asked. Finding that "the white man's days of domination are numbered," she saw no point in trying to integrate. "I am an Afroamerican and I want to maintain my ethnicity and humanism. I never want to be an All-American."[16]

In 1969 a researcher visited fifty colleges to assess Black student views, and found idealistic expectations of campus life. "Large numbers of Black students believed that all they had to do was present themselves and they would be accepted." But their disappointment was giving rise to a determination to assert greater control over their education. He reported a "generalized suspicion and distrust of educational authority figures" and a strong desire for student participation in campus decision-making. They were "tired of having to prove their humanity again and again to every white they met" and of "living in a fishbowl." They resented the pressure to assimilate into the white majority on white terms. According to this researcher, the students' "whole conception of integration changed." It should be a two-way process.[17]

A Yale sophomore reinforced this rejection of racial ambassadorship. "I came here to be a student, not to educate whites about blacks. I'm tired of being an unpaid, untenured professor teaching these guys the elementals of humanity."[18] A Wellesley student describes the college's conception of integration in the mid-1960s: "It was very much a one way street, in that there was no recognition of the African American experience. This was our opportunity to become like them, not for Wellesley to become more like us or learn from us. That kind of idea just didn't exist."[19] Moreover, students in this era were increasingly coming to believe that it was white racism, not a deficiency in skills or preparedness among African Americans, that explained racial inequality in society. This new perspective moved Black students to embrace a Black identity, actively reframe Blackness in a positive fashion, push back against white conceits, and organize new, Black-identified social, cultural, and political spaces on campuses, with Black student unions being the most prominent and well-known example. "They never let you forget you were black," a Berkeley student observed in 1967, so "we decided to remember we were black."[20]

In a study of Black student outlooks, political scientist Charles Hamilton, who coauthored *Black Power: The Politics of Liberation*, found that students had begun to explicitly critique integration, seeing it as synonymous with racial assimilation. "Integration has traditionally

FIGURE 1. Political scientist Charles Hamilton coauthored *Black Power: The Politics of Liberation* and pioneered the concept of a Black university.

meant that blacks should try to be like whites. It has implied that black people were being done a favor by whites. This is part of what the black students are rejecting, and they believe that the institutions of higher learning have been and are insensitive to this." They expressed, he found, a "profound distrust of national government institutions as well as the schools of higher education that they attend." He expressed surprise at the pace of their politicization. These students, Hamilton wrote, "have formed judgments about the nature of political and economic and educational systems much faster than previous generations of activists—especially civil rights activists."[21]

Students expressed this new consciousness in powerful, forceful terms, and they did so on campuses large and small, all over the nation.

A recurring theme in the students' activism was a desire to show their loyalty to poor Black communities and not let their entrance into white academia be seen as a rejection of their culture and communities. "They talk of the university being 'relevant' to the needs of the black community," Charles Hamilton observed after visiting sixty-six colleges. "They have in mind the university as a place where not just a few black students come and graduate and move up and out (to the suburbs), but where new ideas and techniques are developed for the political and economic benefit of the total black community. In other words, they look to the university, naively or not, as a beginning place for social reform or 'revolution.'"[22] Protesting Black female students at Vassar wrote this preamble to their demands: "We refuse not only to waste four years of our lives, but to jeopardize four years of our lives becoming socialized to fit a white dominant cultural pattern. For the Black student to be asked to submit to such acculturation is to ask the student to willingly accept his own deculturalization—his own dehumanization. We refuse to have our ties to the black community systematically severed; to have our life styles, our ambitions, our visions of our *selves* made to conform solely to any white mold."[23]

Along with the critique of cultural assimilation, the turn toward Black Power affected the rhetorical style of Black student leaders. Stokely Carmichael, coauthor of the influential text *Black Power* and longtime leader of the Student Non-Violent Coordinating Committee (SNCC), was pivotal in the rapid spread of revolutionary rhetoric and a confrontational style among students. Because SNCC was unraveling in the late 1960s, and because Carmichael moved to Africa in 1969 and disappeared from the American media radar, his popularity has been underappreciated. In many ways, he picked up the mantle left by the slain Malcolm X, whose posthumous *Autobiography of Malcolm X* was a similarly influential text. Also pushing this generation to feel that they were part of a seismic change was the urban unrest, especially the uprisings in Newark and Detroit in the summer of 1967 that rocked the nation, unnerved the establishment, and made many young African Americans feel and understand the power, danger, and threat of widespread Black rebellion. This turn toward militant rhetoric and Black Power not only unsettled and alarmed whites but also divided African Americans. "To be authentically black became highly subjective and depended very much on the eye of the beholder," one scholar found. And militancy raised the stakes, serving "as a means of disciplining black students as a whole and policing the boundaries of blackness."

The "scathing epithets 'Tom' or 'Oreo' kept less-militant, less-separatist black students in line."[24]

Alongside this process of politicization, social pressure, and rejection of older paradigms was the search for new ideologies. Students were rejecting fundamental pillars of American society but did not have a clear replacement. In Hamilton's view, they were "almost frantically searching for new ideas and ideologies to explain society" and engaging in "endless hours of ideological discussion."[25] Capturing their attention was a new breed of revolutionaries. Fidel Castro, the socialist president of Cuba, had defeated a U.S.-backed invasion at the Bay of Pigs and pledged Cuban support for national liberation struggles in Africa. Castro was also a staunch supporter of the African American struggle, and famously stayed at the Hotel Theresa in Harlem during a visit to the United Nations. Robert F. Williams is another figure whose early 1960s radicalism impressed Black students later in the decade. An NAACP leader in North Carolina, Williams advocated and practiced armed self-defense, faced down the Klan, and fled first to Cuba and later to China. While in Cuba, his radio show, *Radio Free Dixie,* reached listeners in the United States, and *Negroes with Guns,* his account of his use of armed self-defense in North Carolina, inspired the founders of the Revolutionary Action Movement, an underground Black organization that for a time in the mid-1960s attracted a coterie of college students.[26]

The phrase *Black Power* may bring to mind ghetto uprisings and incendiary rhetoric, but the rise of Black Power on campus had a strong intellectual dimension. Campus study groups were extremely significant in shaping new racial identities and consciousness. Coinciding with the Black arts movement, whose poetry, painting, and performance deeply stirred students, an outpouring of new journals, manifestos, newspapers, magazines, and radio and television programming featured debates and discussions of the new ideas percolating through the Black Power movement. Black students across the country read and debated the ideas of Frantz Fanon, Harold Cruse, Melville Herskovits, E. Franklin Frazier, W.E.B. Du Bois, Nathan Hare, Karl Marx, and Malcolm X. The students were passionate about finding ways to translate theory into practice. Their models were wide-ranging: Gillo Pontecorvo's film *The Battle of Algiers* gave Northwestern students a strategy to maintain secrecy in planning their building takeover; at the University of Oklahoma, the Afro-American Student Union applied the ideas of Chicago community organizer Saul Alinsky. But "if Alinsky was our tactician, Fanon was our fire," remembers the students' faculty mentor, George Henderson.

"His books were widely read by black collegians throughout the United States. It was not a far stretch," he notes, "for most of the black students at the University of Oklahoma to identify with the colonized people of Africa."[27] This identification and solidarity with others struggling in Africa, and in Asia and Latin America too, grew in the 1970s. A key distinction between civil rights and Black Power was internationalism—seeing the past and present of Black Americans as inextricably linked to colonized and formerly colonized people worldwide. Study groups encouraged this new consciousness, and later, overseas travel would as well.

For some, the most startling aspect of the radicalization of Black students was their consideration of the idea of armed struggle. I write *idea* because this development should not be exaggerated and it proved to be more posture than practice. Moreover, it is important to note that, during the long Black freedom struggle, violence was used overwhelmingly against Black people, not by Black people. Nevertheless, militant rhetorical strategies by student leaders and widespread admiration for the tradition of armed self-defense as exemplified by Malcolm X and the Black Panther Party influenced the media's depiction of student activists—sometimes unfairly and inaccurately—and shaped outcomes. The larger social context is critical in understanding the skepticism, especially among young males, toward the rhetoric of nonviolence and the practice of turning the other cheek that is most associated with Martin Luther King Jr. and the southern civil rights movement.

Many factors propelled this skepticism. Young people in the late 1960s witnessed a sharp escalation in American involvement in Vietnam and very high casualty figures, all for an anticommunist rationale that they increasingly came to reject. For them, Dr. King's statement in a 1967 speech that the United States government was "the greatest purveyor of violence" in the world seemed true, and it heightened the hypocrisy in the government's urging of nonviolence on protesters. Moreover, eighteen-year-olds in 1968 had spent their childhoods watching television news footage of racist violence inflicted on nonviolent Black southerners, including children. The rioting that broke out in cities beginning in the summer of 1964 and peaking in 1967 and 1968 led to hundreds of deaths, mostly of African Americans at the hands of police officers, but the violence also seemed to shake up political establishments and spark efforts to placate restive urban centers. Moreover, many Africans had embraced armed struggle in the fight to overthrow European colonial rule. This context altered the discursive strategies of many Black student activists, leading to new motifs, tactics, slogans, and all-around style. For example, in an episode of *Black Heritage,* on WCBS-TV in New York, student leaders passionately discussed "racism and education" and "the new role for Black students," and as the show came to a close, an unidentified man offered this suggestion to move forward: "If students took up the gun on the campus and begin to act out on the basis of gun power . . . that might be one basis on which you can do some challenging."[28]

Charles Hamilton found that students were seriously questioning nonviolence. "They do not believe in the efficacy of nonviolence as a philosophy or as a tactic. In fact, many are of the opinion that unless violence is used in some form, there is little likelihood of getting attention from 'the power structure.'"[29] Students began using new language: embracing "revolution" and "revolt," questioning "working within the system" and openly challenging "the white power structure." "The rhetoric gave them a meaningful frame that fitted what they saw around them. And their political consciousness developed." Hamilton also found that rhetoric was used to "shock whites," a tactic displayed over and over again in campus confrontations.[30] But at most campuses, even as students embraced many aspects of Black nationalism, they remained nonviolent in both theory and practice. In describing the popularity of anticolonial writer Frantz Fanon among Blacks at the University of Oklahoma, George Henderson stresses the appeal of "his strategies for achieving black solidarity and positive self-images. There was little attraction among blacks on our campus for a violent revolution."[31] Still, a 1970 study of Black high school students found that "nearly half of the activists agreed with the statement 'violence is cleansing,' as did more than a third of the nonactivists." Even more telling, only 7 percent of all the Black students thought that whites could be "persuaded" to change.[32]

Black student organizations became the most common vehicle for Black student protest. Some Black student organizations began in the early 1960s and were more social than political, but most began in 1967 or 1968 and were steeped in activist culture. The title Black Student Union was common on the West Coast, while many groups on the East Coast were named Student Afro-American Society, but there was great diversity. At Northwestern University, the new organization was called For Members Only, after a sign students had seen on an exclusive club on Chicago's north shore. The word *Black* had negative connotations among most Americans, but Malcolm X, in particular, reversed its meaning for a younger generation of African Americans, who ushered in a lasting change in group nomenclature and identity. By "thinking black" as Malcolm X urged, they "transformed blackness from an inherited set of physical characteristics to a deliberate political and cultural stance."[33] There were many attempts to establish regional and national student formations. In the spring of 1968, Black students from thirty-seven colleges in nineteen states met at Shaw University and formed the Congress for the Unity of Black Students. There were efforts to unify Black students in regional alliances over the next few years, notably in California, but also in Chicago, New York, and elsewhere. Most striking is the similarity of student grievances and reform goals, given this autonomous, local organizational structure.[34]

The Black Power movement elevated male leadership, reflecting the patriarchy of the larger society as well as the tactics and ideology of the late 1960s Black liberation movement. The reappraisal of nonviolence and embrace of more militant rhetoric increased the visibility of male leaders, as did the fallout from a report authored in 1965 by Daniel Patrick Moynihan of the U.S. Labor Department, which identified a rise in female-headed Black families as a worrisome economic indicator and unnatural social development. The Moynihan report would eventually help propel the rise of Black feminism, but at the time it dovetailed with the rise of Black nationalism, which had typically seen the cultivation of patriarchal gender roles as essential to race advancement.

In a sign of the masculine tenor of the times, Darlene Clark Hine, an undergraduate at Roosevelt University in Chicago in the mid-1960s who went on to become a leading scholar in African American women's history, remembers reading, studying, listening to, and valorizing Black men almost exclusively. Black men and their words and experiences represented the race. She found "ample opportunity to study and learn about black men, including, for example, Muhammad Ali, Malcolm X, Martin Luther King Jr., Huey P. Newton, Bobby Seale and Eldridge Cleaver." She applauded their strong images, calling them a "powerful antidote" to the widespread negative depictions of Black men in U.S. culture. "Articulate, handsome, fiercely self-conscious freedom fighters, these men garnered massive media coverage" for their demands for Black rights and social transformation. Like thousands of other Black college students of her generation, Hine read the *Autobiography of Malcolm X,* Claude Brown's *Manchild in the Promised Land,* John A. Williams's *The Man Who Cried I Am,* Richard Wright's *Native Son,* James Baldwin's *Notes of a Native Son,* and Ralph Ellison's *Invisible*

Man. And like so many of her peers, she listened to John Coltrane, Miles Davis, and Pharoah Sanders. She was "oblivious" to the lack of attention paid "to black women's experiences" and even felt she had developed a "black masculine consciousness" by the time she entered graduate school in 1968.[35]

But male dominance did not go entirely uncontested. On several campuses, female leaders of Black student organizations were pressured to give way to male leadership: some relented, others held on. Deborah Gray White was president of her college's Afro-Latin Alliance when a rise in Black student admissions in 1968 spawned demands for a separate Black organization. "Some of the more nationalist black students called those of us who wanted to keep the Afro-Latin Alliance names like Oreo or Uncle Tom." White felt "particularly set upon as president of the Afro-Latin Alliance because the new students demanded masculine representation." She "never got used to being a moderate among black nationalists," but she "persevered."[36]

In his survey of Black student activism, Charles Hamilton found an occasional but "conscious effort to distinguish the roles of men and women. This was especially the case," he found, "where the groups had, as at one midwestern university, adopted a Nation of Islam (Black Muslim) motif. The men served as snappy, disciplined, military-type guards. The women studied their role in the revolutionary vanguard." Whatever the outcome, he found that the Black consciousness upsurge had sparked "serious questioning of the relation of the sexes." On many campuses, "some of the males, sensitive to the theory of black male emasculation, argued that leadership roles should be assumed by men—especially in such matters as occupying buildings, negotiating with school officials, and talking to the press. Their view was that the black man had to speak for the 'Black family of students and be out front in a position to protect the black women.'" But Hamilton also observed some young women push back. "Some of the women were reluctant to give up the egalitarian method of rewarding position," he noted. In the end, he emphasized an important feature of the movement: "Whatever the situation, it was quite evident that men *and* women students, generally, were about equally active in the groups." Notwithstanding the popularity of patriarchal norms or rhetoric, this was an era of youth revolt, incipient women's liberation, and overall questioning of authority. Young women were full participants in the Black student movement.[37]

Black women students on white campuses had particular grievances that arose from the interplay between their racial and gender experience.

The social scene became a point of tension and contestation. A student at the University of Bridgeport told a reporter: "It's much easier for a boy to get along here. If he's a good athlete and a good dancer, he can get into a fraternity and no white girl is going to turn him down if he asks her to dance. But we can't ask a white boy for a date, and you can be sure they don't ask us. With lots of the black boys dating white girls, we just sit around the dorms and get angry."[38] Still, Black women students were hardly passive participants in the negotiation of campus gender relations. Charles Hamilton recorded "a vivid example" of such a negotiation in a meeting at Northwestern University in March 1969. "A black co-ed had accused a white fraternity member of insulting her," and "Black students subsequently invaded the fraternity house and damaged some property." At the meeting "the black co-eds were asking for commitments from the black male students to defend black woman-hood. One after another, the black men spoke—some vehemently in defense of the co-eds (they were judged Men); some equivocated in their willingness to fight 'by any means necessary' (they were put down as Mice). The session became very heated; egos were strained and challenged. Physical blows were almost passed . . . . 'It really got rough there at one point,' a black graduate student said. 'Cats were outdoing each other and that whole black masculinity thing was coming out. At one point, I was sitting there just hoping that some white person would throw a brick through the window just to bring us together again.' " He continued: "The Sisters were really coming down hard on the dudes who didn't sound right."[39]

Black nationalism married the repudiation of interracial dating with authentic Blackness. Greensboro student leader Nelson Johnson remembers being exposed to Black Power ideas and Pan-Africanism by the charismatic activist Howard Fuller. His critique of interracial dating stood out. "He talked a strong black power line," he says of Fuller. "There was a lot of interracial dating among activists at that time and he challenged us to stop it. He whipped on any black man dating white girls so hard it was no longer in vogue."[40] Some students who persisted in dating or marrying "outside the race" felt their loyalty to the cause was unfairly called into question. This was true for a Black female student leader at a major midwestern university whose white boyfriend marked her as racially suspect in the eyes of many Black nationalist students, even with her tireless work and devotion to the movement.

What were the social origins of the students who engaged in such militant action? Student activists were a mix of preaffirmative action children of college-educated parents, first-generation college students from migrant, working-class families, and some (hailing from either group) who had already had some experience in the Black freedom struggle. While many colleges and universities began to implement modest Black student recruitment programs in the early 1960s in response to the stirrings of the southern civil rights movement, the 1965 Higher Education Act propelled greater desegregation and also sparked change in the class composition of Black students. Between 1966 and 1968, crucial seedtime for subsequent demonstrations, there was a dramatic increase in students from low-income families in predominantly white colleges. Leon Denmark recollects that of the approximately thirty-five Black students who entered Columbia College in New York in 1966, "all were from public school." And "we had a certain attitude," he recalls.[41]

According to a study Charles Hamilton conducted in 1969 with 264 students at fifteen colleges, half were getting some kind of scholarship aid. Only one-third of students reported a parental contribution. The vast majority of students were financing education through a combination of sources: scholarships, employment, parental contribution, and loans. Seventy-four percent of the parents had no college education. The single most-frequent parental occupation was "blue collar worker," a category that would virtually disappear in twenty years. These students hailed from what Hamilton termed upper-lower- or lower-middle-class families.[42] Harvard law professor Charles Ogletree entered college in 1971, and remembers that the experience was a jolt for all of them. "Most of the black students who entered Stanford in the fall were the first members of their families to attend college." And of those parents who had attended college, most had attended historically Black colleges. So they were all integrating.[43] Interestingly, Hamilton found a pronounced break from religion among these students. Eighty-five percent of students in his sample grew up in religious families, yet 65 percent of them indicated that they were not personally followers of a religion. "Today's black student is clearly rejecting the organized church of his parents," Hamilton reported.[44]

In addition to the politicization of Black students on white campuses, students at historically Black colleges underwent their own process of politicization. The spread of the Black student movement at both white and Black colleges helps account for its national breadth. Black colleges have a reputation for conservatism. They do not typically come to mind as locations that give rise to protest. But the first large-scale protests by Black college students directed at campus policies occurred at historically Black colleges and then spread to white colleges. Given that popular and scholarly accounts so often portray the Black Power movement as taking place in the urban North and West, it is important to acknowledge that Black student protest around the country was largely inspired by southern campus struggles that were part and parcel of the Black Power upsurge. "Without question, the Black Power–Black Consciousness movement has been felt in the South," wrote Charles Hamilton, formerly a professor at Tuskegee University.[45] A tidal wave of protest swept historically Black colleges and universities (HBCUs) in the 1960s and 1970s, inspired by a range of student grievances, most notably white financial and administrative control, excessive regulation of student life, excessive discipline, inferior facilities and faculty, and outmoded or Eurocentric curriculum.

Given that schools like Howard University in Washington, D.C., and the Atlanta University Center had been home to pioneers in Black scholarship—such as historian and sociologist W.E.B. Du Bois, political scientist Ralph Bunche, historian Rayford Logan, philosopher Alain Locke, and sociologist E. Franklin Frazier—what provoked the charge of Eurocentrism? Darwin T. Turner, dean of the graduate school at North Carolina Agricultural and Technical State University, argued that a move away from studying Black subjects emerged from the optimism spawned by early legal decisions supporting desegregation, the defeat of Fascism, and postwar affluence. Political repression, too, was most likely a factor. "The tendency for black educators to neglect materials related to Afro-American heritage intensified, I believe, during the early 1950s," Turner wrote. The many "indications of opening doors persuaded many blacks to discourage any education which emphasized the existence of Afro-Americans as a body separate from the rest of America." As a result, "studies of Afro-American history, literature, sociology, economics, and politics were stuffed into the traditional surveys, which were already so overcrowded that important materials must be omitted." He felt that "integrated surveys" were necessary but insufficient "to provide Afro-Americans with the necessary understanding of their culture."[46] Indeed, in 1968, several members of Howard's board of trustees "were shocked that courses in Black history, jazz and literature were not presently offered. 'We had many of these things in the 1930s,' commented one member."[47] A 1968 graduate of the prestigious Spelman College complained of "being taught a super kind of European history." Of fifteen courses in a literature department at the Atlanta University Center, she said, "fourteen of them will be on European Renaissance or medieval literature, Elizabethan poetry." She also lamented a "super kind of paternalism" and "Puritanism," but nevertheless acknowledged the important history of black scholarship at the Atlanta University Center and what she termed "a healthy kind of racialism."[48]

Students at scores of Black colleges organized campaigns to reverse these trends, a story that will be taken up more fully in chapter 5, but events at three campuses need to be highlighted because they marked the beginning of the national Black student movement. Clashes at HBCUs in 1967 and 1968 inspired Black students nationwide, in part because students on these campuses faced extraordinary police invasions. In May 1967, police led a full-scale assault on Texas Southern University in Houston. One night a person or persons threw rocks and bottles from a dormitory and allegedly fired a gun as well. At two o'clock in the morning police officers invaded the campus, firing "3000 rounds of pistol and automatic gunfire" into the dorm. Their rampage left one of their own killed by a police officer's bullet, two other officers wounded, at least two students wounded from gunfire, several students bitten by police dogs, and many other students with physical injuries. The Houston police invaded the building, tore up rooms looking for weapons, and arrested 488 students. "No bull horns were used to inform the dormitory residents of the impending attack and no tear gas was used at any time. Instead, there was a barrage of rifle and pistol fire that could have killed scores of students."[49] Mrs. Hattie Harbert, a housemother in the dormitory, said police "made me lie on the floor and two or three of them walked on me." She also saw police carry out "five or six students bloody as beef."[50]

As an NAACP official wired to the U.S. Attorney General the following morning: "It is clear that Houston police engaged in a vengeful and destructive rampage against persons and property at Texas Southern University."[51] The confrontation came after two months of almost continuous demonstrations against police mistreatment of TSU students and substandard conditions generally in the Houston Black community. No weapons were ever found in the dorm. Five students, known as "the TSU five," were charged with the officer's murder, even though he was felled by an officer's bullet. All the students were ultimately cleared, but their prosecution distracted attention from the true culprits. According to opinion surveys shortly afterward, the TSU police riot increased pro-Black Power sentiment among African Americans in Houston; and with the extensive print and broadcast media coverage of the riot, this effect was likely felt beyond Texas.[52]

Perhaps the massive firepower at TSU resulted from the highly militarized riot response plans developed in police departments after the Watts uprising of 1965; perhaps it reflected a particular hostility toward increasingly assertive Black students. Whatever the explanation, the invasion was a disturbing harbinger of things to come, and while it prompted many regional protests by Black students, it did not give rise to a national outcry. But this national outcry was soon to come. Less than a year later, in February 1968, officers with the South Carolina Law Enforcement Division shot and killed three African Americans—Samuel Hammond, Henry Smith, and Delano Middleton—on the campus of South Carolina State University in Orangeburg. Known as the Orangeburg Massacre, the killings outraged and mobilized Black students nationwide. However, the rapid string of assassinations, street clashes, global upheavals and military battles of 1968 soon overshadowed the Orangeburg killings in the major media, leading to the mistaken impression that they had generated little impact.

Students at Orangeburg had been engaged in protests against a city bowling alley and other public facilities that were still refusing service to African Americans four years after passage of the Civil Rights Act. On February 8, state highway patrolmen, newly outfitted with the latest antiriot armaments, converged on a campus gathering and opened fire into a large group of students. Most of the students were already fleeing, so the bullets hit them from the back. The white police officers killed three youths and wounded thirty more people. As at Texas Southern, this was an extraordinary display of firepower, and shows how law enforcement nationwide reacted to the urban uprisings by amassing greater weaponry and firepower and, in some instances, unleashing it on student protesters. Afterward, the police rushed to whitewash the incident, claiming falsely that the students had opened fire. Under pressure from civil rights leaders, the federal government stepped in and tried nine officers, but the white jury acquitted them. No officer was ever held accountable for these murders, and incredibly, the only person ever convicted and sentenced as a result of the Orangeburg Massacre was a SNCC activist who had been shot in the back, Cleveland Sellers.[53]

The Orangeburg Massacre is widely considered one of the "forgotten tragedies" of the civil rights and student movements, but it sparked a wave of sympathy protests by Black college students across the country. These students identified with the slain young men. From Howard University in Washington, D.C., to Crane College in Chicago, students were hurt and angry and held their own commemorations and memorials for the students. "The Orangeburg massacre went through the emergent black power movement like a bolt of lightning," recalls Nelson Johnson, who was a student leader at North Carolina A&T. Black student leaders from sixteen colleges in North Carolina gathered in Durham and agreed to hold "creative demonstrations" on their campuses. At North Carolina A&T, they burned the governor of South Carolina in effigy and conducted a mock funeral procession for the slain young men in what became one of the largest demonstrations in Greensboro. The Orangeburg Massacre was one of a series of catalysts that generated a national student demand for Black studies. In just one example, a year later a commemoration of the massacre at the University of North Carolina in Charlotte led to the creation of a Black studies program.[54]

Students at HBCUs inspired and shaped the Black student movement nationally not only by their martyrdom but also through their efforts to improve and preserve Black colleges. In an extraordinarily important, though strikingly forgotten dimension of the Black Power movement, students fought for the survival of Black colleges in this era of desegregation. The quest by militant Black youth to "save" Black colleges was an outgrowth of their commitment to Black self-determination, yet it dovetailed with the professional desires of Black administrators, who tended to be more politically and socially conservative. Despite this shared long-term goal, conflict and hostility defined the student-administrator relationship. Struggles at HBCUs brought into sharp relief the twin targets of Black Power: white control and integrationist Negro leadership. Students often criticized administrators in biting, acerbic terms, as "Uncle Toms" working to manage the plantation at the expense of a younger generation of Black people eager to transform racial dynamics across American society. The students were seeking to make Negro colleges "blacker," and this was controversial among African Americans. At the same time, the students assailed southern white legislatures for inadequate funding of public HBCUs, and whites on the boards of directors of private HBCUs for their paternalistic control of Black institutions. And there were undeniable generational cleavages as well. Students opposed the strict curfews, dress codes (especially for women), and other in loco parentis rules,[55] which they increasingly framed as excessive and oppressive. Indeed, in a sharp rupture, the students were forgoing the "politics of respectability," forged in the era of

Jim Crow, in favor of more assertive forms of Black representation and protest.

Many students at Howard, most famously Stokely Carmichael, had been involved in the civil rights movement in the early 1960s and even interrupted their schooling to go south and join the movement. By the mid-1960s their gaze had shifted to the universities themselves. Howard students staged a series of major campus protests in 1967, 1968, and 1969. They protested the war in Vietnam, the draft, and in loco parentis, but most controversially they argued that Howard should declare itself a "Black university" in service to Black communities. Surprisingly, the curriculum at Howard had few courses in either African American studies or contemporary urban and social problems. According to one observer, "Professor Sterling Brown was for years alone in including Negro writers in literature courses," and "the college had made few efforts to study or actively participate in the black community around it."[56] The rise of Black Power inspired protest at dozens of historically Black colleges: Howard was simply one of the first. A catalyst for the surge in Black nationalist feeling was President James M. Nabrit Jr.'s declaration in the fall of 1966 that Howard should raise its admissions standards and admit more white students. This statement came amid a larger context of anxiety over what integration portended for Black institutions. In response, students, along with Nathan Hare, a professor of sociology who became an important mentor and ally to Black student activists nationwide, organized the Black Power Committee to promote Black consciousness among the students in order to prepare them to challenge the university's new direction.[57]

In addition to students, a cohort of young Black professors began to envision a new and leading role for historically Black colleges in the post-Jim-Crow era. Charles Hamilton first articulated the conception of a "black university" in a 1967 speech, "The Place of the Black College in the Human Rights Struggle." He called on Black colleges to reject the white middle-class character imposed on them by white funders and to redefine their mission to provide greater aid and assistance to Black communities. Later published in the *Negro Digest,* Hamilton's article spawned a yearly tradition of devoting an entire issue of the *Negro Digest* (later the *Black World*) to the idea of a Black university. According to Hamilton, the mission of the Black university was to develop a distinctive Black ethos; to prepare students to help solve problems in poor Black communities; and to offer a new curriculum, one that was relevant to contemporary needs but which also required a course in ancient

African civilizations. "I am talking modernization," Hamilton asserted. "I propose a black college that would *deliberately* strive to inculcate a sense of racial *pride* and *anger* and *concern* in its students." The ideas in his essay illustrate the emerging view that the Black intelligentsia was a relatively untapped and potentially radical leadership resource for the Black liberation movement. In some respects, Hamilton was advancing an updated version of W. E. B. Du Bois's idea of a "talented tenth," an educated elite cadre who would advance the interests of the race as a whole. "We need," Hamilton declared, "militant leadership which the church is not providing, unions are not providing and liberal groups are not providing. . . . I propose a black college," he wrote, "that would be a felt, dominant force in the community in which it exists. A college which would use its accumulated intellectual knowledge and economic resources to bring about desired changes in race relations in the community." It would dispense with "irrelevant PhDs," he wrote, and "recruit freedom fighters and graduate freedom fighters."[58]

Howard became the locus of this struggle, but the quest for a Black university did not take place in isolation. It coincided with the broader social justice movement of the era, especially the struggle to end the war in Vietnam, the draft, and compulsory military training courses. A visit to Howard by General Lewis B. Hershey, head of the Selective Service System, in the spring of 1967, triggered an escalation of protest that would shake the campus for the next two years. Someone in the audience yelled, "America is a black man's true battleground," and about forty students rushed the stage, preventing Hershey from speaking.[59] In the aftermath, Howard suspended twenty students and dismissed six politically active professors, including Nathan Hare. The university labeled these faculty members, four of whom were white, as "a dangerous element" for allegedly promoting Black Power. But the student newspaper, the *Hilltop,* reminded readers that the charge of communism had been used in the McCarthy era to discredit reform in general. "In effect the university used public hysteria over black power," the student-editors wrote, "to cloak its efforts to get rid of controversial teachers who encouraged students to ask questions about the administration of the university or the position of black people in this country."[60] Nathan Hare was immersed in student radicalism at Howard and in his next job, at San Francisco State College; at both he adopted the rhetoric and style of student leaders and stood with them shoulder to shoulder, a choice that landed him in hot water with his employers on both coasts.[61] Upset that Howard had no code of conduct or student inclusion in disciplinary procedures, the suspended students hired attorneys from the American Civil Liberties Union and sued Howard in federal court.[62]

Protest continued the next academic year, including a victorious sit-in in the fall that brought an end to compulsory ROTC classes. Michael Harris, president of the freshman class, led many of the anti-ROTC protests and also served as political director of the Black nationalist student organization, Ujamma. The son of a police officer and a secretary, Harris said that his Catholic high school experience in Chicago had turned him off to integration because he couldn't be himself. In his view, "Howard University should serve another purpose other than preparing people to fill slots in white society." Students, he felt, "want Howard to belong to the black people in Washington, D.C., the black people surrounding the university." Harris's comments in 1968 reflect the intense pace of change in the country and the sense that the United States was undergoing unprecedented confrontation that was likely to intensify. "I think that in about five years there's going to be an all-out race war," he declared that summer, fresh from visiting the Poor People's Campaign's encampment at the Capitol, known as Resurrection City, where he says police were threatening a violent takeover and using tear gas against women and children. "To me, black power is simply a means of getting ready for the confrontation."[63]

In February 1968, hundreds of students at Howard staged a sympathy demonstration for the slain students in Orangeburg, which quickly turned into a protest against Howard's administration. They called for the resignation of the president and issued a long list of demands pertaining to student rights, reinstatement of professors, and Black awareness that came to be known as the "Orangeburg Ultimatum." Reportedly, Nabrit and the faculty found it "reprehensible."[64] A month later at the Charter Day ceremony celebrating the anniversary of Howard's founding, students stormed the stage and took control of the podium. They passed out an alternative charter for a Black university, which renamed Howard "Sterling Brown University," gave control of academic matters to faculty, and gave students a seat on the board of trustees and responsibility for regulating student life and conduct. According to student leader Anthony Gittens, "We are trying to bring democracy and a concern for the black student to Howard."[65]

But not everyone saw it this way. It was an extraordinary disruption of Howard decorum. "In a monumental show of rudeness, discourtesy, and vulgarity," wrote a *New York Amsterdam News* reporter, who was a 1966 Howard graduate, students grabbed the microphone and said,

"We declare today the end of Howard University. A new Black University is being born." She noted that firebombs had recently been thrown into the homes of Dean Frank Snowden and President Nabrit. Two students were later arrested.[66] Indeed, Black Power was a critique of liberalism for having failed to eradicate racial inequality, and of the civil rights old guard for still hewing to this failed course. SNCC leaders Charlie Cobb and Courtland Cox echoed this view: "In the eyes of many students, the Howard administration has come to represent all that is negative of older generation Negro leadership." They were colluding with white America to resist the inexorable rise of Black Power.[67]

When the administration summoned thirty-nine students involved in the protest before a judiciary board, it rekindled widespread student displeasure with the disciplinary process. At a rally in protest, student leader Ewart Brown called for a sit-in at the administration building, and hundreds gathered there in the president's office and throughout the building, causing administrators to make a hasty exit. For five days in late March, roughly two thousand students gathered inside or around the administration building. Even with the recent history of tumult, this was a dramatic, unprecedented act of student rebellion at Howard. The administration quickly suspended most classes and closed down the campus, inadvertently furthering the students' sense of having seized power. The Howard sit-in became a focal point of the budding Black Power movement and attracted visitors from around the region, including SNCC leaders like Stokely Carmichael. The students' sixteen demands included "a black democratic university," the resignation of President James Nabrit, greater faculty and student rights, African American studies, a "black awareness institute," and the dropping of charges against the thirty-nine students, because "Howard is run by a dictatorial system."[68]

Students worked hard to project the protest—to administrators, the media, and supporters—as respectful and disciplined, yet, as in most such protests, they also sought to construct a visible counterculture. There was "a continuous atmosphere of black awareness and cultural pride," one professor noted. Leaders in the Black arts movement came to perform, and many parents came to offer solidarity. Robert Anderson, the parent of a freshman, said the sit-in "was done in such a manner as to make parents proud to have a child here."[69] Howard administrators, including the president, largely absented themselves from the conflict, leaving a leadership void that was eventually filled by a group of distinguished members of the board of trustees—Judge Miles Paige,

FIGURE 2. In March 1968, students at Howard University occupied the administration building and issued a series of demands, including the call to transform Howard into a Black university.

Dr. Percy Julian, and Dr. Kenneth Clark. Clark was a well-known advocate of integration, having testified before the U.S. Supreme Court for the plaintiffs in the *Brown* case. But he knew that bringing the police on campus risked a bloody confrontation. In contrast to most Howard leaders, these prominent trustees did not want to use force to clear the building. As the protest wore on, students increasingly demanded that Howard declare itself a "Black university," but this proved unattainable. In the end, Howard agreed to grant the student assembly power to create a disciplinary system; to make Howard more attuned to the times; to create a student/faculty board to work on student problems; and not to discipline students involved in the takeover.[70]

Not everyone was happy with the settlement. Many of the more militant students saw it as a betrayal of the longer list of demands, and former professor Nathan Hare urged rejection, saying too little would be gained. Adrienne Manns, a leader of the sit-in and a rare female spokesperson in the Black student movement, supported the settlement. She had headed the student negotiating team. The cry of "nonnegotiable demands" would take off in the coming year, but Manns employed a pragmatic approach to resolving the five-day protest; moreover, she hoped to avoid a violent showdown. "We came under fire," she re-

flected later that summer, "for selling out the students from local organizations like the SNCC and other people. I guess they had been down
in Orangeburg and have seen people get killed, and they thought that's
what should happen up here." Manns felt that reaching a victory was
more important than continuing confrontation; still, her comments re-
veal the difficulty many student leaders faced of knowing when to call
off a protest. "I was not going to stay there to satisfy my ego. I wanted
to stay very much, but I realized it was a totally emotional reaction to
the situation. I was not prepared to sacrifice things for people next year
because of my own emotional needs." Some people, she said, wanted a
violent confrontation with police, but she "refused to go along with the
cowboy-on-television revolutionary stuff about just dying for its own
sake." In her view, the threat of retaliation was real and would do little
to advance their cause. "We have been subject to police action for a long
time, and we don't need that novelty experience of getting our heads
beat," she said.[71]

The media gave extensive coverage to the sit-in—WNET in New York
even produced *Color Us Black*, an hour-long documentary devoted to
the Howard story.[72] This coverage sparked protests at other HBCUs,
including Fisk, Morgan State, Cheyney State, and Tougaloo. According
to a visiting lecturer at Howard, the "dramatic occupation" of the administration building ended an era "of internal calm, led to a series of
demonstrations on other Negro campuses, and laid their peculiar institutional problems before a public audience."[73] To some extent, this effect was obscured by the assassination a few days later of Martin Luther
King Jr. His murder galvanized Black student protest all over the country, leading many observers to miss or forget the emergence of Black
student unrest prior to April.

Booker T. Washington might have rolled over in his grave if he knew
what students were up to at the school he founded, Tuskegee Institute
in Alabama, in late March and early April 1968. The Howard protest
had spurred student activists there to boycott classes in order to end
compulsory ROTC training, gain scholarships for athletes, and upgrade
conditions in housing and dining halls. A week later, frustrated with
administrative apathy, students locked twelve trustees in a guesthouse
for twelve hours. The police response was swift, and as at other protests
at Black colleges, dramatically disproportionate to the offense. Three
hundred National Guardsmen and seventy state troopers converged on
campus, but departed after an African American sheriff persuaded the
students to release their influential captives. They had already released

retired General Lucius Clay so he could catch his plane to New York. "There was no threat of violence," Clay said. We could have called for assistance at any time." Nevertheless, the college closed for three weeks, ten students were charged with crimes, fifty others were suspended, and seventy-five students were placed on probation.[74] U.S. District Court Judge Frank M. Johnson, lion of the liberal judiciary throughout the civil rights era, later ordered that the fifty suspended students be readmitted, because they had not been permitted a hearing.[75]

The assassination of Martin Luther King Jr. on April 4 intensified the sense of responsibility among African American college students that they needed to become leaders and wage battles to widen opportunities for Black youth. Yet the murder of the foremost advocate of nonviolence embittered many, causing them to see the fight for inclusion as less about moral suasion and more about organizing student power. Moreover, the assassination seemed to stand for the crushing of nonviolent means to social change, making many young people feel increasingly justified in resorting to confrontational tactics to spur change. That spring saw an upsurge in Black student protest. At Wellesley College, an all-women's liberal arts college in Massachusetts, Black students, including future historian Francille Rusan Wilson, threatened a hunger strike to get the college to admit more Black students and hire Black professors. Students at Boston University demanded that the school of theology be named in honor of their slain alumnus Dr. King. Two hundred male students at the predominantly Black Cheyney State College in Pennsylvania seized a building, while their female allies formed a human chain of support outside. They demanded a student voice in governance, more courses in African American and African history and culture, and, crucially, more scholarships. The president resigned a week later under pressure. Confrontational tactics became commonplace: at Ohio State, Black students occupied the administration building and reportedly held two vice presidents and four employees "captive" for eight hours. What demands prompted such radical action? They wanted more Black professors, counselors, and courses. This upsurge of Black protest at so many campuses across the country began to assume the shape of a movement. Only three months after expressing outrage at the behavior of Howard students, a reporter for the *Amsterdam News* now gave voice to a rapidly shifting national mood: "These comparatively new student campus seizures have triggered a much needed reexamination, re-evaluation, and revamping of the future of America's universities," she wrote.[76]

In addition to students at HBCUs, Black students in California were pioneering in launching this new chapter of Black Power campus activism. Many factors pointed to the significance of California. In the early 1960s, the state greatly expanded its system of higher education in order to guarantee a seat in college for all high school graduates. For southern Black migrants and their children, this would prove critical to social mobility and went a long way in shaping their political activism.[77] Harry Edwards, an activist sociologist who wrote about and organized "the revolt of the black athlete," helped turn Black collegiate athletes in California into a leading force for social change.[78] Finally, the Black Panther Party played a galvanizing role in California student activism, especially in the Bay Area, although, oddly, studies of the party have neglected this.[79]

Before they founded the Black Panther Party, Bobby Seale and Huey Newton had participated in the Berkeley-based Afro-American Association, a study group promoting Black history and Black consciousness. As students at Merritt College, a two-year public college in Oakland, they helped to win the addition of a Black history course in 1965–1966, and with little fanfare or media attention a Black studies department was launched in 1968.[80] The demographics at Merritt College forecast the racial change occurring in many American cities. Black student enrollment shot up, from 10 percent in 1963 to 40 percent five years later, giving Merritt the largest concentration of Black students at a predominantly white institution in the United States.[81]

For the students at Merritt, winning Black studies was just the beginning of an effort to gain Black power at Merritt, and beyond. Charles Hamilton visited there in 1969 and quoted a student leader's summation of their remarkable achievements: "For the last seven years the Soul Students Advisory Council . . . of Merritt College has fought a long, hard battle without compromise for a Black studies department. During this time, we have increased the number of our Black faculty, acquired a Black president, gained total control of our student body, and Black students sit on the major decision-making bodies of this college." Community colleges were, in many cities, the first large, public institutions where African Americans assumed administrative leadership. Student activism played an important role in hastening and shaping this demographic shift. But as would occur again in the Black studies movement in California, the students almost immediately launched a critique of the Black studies department for allegedly depoliticizing the struggle and reorienting Black studies toward academic respectability rather than community engagement. "We watch as the Black studies department we fought so hard for is bastardized by and pimped off by Negroes and Whiteys," they wrote.[82]

According to historian Donna Murch, "Merritt clearly demonstrated how the integration of black youth into 'historically white' institutions inspired new and influential expressions of racial militancy."[83] San Francisco State College, another public institution of higher education in the Bay Area, did so as well, but on a much larger, more contentious, and more publicized scale. The Black Power movement among students had important southern origins, but it very quickly spread nationwide, and San Francisco State was its most momentous battle. Here the students aimed for revolution.

CHAPTER 2

A Revolution Is Beginning

The Strike at San Francisco State

In November 1968 the Black Student Union (BSU) at San Francisco State College (SFSC or State) called a student strike. For five months the strike rocked the Bay Area, led to nearly eight hundred arrests, galvanized local and national media, and put Governor Ronald Reagan, the Black Panther Party, students, faculty, administrators, and the board of trustees on a collision course. The students wanted to fundamentally redefine higher education. California's reorganization of its three-tier system of higher education, together with the introduction of the SAT in the mid-1960s, had toughened admissions criteria at the state colleges, leading to a sharp drop in Black students at SFSC at precisely the moment when African American baby boomers and children of southern migrants were coming of age and possessed of a strong desire for upward mobility and access to education. Deeply affected by the broader civil rights movement in which many had taken part, SFSC students organized a mass movement with a strong base on campus and in nearby Black communities, calling for sweeping reforms, including the admission of all Black high school graduates and an independent department of Black studies. Overnight, the strike put Black students at the center of the civil rights struggle in California and, increasingly, the nation. This epochal battle took place on a liberal campus famous for its innovation and student autonomy, but the liberal administrators were all sacked during the conflict and conservative state leaders fought hard to quell the strike and punish its leaders. The aftermath was paradoxical:

the tools to create a multiracial university were won, but in the short term a vision for a "revolutionary" student-controlled Black studies movement was crushed.[1]

In 1968, nine hundred of San Francisco State's eighteen thousand students were Black, and their average age was twenty-five. It is vital to grasp these demographics in order to appreciate the significance of the strike. How did Black students manage to wage a long strike for Black studies on a majority white campus? How did students inspired by the controversial politics of Black nationalism gain the wider multiracial and intergenerational support that would be essential to pulling off a strike? The answer lies in the complex mix of community organizing, working-class aspiration, and coalition-building that came together during the strike. Before entering college, many of the strike leaders had been active in the Black freedom struggle, and their consciousness had been shaped by the rise of revolutionary Black nationalism in the Student Non-Violent Coordinating Committee (SNCC) and the Black Panther Party. As a social movement, the strike was the culmination of a long process of political education, organizing, and relationship-building both on campus and in the Bay Area.

Jimmy Garrett was pivotal to the development of a politically conscious Black student community at State. Widely regarded as "a visionary,"[2] Garrett was a seasoned organizer before transferring from Los Angeles City College to SFSC in February 1966 at the age of twenty. Like many young men of his generation, Garrett enrolled in college to avoid the draft. Born in Texas, he moved with his family to Los Angeles, where he joined a street gang but became socially aware. He credits his mother, a domestic worker and "great reader," as a "pivotal political influence." At age fifteen he went south—participating in sit-ins and freedom rides—and brought these influences back to California. Garrett cites the SNCC Statement on Freedom Schools written by Charlie Cobb and Bob Moses as an influence on the "liberation school" he helped to later set up in Watts. "How do you liberate education from the domination of the system?" was the critical question he learned and applied in his northern organizing, including at San Francisco State.[3] Another legacy of Garrett's experience in SNCC was a critique of the role of white activists in Black movements. At a 1965 conference of the Students for a Democratic Society (SDS), Garrett argued against interracial student organizing. "That failed in Mississippi," he said. "It failed all over."[4] Instead, he championed organizing Black students around student-centered issues, with an approach grounded in both politics and culture. "We are no longer striving for an integrated society," Garrett declared. "Those days are gone. We are struggling for self-determination. Self-determination for our black lives; self-determination for our black communities; and self-determination for a black education."[5] His political instincts proved prescient, as this cultural-political approach characterized the Black student uprisings of 1968–1972.

While State did not have Berkeley's reputation for radical activism, it was a cosmopolitan, liberal campus. Strike leader George Murray entered as a seventeen-year-old in 1963. It was "a contentious kind of place philosophically," he recalls, where he encountered "elaborate critical thinking." The campus was "very integration-oriented," and many organizations recruited there, including SDS, the Congress of Racial Equality, the United Farm Workers Union, SNCC, and the Southern Christian Leadership Conference. Murray first became politicized as a teenager in Oakland, where he knew Bobby Seale and Huey Newton. They had an internationalist outlook from an early age, and all three future Panther leaders participated in protests against apartheid at the South African consulate in 1964. FBI agents subsequently visited his house, showed his mother pictures of him demonstrating and asked, "Do you know your son is hanging around communists and socialists?" Murray, who stayed at State to get his master's degree and taught Danny Glover in freshman English, became the minister of education for the Panthers. "They needed someone who could teach the political education courses and write," he recalls.[6]

Born in Mississippi, where he was expelled from high school for joining the NAACP, Jerry Varnado entered SFSC in 1963 after serving in the U.S. Air Force. He loved college so much that when he had compiled enough credits to graduate, he changed his major. Varnado learned a lot at BSU political education sessions. "We read everything," he says, and he attended frequent debates on campus. It was competitive; you "had to know what you were talking about." As the BSU's on-campus coordinator, he helped build support for the strike among Black fraternity members: "That's how the whole strike got started," he recalls. The administration would not permit Black fraternities and sororities to use campus facilities. "Students were outraged by this."[7] Ben Stewart was twenty-three years old and chairman of the BSU when the strike began. He had grown up in Oakland but came to State from "San Francisco's most prestigious public high school," where he had run track. According to a student journalist who covered the strike, "Stewart learned to play the role of the black militant. He customarily wears a frown on his face, attempting to project an image of uncompromising toughness." "Stewart," he wrote, "wears sunglasses, even under cloudy skies."[8]

A second-generation Indian American, Hari Dillon entered SFSC in the fall of 1966. His grandfather was among the Indian immigrants in the United States and Canada who were founders of the Ghadr Party, which sought to liberate India from British colonial rule. Hari Dillon was shaped by his family's tradition of anticolonial nationalism and socialism, but more immediately by the civil rights and anti-Vietnam war movements. He had participated in the Meredith March in Mississippi, where the slogan "Black Power" exploded into national consciousness, and later at State he was active in the BSU. In Dillon's view, the student struggle in San Francisco turned the slogan "Black Power" into a mass movement, giving it its most sustained application in social struggle.[9]

As in other Black Power–era struggles, men ran the student movement in San Francisco, but it was nevertheless shaped and sustained by a courageous and militant group of Black women, who were coming of age on the eve of women's liberation. Jimmy Garrett launched his career at State with a dramatic act of male chauvinism. Walking into a meeting of the Negro Students Association in 1966, he blurted out, "The first thing I want to know is why a woman is up there," referring to the group's president, Maryum Al-Wadi. Al-Wadi stepped down under Garrett's pressure, but she and another female student, Tricia Navarra, prevailed in insisting that *Black* replace *Negro* in the title of their organization. A respected leader, Al-Wadi was seen as "far ahead of her time in wearing African garb." While Garrett's gendered power play exemplified a prominent strain of Black Power politics, Al-Wadi's Pan-African style and strong womanhood did as well. But still, an overall deference to—even investment in—Black male leadership shaped Black nationalism, even as the seeds of future feminist assertion were being planted.[10]

The activists at San Francisco State were extraordinarily creative and resourceful. Like the Black Panther Party, they built their own programs. They did not just advocate instituting a Black studies department, for example, they created one. Black studies first got under way in the Experimental College, a student-run, highly innovative program that began in 1965 and quickly became a national prototype. Spreading to many other universities the following year, experimental colleges were a means of infusing the curricula with the social tumult of the 1960s and of incorporating student energy and initiative. The first Black studies course at SFSC was titled Black Nationalism, taught by Aubrey LaBrie in the spring of 1966. In the fall the BSU launched a Black Arts and Culture series within the Experimental College, which stood as an exemplar of what Black studies might offer. Poets Leroi Jones and Sonia Sanchez, luminaries of the Black arts movement, taught courses. Jones, who soon afterward took the name Amiri Baraka, also ran a theater company that staged plays in Black neighborhoods. For BSU secretary Ramona Tascoe, "cultural enrichment and empowerment, combined with courses in the Experimental College," were the foundation for their new consciousness and identity. The Experimental College "was something I had never been exposed to. It was like a dream come true." She took Black Economics taught by Jerry Varnado and read the best-seller *The Rich and the Super-Rich* by Ferdinand Lundberg, which stressed the role of inherited wealth in the United States. For her, such courses provided the data and evidence to back up the charged slogans and rhetoric of the movement. The following year, eleven Black studies courses were offered in the Experimental College. The instructors were alumni, students, and community members, including Jimmy Garrett, whose course The Mis-education of the Negro promoted a critique of the Black student/intellectual's estrangement from the Black community.[11]

In addition, a few Black-content courses were offered in the college. Sonia Sanchez taught a Black literature course in the English department. "At that time," she said, "it was a revolutionary idea to insert into the English Department the study of African-American literature." Many of the texts were out of print, so she often read aloud from her copy and reproduced excerpts, using mimeograph machines with messy ink. "My hands were always blue and purple," Sanchez recalls. "I thought they would never get clean again." Sanchez thinks an important contribution of collegiate Black studies was its revival of attention to forgotten or censored Black writers, such as W.E.B. Du Bois, Paul Robeson, and Marcus Garvey. One day an FBI agent visited her home in San Francisco to interrogate her for teaching the communist Du Bois. "We resurrected people who had been hidden, and by doing that, of course, I got on the list," she observed, noting that the cycle of surveillance continued.[12]

San Francisco State gave rise to the first grassroots, bottom-up Black studies program at an American college.[13] Many of the principles that would shape the quest for Black studies nationally were first articulated in Bay Area struggles, especially at State, notably the desire for as much autonomy in form as possible, student leadership, and a strong connection to off-campus Black communities. In March 1967 Jimmy Garrett submitted a proposal for Black studies to the college. Imagined as an institute with a ten-person board of directors, seven of whom would be selected by Black students, the design exemplifies the student-centeredness of Black studies as envisioned by students. It emphasized that Black educators would shape the institute, and that Black students would form the majority in the classroom, but it rejected a narrowly nationalist approach. "There is room for a minority of whites, because everybody must learn," Garrett wrote. The proposal also included a plan to help Black high school students gain entry to State. In fact, re-forming admissions requirements and heavily promoting higher education to Black high school graduates would increasingly move to the forefront of BSU activism over the next two years. Garrett's efforts began to pay off. A committee quickly approved the proposal, but it needed to pass through several more stages, a process that the students insisted should not apply in this unique, volatile situation. A big source of student discontent was dealing with what they saw as a slow, inflexible bureaucracy that was controlled by Sacramento as much as by San Francisco. For their part, administrators tended to have more respect for the regular procedures of curricular change, even as they saw themselves as sympathetic to the students' goals.[14]

On Garrett's recommendation, the college hired Nathan Hare, a sociologist recently dismissed from his teaching position at Howard University, to set up and direct Black studies.[15] Hare was a Black nationalist scholar-activist who supported the students' desire to take power into their own hands. He began in February 1968 with the mission of gaining departmental status, a large budget and faculty, and as much autonomy from the administration as possible.[16] SFSC was unusual in that it offered an array of Black studies courses before the creation of a formal program in Black studies. When Hare arrived, there were fifteen Black-studies-oriented courses offered throughout the college, including History of the Third World, Sociology of Black Oppression, and Avant-Garde Jazz. Roland Snellings, the poet who soon changed his name to Askia Toure, and who was a coauthor of SNCC's position paper on Black Power, taught a course in the Experimental College on ancient African History. Hare and the BSU proposed moving these courses to a new department. The BSU prized the quest for "autonomy," a buzzword from the era that signaled, in essence, their desire to be free from white and traditional disciplinary oversight and control—something that departmental status, with its practice of allowing faculty to hire each other and control budgets and curriculum, seemed to offer.

A year after Garrett's first proposal, Hare submitted "A Conceptual Proposal for Black Studies," which stressed the goal of serving the educational needs of the Black community as a whole.[17] A commitment to advancing the interests of all Black people, not just students, was a core, animating principle of the Black student–Black studies movements.[18] Previewing the controversy to come, political science professor John Bunzel assailed Hare and his vision. He described Hare as a man "seething with anger about the path of Negro leadership, duplicity of many whites, and fallibility of many Negroes who follow it." He also criticized the students' Black nationalism, warning that the "emphasis on collective identity and community fealty will produce group think rather than critical inquiry."[19] This fear was expressed again and again among critics of Black studies over the next several years. At San Francisco State, Bunzel was harassed in a variety of ways over the next year or so after his article appeared; his car was painted and the tires slashed.[20]

Strikingly for an academic initiative, Black studies elicited an intense response. It arose, and acquired political symbolism, at precisely the juncture when the concept of self-determination was challenging integration as the goal of African American activism. Reactions to Black studies, then, often expressed a range of social and political anxieties. Berkeley City councilman and future congressman Ron Dellums warned, "If black studies is perceived as a separate entity, completely unto itself, for time immemorial, then it is a bad bag." The ultimate quest, he argued, "is to change the institution."[21] The sole Black member of the state college system's board of trustees became "irritated when Board members begin to express" concern that the staff of a Black studies unit would be all Black. They never worried about all-white departments. "Nor do I see them talking in terms of integrating all white departments right now."[22] The role of whites in Black studies often became a charged point of debate. Nathan Hare thought white scholars might eventually teach in the department, but felt "there are very few whites who could do it now." He acknowledged a white member of the department at Merritt College whom students liked and who taught "from a black point of view."[23]

Pivotal to the students' ability to sustain their long protest at State was the support of prominent community leaders. Cecil Williams, a minister at Glide Memorial Church in San Francisco, often joined the students at meetings with administrators and faculty. He experienced

FIGURE 3. Sociologist Nathan Hare was hired to design a Black studies department at San Francisco State. He was a staunch supporter of the Black Student Union and their decision to go on strike.

considerable frustration in trying to explain their desire for Black studies and the rising appeal of self-determination, and found university responses "unreasonable." He considered the liberals worse than conservatives because they acted as allies but slowed the process. Frustration over the pace of change was a significant factor in causing the strike. "They didn't understand the need for immediate action. Everything would always be two to five years off, " Williams said. As radical youth moved to the forefront of activism in the Bay Area, Rev. Williams felt that support from elders was important: "No longer are the Black students going to be able to say: 'Those old folks don't know what we are talking about or what we are trying to do.'" He admired the fact that "Black young people feel they can change society," and believed that civil rights leaders had an obligation to support them.[24]

Coinciding with the push for curricular change, Black students and, increasingly, other students of color demanded an increase in the admission of students of color in the state college system. California was home to an extensive public system of higher education, but restructuring in 1960 had the effect of reducing the numbers of Black students at four-year colleges and concentrating them in the two-year junior colleges. With the Master Plan for Education, California implemented a tracking system in its three tiers of higher education that offered a seat at college for every high school graduate, but Black students were overwhelmingly relegated to junior colleges, the lowest rung. The Master Plan dramatically reduced the percentage of those admitted to state colleges, from the top 70 percent of high school graduates to the top 33 percent. A major cause of Black student discontent was the sharp recent decline in Black enrollments. In contrast to virtually every other predominantly white college or university in this period, where Black student presence prior to 1968 was extremely limited, San Francisco State had had larger numbers of Black students before the Master Plan and before the introduction of standardized entrance tests in 1965. In just four years, Black student presence plunged, from 10 to 4 percent of the student body.[25]

Ironically, in 1964–1965, at the exact same time that the Black student presence at San Francisco State was in decline, the Educational Opportunity Program (EOP) began at the University of California; by 1969, EOP programs had been established on nine California campuses, including SFSC. This modest affirmative action program waived admissions criteria for 2 percent of incoming students. There had long been a special admissions category applied to students with special skills, such as musicians and athletes, but African American activists fought to extend this program to students who had the talent to succeed in college but who had been deprived of an adequate secondary education. After King's assassination, the board of trustees doubled the quota to 4 percent and projected it as a way to increase the numbers of African American and Mexican American students. Yet, the program remained multiracial. In 1968, for example, EOP students at the University of California included 147 whites, 918 Blacks, 500 "Mexicans," 217 "Orientals," 150 unidentified, and 16 American Indians. The EOP provided financial aid, tutoring, counseling, and housing aid.[26]

Just as Black studies emerged out of a student-led, grassroots struggle, so too did the character of this early "special admissions" program. Students, not admissions officers, went out looking for Black students, and they had to lobby for their entry. BSU leaders had to convince skeptical administrators that the slots used to recruit musicians and athletes should be used to admit more Black students, and that the Black students they identified were qualified. The BSU recruited Clarence Thomas and Danny Glover from San Francisco City College in 1967. Thomas remembers watching Garrett, Stewart, and Varnado advocate in his behalf at a meeting with college officials. After his admission, he went through an extensive BSU-organized orientation, which included readings by Che Guevara, Frantz Fanon, and Nathan Hare, as well as W. E. B. Du Bois's *Souls of Black Folk*. For Thomas, the whole experience was "Black Power in action."[27]

An event in November 1967 put the BSU in direct conflict with the administration and set the students on a more assertive, confrontational path. A group of BSU members, including George Murray, Clarence Thomas, and Danny Glover, visited the offices of the campus newspaper, the *Gater*, to protest a description of Muhammad Ali as a "clown" and the likening of the Nation of Islam to the Ku Klux Klan. Moreover, editor Jim Vazcko had editorialized that the college's new affirmative action program had tarnished its image. The visit was in keeping with the BSU policy of boldly confronting acts of racism on campus. A melee developed, and the students beat up Vazcko and were caught in the act by the paper's photographer. A few students were suspended, and six, including Murray, were arrested and given six-month suspended sentences. The suspensions prompted another round of protests, including a building occupation after President John Summerskill reversed an unrelated suspension of white students. The Republican establishment assailed Summerskill's decision to briefly close the campus rather than risk calling in police to end the occupation, even though this decision had been reached in consultation with the San Francisco police, and even though student leaders, including Jimmy Garrett and Hari Dillon, were later arrested. The "*Gater* incident" and its legacy signified Black student assertion, a punitive response, an unsympathetic media, and external political pressure to reject negotiation in favor of bringing in the police, a scenario that repeated itself many times over during the next couple of years.[28]

Student leaders felt that the extremely modest special admissions program at SFSC was insufficient to meet the demand for college by students of color. By 1970, half the population of San Francisco was Latino, Asian American or Black. Inspired by the BSU and seeking to build a broader student movement on campus, a group of Mexican American, Black, and Asian American students formed the Third World Liberation Front. Together with the SDS, they took over the administration building in May 1968, demanding, among other things, the rehiring of a popular Chicano professor and a sharp increase in the admissions of "Third World" students. Hari Dillon believes the creation of the TWLF, and this protest with its strong message "challenging institutionalized racism on campus," were crucial to developing the coalition that would sustain the strike the following year.[29]

The students faced enormous obstacles in their quest to build Black Power on campus: not only were they pushing charged questions of race and usurping traditionally adult areas of authority, but they were also facing a conservative state government wedded to principles of tax cutting and government shrinkage. Just as the baby boom generation was entering higher education, the state of California sharply cut its funding of state colleges. And just as students were fighting for greater admission of Black, Latino, and Asian American students, the state was cutting financial aid. Over the summer, Republican governor Ronald Reagan struck $250,000 from the Educational Opportunity Program, and his next budget failed to include the $2.5 million recommended for the EOP.[30] This conservative vision clashed with the rising expectations of working-class college-bound youth. In the words of one student, Reagan's public demeanor toward state financed colleges was "one of barely concealed, unremitting hostility."[31] But administrators felt the pinch as well, especially as newly centralized control over budgets in the chancellor's office tied the hands of college presidents. Student unrest may have caught the media's attention, but the faculty and administration were equally at loggerheads with the chancellor and board of trustees during this same period. Fatefully, John Summerskill, a liberal administrator who had hired Nathan Hare and preferred negotiations with students over calling in the police, resigned early in 1968, contending that the college was "being seriously eroded by political interference and financial starvation." State officials were leading attacks on public higher education in California, he charged. He was gone by May.[32]

Jimmy Garrett also left San Francisco State in the spring of 1968. He had been arrested for his role in a December protest over the *Gater* suspensions. More than a dozen police officers had come to arrest him, or as Garrett remembers thinking, "they came to kill me." Garrett had a gun in his possession that day and was convicted of assault on a police officer with a deadly weapon, a felony. His attorney, state assemblyman Willie Brown, and "the black lawyer elite" persuaded the judge to offer an alternative to prison. His choice was five to twenty-five years or to leave San Francisco. "So I left San Francisco." He was barred from entering the city or county until 1973 and had to finish school by mail. Coincidentally, Garrett was also ousted from leadership of the Black Student Union that spring. "I began to believe my own press notices," he recalled, letting leadership go to his head. "I centered much of what was going on around myself." And he had less time to devote to State: as the leader of the sixty-member Western Regional Alliance of Black Student Unions, he was traveling around the West, building Black studies programs and Black student unions. Garrett relocated to Washington, D.C., where he continued in the same work, building the Black studies program at Federal City College, which later became the University of the District of Columbia.[33]

By the fall of 1968, with new president Robert Smith at the helm, the promises made to Nathan Hare and the BSU seemed farther off. The fledgling Black studies department had only 1.3 positions: Hare plus a part-time staff person. A highly contentious meeting in September with BSU leaders, administrators, and community leaders Willie Brown and the Reverend Cecil Williams revealed sharp differences in how various people understood Black studies. In a major sticking point, President Smith refused to move Black content courses taught in other departments into the new unit. Smith and the other administrators bristled at the idea of autonomy for Black studies and reaffirmed the need to go through many stages of university approval for the creation of a Black studies department.[34] In his own account, Smith wrote that he promised to set up Black studies by the spring but worried that board of trustees approval for a new major would be stymied by concerns over "black separatism and possible indoctrination."[35] For its part, shortly after this meeting, the BSU issued a statement declaring, "In the coming semester we will be engaged in revolutionary political activity."[36]

The fall of 1968 was marked by student rebellions up and down the state of California. In October, Black students at UC Santa Barbara occupied the computer center. At San Fernando Valley State College in Northridge a Black student occupation of the president's office in November produced a mass felony arrest—the largest arrest of college students in U.S. history. That fall "Bay Area schools and colleges were requiring police action at one or another campus almost daily."[37] The Black Panther Party had close relationships with Black student activists in California. SFSC student Ramona Tascoe sometimes wore the Panther uniform. It was a way to say, "Be afraid of us," she recalls. Notwithstanding the militant image, the Panthers wanted students to stay in school, thrive, and succeed. "Our education was central to the masses," was their philosophy, according to Tascoe. Being on the frontline of the BSU—"that was your assignment for the cause of the people."[38] Students at Berkeley had invited Panther leader Eldridge Cleaver to give a series of lectures in an experimental course, outraging Governor Reagan and Superintendent of Public Instruction Max Rafferty, who called the appointment of Cleaver "asinine and ridiculous" and blocked his paycheck. The clash generated vitriol and condemnation until Cleaver's flight into exile ended his brief teaching career at Berkeley.

Similarly, when the media discovered that Panther leader and graduate student George Murray was slated to teach at State in the fall of 1968, they ran headlines exposing his "foreign" radicalism and questioning the appropriateness of his hiring. "SFS Puts Admirer of Mao on the Teaching Staff," declared the *San Francisco Examiner,* and reminded readers of Murray's speech in Cuba over the summer assailing U.S. imperialism and supporting the Vietcong.[39] That same summer, Panther founder Huey Newton was tried for the murder of Oakland police officer John Frey and convicted of voluntary manslaughter in September. In October, Murray gave a speech in Fresno, "The Necessity of a Black Revolution," in which he proclaimed: "Political power comes from the barrel of a gun." His alleged statement "We are slaves and the only way to become free is to kill all the slave masters" prompted the board of trustees of the state colleges to order President Smith to fire Murray. The fiery rhetoric of a Panther leader notwithstanding, Smith felt that firing Murray, whose classroom performance was by all accounts solid, would violate personnel procedures and certainly inflame the faculty and students, so he tried to buy time.[40]

At the same time, seeking new means to pressure the administration, Jerry Varnado broached the idea of a student strike. He was inspired to step up students' militancy after seeing *The Battle of Algiers,* a highly influential film for student activists of this era, which documented the Algerian people's struggle against French colonialism. At a meeting of Black faculty and students, Varnado and Murray proposed a one-day Black-community strike for November 6.[41] On October 28, the first anniversary of Huey Newton's arrest, BSU leaders led a march across campus to test the waters and assess the degree of Black student awareness and interest. They chanted common slogans of the Black Panther Party: "Free Huey" "Black Is Beautiful," "The Revolution Has Come," and "Off the Pig."[42] In the cafeteria, Murray gave a speech decrying the low numbers of Black students at the college and complaining that "four and one-half million black and brown people in California pay taxes to pay for the racist departments here, but none of their taxes go to black and brown people." He defended the Panthers' policy of self-defense and carrying arms and urged the students to join the fight. "If a fraternity takes up guns to defend our communities from the pigs, then it is doing something. Otherwise," he declared, "it's not."[43]

At a press conference on November 4, the BSU announced: "Black people, including students, staff workers, teachers and administrators, will be striking on November 6."[44] Nathan Hare and other Black administrators attended in support. Hare was thirty-four and very close to the student leaders, whom he described as "the most sophisticated in the country."[45] Of the BSU's ten demands, the first called for the transfer of all Black content courses offered in the college to a new Black studies department. "We, the Black students at San Francisco State College," they wrote, "feel that it is detrimental to us as Black human beings to be controlled by racists, who have absolute power over determining what we should learn." The students felt that, after two years of struggle, all they had was a paper department, without funds and faculty. Some of the demands pertained to Nathan Hare's rank and salary, because he was paid less than initially promised. They called for admission of "all Black students wishing to be admitted in Fall 1969," a demand for open admissions that would be made at many other urban campuses the following year. The students demanded twenty full-time positions in the Black studies department. George Murray had finally been suspended on October 31, and his rehiring became one of the strike demands. In a controversial stance, the BSU declared the demands "non-negotiable."[46] Jerry Varnado told a *New York Times* reporter, "What we are doing is revolutionary. We are going to have a black studies department that we control. Where we can hire and fire who we want. . . . There's not a department like that in the country."[47] For the students, the overriding goal was to achieve the Black nationalist idea of self-determination: for Black people at SFSC to gain control of their educational destiny.

On the eve of the strike, Stokely Carmichael gave a fiery speech to a packed Blacks-only audience urging the students to recognize the necessity of "protracted struggle." "Our fight is a fight of this generation," he declared. "The entire generation has to give its blood, its talents, its skills, its sweat . . . and its life to this struggle. It's not a fight that's gonna be over tomorrow, next year, two years from now. . . . We've got to fight our whole lives."[48] His speech helped to inspire the devotion and commitment that would be needed to sustain a strike. The next speaker was BSU president Ben Stewart, who tried to persuade the audience to adopt the "strategy of the flea," which he had learned from Robert Taber's book, *The War of the Flea*. Taber captures a brief but politically explosive moment when American power was under siege. Events in Cuba and Vietnam appeared to confirm that well-organized, nationalist forces could withstand the military might of the United States, while domestic dissent had helped to bring down President Johnson. This surging realignment of power, globally and locally, made a deep impression on this generation and reinforced its own sense of being able to decisively shape the flow of history. But Stewart was more interested in the book's explication of guerilla tactics. He told the students that the "war of the flea" was a series of actions intended to frustrate authorities. "You just begin to wear them down. Something is always costin' them. Something happens all the time. Toilets are stopped up. Pipes is cut. Water in the bathroom is just runnin' all over the place. Smoke is coming out of the bathroom."[49]

On the first day of the strike, during a large meeting on campus, students debated what to do. In a decisive moment, a young man stood up and asked, "If we're on strike, why are we sitting here? Let's go shut it down." And "on strike, shut it down" quickly became the strike's rallying cry. At once, the idea of a symbolic Black community strike changed decisively to a campuswide shutdown. The students divided into "flying squads" to go around campus and persuade students, staff, and faculty to join them. Groups of ten or so Black students entered classrooms, explained the strike demands, and urged professors to halt teaching. BSU secretary Ramona Tascoe was in a group that visited the anthropology office. As she began reading the demands, someone threw a typewriter out a window, another student cut phone wires, and sparks began to fly. The students began to flee, but she "was either too naive or too foolish to run" so she just kept on reading. She was on the third demand, when a secretary told her, "Honey, you'd better go." Her more emphatic "Go!" finally sent Tascoe running. She broke, fell, got up and ran; and then fell and got up again. The third time she fell was over the foot of a plainclothes officer, several of whom were undercover in various departments, waiting for the strike to commence. The first of nearly eight hundred arrests during the five-month strike, Tascoe immediately imagined her face plastered on the city's front pages and dreaded her parents' reaction. She hailed from a large, socially conservative Louisiana migrant family and had attended Catholic school all her life before entering State. Her parents had no idea that their daughter was a Black Panther, and she certainly wasn't going to tell them she got arrested. So, the San Francisco State coed arrested that day was identified in the press as "Mona Williams." Her attorney, Assemblyman Willie Brown, got the two felony charges down to a misdemeanor and a sentence of two to three years of probation. While some students engaged in vandalism or other disruptive tactics in order to shut the campus down, the main tactic was the boycott of classes and the enormous rallies and picket lines that became a near daily occurrence.[50]

The Black Student Union had an elaborately defined structure with strong gender divisions, even as gender roles in society were on the verge of major change. Wanting to avoid investing leadership in one person, the BSU was run by its twelve-member central committee.[51] And it was all male, consisting of "the most vocal, the most assertive, the most recognized brothers."[52] Reflecting their belief that a revolution was possible, BSU members wore green fatigues throughout the strike, and some practiced at firing ranges to become familiar with weaponry. The next layer of leadership, the presidium, was mostly female. According to Ramona Tascoe, the gender division was "part of the culture of the times. It was a time in history when women were still actively subjugated to supportive roles." But, she noted, if membership on the central committee had been "determined by the work people did," she "would have been on it." Like other Black women on campus, Tascoe fought shoulder to shoulder with the male students, getting arrested, walking picket lines, and attending rallies, but her BSU duties were traditionally female tasks: she typed speeches for George Murray and other leaders, scheduled meetings, and sent out notices.[53] This period was marked by strong women and high levels of female participation—Varnado described the women in the BSU as "fighters" who "were on the front lines"[54]—but also, as in society at large, by pervasive chauvinism and presumptions of male leadership. On the first or second day of the strike, a large group of students went to the BSU off-campus office for a meeting. As it was about to start, one male student said to a group of other males: "We're ready to start; we should send the women out." They debated and ultimately decided against it, but it didn't change the all-male leadership structure, which lasted throughout the strike.[55] In Tascoe's view, theirs was "a generation of African American brothers and sisters who were transitioning from an era of male chauvinism and overt oppression of women toward an affirmation of, and making of room for, women as comrades."[56]

Two days into the strike, the Third World Liberation Front endorsed it and attached five more demands, including a call for a School of Ethnic Studies, which would encompass the study of other racially oppressed groups. The TWLF endorsement broadened support for the strike, and serious coalition-building among diverse organizations of students of color developed over the next several months. But members of the Black Student Union remained the primary leaders. As Tascoe remembers it, "They assimilated behind us respectfully. It was an affirmation of Black student leadership."[57] The decades-long civil rights movement had given Black students valuable experience, which other students recognized and admired. "We would tell them: just watch what we do," Varnado said, because "blacks have been struggling for years and years."[58] In fact, Jimmy Garrett had helped form the TWLF the previous spring, and the BSU helped publicize its existence, leading to the creation of chapters on other California campuses.[59]

There was a genuine effort to bridge Black nationalism and Third Worldism—a term the radical students of color used to signify their sense of shared condition and perspective—but differences still remained. Like the BSU, the TWLF included both seasoned radicals and many students who were new to political struggle, as well as more traditional first-generation college students. According to TWLF leader Roger Alvarado, Black Power "affected non-black Third World people too," but he did not see an alliance as inevitable or natural. Rather, he saw each group's relationship to their community of origin as the bond that held them together. "That is essentially to us the key that has brought us to where we are now," he said. "Being able to refer to our communities and being actively involved in the different aspects of those communities has developed for us some attitudes and perspectives, which has taken us from the bourgeois context of higher education." For Mason Wong, a Chinese American student, the TWLF provided an opportunity to educate others about the plight of Chinese American workers and dispel the image of Asian Americans as the model minority. The "Chinese community has the same basic problems as all other non-white communities," he argued, pointing to the exploitation of Chinese workers in the sweatshops, laundries, and restaurants of Chinatown. "Another fallacy" according to Wong, "is the myth that Orientals are the best educated minority in the United States." In actuality, the "formal educational grade level of Chinese people under 25 years old" in Chinatown is 1.7, "not even a second grade level."[60]

To succeed, the BSU and TWLF also needed the support of white students and faculty. The decision to shut down a majority white campus clearly entailed enlisting as many students and faculty as possible. The local television stations gave extensive coverage to the strike, and their footage illustrates that large numbers of white students walked picket lines and attended rallies.[61] In addition to the many liberal whites, there was a smaller but well-organized group of radicals, many of whom were affiliated with the Students for a Democratic Society; and in turn, many SDS members at State were part of the Worker-Student Alliance, which was a satellite of the Maoist Progressive Labor Party. A few members of the BSU were also in the Progressive Labor Party. When the strike began, SDS members debated whether to insist upon an antiwar plank in exchange for their endorsement. But they concluded that the strike was not about Vietnam anymore than it was about the grape boycott or any other struggle. It was "a strike about racist policies and practices of the university," and since "destroying racism was key to the revolutionary goal," they voted to give the strike and the BSU and TWLF their full support. According to SDS leader John Levin, white supporters were not just sympathetic observers but also active participants who saw the strike as their fight too. "It was a different time," and the general attitude toward the fifteen demands was that "these were good things" that would improve the college. Still, he recalls, some students "were scared of the militancy of the Third World students, who often attended meetings with side arms, and by the fiery nationalism of their rhetoric." But he felt that Hari Dillon's view that "nationalism was aimed at white racism not white people"

FIGURE 4. Strike leaders address a rally. Black Student Union members Nesbit Crutchfield, on the left, Bridges Randle with the improvised megaphone, and Don Smothers
between them.

helped give political clarity and build unity between Third World and
white students.[62]

Many white students and faculty at State also felt that the board of
trustees, chancellor, and elected officials were interfering with local affairs in an aggressive, unwarranted manner. The calls for due process,
student rights, and local autonomy were important factors in pushing
white students and faculty to support a strike led by Black and Third
World student groups. And their support grew as the city's infamous
tactical squad adopted aggressive policing. Hundreds of white students
were arrested during the five-month strike, creating solidarity with the
TWLF "forged in blood and struggle." White students, led by Margaret
Leahy, ran the bail campaign, traveling to churches, unions, and other
campuses to raise funds. "Students had massive support in the community," Levin remembers.[63] Some of the more militant white students used
stinkbombs, smoke bombs, or other forms of vandalism to help shut the
campus down. Indeed, a government observer reported that "far more
whites than blacks or other minorities could be seen throwing rocks or
shouting insults at police."[64]

A violent confrontation between hundreds of San Francisco Tactical Squad police officers and students on November 13 shocked many on campus and set in motion a shift toward much greater campus support for the strike. As on many college campuses in 1968 and 1969, excessive use of force by police pushed moderate students over to the side of radicals. Ironically, after a week of intense strike activity, many BSU leaders were exhausted, and they planned to have a press conference the next day to help lay the groundwork, possibly, for a end to the strike.[65] But police aggression changed everything. President Smith sought to cool tempers by temporarily closing the college and holding a campus-wide convocation. A television news reporter called the convocation historic: "It's the first time an American college has stopped all its academic pursuits to devote its entire attention to the educational needs and demands of American minorities." But Sacramento wanted a hard line, and on November 26 Robert Smith resigned the presidency under pressure from the trustees.[66]

Ronald Reagan offered the job to Professor S.I. Hayakawa, a Japanese American semanticist, who came to relish his public image as a hard-line president, arranging a stream of television and radio appearances.[67] As one colleague put it, "Hayakawa felt that somebody should stand up to these kids and not be bullied by them."[68] That's exactly what he did. Hayakawa set out to crush the strike. On December 3, "Bloody Tuesday," the new president declared a state of emergency, suspended civil liberties, and called in hundreds of heavily armed members of the tac squad. The police swarmed onto campus in full riot gear, with billy clubs at the ready as they marched in formation. "It was the most riotous [day] in the school's history," according to one reporter. Hayakawa, Governor Reagan, and San Francisco Mayor Joseph Alioto held a press conference announcing arrest warrants for seven strike leaders: Jack Alexis, Roger Alvarado, Nesbit Crutchfield, Hari Dillon, John Levin, Tony Miranda, Bridges Randle, and Jerry Varnado. The police aggressively moved to break up the now banned demonstration and knocked down and arrested many. This marked the start of a period of bloody police-student clashes known as the "December days." But instead of crushing the strike, Hayakawa's repression widened its base of support. "We were not intimidated," remembers Dillon, and "the strike became more massive and determined."[69] Police arrested Alexis, Dillon and Randle a few days later. "They seized Randle after he spoke to a rally of hundreds with a makeshift cardboard megaphone." In former president Smith's view, "nothing radicalized the SFS student

FIGURE 5. Strike leaders at the head of a mass march of ten thousand students on campus during "December days." From left, Thomas Williams, Roger Alvarado in sunglasses, Carlotta Simon, Bridges Randle with fists in front, Hari Dillon with raised fist, Don Smothers, Claude Wilson with megaphone, and Paul Yamazaki with neck scarf.

body and faculty as much as the sight of the brawny, helmeted Taq Squad chasing a single student, felling him with a truncheon blow, then striking him several times on the ground as the blood spurted out." While not typical police behavior, he said, this happened often enough, "in sight of thousands," that it created many strike sympathizers and "police-and-Hayakawa haters."[70] Overall, eighty students were injured during the course of the strike while being handled and arrested by the San Francisco Police Department. Hayakawa's tenure was marked by a massive police presence, frequent and numerous arrests, ongoing clashes with students, and other less visible curtailments of student power.[71]

Bystanders were not immune to police abuse. A nonstriking student objected when he saw a police officer clubbing a woman lying on the ground. After being arrested and charged, his view of the strike changed. He subsequently dropped his economics major, saying he wanted to learn "something that will help people socially."[72] On December 3, an African American apprentice reporter with KQED witnessed police "running at students and hitting them. I actually saw them run up and hit a girl across her behind and laugh about it, you know, actually laughing, in public." Unfortunately, his press credentials did not protect him from the officers' wrath. The police clubbed him, called him racial epithets, beat him again in the paddy wagon, and arrested and strip-searched him at the station. "I have never seen anyone carry a weapon in their asshole before.... In other words, they break you down to where you don't even feel like a human being anymore."[73] In an effort to resolve the strike, eighty African American leaders met with President

FIGURE 6. Tactical squad police brutally beat and arrested Don McAllister on Bloody Tuesday, December 2. A second striking student—being pulled with a nightstick at his neck—was another of many arrested.

Hayakawa in early December at the offices of the *Sun-Reporter,* a newspaper published by physician and activist Dr. Carleton Goodlett. In 1937 at the age of twenty-three, Goodlett had received a PhD in psychology from the University California, Berkeley, but it was thirty more years before Berkeley awarded another PhD to a Black person, a striking illustration of what the Black student movement was trying to change. At the meeting, Hayakawa was by many accounts rude and tone deaf to the sentiments of Black leaders. His condescending remark to a woman, "Now look, baby, you people have got to understand . . . ," unleashed a heated exchange. And then, abruptly, Hayakawa got up and walked out. Ron Dellums was in the room and heard Hayakawa say, "I, as a minority, see my role as interpreting your concern to the white community." Dellums was stunned. "Man, if black people ain't said nothing in the last two years, they said don't be speaking for me.[74] Similarly, Willie Brown saw Hayakawa as "plantation oriented." Calling the college president's behavior "bizarre," Brown stated that Hayakawa "said, 'You be good boys and girls and help me on the campus, and I will go back and tell all the white folks what you did.' . . . Those were his exact words. He was almost lynched."[75] According to another participant, the meeting united "the black community in total support of the student strike, even though many of us did not have all the detailed information that was the basis of the strike."[76]

The strike generated considerable controversy in San Francisco and nationally. San Francisco Mayor Joseph Alioto convened a Committee of Concerned Citizens chaired by Catholic Archbishop Mark Hurley, which began negotiating a resolution to the strike in December, but at that time the BSU wasn't ready to negotiate.[77] The federal government dispatched a team of researchers who were studying urban violence. Appointed by President Lyndon Johnson in the spring of 1968, the National Commission on the Causes and Prevention of Violence visited San Francisco in the fall and interviewed many participants in the conflict, as well as African American leaders in the city. Anxious about the students' revolutionary rhetoric and confrontational tactics, the researchers found community leaders who, while not necessarily endorsing the tactics, overwhelmingly defended the students. Willie Brown explained that the Black community saw the young activists not as irresponsible but instead "as persons to be loved, nurtured and guided."[78]

In fact, in terms of legal, political, and moral support, community leaders—especially Dr. Carlton Goodlett, a longtime civil rights activist; Brown; and the Reverend Cecil Williams—were very important allies to the striking students. One reason for the solidarity of Bay Area leaders was the fact that the students had long been involved in community struggles. The students "have taken out a membership of some kind in every organization that is attempting to improve the life of people in this ghetto," noted the Reverend Hannibal Williams, including involvement in his own Western Addition Community Organization, helping to halt a redevelopment project that threatened to displace poor Black residents of Fillmore. Williams applauded the BSU for taking the view that "college for the black student is not an ivory tower but a place where he gets some kind of preparation to come back to these ghetto communities." In Williams's view, the police, who "come in with the blessing of the authority structure . . . to establish law and order," and who were "vicious and violent," deserved public scorn and condemnation.[79] More than anything else, witnessing excessive use of force on campus brought community leaders to the side of the students. Moreover, the Black Student Union gained the support of many Black faculty and administrators. EOP director Reginald Major defended the verbal brashness of the BSU leaders, calling their willingness to speak openly about racism and to assail authority, and their decision to cultivate a "hostile, aggressive style," their "most potent weapon."[80]

But the San Francisco State strike wasn't simply another version of Birmingham or Selma, where nonviolent protesters endured brutal police violence. Some students used violent tactics, and this certainly influenced the media's framing of the event. Eight bombs were planted during the strike, and four were detonated, in mostly deserted areas.[81] On the second day of the strike, a twenty-eight-year-old Nigerian student was arrested for carrying a small homemade bomb.[82] The office of a vice president was burned, and two firebombs were hurled into the house of an assistant to the president. And on March 5, freshman Tim Peebles attempted to plant a bomb in the creative arts building, but it went off prematurely and he suffered hand and face injuries. He was partially blinded.[83] William Pulliam, another student, was also injured, and both young men were arrested. Ramona Tascoe said the accident "jolted them into reality."[84] Central committee member Jerry Varnado claims that individuals who set off bombs or vandalized automobiles were doing "their own thing." . . . "We did not want to destroy anything. We were trying to build something." He says their main goal was to shut the school down. "Some people did those things on their own. We might hear about it later, and they would come to us and say, 'Well, what did you think about this or that?' We tried to persuade people not to do that kind of stuff." Still, Varnado himself was arrested seven or eight times during the strike and was sentenced to a year in jail for "tossing a firebomb at a building." He pled guilty to a felony, though he insists he was innocent. A campus police officer identified him as the culprit, and Varnado says he "couldn't prove [he] didn't do it" and felt it was too risky to go to trial.[85]

The strike garnered daily coverage by television, radio, and print journalists, and, as a media event, its framing swung beyond the students' control. The media tended to portray the students as intent upon destroying the university, which increased the clamor for punitive crackdowns.[86] A mediator who had been brought in by the city to help settle the strike complained that the media was only focusing on radical slogans and failing to see the substance in the students' demands.[87] Conservative Californians sent thousands of letters to Hayakawa and the board of trustees. After seeing a televised interview with George Murray, one person wrote, "In the course of the interview he expressed disdain for the United States, and in particular, said, 'To Hell with America.' I wish to express to you my amazement and dismay that the California state college system is persuaded to employ this type of man." Many in the public absorbed the image of spoiled youth whose radicalism was paid for by hard-working taxpayers. But that picture was far from accurate: 80 percent of SFSC students were employed, and their average age was twenty-four.[88]

Meanwhile, the strike was fairly effective in closing down the campus. A survey of the classes that met on January 14, 1969, at a time when 115 classes were scheduled, indicated that forty-three classes were held, or 37 percent. And all of these reportedly had an attendance rate below 50 percent.[89] The academic senate found that class attendance was off by 50 percent: "Although still 'open' in some legal or political sense, . . . the college is rapidly closing intellectually and spiritually."[90]

The strike's reverberation into the broader San Francisco community widened when the campus chapter of the American Federation of Teachers struck on January 6, 1969. The city's labor council sanctioned the strike, giving the faculty, and indirectly the students, the backing of scores of workers across this pro-labor town. In one example of material support, the International Longshore and Warehouse Union offered casual jobs to individuals affected by the strike. The father and grandfather of BSU leader Clarence Thomas had been members of that union, and Thomas would later become a leader in the union. Walter Riley was a bus driver during the strike and organizer of a Black caucus in the militant Transport Workers Union. He had also attended SFSC the year before and was active in the BSU and SDS. He brought groups of bus drivers in uniform to the picket lines to offer visible strike support.[91] The faculty struck to protest the state of emergency, suspension of civil liberties, refusal of Reagan and the trustees to negotiate, mass arrests, and daily presence of several hundred police. With a picket line now circling in front of the campus gates, the location of protest activity shifted off-campus and violence declined. The 350 teachers who struck also had their own professional demands, including the desire for a contract. Their strike lasted two months.[92]

The height of the strike coincided with the Federal Bureau of Investigation's effort to destroy the Black Panther Party through a range of secret methods known as counterintelligence programs, or COINTELPRO.[93] These methods included surveillance, false arrest, disinformation, and even assassination and went a long way toward decimating the party by the early 1970s. A slight detour southward, to the movement in Los Angeles, will help illustrate the wider context of California Black student activism, the lethal affects of repression on college campuses, the intense ideological ferment in the student movement, and a contrasting example of a student vision for African American studies. In distinction to the Bay Area, where the Panthers were predominant, the Los Angeles chapter of the Black Panther Party was embroiled in a sharp rivalry with US, a cultural nationalist organization headed by Maulana Karenga. Both groups emphasized physical prowess and training in weaponry. But in contrast to the leftist, anti-imperialist politics of the Panthers, who criticized the government and built dynamic community-based programs, cultural nationalists tended to emphasize African roots, cultural grounding, and gender hierarchies as remedies for contemporary racism. Their conflict culminated on January 17, 1969, with the shooting deaths of Panther leaders Alprentice "Bunchy" Carter and John Huggins by US members after a Black Student Union meeting on the campus of the University of California at Los Angeles. Subsequent accounts revealed that the FBI had infiltrated and provoked discord between the two groups.[94] Strike leader and Panther Minister of Education George Murray believes those bullets were actually meant for him.

Even though the Black student movement in Los Angeles was deeply marked by the Panther-US rivalry, the students who spearheaded the creation of the Center for Afro-American Studies at UCLA endeavored to withstand these ideological currents. And in many respects they stood in contrast to the students who devised Black studies at San Francisco State. Black students did not always agree on the form or function of African American studies, and the local political landscape shaped their thinking. The UCLA student leaders tried to resist the efforts of community leaders to gain influence over Afro-American studies, and endeavored to imbue the program with academic rigor and independence. The creation of the center gave rise to a fierce battle for "control" between these student leaders and members of the Community Advisory Board, who wanted the center to be a social and political force in the Black community. The Black Student Union itself was divided over this issue. According to Mary Jane Hewitt, an African American administrator and advisor to Black students at UCLA, "The prime movers in getting that Center started" were Virgil Roberts, Arthur Frazier, Mike Downing, and Tim Ricks. She remembers them as "a group of very bright, very energetic, and very determined young African American students." They also helped design and administer the High Potential Program, an affirmative action program that actively utilized Black students in student recruitment. Members of the us organization as well as the Black Panther Party, including Bunchy Carter and John Huggins, were recruited to UCLA through High Potential. Beginning in the summer of 1968, Roberts, Downing, Frazier, and Ricks researched Black studies programs and proposed an interdisciplinary center consisting of four ethnic studies units. As part of their proposal, they called for support for an academic journal (which later became the important *Journal of Black Studies*) and funding for conferences and research. The students visited San Francisco State to examine how Black studies was evolving there and borrowed some of their ideas. But in the end, they advocated creating, and won, a center rather than a department, incorporating Asian American, Mexican American, and Native American units, because, in their view, this promised to "be more salable politically."[95]

It was a time of intense nationalism, but they built alliances, in part because the number of Black students at UCLA was small. Roberts recalls that Black students and faculty were unified in their desire to create the center. "The conflict later on came over who the people were going to be. We had this conflict with Maulana (Ron) Karenga and our Community Advisory Board." But the president of the BSU, history graduate student Floyd Hayes, opposed the plan and virtually "excommunicated" Roberts, Frazier, Ricks, and Downing. "There was a meeting in which the BSU members said they felt we were selling out to white folks, and they were going to kill all of us," Roberts recalls, still taken aback at the threats and level of vitriol. The four students felt betrayed and ostracized, he says, after having given so much of themselves to build the center, so much so that Virgil Roberts stopped wearing his dashiki in favor of a suit and tie when he came to campus, so as not to be associated with the BSU.[96]

Students and community leaders had contending visions for the center. Dr. Alfred Cannon, a psychiatrist at the medical school and prominent community leader, sat on the Community Advisory Board for the Center for Afro-American Studies and promoted as director of the new center Dr. Charles Thomas, the director of a health center in Watts. Ron

Karenga, who also sat on the Community Advisory Board as head of the US organization, supported Thomas as well. "Take the community to the campus, bring the campus to the community—there's no way around it," Karenga later described his stance.[97] Hewitt, who directed the EOP and High Potential programs, recalls that US members had given the very first director of the center, UCLA political scientist Sylvester Whittaker, "a bad time," helping hasten his departure to Princeton. Among some students and faculty, there was a concern that Karenga and the advisory board were overreaching in campus affairs. Roberts and several of the other students came to view Thomas as "unacceptable" after he visited campus and gave a job talk. They questioned his ability to hold his own in a rigorous academic environment. "We wanted to have a really heavy brother come in who could deal with UCLA, and we were convinced at the meeting that there's no way he could deal with UCLA—you know the faculty would be able to just push him over."[98]

At a packed meeting in Campbell Hall—where the shootings would happen two days later—the students related their opposition to Thomas to the Community Advisory Board. Virgil Roberts was there, along with Bunchy Carter and John Huggins. The Simbas, the appointed muscle for the US organization, were out in force. Roberts remembers that advisory board members went "ballistic, especially Maulana." The students adjourned to another room and Karenga began lecturing them about what was in their best interest, when Mary Jane Hewitt stood up and confronted him. "I just remember saying to him I thought he was damned irresponsible to be playing this kind of role and bringing this kind of madness to campus," she later recalled. "I chastened him. I can remember saying that 'you ought to know better than to do this kind of thing, manipulating young people like this.'" Community groups should advise, she told him, not dictate. Virgil Roberts remembers her upbraiding Karenga: "The students (were) cheering and stuff," but Karenga "was totally upset." Meanwhile, Panthers and US members lined the hallways of Campbell Hall in long coats, which allegedly concealed their weapons. Before departing, the students formed a new search committee, on which Carter and Huggins were appointed to serve.[99]

Two days later, an alleged FBI operative in the US organization gunned down Carter and Huggins in Campbell Hall, killing them both. Claude Hubert, the alleged gunman, was never apprehended, but Donald Hawkins and brothers Larry Stiner and George Stiner were convicted of conspiracy and second-degree murder. In 1974 the Stiners escaped from the maximum-security prison at San Quentin and went to live as fugitives in South America. All three men had been members of the Simbas. A group of Simbas, Virgil Roberts said, "came in, walked in, shot in the hall and ran out."[100] The killings traumatized students and ushered in a long period of political quiescence, anxiety, and fear on campus. There were many witnesses, including some who lived under police protection for the rest of the quarter. FBI counterintelligence operations against the Panthers, including assassination, have been well documented, yet neither the Panthers nor us shied from armed struggle. Members of both groups carried weapons and "physically disciplined" members; Karenga was himself imprisoned in 1971 for ordering the beating of a woman.[101] But after gaining an early release, he embarked on a long career teaching Black studies at California State University in Long Beach and, most famously, developed the African-inspired holiday Kwanzaa, which became popular among many African Americans nationwide.

As noted, San Francisco State strike leader George Murray thinks the bullets in Los Angeles that January day were actually intended for him. The twenty-three-year-old was meant to have been at UCLA as a guest of the Los Angeles Panthers, but because of the demands of the strike, his exhaustion, and his wife's pregnancy, he cancelled at the last minute. "I was supposed to have been there," he says, and remembers learning the news over the radio. He assumes he was the real target because of his intense notoriety in the state and his leadership position in both the BSU and the Black Panther Party.[102] At the same time, authorities in San Francisco were determined to arrest strike leaders and remove them from the scene. About one month later, Murray was sentenced to six months in jail for violating the terms of probation he received following the *Gater* melee. After he was rearrested, police said they found two guns in his car, although Murray contended that the us organization had broken into his car and planted the guns. In a courtroom packed with eighty spectators, "many of them militant blacks," Panther leader Bobby Seale testified that Murray could not have had the guns.[103] Murray thinks that authorities hoped his incarceration would end the strike. The judge "had it in for us," he remembers. "He must have been under a lot of pressure."[104]

Meanwhile, Bay Area support for the students continued to grow. On January 23, close to two hundred community supporters joined a rally on campus. Hayakawa had banned all demonstrations, and when police surrounded the large crowd, demanding that they disperse, the elders inserted themselves between police and students. "It is not necessary to brutalize us in order to arrest us," Dr. Goodlett declared through a bullhorn.[105] Four hundred and fifty people were arrested that day, the largest mass arrest in San Francisco history, leading to more than a year of mass trials and harsh sentencing. Importantly, it was not simply police or administrative overzealousness that brought students deep local support. The BSU and TWLF demands reflected community aspirations, and symbolized the new direction of the Black freedom struggle as it was expanding across the country. Students were trying to open up institutions of higher education to underserved Black and Latino communities. Adults in these communities recognized that the outcome of these protests had significant long-term implications. The doors to college, said Ron Dellums, who was soon to be elected to Congress, "should be open to all interested ethnic minorities who seek admission." Moreover, he felt, taxpayers should view this quest for upward mobility as a smart antipoverty program. "Colleges must spend more on tutoring, counseling, [and] support services to help students thrive," he also insisted, reminding us that advocates of expanded admissions still believed in academic rigor and proper preparation. He too thought the media's and government's focus on tactics was a distraction from the substantive issues of the strike, and he resisted pressure to condemn the students. "Some people get hung up on the tactics," he thought. But "that is a bad bag for us as community people to get into. It is a divisive bag." The students had already "gone through eighteen months of negotiations" and "committee meetings and more committee meetings," only to get broken promises and extended negotiations.[106]

As the violence, arrests, and media attention intensified, officials stepped up efforts to find a resolution. Joseph White thought the students were frozen in revolutionary rhetoric and should have begun talks much earlier. "You see the students did not know how to negotiate, so we went into the Black community to get the elders and senior ministers to show the students how to negotiate with the administration." He helped, he said, even though the students had viewed him skeptically as a "house Negro."[107] According to BSU secretary Ramona Tascoe, the strike ended in March because "the crescendo had peaked," and "because the brothers were gone and they were the lead strategists."[108] After the mass arrest in January, authorities began to seek out the strike leaders in earnest to either lock them up or make them afraid to come on campus. But it wasn't just arrests and repression that brought the strike to a close. BSU off-campus coordinator Leroy Goodwin said it was simply very challenging to keep a coalition of different organizations and constituencies united and mobilized for so long. Black student support and morale was weakening. In his view, class differences between BSU and TWLF members were more pronounced than initially anticipated, leading to different political approaches and sensibilities. Not insignificantly, the administration seemed poised to offer many of things the students had been fighting for.[109]

Several committees negotiated an end to the strike, and a settlement was signed on March 20, 1969. The college agreed to design a School of Ethnic Studies and to move all Black studies courses to the new Department of Black Studies, to be launched in the fall with 11.3 staff positions. The school was later renamed the College of Ethnic Studies and also included programs in Chicano, Asian American, and Native American studies. Hayakawa had fired Nathan Hare in February after Hare and several students disrupted a speech in which Hayakawa was boasting of the recent mass arrest and claiming victory. Hare was never reinstated, never had the opportunity to build the department he had envisioned, and feels he was blacklisted from future employment in the state college system because of his strike activities. San Francisco State has developed the reputation of launching the first Black studies department in the United States, but because of the delay caused by the strike, a Black studies department apparently got under way at Merritt College first. But the long birth of Black studies in the Experimental College and its final creation as part of a new School of Ethnic Studies was pioneering and unprecedented. The college agreed to undertake steps to increase the enrollment of students of color and to withdraw police from campus. More significantly, California enacted an EOP law in 1969 that gave affirmative action greater legal and political footing. Hayakawa was determined to discipline strike supporters even though the settlement recommended leniency. In the end, most ordinary students got amnesty for strike participation, but most strike leaders went to jail and were banned from campus.

All the BSU and TWLF leaders had been arrested, many several times. And many served time in jail. According to Hari Dillon, "Reagan and Hayakawa's assault on the strike was a severe blow." George Murray served two and a half months in jail. The judge called him "all kinds of names" and accused him of rending "the social fabric of San Francisco," but "progressive forces in the legal system" assisted Murray. His lawyer announced that he had undergone a spiritual awakening and was committing himself to the church, and indeed the former Panther minister has led an Oakland church for decades.[110] Still, after jail, Murray remembers, "I was watched everywhere I went."[111] Several student leaders went on trial in the spring. Dillon, Bridges Randle, and John Levin were tried together; as a tactic to put the power structure and police on trial, they declined an attorney and Dillon acted as the lead counsel. But Dillon doubts an actual attorney could have mitigated the outcome. They faced the charge of inciting to riot, and authorities had film footage of all the defendants playing leading roles at strike rallies and marches. Dillon and Bridges each got a year in the San Bruno jail, while Levin, the white defendant, got six months. BSU leader Jack Alexis was deported to his native Trinidad.[112]

Jerry Varnado faced a lot of time, so he concluded that going to trial was too great a risk. He got a year but was released a couple of months early on the condition that he begin law school. Varnado stayed in the Bay Area, but it was twenty years before he set foot on campus again.[113] Danny Glover spent a couple of months in jail. Nesbit Crutchfield, a BSU leader who was clubbed and arrested in November, did sixteen months in jail and earned a criminal record "that follows me around to this day." Yet Crutchfield says he would do it all again. As a result of their struggle, "many, many young people throughout this state and nation, and the world, are seen now as whole people, as people who have the ability to excel, as people who should be evaluated based on their worth rather than on something as arbitrary as their race or background."[114]

It took some time for the progressive legacy of the strike to emerge. In the first couple of years, Hayakawa pursued a revanchist regime. He fired about twenty-five professors; battled the Black studies department; used financial aid to intimidate students; deprived student organizations of funds; attacked student government; and barred many students and teachers from involvement with the Educational Opportunity Program. In the summer of 1969, the college announced that anyone who had been arrested in the strike could not teach in the new Black studies department. This happened at several colleges in California, alienating student activists from the departments that their sacrifices helped spawn. Hayakawa precipitated an exodus of Black administrators, including Joseph White, Elmer Cooper, and Reginald Major. "I'm glad to see them go," the future U.S. senator declared. For his part, Major called Hayakawa "the biggest single disaster that non-white people at San Francisco State College have ever experienced."[115]

The Educational Opportunity Program became a target of conservative retribution, since some critics claimed that EOP students had caused campus rebellions. But a report by the state assembly found that only 58 of the 958 arrests on state college campuses were EOP admits, and these students represented only 2 percent of EOP enrollment.[116] In 1969 California put the board of trustees more squarely in control of the EOP and solidified the "professionalization" of affirmative action and the move away from student-activist-community control. This coincided with Hayakawa's move locally to keep activists out of the EOP program at SFSC, turning the EOP, in Nesbit Crutchfield's words, "from a people's program to a pig's program."[117] For his part, even though he cosponsored the EOP bill in the state legislature, Willie Brown called it "only a band-aid where surgery is required." Reflecting the sense of revolutionary change so prevalent in this era, Brown called for a redefinition of the mission of the university and a fundamental "redistribution of campus power" toward students. "We must give them the opportunity to reshape the society that they will inherit," he argued.[118]

As soon as the strike was settled, Joseph White and Robert Chrisman, an assistant professor and founder, along with Nathan Hare, of the important journal *The Black Scholar*, convened a group of African American faculty (and Black Student Union members) to recommend professors for the new Black studies department. They hired six full-time and twelve part-time instructors, who taught five hundred students (almost all Black) in thirty-four courses that fall.[119] A female scholar, Lucille Jones, was hired as chair, an interesting outcome given the all-male leadership of the strike. Her spouse, Woodrow Jones, was also hired, and both, with PhDs, were considered traditional academics; but the couple lived near the campus and had been supportive of the students during the strike. Four more women were hired, including Judith Thomas, who had graduated from SFSC that spring; she had served as editor of the BSU newspaper *Black Fire* and as the first female editor of the *Black Panther*. She taught the course Black Journalism. Other courses included Black Psychology, Black Economics, and African American History. Reflecting the strong influence of the Black arts movement on the early Black studies movement, a visual artist joined the faculty, as did the famed saxophonist and composer John Handy. Clarence Thomas, who was active in the BSU that year, had recommended hiring Frank Kofsky, a white writer on politics and jazz, but he was voted down. "It was too early to bring white folks in," Thomas concluded.[120]

After waging a bitter five-month strike, the Black Student Union was determined to play a leading role in shaping the mission of Black studies at San Francisco State. The students felt that they had won this right. "We created it," emphasized Clarence Thomas. "It was our vision." And that vision was to "educate black students on the question of self-determination." According to Thomas, the students helped "develop a curriculum that was informed by a basic principle: preparing black folks to carry out self-determination in the black community, teaching students how to gain political and economic control of the community."[121] Trickier for Dr. Jones was the BSU's view that Nathan Hare was the rightful chair. She resigned after only a month because of threats, she said, from "disgruntled students" who wanted Hare rehired.[122] Hare stayed close to the BSU that fall, but after a gun-possession arrest in December, and continued opposition by Hayakawa, he finally abandoned efforts to be reinstated. The students were loyal to Hare, a scholar of working-class origins and militant sensibility whom they saw as an important ally.[123]

The first year of the Department of Black Studies was marked by clashes between the students and administrators over control of the department. The BSU was committed to making the department an arm of the Black revolution and to win for it as much autonomy from the State administration as possible. Acting director of ethnic studies Urban Whittaker said the overriding points of contention that year were: "Who shall control the Black studies program, faculty or students? What shall be the purpose of the program, education or revolution?" The BSU's central committee, Whittaker said, "insists on control of Black studies by the students for the purposes of perpetuating a revolution." Nesbit Crutchfield defined revolution as "a radical and abrupt change in direction and attitudes." But Lucille Jones expressed a more critical view. "They aren't much like real revolutionaries," she felt. "Some of them can't even wake up in time to come to class." In her view, the time had come to switch from protest to education, but for many students in the BSU the struggle continued.[124]

That fall the BSU sought to exercise influence in the classroom, assigning student assistants to each class to "to organize the students to form collective student power" and "to talk about the strike if necessary—tell how the students got their heads beat in and how they are now facing unjust charges because they were fighting for their beliefs—the troubles they are having in the courts and in jail." Whittaker complained that the faculty refused to meet with him all semester.

Moreover, he stated that faculty who had resisted control of their classes by students faced harassing phone calls, vandalized personal property, intimidation, and physical threats. According to Whittaker, some sought police protection and transfer of their classes out of the Black studies department, but none made formal charges or complaints. In March 1970, declaring that the department was "a mess and has been mishandled," Hayakawa fired the faculty.[125] BSU leaders felt betrayed. A photo in a student newspaper pictured two members, including Danny Glover, burning the strike agreement. "We learned," said Clarence Thomas, "that just because you get a Black studies department doesn't mean you get the faculty you want."[126] Two years later, instructors were still at odds with Hayakawa, complaining that he had starved them of resources, faculty, and status.[127] In essence, the students failed to achieve either autonomy for the department from university oversight, or student control of departmental affairs and governance. And compounding matters, the department had to endure a general punitive crackdown from the administration.

In contrast, for Hayakawa, the strike's aftermath brought immediate benefits. The strike increased his administrative power on campus, propelling him into the political limelight and into the U.S. Senate in 1976. As a one-term senator, he opposed many liberal causes, from bilingual education to reparations for Japanese Americans interned during World War II. An advocate of immigrant assimilation, Hayakawa introduced an amendment to make English the official language of the United States.[128] The crackdown at SFSC and other California campuses left a bitterness and sense of failure among many of those who had participated in the struggle. As the director of ethnic studies at Mills College observed, "Most of the pioneers have moved on, the vast majority involuntarily." Nathan Hare exemplified this outcome. Three years after the strike, he viewed most Black studies programs as "polka-dot studies," as too traditional and not taught from a Black perspective. Black studies "has to express the ideology, goals, and thought of the black struggle," he insisted. An ousted professor at Berkeley concurred: "The potential and wealth of scholarly potential is there, but I'm not sure on a racist campus one can ever have a black studies program."[129]

Despite the fierce crackdown from state officialdom, most of the student activists thought the gains were worth the fight. Bernard Stringer, the first student to graduate from State with a degree in Black studies, said the strike "was the beginning of making education relevant for Black people." It "was hard," he conceded, but "we did what we thought was best to improve the education of black people."[130] In a keynote address at a twenty-year commemoration of the strike, Hari Dillon declared that "the ultimate measure of the moral veracity and social significance of any mass movement is the verdict of history. Hayakawa and the Tactical Squad are gone, but the Educational Opportunity Program is standing strong!" He cited the thousands of students of color who had gone to college as a result.[131] But in more recent years, affirmative action in college admissions has come under heavy assault, and it was legally dismantled in California, causing a decline in the proportion of African American students at University of California campuses, the state's flagship campuses. George Murray feels the incarceration and intense opposition was the price they paid for being agents of change. "You pay an extreme penalty for being ahead of your time," Murray said.[132] Carleton Goodlett's view in 1969 proved prescient. "There won't be a college in the country now that won't have black studies," he predicted. But "in the meantime, there are going to be some casualties."[133] Even though he feels that the strike went on for too long, Joseph White thinks it succeeded in giving legitimacy to the idea that a public university should reflect the ethnic makeup of the people in the community. "The university did not look like America before that," he says. While inclusion may seem like a modest, reasonable aspiration, it was "difficult and controversial," White believes, "because young people were telling old people how to run the university, and black people were telling white people how to run the university."[134]

The explosion of Black student protest in California was especially militant and dramatic, but it was not unique. Black students rose up in protest nationwide in the late 1960s. Cities like San Francisco, Chicago, New York, and Washington, D.C., were particularly important as movement centers because they brought students into closer contact with other campuses, civil rights leaders, ministers, attorneys, and community members. While the beginnings of student protest were in historically Black colleges and the Bay Area, the movement spread nationwide very, very quickly, assuming a character of simultaneity.

CHAPTER 3

A Turbulent Era of Transition

Black Students and a New Chicago

Conflict and confrontation may have characterized the student movement in California, but in the Midwest the movement unfolded in less
violent, if still dramatic, form. If San Francisco State showed that a
revolutionary conception of Black studies would be difficult to realize,
the movement in Chicago demonstrated that it was still possible to
achieve a significant transformation of educational institutions. And in
a city with a Black political class closely tethered to the machinations of
Mayor Richard M. Daley, student protest helped usher in changes that
reverberated more broadly in the city's political, cultural, and institutional life, laying the groundwork for a wider upsurge of independent
Black organizing and assertion. Student protest at Northwestern University, an elite, private research university in suburban Evanston, and at
Crane Junior College, a two-year public institution on Chicago's west
side, illustrate the diverse locations and goals of the Black student rebellion. Both campuses produced disciplined and savvy organizers who
championed campus improvement and greater African American access
to higher education. Studying these two campuses together underscores
the diverse institutional base of Black student activism, as well as the
importance of urban culture, politics, and institutions in shaping student
demands and strategies. In later years African American studies would
become associated with elite professors and Ivy League universities, but
the movement began close to urban Black communities and was inspired, shaped, and galvanized by the broader Black Power upsurge.

Black students claimed the right to shape their education in a variety of ways. At Northwestern they pressured the university to adopt African American studies, affirmative action, and other initiatives to promote greater inclusion and equality for Black students. In many respects, Northwestern typified Black experiences at elite, private historically white universities. There was an emerging liberalism, and many openings for change, side by side with the legacy of a racist cultural and institutional history. In Evanston, as elsewhere, the students forcefully and creatively asserted themselves. In contrast, the students at Crane aimed not for a Black studies department but the infusion of Black content across the curriculum. Crane came to exemplify the quest for Black control of an institution in a Black community, as it was renamed Malcolm X College and gained an African American president. Well before victories in city hall, public two-year colleges in cities such as Chicago, Oakland, Detroit, and New York became early sites of Black administrative management in a context of urban "white flight." Northwestern and Malcolm X both produced a generation of student-leaders who went on to play important roles in academia, government, law, and politics for decades, in Chicago and across the country.

It is impossible to write about the Black student movement in Chicago without acknowledging the significance of Roosevelt University, an important incubator of collegiate activism well before the 1960s. Roosevelt was founded in 1945 by a group of professors who had quit the Central YMCA College in protest over the use of racial and religious quotas in student admissions. With an explicit policy of nondiscrimination, Roosevelt was one of the few private colleges, outside of historically Black colleges, where Black scholars could find employment and significant numbers of Black students could gain admission. Scholars St. Clair Drake, Lorenzo Dow Turner, Charles Hamilton, and Hollis Lynch all taught there. The student body was similarly diverse. Bennett Johnson entered in January 1948. An Evanston high school graduate and future publisher and civil rights organizer, Johnson joined a formidable Black student group that included future congressman and mayor Harold Washington; future congressman Gus Savage; future real estate mogul, activist, and writer Dempsey Travis; future novelist Frank London Brown; and future historian Tim Black. "We were all there," Johnson recalls, and the group forged lifelong political and social ties. They won election to student government and waged direct action protest to desegregate downtown establishments, learning organizing skills that they put to use for years after graduation.[1] Many pioneering scholars in Black studies took their undergraduate degrees at Roosevelt, including Charles Hamilton, Christopher Reed, Darlene Clark Hine, and John Bracey. And the campus continued to be a launching pad for civil rights activism in Chicago throughout the 1960s. In contrast, this activist interracial culture did not characterize life at Northwestern University, a private "Big Ten" university located just over the city limits, in Evanston. Northwestern first admitted a Black student in the early twentieth century, but admitted only a very small number until the 1960s, when it began to recruit student athletes.

In 1968 the quiescence of this tony north shore campus unraveled as Black students launched a struggle that would push Northwestern into the modern era. In the early morning hours of May 4, exactly a month after the assassination of Martin Luther King Jr., about 100 Black students at Northwestern occupied the university's business office, with its enormous mainframe computer, which happened to contain financial and admissions records for the entire university. With a well-organized supply and communications network and, eventually, a large group of white student sympathizers surrounding the building, they vowed to stay until the administration met their list of demands. A few days earlier, New York City police had forcibly ejected Columbia University students from several campus buildings, arresting 700 and injuring 150. Northwestern students feared a similar police raid, and the Evanston police were reportedly eager to move in. What provoked virtually every Black student to join a protest that might lead to arrest, expulsion, or loss of financial aid?

In 1965 there were twenty-six Black students at Northwestern, twenty of whom were athletes. The athletes' experience of "integration" was telling. One day after class in the early 1960s, Don Jackson, who played on the basketball team, was walking down Sheridan Road with his white male and female classmates. A member of the university's board of trustees happened to drive by and saw Jackson, who was summoned by his coach and instructed to avoid being seen in public with white coeds. Such hysteria over Black male–white female intimacy is perhaps more associated with the Jim Crow South, but this anxiety and prohibition was widespread across the nation. Many Black student athletes reported strong pressure from athletic departments not to date white females. Such surveillance and regulation doubtless sent them a message that the university valued their athletic talents and skills but opposed their full integration in campus life.[2]

The Higher Education Act of 1965, part of President Lyndon Johnson's Great Society, increased federal aid to universities and created scholarships and low-interest loans, spurring colleges and universities to increase the admission of African American and other underrepresented students. This marked the beginning of a more significant Black student presence on many historically white campuses. In addition to admitting more Catholic and Jewish students, Northwestern admitted fifty-four African American freshmen in the fall of 1966, up from five the year before, and during that summer the university established the Chicago Action Project "to orient and acclimate incoming freshmen recruited from Chicago."[3] In a classic articulation of postwar liberalism, Northwestern labeled the Chicago Action Project students "culturally deprived," and required their participation in weekly cultural outings. "It was so shocking to me," former participant Sandra Hill said, "that they would tell me with a straight face that I was culturally deprived." More Black female students entered that fall than ever before, and a few faced rejection from their white roommates, who had the option of choosing a same-race roommate, a right that Black students were denied. When it was discovered that Sandra Hill had been assigned a Black roommate, evidently by mistake, Northwestern offered the students single rooms. "They did not want two African Americans rooming together," Hill says. Students who took over the bursar's office in 1968 demanded all-Black living units in order to give African Americans the same option whites had enjoyed. "They treated us like objects," Kathryn Ogletree recalls, "and wanted to maximize our exposure." In addition to housing, the other major source of racial animus and friction on campus was the all-white Greek-letter organizations, which were recurring sites of physical clashes and racial insult during this entire period.[4]

Events in 1967 spurred a new militancy among the students. In January, undergraduate Leslie Harris penned an open letter interrogating liberalism at Northwestern. "We Negroes have not been accepted as part of Northwestern's family," she wrote, and asked her fellow students: "are we going to be satisfied with this worn and tattered form of pacification, known as token integration, or are we going to attempt to obtain the type of equality upon which our country was founded?"[5] That summer, Detroit and Newark exploded in the most serious domestic unrest since World War I. Fifty Black people were killed, more than a thousand people were injured, and thousands more were arrested. The student counselors in the Chicago Action Project organized a new

Black student organization, called For Members Only (FMO), in order "to nurture and unite the community."[6] And a few months later, other students formed the smaller, more politically conscious Afro-American Student Union (AASU).

The two organizations worked together to build unity among Black students, negotiating differences between athletes and nonathletes, students of different class and regional backgrounds, and Greeks and non-Greeks. The president of FMO, Kathryn Ogletree, a freshman from Chicago's west side, was a rare female leader in this Black nationalist era. James Turner, a charismatic graduate student in the sociology department headed AASU. Two other graduate students, James Pitts, also in sociology, and John Bracey in history, were key sources of counsel for the undergraduates. Influential undergraduate activists Eric Perkins and John Higginson led regular rap sessions on the works of revolutionary theorists like Frantz Fanon, Amilcar Cabral, and Karl Marx. "The level of consciousness-raising was extreme," remembers Michael Smith, now a sociologist.[7] A few student activists had been exposed to radical politics or involved in the civil rights movement, but the majority of Black students had not been politically active or especially socially conscious before 1968.

Active in the wider Black freedom struggle, John Bracey enrolled in graduate school at Northwestern in 1966 in order "to cool down after things got kind of hot in Chicago." He took a seminar, "History of the South," taught by white historian George Frederickson, along with another African American graduate student, Sterling Stuckey. "All the books were by white people," he recalls. There "was no Black history." They challenged Frederickson, and for Bracey, the outcome was significant. "Within two years he had switched over," Bracey says, noting that Frederickson eventually became a faculty ally in the struggle to wrest a commitment from the administration to implement Black studies. Frederickson went on to write *The Black Image in the White Mind: The Debate on Afro-American Character and Destiny; Black Liberation: A Comparative History of Black Ideologies in the United States and South Africa;* and *Racism: A Short History.* In Bracey's words, "Now Frederickson's like a world famous expert on Black people."[8]

When Martin Luther King was murdered on April 4 in Memphis, the students at Northwestern quickly turned their attention southward to assist besieged Black communities in Chicago. Activism on campus could wait. Students worried about the welfare of friends and family after rioting broke out on the west side and the National Guard sealed off the neighborhood. In one dramatic example of their desire to help, students secured a large truck and loaded it with food donated by a supermarket chain owned by the parents of a Northwestern student. John Bracey and Wayne Watson, an undergraduate on the wrestling team, were able to talk their way through roadblocks in order to distribute the supplies to various shelters on the west side. But the assassination also stepped up their determination to win change on campus and open more opportunities for young Black Chicagoans to enjoy a Northwestern education. As Bracey puts it, "Our goal was to get Chicago's black population a beachhead at Northwestern."[9]

After many months of student research, discussion, and organizing, on April 22, 1968, FMO head Kathy Ogletree and AASU head James Turner presented a detailed list of demands to the university administration. They asked for many things, including that Northwestern declare its opposition to racism on campus and in Evanston; admit more Black students, with half coming from the inner city; shift its financial aid policy, away from work requirements to grants; change its housing policy so that Black students who had previously been required to live apart could choose to live together; establish Black studies courses with Black professors chosen by the students, "since no one in the administration is capable of adequately judging their qualifications"; hire a Black counselor to aid students in coping with tensions resulting from "the dualism of our existence as 'black college students'"; and designate a facility to house Black student organizations and activities, since "Black students have nothing at Northwestern to call our own"; and finally, they asked that Northwestern fully desegregate its real estate holdings in Evanston. The tone was insistent: "We have been to the administration before but with very little consequence. We want tangible results, not excuses or even promises." Two days later, the administration responded with a couple of concessions, several rebuffs, and, according to the students, a rejection of "the basic principles on which our demands were based."[10]

A small group of student leaders began to plan for a major action. Later, the media would focus on graduate student leaders, but Bracey emphasized that it was the undergraduates who took the lead in initiating and planning the takeover of the bursar's office. Graduate students tried to assist and protect them as much as possible, "but it was the undergraduates who had the courage to say, 'We're taking this thing over the edge.'"[11] In planning their protest, the students wanted to protect each other and guard against infiltration by an informant, so, borrowing from Gillo Pontecorvo's film *The Battle of Algiers*, they used a system of secret cells to organize resistance. Students worked in groups, or cells, of three; this way, nobody knew more than two other people involved. Their caution turned out to be justified. At a mass meeting the night before the sit-in, student leaders announced plans to occupy the administration building. They intentionally gave false information, assuming that word would get back to the administration "even though no white people were present." "Sure enough," according to John Bracey, "the next morning the administration building was filled with Northwestern police."[12]

The choice of the building to occupy reflected the careful planning and strategizing that went into every facet of the protest. The students wanted a building that was manageable in size, somewhat isolated, with easy access, but one that was critical to university functions. The small, two-story building that housed the bursar's office fit all these criteria, and it housed the university's central computer system as well, where all financial and admission information was stored. Indeed, the fact that one of the student leaders was a computer whiz was made known to the administration at a crucial juncture in the negotiations. In order to cultivate wide support and participation in the protest, every student was assigned a task. Steve Colson, who later became a prominent jazz musician, had to investigate and ensure there were no underground tunnels linking the bursar's office to other buildings, as rumored. Along with Eric Perkins and Michael Smith, he also had to procure chains and padlocks. Victor Goode, a future director of the National Conference of Black Lawyers, was part of a diversion team charged with luring the police away from the bursar's building. Wayne Watson, who later became chancellor of Chicago City Colleges, coordinated the acquisition of a large supply of food with the assistance of Evanston teenagers. Unbeknownst to the administration, the students were prepared for a very long sit-in.[13]

One hundred members of the total Black student population of 115–120 took part in the protest, so the overwhelming majority of Black students on campus participated. And evidently those few students who did not participate agreed to go to the movies downtown or otherwise be away. They agreed to say nothing to the press and support a public stance of Black unity. By many accounts, student leaders were remarkably successful in building trust with the students. Students showed up on the appointed day and hour with overnight provisions in tow without knowing further details. Early on the morning of May 3, 1968,

FIGURE 7. Students in front of the Northwestern building that housed the bursar's office. Stephen Brousard is standing to the left, Michael Hudson is seated next to Jocklyn Harris, center.

students gathered in an alley near the business office, and when the diversion team raced off toward the administration building to distract the African American security guard, they rushed into the building. They heard him report, "The building has been occupied." Bracey feels that both the guard and white clerical staff were sympathetic. Northwestern "treated their help badly," he recalls. As the secretaries were leaving the bursar's building they smiled at the students and gave them thumbs up.

Naturally, parents were concerned about their students' participation in a building takeover, and in one instance a father commanded his daughter to leave the building. Eva Jefferson (later Eva Jefferson Paterson), called her parents after they had taken over the bursar's office.

"They told me to leave or they would cut off my money for school," she said. "All our parents were afraid for us." Paterson left through a window and began collecting supplies for the students. But the experience changed her. "The next day I decided I would support myself at NU and went back inside." She stayed in Evanston over the summer and "ended up getting teargassed at the demonstrations around the Democratic convention." In many respects, her life revealed in microcosm a process that many others in her generation were undergoing. They were going through formative activist experiences, not in any year, but in 1968, a year of intense political upheaval and mobilization in the United States and around the world. Paterson went on to become a leader in the antiwar movement and was elected the first African American president of the Associated Student Government at Northwestern; she has spent her professional life as a civil rights lawyer in California.[14]

The students developed a sophisticated media strategy that illustrated their commitment to the idea of self-determination. Fearing that the mainstream media would likely misinterpret or distort their actions, they wanted to personally control the framing and dissemination of their story. They had cultivated ties with Jeff Kamen, the host of a popular talk radio show in Chicago who had previously covered the southern civil rights movement. Kamen was told to be on a particular street corner in Evanston at a specified time on May 3, 1968. When the students had taken over the building and decided the time was ripe to announce their demands, they used his microphone to directly state their demands to the thousands of listeners in Chicago.[15]

Northwestern president J. Roscoe Miller was at a meeting of the board of directors of the Sears Company when he learned that Black students had taken over the university's business office at 619 Clark Street. He directed his subordinates to "throw the recalcitrants (sic) out, call the cops, and throw them in jail." A college dean later cited the "decisive role" played by Franklin Kreml, vice president for planning and development, in persuading Miller to agree to negotiations. A former police officer, Kreml "was aware of what happened at Columbia" and feared there would be "disastrous results" at Northwestern if the police were summoned.[16] He was referring to the massive police bust at Columbia University a few days earlier, which resulted in hundreds of student arrests, scores of injuries, and damaging front-page publicity. The fact that the students at Northwestern were African American likely increased the concerns among some administrators about calling in the police. Lucius Gregg, the only Black administrator at Northwestern,

FIGURE 8. Northwestern student Eva Jefferson (later Eva Jefferson Paterson) speaking at a women's liberation rally in Chicago.

was immediately summoned to join the negotiating team. Concerned parents of students inside the bursar's office had been telephoning Gregg and were relieved to hear that the protest would be resolved without the police.[17] The student negotiating team also credited Kreml's constructive role in negotiating a settlement. Kreml was "not a liberal" but "a money guy," who had a person with a calculator next to him adding up the cost of every demand. In John Bracey's recollection, Kreml thought the demands were quite reasonable and wanted to accede to all of them, but felt the university needed "to save face," so they crafted a statement in which the settlement appeared more balanced. But the students understood: it was a big victory.[18]

Dean Gregg recalls that the toughest part for the administration was simply acknowledging that Northwestern shared in the racism of the broader society. The students felt—accurately as it turns out—that genuine change would begin only after such an admission. The first paragraph of the May 4th agreement began: "Northwestern recognizes that throughout its history it has been a university of the white establishment." Gregg says they debated this plank for hours, spending more time on it than anything else.[19]

Clearly, the thirty-eight-hour sit-in at Northwestern was not as traumatic as the five-month strike at San Francisco State, but it shook the university community and marked a turning point in racial conditions at Northwestern. "One of the many consequences of the student demonstrations," the president of the Alumni Association declared, "has been an active reexamination of Northwestern's proper role as a leading privately-supported university in the second half of the twentieth century."[20] In essence, the agreement reached between the administration and Black student leaders projected a new paradigm for racial reform—rejecting an ostensibly color-blind approach, which had left white status unchallenged and not made meaningful space for Black participation, in favor of more race-conscious efforts toward inclusion. The agreement even narrated this shift: "For many of us, the solution has always seemed to be one of simply obliterating in our laws and in our personal relations the distinction between the races: that is, if only man would ignore in his human relations the difference in skin colors, racial problems would immediately disappear. We are now learning that this notion does not come fully to grips with the problems of the present turbulent era of transition. In short, this means that special recognition and special concern must be given, for some unspecified time, to the black community that is emerging within our institution."[21]

Of the several demands that FMO and the AASU persuaded the administration to grant, a few were new, while others involved processes already under way, such as the university's pledge to continue to increase Black student enrollment. Northwestern would not explicitly commit itself to a 10 to 12 percent Black student body, but the university did

FIGURE 9. White student sympathizers surround the bursar's office in a show of support.

FIGURE 10. Graduate student James Turner explains the goals for the sit-in to the media. The protest was a major media event in the Chicago area.

agree to seek 50 percent of Black students from inner-city schools. The students felt a strong sense of responsibility to serve as access points for young people from poor urban communities. Their sensitivity to class was not an anomaly in the Black Power era: the riots forced attention to socioeconomic conditions, and as young people from these neighborhoods became politically active, they carried this awareness with them to college campuses. Northwestern agreed to create salaried positions for Black students in the admissions office (five students were employed in the admissions office in 1970); increase financial aid; create space for Black student activities; and expand "studies of black history and black culture in the University." The university also agreed to reserve residential space for Black men and women, but the Department of Health, Education, and Welfare, the federal entity charged with enforcing Title VI of the Civil Rights Act, objected to explicitly race-based housing. On many campuses, including Northwestern, administrators found ways to resolve this by allotting space, usually a floor in a dorm, to those with a cultural or other interest-based affiliation, or by opening Black-identified housing to any interested student. Interestingly, Northwestern had reversed its opposition to Black-identified housing only after students forced it to acknowledge the inconsistency

of tolerating the exclusionary policies of white fraternities and sororities. The May 4th agreement, as the settlement became known, was a
major victory for the students, even though they did not gain the
decision-making power over faculty hiring or distributing financial aid
that they had sought. They did, however, carve out new roles for student leadership, participation, and consultation in many matters of
university life, including the selection of a chair in African American
studies.

Media reaction to the protest was mixed. As had happened in California, conservatives wrote lots of letters to newspapers. In the *Chicago
Daily News,* Helen Welker declared, "I speak for all middle class white
and black people, who pay their taxes, respect the law, work hard, and
try to bring our children up the same way. Start a real crackdown on
lawlessness. Quit coddling lawbreakers or this country is headed for
ruin!"[22] This was a common reaction to student protest that was voiced
around the country. Many of the more conservative news outlets criticized, even assailed, the decision not to call the police. The *Chicago
Tribune* published an editorial denouncing the university's handling of
the crisis and portraying the Black students as ungrateful, criminal militants. Northwestern had "condoned lawlessness" and agreed to a "hu-
miliating" and "complete" capitulation. "Forgotten in the disgraceful
articles of unconditional surrender signed by university officials," wrote
the editors, "was the fact that friends and alumni who had given count-
less millions of dollars to Northwestern were not contributing to a
Tuskegee or a Howard university and had never conceived that their
gifts were directed toward creating a racial enclave and calling it Northwestern university." The *Tribune* ridiculed the deans for having negotiated, and it described the sit-in as being more like "an outbreak in a
penitentiary" than "a university dedicated to intellectual freedom." The
Tribune was especially incensed at the university's acknowledgment of
white racism, "that invidious term coined gratuitously by the Kerner
commission and eagerly accepted by every masochistic breast-beater in
the white 'liberal' community." Finally, the paper accused the students
of seeking "apartheid" on campus and of harboring "hatred" toward
whites.[23] The significantly different response by the *Chicago Daily
News* began: "Northwestern has never been regarded as a pacesetter of
liberalism, and one of the surprises to come out of its showdown with
black students was the university's ability to cope with radical change."
The paper condemned the students' tactics, but noted with approval
that violence had been avoided.[24]

In a public statement on May 13, President Miller indirectly responded to the *Tribune* and other critics. Yes, the "sincere but misguided students" had engaged in an "illegal trespass," but "the grievances of the students were real and deserved relief," and the university had "failed to understand the depth of the problems presented by prior petitions." Moreover, "far from the complete capitulation to the demands of the students that has been charged in some quarters, the university refused to grant many of the demands."[25] The May 4th agreement exposed Northwestern to a period of intense scrutiny and criticism, but backing from the board of trustees and timely donations from local corporate and financial titans shored up the administration's position. Associate Dean Lucius Gregg vividly recalls the day in May when the director of the Chicago-based Harris Bank walked into the president's office and wrote a check for a very large sum. He had been intending to make a donation for quite some time, he reportedly told the president, and concluded that now seemed appropriate. Gregg believes the May 4th agreement helped catapult Northwestern onto the national stage and increase its competitiveness. The development and admissions offices closely monitored the aftermath of the protests for effects on giving and applications, and both went up.[26]

The university had recently launched its "First Plan of the Seventies," a $180-million fund-raising campaign, and by the end of May, Jewel Food Stores, a large area chain, had made a pledge, and corporate giants Esso, Swift and Company, and United Airlines quickly followed suit.[27] Corporate America was making peace with racial change, perhaps finding it preferable to the annual summer riots. In the words of student leader John Higginson, "We made Northwestern more than what it was. They were compelled to face up to the world in which they lived."[28] In a reflection on the legacy of the bursar's-office sit-in twenty years later, former dean Robert Strotz said, "I think we moved into the modern era. We became less of a country club school and more of an intellectual center with political and social concerns, and at the same time, we didn't surrender anything of importance to us."[29]

The May 4th agreement did not specify the form that Black studies should take, and, surprisingly, this seemingly arcane academic question was quickly becoming a source of volatile conflict nationwide. A key question was whether Black studies should be a full department, with its own faculty, or a weaker program, borrowing faculty from departments. Both of these formations were, and are, interdisciplinary, but since a discipline was often conflated with departmental status—such as history, English, or chemistry—*interdisciplinary* in this period was almost always understood to refer to a program rather than a department, since it was understood to signify an interdepartmental entity. At Northwestern, the May 4th agreement offered a vague commitment to "expanding studies of Black history and culture in the University" but left the matter entirely in the hands of the faculty to decide.[30] Students did propose suggestions for visiting lecturers, and this led to the greatly acclaimed and popular Lerone Bennett and C.L.R. James coming to campus as visiting scholars in 1968–1969. The students' preference for James and Bennett shows their desire to inject a movement sensibility and critical edge to the forging of a Black studies curriculum in Evanston. Both Bennett and James were prolific exemplars of nonacademic Black history writing; and as it happened, neither man was particularly interested in a career in academia. Northwestern experienced major challenges, successes, mistakes, and conundrums in hiring faculty for Black studies, and this experience exemplified patterns nationwide.

C.L.R. James electrified students. A Trinidadian-born journalist, novelist, playwright, historian, anticolonial agitator, and Marxist theorist, C.L.R. James was the leader of several small socialist formations, including the Johnson Forest Tendency, the Correspondence Publishing Committee, and Facing Reality. He became well known and admired among Black college students in the late 1960s as the author of *The Black Jacobins: Toussaint L'Ouverture and the San Domingo Revolution,* an account of the Haitian Revolution that became required reading in the early Black studies movement. James was a transatlantic radical who did political organizing and writing in London, Trinidad, New York, and other cities. The United States government deported him during the McCarthy era, and his hiring by Northwestern illustrates an interesting, unintended consequence of the early Black studies movement. Many radical thinkers or activists from other countries had been barred from entering the United States since the 1950s, but the easing of these restrictions by the late 1960s and early 1970s, and the creation of academic positions as a result of the emergence of Black studies programs, enabled many overseas intellectuals and activists to work and speak in the United States. James was able to return to the United States for the first time since the 1950s. But despite the opportunity that the Black studies movement opened up for him, James never felt politically at home in the academy. According to John Bracey, James grew restless in Evanston and often posed the questions "What is a university? Where is the self-activity of the masses?" After his stint at Northwestern, James moved to Washington, D.C., where for a short time he taught Black studies at Federal City College (now the University of the District of Columbia). James had been invited to teach there by Jimmy Garrett, the legendary organizer who moved to Washington after a felony charge forced him out of the San Francisco Bay Area.[31]

Born in Mississippi, Lerone Bennett was the executive editor of *Ebony* magazine and author of the best-selling text *Before the Mayflower: A History of Black America, 1619–1962*. During Bennett's visiting professorship in the history department, his lectures on African American history were packed, helping to put him atop the students' wish list as a permanent professor and possible department chair. The following year, the history department hired pioneering journalist Vernon D. Jarrett to teach African American history, upon the recommendation of graduate student Sterling Stuckey, who specialized in African American history. Jarrett and singer-activist Oscar Brown Jr. produced the first Black daily radio show, *Negro Newsfront*, in 1948, and in 1970 Jarrett became the first African American columnist for the *Tribune*. He also hosted a Black public affairs television show in Chicago for thirty years and was a founder of the National Association of Black Journalists, initiatives that paralleled the emergence of Black studies and sprang from a similar politics and strategies for Black professional inclusion and advancement.

Several months after the bursar's-office takeover, a faculty committee issued a report opposing the creation of a Department of Afro-American Studies. "We do not believe in a separate degree for black studies, or in an exclusive or separatist pursuit of this knowledge," they stated, illustrating just how much Black studies lacked academic legitimacy and was seen as a Black nationalist intrusion in academia. They faculty opted instead for a program: "The courses planned are conceived as a 'Program in Afro-American Studies,' a collection of courses offered in various departments dealing with the Negro in America and with what he identifies as his cultural heritage." They offered two reasons for opposing a department: "'Black Studies' does not constitute a distinct discipline" and it would distract students from the disciplinary training they need.[32]

But students immediately pushed back and insisted on a department. The debate over the structure of Black studies was a debate about race, control, and self-determination. "The most crucial question," according to student John Higginson, is: "who will control the program, black people or white people?" Northwestern, or any other white college, "must have the courage to believe that Black people know what they want and have the facility to realize their interests and needs." In the

FIGURE 11. Lerone Bennett, executive editor of *Ebony* magazine and author of *Before the Mayflower: A History of Black America,* was a visiting professor at Northwestern and was later hired to be the first chair of the Department of African American Studies.

spring of 1969, Dean Robert Strotz appointed a Committee on Afro-American Studies to launch a unit and hire faculty. He projected ten positions by 1971–1972. But over the next two years, Black students frequently disputed the committee's legitimacy, causing a series of skirmishes and resignations, as a result of the students' view that they should have more say in the design of African American studies, and that the university should explicitly commit to establishing a "respectable, continuing academic department." As they put it, "We view the appeasement tactics of making one- and two-quarter appointments to a nonexistent Afro-American Studies Program as mere paternalism." They charged the committee with a "profound lack of direction and purpose.[33]

Tension also arose over how to structure appointments—whether to house faculty fully in the new department or share the appointment with the discipline of their training. This issue was similarly politically charged. In the fall of 1970, the mostly white committee urged the college to move ahead with hiring Black faculty, postponing a decision about structure until more specialists in the field could be present and involved in the decision. "It is our impression," the committee chair wrote, "that many black scholars identify with an existing academic discipline and would prefer to have at least a joint appointment in an existing department rather than to receive an appointment in a Black Studies Department alone. However, until we have more faculty who enjoy credibility with our black students, this argument may continue to be met with skepticism."[34]

The administration dragged their feet throughout the following year until a revival of student pressure got things rolling again. In June, FMO leaders demanded a restatement of the university's commitment to developing African American studies and called for a new committee with a Black majority and student participation. The students at Northwestern fought hard to create an independent, robust Black studies department, and this resurgence of protest had an effect.[35] In October 1971, the board of trustees finally approved the creation of a Department of African American Studies, and the college reconstituted the Committee on Afro-American Studies under the chairmanship of white historian George Frederickson. Two Black professors joined the committee: Sterling Stuckey, who was on his way to becoming a leading scholar in African American history, and Joshua Leslie, a highly regarded professor in the Department of Mathematics. A Northwestern PhD, Stuckey joined the history department in 1971. Strikingly, the college had tried to entice Stuckey with the opportunity to chair African

American studies a couple of years before, while he was still a graduate student. He declined and never joined the department during his many years at Northwestern, but he often assisted in faculty searches.[36] Stuckey's interest in Black history was deeply rooted. Son of a poet, and graduate of Du Sable High School, Stuckey was close to his mother's friend Margaret Burroughs, a poet, artist, and founder of the Du Sable Museum of African American History and Culture, and he defied anti-communist pressure to host a reception for "his hero" Paul Robeson at his parents' home in 1951. After going south in 1960 with the Congress of Racial Equality to join the civil rights struggle, Stuckey returned to Chicago, taught history at Wendell Phillips High School, and was one of the founders of the Amistad Society, a little-known but important precursor to the Black studies movement. "The work of the Amistad Society was pointing toward Black studies," Stuckey recalls. "It was certainly creating an atmosphere in which Black studies would be found desirable." Interestingly, John Bracey, another Chicago-based activist who would go on to graduate school at Northwestern, was also active in Amistad. The group hosted talks by prominent artists and scholars, including Sterling Brown, John Oliver Killens, and Lerone Bennett.[37]

With Black student consultation and support, the Committee on Afro-American Studies fairly quickly settled on Lerone Bennett as their choice to direct the new department, and in February 1972 Northwestern hired Bennett to chair and set up a new Department of African American Studies. Adamant that the college commit to a sizeable department, Stuckey, Leslie, and graduate student leader Freddye Hill urged Bennett to demand several faculty positions. And on paper at least, Bennett prevailed. In their agreement with Bennett, administrators pledged to build a "first rate" interdisciplinary department with attention to economics, history, literature, and music, among other fields, and to include within its scope the study of Africa and the Caribbean. They agreed to hire four professors during the coming academic year and four more over the next two years.

A sharp dispute, however, quickly arose over whether the Committee on Afro-American Studies should continue to play a role in hiring additional faculty or should dissolve with the arrival of a chair. Bennett objected to the committee's continuing to play a role in the formation of the department. He felt his promised authority over hiring was compromised by having to collaborate with the committee. He was, he said, "not prepared to take orders on the interpretation of the Black experience."[38] Stuckey and Leslie took a very different view. Stuckey

FIGURE 12. Historian Sterling Stuckey, a professor at Northwestern, helped launch the Department of African American Studies.

complained that Bennett's style was "authoritarian," and that he had declined to share information with the committee about hiring and would not allow their input. "His way of doing business made cooperation impossible," Stuckey said, and, in his view, jeopardized the future of the department.[39] And so, after only a few months, and before even moving into his campus office, Bennett resigned. When FMO leaders returned in September, they were incensed. Feeling that Bennett's judgment and leadership had been unfairly called into question, and convinced as well that his lack of a PhD might have played a role, they mobilized an effort to bring him back, even marching on the president's house as a group one hundred strong. At a large, very heated meeting of the Northwestern Black community at a church in Evanston that fall, there was "an ugly scene" between the students and Professors Leslie and Stuckey, who walked out. This student-faculty conflict was clearly an inauspicious way to launch the department. Even though Bennett never came to Northwestern, Robert Hill, a Jamaican-born scholar of Marcus Garvey, and Mari Evans, the Ohio-born Black-arts-movement poet, entered that fall as the department's first hires, with math scholar Leslie serving as acting chair. The Guyanese novelist Jan Carew was set to come in January and assume the chairmanship.[40]

Ironically, in light of the fact that the new dean, Hanna Gray, had supported Stuckey and Leslie's view that the Committee on Afro-American Studies should continue to play an active role in hiring, her January offer to Jan Carew signaled the success of the students' fall mobilization. She granted him considerable authority in initiating hiring and stressed that the committee's role would be purely consultative. Robert Hill recalls that the department began with "high hopes but then everything fell apart." First Bennett withdrew, and then "things got worse" as a long period of internal acrimony, poor leadership, and irregular procedures followed. In the spring of 1973, chagrined at not having been consulted in the selection of Carew as chair, FMO called a boycott of African American studies classes, as well as those taught by Professors Leslie and Stuckey. The newly hired faculty Hill and Evans were obviously in a tight spot, and both supported the students and their principles. Reflecting the students' long-simmering discontent over feeling marginalized in the formation of African American studies, the boycott was a success. By October 1973 there was "a virtual absence of black students from African American Studies," with seats filled instead by white and Asian American students. After two quarters, FMO called off the boycott. They had flexed their muscles and made their point; and in the aftermath, faculty in the department worked harder to forge closer relationships with Black student leaders. Carew in particular cultivated ties with students and helped raise financing for overseas student travel.[41]

Despite consternation over various aspects of Carew's term as chair, his tenure was notable for launching African American studies within an African diaspora rather than a U.S.-centered context. Carew wrote that the new department must embrace the "Afro-American core," but "if these studies are to validate themselves, they must of necessity deal with the other Black peoples of the New World diaspora and with Africa, the continent from which the African American people derived." Yet approaches to the study of diaspora have varied greatly and changed over time, and Carew, for his part, urged the inclusion of linguistic anthropology, folklore, oral traditions, and expressive culture in the curriculum. Illustrating another important characteristic of early Black studies, Carew offered a definition of the new discipline that emphasized its expansive, humanist, and searching character. "Black Studies," he wrote, "must be both local and international in character, must be based on a worldview that is particular for Afro-Americans but also universal." Moreover, "these studies must fearlessly cross new frontiers of knowledge; must allow no forces, no philosophy of expediency, no plastic anger or superficial rage to divert them" from this principled path.[42]

Even as the Department of African American Studies sponsored innovative symposia, workshops, and lectures, and offered popular courses, it struggled for many years with mostly assistant, adjunct, and visiting professors. This was typical of early Black studies programs, even in research universities. Although to be sure, there were young scholars in Black studies departments who would later become leaders in their fields, including the historian Barbara J. Fields at Northwestern. Strikingly, the tenured faculty in the department at Northwestern all happened to be novelists rather than academics, including the highly acclaimed writer Leon Forrest and the department's next chair, Cyrus Colter, who was also a longtime member of the Illinois Commerce Commission. It is very likely that many administrators and scholars saw these creative artists as outsiders; but without the willingness of the latter to take on leadership roles in Black studies, the department, like others around the country, would probably not have survived. The department hung on, proving itself and laying the groundwork for expansion, as Northwestern finally approved a major in African American studies in 1982, fourteen years after the bursar's-office takeover.[43] As elsewhere, the foresight of Black students in calling for departments over programs helped to ensure the survival of this newly incorporated and controversial discipline.

In many cities, the Black student movement was based, to a large degree, at community colleges. The first Black studies course on the West

Coast was established at Merritt College in Oakland. Crane Junior College, founded in 1911 and one of the Chicago City Colleges, became a center of the Black liberation movement in Chicago: Black students virtually took over the school, won a Black president, redefined the college's mission, and rechristened it Malcolm X College. By the late 1960s, this public institution located on the predominantly Black west side had a majority Black student body but a largely white faculty, curriculum, and administration. Crane may have seemed ripe for change, and some administrators likely grasped the tide of history, but the students still needed to engage in extensive organizing and even class boycotts to win reforms. Black student activists at Crane began their campaign with a Negro History Club but came to embrace a more sweeping mission. "We wanted to change the mission and character of the whole campus," said Henry English, the first Black student body president. The student leaders that emerged at Crane were slightly older than traditional students. In their midtwenties, many were raising families, and many had served in the military. As on other campuses, most of the formal Black student leaders were male, but females played critical if less visible or recognized roles. Women would begin to assert more claims to leadership in a couple of years; but from 1966 to 1969, young men took the lead.

Standish Willis was a leading activist at Crane. Born on the west side to southern parents, he graduated from Crane High School, became a father at age seventeen, got a job, flunked out of Crane Junior College in his first semester, and then joined the Air Force for four years. He reenrolled in Crane Junior College in 1966 while also working as a bus driver. After hearing a white female historian lecture on African American history, Willis experienced his first "real awareness of the dimensions of African American history." "I started the Negro History club," and students began reading and discussing history. Not long after, the popular club changed its name to the Afro-American History Club and linked up with students doing Black-history-related initiatives on other Chicago City College campuses. The club brought in many speakers; among the most popular were Nahaz Rogers, a local follower of Marcus Garvey who later had his own cable television show, and Lerone Bennett, the historian and the executive editor at *Ebony*. Henry English, too, became active on campus. His family moved to Chicago from Mississippi when English was six. He served in the Marine Corps for five years and entered Crane in the fall of 1966 as a part-time student. He worked at an aluminum company, and, taking advantage of a vacation clause in his union contract, he was able to go to school full-time in January and quickly got involved in student government.[44]

According to Willis, Malcolm X stimulated an interest in Black nationalism among his generation, yet the students' nationalism was new and controversial even in Black communities. "I remember in my household people saying, 'Why you growing your hair like that?'" But "after a while the whole community was kind of feeling it." Black nationalism in Chicago was an indigenous development, but outside groups like SNCC were powerfully articulating the new mood. "We had a lot of respect for them, and we followed them," Willis remembers. In keeping with the Black nationalist inclination toward self-determination and institution building, the activists at Crane went beyond critique to building alternatives. For example, they complained that the regular student newspaper "prints no news that is controversial or thought-provoking" and "avoids contact with the radical elements on campus." So they created the *Phoenix*, which became a fount of creativity and gave students space to explore and debate new cultural and political ideas.[45]

In 1968, contributors to the *Phoenix* devoted considerable attention to the issue of identity, particularly to the political valence of the terms *Negro, Black,* and *African American*. Christine C. Johnson, the principal of the University of Islam, the Nation of Islam's high school in Chicago, contributed a poem called "No Longer a Negro," which began "I am an African American/No longer shall I be called Negro./I give this name back to my oppressors." She continued: "I am a Man,/Not a thing." Her declaration "I am a Man" is striking and reflects the Black nationalist investment in promoting images of strong Black men or, more generally, the equation of manhood with strength and power. Another student wrote an essay arguing that the most insidious aspect of white supremacy in the United States is the way it disguises itself in the myth of American exceptionalism. "Our biggest problem," he wrote, "is getting ourselves together mentally. When we do this, the rest will come naturally." The critical mental shift entailed seeing the United States not "as the land of the free and home of the brave" but as "a racist, sickening society." This more critical posture toward the nation as a whole, not just the South, set many Black Power advocates apart from classic integrationists.[46]

The students were audacious and set out to build a movement that would enable them to reshape the culture, mission, and curriculum of Crane College. "We were energetic and idealistic," English perceptively recalls, "and in some ways out of touch with reality. Because of that we didn't see any restrictions; and because of that we were able to bring about a lot of change."[47] The students built power through many channels. "Our first strategy was to take over student government," recalls Stan Willis who was elected president of the student senate in 1967. Robert Clay, also a leader in the Afro-American History Club, succeeded Willis, and Henry English succeeded Clay. Additionally, English was a founder and the first president of Chicago City College student government. At the same time, English became a leader in the Chicago chapter of the Black Panther Party. "We became a formidable group," he recalls. As Willis puts it, "We were all working-class kids who, for the most part, lived on the west side of Chicago."

The students also began to build support in the surrounding community. After the massacre of three young men on the campus of South Carolina State University in Orangeburg in February 1968, Willis organized a march through the neighborhood in the guise of a funeral procession, complete with a casket. "This march will also give notice," Willis wrote in the *Phoenix*, "to the city, nation and the world, that the members of Crane Junior College have thrusted themselves into an all out fight against human injustice and human misery." It "really had an impact," Willis recalls. Crane was becoming a center of student and community activism, and students even began to gain support from staff, administrators, and faculty. "They were really beginning to listen." Henry English says that, while Crane was comparatively a small school, "it became a focal point for Black activism in the city." There was always a lot of activity, and politicians regularly made the campus a destination. Longtime Chicago activist Edward L. "Buzz" Palmer was working in security at Crane when he and Renault Robinson organized the Afro-American Patrolman's League in 1968 in the aftermath of riots that shook the west side. Stan Willis took part in a major two-week wildcat strike by Black bus drivers in 1968. Muhammad Ali, Dick Gregory, and Jesse Jackson spoke at rallies, and Black and white college students walked picket lines in support. Many of the Black student leaders at Chicago City Colleges were themselves union members or came from families whose wages and benefits flowed from union membership.[48]

Black students from Malcolm X, as well as those from Northwestern, the University of Illinois at Chicago, Roosevelt, and the University of Chicago, connected with each other and the broader world of Black Chicago via a lively and vibrant Black arts movement in the city. Willis remembers frequent trips to the Affro-Arts Theater, at Thirty-Ninth Street and Drexel Boulevard, which was owned by legendary Chicago musician Phil Cohran, a founder of the Association for the Advancement of Creative Musicians (AACM). According to a scholar of the AACM, the Affro-Arts Theater was part of "a complex network of forces operating around black cultural consciousness in Chicago," which included AACM and the Organization of Black American Culture. Steve Colson, a Northwestern student who took part in the bursar's-office sit-in, was a member of the AACM. Willis remembers the Affro-Arts Theater as the "most popular gathering of artists in city."[49] Poets Haki Madhubuti, Gwendolyn Brooks, and Amiri Baraka performed there, and political activists such as Stokely Carmichael attracted large crowds. Carmichael was at the height of his influence among Black college students. "Wherever he was," Stan Willis says, "we went." Unfortunately, the theater's connections to radical activists and artists brought police attention, occasional raids, and other harassment, leading Phil Cohran to close it in 1971.[50]

The students at this working-class community college on the west side of Chicago played leading roles in developing citywide Black student conferences and organizations. A large Black student conference was held in November 1967 at Christ United Methodist Church in the south side Englewood neighborhood, whose pastor, John Porter, was an important figure in the Chicago Freedom Movement. Willis remembers it as the largest meeting Black students had had up until that time. Evidently, James Bevel, a leader of the Southern Christian Leadership Conference, got into a heated argument with the head of Roosevelt University's Black student organization after Bevel argued that "black men should mate with white women" in order to create "a mixed race of kids." The students felt insulted by his theory, and Willis recalls that it led to a shoving match.[51] The following year, students from sixteen area colleges formed the Black Student Congress in order "to organize Black students for liberation." Its positions reflected the radicalism of 1968; in addition to "support for all revolutionary movement of nonwhite people in their struggle for liberation against oppression," the Congress opposed "the present political, economical, and social structure of the United States government and other Western capitalist structures and governments in general." Moreover, the students opposed "the racist police state in which the Black community is held" and supported "the right of armed struggle against such a structure."[52] Such a stance was a far cry from the sentiments of the founders of the Student Non-Violence Coordinating Committee in 1960 and shows the extent to which young Americans had been influenced by revolutionary rhetoric and perspectives—from Algeria or Cuba or the ghettos of Oakland, Detroit, Newark, and Cleveland. The cry of the Black Panthers for armed self-defense against the police was particularly appealing.

Crane Junior College's neighborhood was home to a chapter of the Black Panther Party under the dynamic leadership of Fred Hampton. The BPP in Chicago attracted students from Roosevelt, University of Illinois, and many City College campuses, and as a result students played an important role in the local leadership of the Black Panther Party. Moreover, the Panthers targeted community colleges as profitable places to organize. Hampton, as well as future congressman Bobby Rush, came to Crane to organize students, and Hampton even enrolled there in the fall of 1967. Henry English participated in a meeting where "we came together and formed a central committee" and decided to house their office on Madison Street on the west side. "The whole crux of the central committee was students; others came later," according to English. One of his party assignments was organizing students. Other Crane students involved in the Panthers included Willie Calvin, Rufus "Chaka" Walls, who became minister of information, and Robert Clay, who became the party's minister of culture. The Panthers gained considerable status on campus, rivaling that of student groups. In "What Black Students Want," Willie Calvin echoed the Panthers Ten Point Platform in his framing of education as a right of citizenship: "We believe that the city and federal government is responsible and obligated to give every man a decent education as so defined by their jive constitution."[53]

In the spring of 1968, after Dr. King's assassination and a wave of rioting on the west side, students held a memorial on campus. In his remarks, Stan Willis quoted Stokely Carmichael's pledge of undying love for Black people. Fred Hampton, who was under growing police surveillance and would himself be assassinated the following year with the assistance of a Black informant, spoke next. He "attacked my speech," Willis recalls. "Hampton said you can't have undying love for black people, because some black people are betraying us." The feeling of being under siege was actually widespread. Motivated by the Panthers' and Malcolm X's emphasis on armed self-defense, as well as by Mayor Richard Daley's notorious order to city police in April 1968 to "shoot to kill any arsonist," students at Crane contacted Kermit Coleman of the American Civil Liberties Union about starting a campus rifle club, and they eventually did. "We were arming ourselves," Willis remembers.[54]

It was this context of turmoil, activism, high expectation, and solidarity in which student leaders at Crane issued a list of demands to transform their campus. And they did so, not as leaders of a Black student organization, but as leaders of the student senate. They spoke as authorized representatives of the student body. Rather than a Black studies program, the students wanted the "integration of the history of African Americans into the existing curriculum" of the entire college. They boycotted professors who did not support their vision: "If you could not integrate [African Americans] into the curriculum," Henry English says of their view, "then you should find somewhere else to go." When Willis and English had arrived at Crane, there were three African American professors: Elliot Evans, Frank Banks, and J. Neal. Banks had been a Tuskegee airman and a union organizer who served as the teachers' representative on campus. Shortly after, Carol Adams, who would become a prominent cultural and education leader in Chicago for decades, joined the faculty, as did Barbara Lewis King, who served as assistant dean of community services. The students' goal was to bring in more Black professors. Many of the white teachers could not relate to the surge of Black nationalist feeling among students, and many would leave after Crane became Malcolm X. There were some white professors who supported the students, such as Beatrice Lumpkin, who also happened to be one of a few communists on the faculty. "Nobody knew they were communists at the time," Willis remembers. Lumpkin, who was married to Black steelworker activist Frank Lumpkin, later wrote an Afrocentric children's math book.[55]

In May 1968, declaring their "profound devotion to our community," the students issued ten demands designed to make Crane "intellectually and socially relevant to the community as a whole." "Since the student body at Crane is predominantly black, and the community is predominantly black," they felt "the curriculum and academic policies should cater to the needs of the black students of this institution and to the black people of this community." Their demands show their desire to make the community college a vehicle for upward mobility and enhanced opportunity for the students and community as a whole. The first demand was for a formal policy enshrining student rights, and the second asked for the right of students to name the college's modern new campus. They demanded a Black president, more Black instructors, more Black clerical personnel, the upgrading of existing Black workers, and new American history texts that covered the African American experience without distortions, as well as more advanced courses in the curriculum to promote greater readiness for transfer to four-year institutions.[56]

A committee of administrators, faculty, and students, including college president Irving Slutsky, found the demands "reasonable, moral and just." In a sign of the students' extraordinary political skills and, certainly the activism and ferment on the west side more broadly, they won virtually every demand. In May 1969, Malcolm X College got a Black president, the first in the City College system. Interestingly, in light of the largely male leadership at the college and the general male thrust of Black Power politics, the students' first choice was an African American woman, Barbara Lewis King, who was serving as dean of community relations. Henry English describes her as "an imposing woman" who "cared about the students." "We didn't understand that this was way ahead of the time," he says, referring to the possibility of a Black woman president. "We didn't get Barbara King." "They were just not going to hire a female," is the way English remembers it. "They advanced a man instead." English was in jail when Charles Hurst, the forty-one year-old Howard audiologist, visited campus, so he missed the interview. But other students were impressed. Hurst got the job and arrived with a lot of fanfare and media attention. "The first thing he did," according to English, "was he did Barbara in." Barbara King moved to Atlanta and became one of the city's most prominent civil rights, education, and religious leaders.[57]

The students had begun calling Crane "Malcolm X" before the name was officially adopted. "We were following international events," Willis remembers. "We knew about Lumumba and Nkrumah," referring to the first postcolonial presidents of the Congo and Ghana, and this "made us feel like Black people should be running this college, and it should be named after a Black person." The City Colleges resisted at first, then encouraged the selection of Booker T. Washington as the new name; but the students stood their ground and ultimately prevailed.[58] In September 1969, "despite stern resistance from a variety of sources to the naming of a public college after the Black Nationalist," Crane was rechristened Malcolm X College.[59] The administration acknowledged that its faculty needed further training in order to competently incorporate African American subjects into their course material, so they proposed a series of mandatory seminars and workshops and hoped to bring in scholars such as St. Clair Drake, John Hope Franklin, and Charles Hamilton as consultants. Under the new administration, the role of Malcolm X was "to establish a dynamic learning community in which all are teachers and all are learners. The ultimate objectives are self-actualization and a new social order through the educational process."[60] There was an open admissions policy. The student handbook for the 1970–1971 academic year featured a bold red, black, and green cover emblazoned with "Malcolm X College" and the words *Education, Liberation,* and *Unity* around a clenched fist. It included a comprehensive, detailed section on student rights and responsibilities. Martin Luther King's and Malcolm X's birthdays were both included among school holidays, and Phil Cohran, founder of the AACM and African Heritage Ensemble, composed the school song, which included the lyrics "We once were the Kings (or Queens) of/the ancient Empires now we/must move from the/slave maker's fire we come/to Malcolm X to find a way."[61]

Charles Hurst was "very theatrical and an excellent communicator. We called him 'sugar tongue,'" English recalls. The students got along well with the new president, even though he resisted some of their efforts to institutionalize the role of students in campus governance. "Hurst gave lip service to this; he didn't really support it." But the students were strengthened by the "tremendous community support in the background," says English including allies on the board of trustees. "While we were out on the front lines doing the battle, they were in the back room doing the deal."[62] The students won not only a new name for the college and a new president but also a new, modern campus, which opened in 1971. Stan Willis remembers Hurst as an advocate of Black capitalism and a supporter of President Nixon. And indeed in his first semester in 1969, he developed an internship program with twenty-five large companies in Chicago and hosted a corporate fair called "Black Excellence Unlimited."[63] But Malcolm X's outreach went in many directions. One of the programs that students had advocated, and which was established during Hurst's tenure, was at the Stateville prison, where the inmates would receive course credit at Malcolm X. Willis taught a course there after he had begun graduate school at the University of Chicago.[64]

African rhythms, courtesy of Phil Cohran's band, infused commencement ceremonies in the spring of 1970, after Hurst's first year as president and the first year ever for Malcolm X College. Dick Gregory was awarded an honorary doctorate, and achievement awards were given to Bobby Rush, Illinois Black Panther Party chairman; two aldermen; and Mrs. Francis Hampton, the mother of slain Panther leader Fred Hampton. In a sign of how interconnected student activism had become across campuses and across the country, James Turner, a former graduate

FIGURE 13. Celebrating a new name and a new president. Jesse L. Jackson, director of Operation Breadbasket, and Betty Shabazz, widow of Malcolm X, flank Charles Hurst, president of Malcolm X College.

student at Northwestern and the recently appointed director of the new Center for Africana Studies at Cornell, gave the graduation address. He urged students not to forget their roots and to choose careers that would benefit their communities. "Your people need you," he intoned in the spirit of nation building. "They need doctors, lawyers, architects."[65]

After the college's first two years as Malcolm X, an accrediting team commended the college for its "utilization of indigenous leadership at all program levels"; it also noted the high faculty turnover of recent years, but reported an ongoing reduction of "faculty tensions." The faculty "seemed to be a very dedicated group of individuals working far above the expected call of duty," yet "there is some observable strain produced by the slight degree of racial polarization." The team praised the continuing education program in particular. "The strength of the program lies in its strong communal base and the recognition by the community that the college is sensitive to, and is organizing programs relevant to, their needs." Malcolm X was building up its occupational training in nursing, business, and engineering and "related technology," but its arts and sciences division still claimed the most students. With open admissions, compensatory and remedial education assumed a new visibility in the college. Also new was a strong Black studies program, which the committee praised for elevating student self-esteem and promoting closer town-gown relations. "The avowed two-fold objective of Black Studies—knowledge and creativity—was evident in the programs" for a week entitled "Focus on Black."[66]

A concluding look at a community-based Black education program called the "Communiversity" reinforces the portrait in this chapter of a loosely connected Black student movement in Chicago—even across public and private school lines—and underscores that the students' desire to "give back" to the community was more than rhetoric. Graduate and undergraduate students from the University of Chicago and other universities, along with independent artists and educators, came together in 1970 under the name Communiversity—a fusion of the words *community* and *university*—to offer weekend courses in a Black neighborhood to Chicagoans who did not have access to formal Black studies programs. In addition to realizing the oft-professed desire to connect town and gown, the Communiversity made visible the ideological developments and splits that were emerging in the Black liberation movement, including the Black student–Black studies movements.

When Stan Willis transferred to the University of Chicago from Crane Junior College in the fall of 1968, he was "very strong in my nationalist beliefs," but in Hyde Park "he met some socialist brothers and sisters who were strong too." He majored in history and studied with John Hope Franklin. The Black students at the University of Chicago were studying Marxism and producing and attracting "very strong theoreticians." Robert Rhodes, a political science graduate student who introduced many Black students to Marxism and briefly taught at the Communiversity, was a leader of these study groups. Stan Willis recalls that Ishmael Flory, an African American leader in the Communist Party in Chicago, was "around all the time" and "tried to recruit me to the party, saying I reminded him of [Paul] Robeson." Also participating in these study groups and teaching at the Communiversity were Harold Rogers, a graduate student who would later chair African American studies at Olive-Harvey College in Chicago and be a leader in the Coalition of Black Trade Unionists, and Linda Murray, an undergraduate who would later become a physician and go on to be president of the American Public Health Association. Willis called her "one of our strongest theoreticians." The weekend courses of the Communiversity, which lasted for a few years, took place in the building on Oakwood Boulevard in Bronzeville where St. Clair Drake and Horace Cayton had written *Black Metropolis* and where the Center for Inner City Studies of Northeastern Illinois University now stands.

Teachers at the Communiversity included Marxists, socialists, and Black nationalists who emphasized the study of classical African civilizations, an orientation later embraced by the Center for Inner City Studies. In addition to Rhodes, Rogers, and Murray, instructors included Ebon Dooley, a poet, lawyer, and activist; Jerry Wilburn, a community organizer; Anderson Thompson, who has taught at the Center for Inner City Studies for decades and leads regular trips to Africa; Bobby Wright, a prominent psychologist; and the anthropologist Leith Mullins, then a graduate student. Robert (Bob) Rhodes, who was a popular instructor in political economy in the early years, said the Communiversity combined "a fascination with ancient Egypt and contemporary politics." According to Stan Willis, "Once [the students] got into Bob's class, they wouldn't go to any other classes; so we had to cancel all the classes that conflicted with Bob. . . . People never heard it before. People really liked it."[67] Still, according to both Willis and Rhodes, the cultural nationalists outnumbered leftist instructors, and several continued teaching there when Northeastern Illinois University moved into the building, while the more leftist instructors finished graduate study and moved on.[68]

As historian Adam Green has argued, a core characteristic of Black Chicago history has been institution building, and the struggle for educational self-determination exemplifies this thrust.[69] There are numerous examples beyond higher education. Acclaimed poet Haki Madhubuti founded Third World Press in 1967 and, with his wife, Safisha Madhubuti, founded the Institute of Positive Education/New Concept School in 1969. Margaret Burroughs, one of the best-known Chicago institution builders, was an artist and educator who built the first African American history and culture museum in the United States. A longtime leftist and founder of the South Side Community Arts Center, the only surviving Works Progress Administration project in the country, Burroughs taught high school in Chicago for decades and with her husband, Charles Burroughs, opened the Du Sable Museum of African American History and Culture. Typifying the community-based, politically engaged educators who populated many early urban-based Black studies programs, Burroughs taught African American art at Elmhurst College and was a professor of humanities at Kennedy-King College, a two-year public college, from 1969 to 1979.

The Black student movement had effects and legacies that went beyond transforming institutions of higher education. It accelerated the push for Black political empowerment more generally. The activists who came out of the Malcolm X struggle have made important contributions to the civic, educational, and cultural life of Chicago. As in many other cities, the political intensity of the late 1960s exerted a long and wide-ranging influence; and in a city marked by formidable machine politics, the rise of new sources of leadership and independent power bases shaped political mobilization as well. An attorney, Standish Willis has been a leader both in the fight against police torture and in the movement to rearticulate domestic civil rights as international human rights. Henry English became president of the National Black United Fund, a philanthropy aimed at promoting collaboration and self-reliance. Carol Adams, formerly on the faculty of Malcolm X, is president of the Du Sable Museum of African American History and Culture. Many former activists at Malcolm X see a direct connection between their victories on the west side and the election in 1983 of Harold Washington as Chicago's first African American mayor. By channeling Black activist energy outside machine politics, and creating alternative sites and sources of power and mobilization, the Black Power movement laid critical groundwork for Washington's electoral challenge. The Black student movement in New York City, too, reverberated well beyond campus and helped to reconfigure power and politics across the metropolitan region.

CHAPTER 4

Brooklyn College Belongs to Us

The Transformation of Higher Education
in New York City

Black student activism exploded in the spring of 1969. It was the high-water mark of the Black student movement, with militant actions and mass confrontations at campuses across the country, most notably at the University of California, Berkeley; Cornell University; Harvard University; Rutgers University; and Howard University. Coinciding with the community-control-of-public-schools movement, the Black student movement in New York City aimed to redefine the relationship between universities and Black communities. Like students in San Francisco, Chicago, and other cities, students in New York wanted some form of open admissions in public institutions of higher education. But as elsewhere, the struggle over higher education in New York was hardly over a single issue: it encompassed admissions, faculty hiring, curriculum, and overall mission. In the spring of 1969, students at every single division of the City University of New York (CUNY) rose up in protest. The two-week occupation of City College in Harlem precipitated a political crisis in the city and ushered in a major shift in public policy; as a result, the protest received extensive local and national media attention, but strikingly it has garnered little attention from historians. Similarly, the struggle at Brooklyn College has been virtually forgotten, even though it was pivotal in reshaping the admissions policy, the university's relationship to communities of color, and the curriculum. As one observer noted, "The integration of CUNY has been the most significant civil rights victory in higher education in the history of the United States."[1]

Yet the Black student movement in New York City has been left out of most narratives of the Black freedom struggle, a striking elision in light of the fact that much of the post-civil-rights backlash has focused on ending affirmative action in college admissions.[2] The quest for open admissions, and the articulation of higher education as a social right of the working class, has been either vilified or erased from movement history. Black students in New York had an enormous impact on university policies, structures, and cultures. These students may have read *Quotations from Chairman Mao,* but they won reforms that dramatically opened up public higher education and opportunity structures in the region, paving the way for the expansion of the Black middle class. While they achieved a great deal, they inspired formidable opposition, previewing the political conservatism that would later gain wider ascendancy in urban, state, and federal governments.

This story, like the stories of other campuses, complicates the widely held view that Black nationalist politics of the late 1960s blocked multiracial alliances, moved class issues off the radar, muted Black women's voices, and alienated and drove away white allies. In fact, this generation had a flexible and dynamic conception of so-called identity politics: they forged alliances with Latino and Asian American activists and kept socioeconomic issues front and center. African American female students, moreover, fought for Black studies and affirmative action as much as their male peers, notwithstanding the prevalence of male leadership. And the students won considerable support from elders in the community. Yet, as elsewhere, the emphasis was not on interracial organizing but on Black student assertion. Black and Puerto Rican students on CUNY campuses took the lead in shaping the tactics and goals of antiracist activism, while radical or liberal white students organized support efforts separately.

Black and Puerto Rican students had long gained entry to tuition-free City, Brooklyn, Hunter, and other colleges under the prevailing admissions standards. Affirmative action, meaning programs and policies aimed at admitting "minority" students who did not meet the prevailing entrance criteria, began with the Search for Education, Elevation and Knowledge (SEEK) program enacted by the legislature in 1966. Reflecting the new clout of a growing block of Black and Puerto Rican legislators in Albany, as well as the efforts of Black professors Kenneth Clark and Allen Ballard in allegiance with enlightened white administrators, SEEK provided promising graduates of city high schools a college education and the extra academic support, counseling, and remediation needed to succeed. It was by far the largest program of its kind in the country. SEEK shows the legislative origins of affirmative action in higher education, as well as the leading role of Black elected officials in making access to higher education a critical public policy issue in the state.[3] Still, the small but growing number of Black students at CUNY colleges in the mid-1960s were troubled by the overwhelmingly white student bodies, faculties, courses, and cultural programming. The fact that these were taxpayer-funded institutions gave students of color the confidence to make far-reaching claims of belonging and entitlement.

Labeled as "culturally deprived," SEEK students were expected to be grateful for their access to an excellent education. The students pushed back against these terms and assumptions. As in San Francisco, student leaders at CUNY interrogated both the mission of public universities and the criteria for determining "merit." They posed a question: Should public colleges be expected to offer opportunity to a broad range of taxpaying New Yorkers, or should they be permitted to adopt the exclusionary practices of private institutions and rely on test scores to determine admission? Moreover, students demanded a new answer to an old but critical question of the civil rights era: How should the United States correct the consequences of segregation, in this case the unequal educational system that it has produced? The prevailing view had been that efforts should focus on improving primary and secondary schools in order to better prepare students for college. But in the late 1960s, African American youth argued that it was the college's responsibility to offer the appropriate remediation. They increasingly framed access to higher education as a right of postwar U.S. citizenship. Fortunately for them, the broader urban turmoil across the United States played a role in encouraging college officials to reevaluate admissions policies. After several summers of very serious and deadly urban unrest, white administrators feared Black militancy and the prospect of riots at their gates.[4]

Even with several new admissions programs seeking to recruit students of color, Brooklyn College was 96 percent white in 1968.[5] In a profound sense, the campus tumult of the late 1960s reveals the snail's pace of court-mandated integration and the stunning lack of preparation for it on American campuses. For its part, Brooklyn College had appointed a committee in 1964 "to look into the need to create educational opportunities for students on the campus, or students who were not being admitted." In the words of acting president George A. Peck, it "worked sporadically at first" and finally came up with a plan to admit two hundred Black and Puerto Rican students in a special program in 1968.[6] What Peck did not mention was that two left-wing student organizations, the W.E.B. Du Bois Club and Students for a Democratic Society, had occupied the registrar's office in May 1968, demanding that one thousand minority students be admitted that fall.[7] The faculty and curriculum, too, lacked diversity. For all the vaunted cosmopolitanism of the faculties at the City University of New York, Brooklyn College offered thirteen courses "with content related to American minority groups," the president's office reported in 1969, and all of these had begun in 1968! A big problem, the administration contended, was "finding faculty to teach them,"[8] a statement that points to the slow pace of producing African American PhDs in the United States fourteen years after *Brown* and twenty years after President Harry S. Truman had appointed a committee to study minority access to higher education.

Among the small number of Black students at Brooklyn College, a few key leaders emerged, notably Leroy (Askia) Davis and Orlando Pile. Both young men were involved in off-campus organizing, and their efforts at Brooklyn College were part of the overall Black freedom struggle. Pile was the student representative on the Ocean Hill–Brownsville community school board and was also involved in welfare-rights organizing. African American women were at the center of both these campaigns, a fact that balances the largely masculinist portrait of Black Power politics and suggests a broader range of influences, especially at the grassroots, on a generation that venerated Malcolm X and Frantz Fanon. Askia Davis came up to New York from Georgia at age fifteen. He saw *The Battle of Algiers,* read *Black Skin, White Masks* and joined the Black Panther Party. But Malcolm X had the most decisive influence on his life. All his boyhood, Davis had eagerly waited for the day he could join the military. "I always dreamed of going to the air force academy," he says, becoming a pilot, and dropping bombs. "That was my goal. I was a warrior." He might have gone to Vietnam like his brother had he not encountered *The Autobiography of Malcolm X.* "Reading Malcolm X really changed me—really, like overnight."[9]

In 1968 Davis and Pile began to reach out to the small number of Black students—approaching them in the library—and soon organized BLAC, the Black League of Afro-American Collegians. In conjunction with the Puerto Rican Alliance, BLAC quickly became a force on campus. BLAC would present eighteen demands to the administration in the spring of 1969, but they also tried to change campus conditions through their own direct action. One tactic they used in order to overcome Black students' sense of isolation in the classroom, especially in the face of offensive or insensitive racial remarks, was to get groups of Black students to register for the same course. In 1969, five or six Black student activists plus several more nonpolitical Black students enrolled in an introductory literature course taught by Robert Fitzhugh. The first day, Askia Davis recalls, Fitzhugh walked in and saw "this sea of Black faces. He was shocked." "We were polite," he remembers. "We wanted to learn." Orlando Pile asked Fitzhugh why there were no Black writers on the syllabus, and he even presented the professor with a list of important Black writers. One imagines that James Baldwin and Richard Wright were probably on this list. Fitzhugh retorted that these writers were "social activists, not major novelists." A "personal confrontation" ensued. Fitzhugh asked Pile why he didn't leave the class if he didn't like it, and Pile replied, "Why don't you?" "And then," says Pile, still incredulous many years later, "the professor walked out!" BLAC leaders arranged with the dean for the Black students to withdraw from the course, and the activists did, but the nonpolitical Black students chose to remain. A couple of weeks later, they had changed their minds and told Pile that Fitzhugh was grading all of their work poorly, and had "disrespected them" when they brought it up. Number eleven on the list of eighteen demands called for the dismissal "of all White professors who have demonstrated racist tendencies," specifically, Robert Fitzhugh of the English department.[10]

The "18 Demands" illustrate the students' political sensibilities and vision. The demands are bold and wide-ranging, yet at the same time, specific and pragmatic, suggesting the students' complex sense of their role. The first demand called for the admission to the college of all Black and Puerto Rican high school graduates who applied.[11] The second demand called for "a free tutorial program" and "basic skills courses" to enable students "to fulfill their scholastic potential." While the first goal seems to reject all entrance criteria, the second one illustrates that the students still took academic success seriously. Even though students were challenging prevailing definitions of who was qualified to enter college, they were not rejecting academic culture or excellence. On the contrary, they wanted to benefit from it.[12] Most significantly, the demands show the students' desire to have Brooklyn College serve the educational needs of the population of Brooklyn, not only of those whose test scores were the highest.

The students called for Afro-American and Puerto Rican institutes to be "controlled by Black and Puerto Rican students with the help of the Black and Puerto Rican faculty and the community." The wording of this demand suggests that the students did not trust the college to set up the institutes, and so claimed this role for students of color and their faculty and community allies. At many campuses, student activists had a conception of Black studies as a social movement—seeing it as a bridge between Black students and Black communities, in addition to its transformative intellectual potential. The thirteenth demand called for a special course that would give academic credit for field work in the community, reflecting this generation's desire to make their college educations "relevant" to community needs, and their desire not to wall themselves off in an ivory tower. Indeed, Brooklyn College set up an entirely new college—the School for Contemporary Studies—that incorporated many of these goals. Echoing a similar demand at City College, the fifteenth demand asserted that students majoring in education—future public school teachers—should be required to take courses in Black and Puerto Rican studies. This reflected the students' sense of obligation to use their position inside the college to affect the education of Brooklyn youth of all ages. The students also demanded the hiring of Black and Puerto Rican professors in all units of the college, showing their desire not to let the creation of the new Afro-American and Puerto Rican institutes create an excuse for the other departments not to diversify.[13]

By early 1969, student activists had engaged in extensive organizing on campus and had gained considerable support. The BLAC faculty advisor was Professor Craig Bell, but all among the small number of Black professors on campus supported them, as did several white professors, "especially and very vocally" Bart Meyers.[14] Reflecting the movement's turn toward self-determination, it was important to Black and Puerto Rican students to organize and lead their own struggle. The largely white Students for a Democratic Society chapter on campus supported the citywide push for open enrollment, and they were engaged in a range of campus actions that spring. Pile said that their support was fine, but "they could not be part of us."[15]

In mid-April, frustrated that neither the administration nor the faculty had yet considered the eighteen demands, a group of Black and Puerto Rican students took over the microphone at a faculty meeting and commanded the professors not to leave. "Militant" students disrupting normal campus procedures and making "demands" to a "frightened" faculty became the archetypical sequence of events at American campuses in 1969. "We want the 18 demands presented now," Askia Davis declared. "You will not shut your eyes any longer," he told the faculty. "Brooklyn College belongs to us, not you."[16] The president subsequently participated in a forum of two thousand people, but the administration, according to the student-radicals, took a "rigid stance."[17]

Student demonstrations culminated in a mass demonstration at the end of April. One hundred and fifty students from BLAC and the Puerto Rican Alliance, as well as forty white students, "squeezed into" the president's office in Boylan Hall, where a meeting among administrators and student representatives over Black and Puerto Rican issues was in progress. They dramatically presented the eighteen demands, but the president was actually out of the office. Some students engaged in minor vandalism, and someone spray-painted the words *power* and *revolution* on walls inside and outside the building. In the meantime, some white students took over other campus buildings, and unknown persons set small fires on the campus. The students stayed in Boylan Hall for a couple of hours and left when they heard that the police had been called.[18] In early May, one hundred students led by SDS held a demonstration inside the dean's office, and acts of arson and vandalism continued, alongside daily and increasingly large rallies. On May 6, President Peck alleged that a hundred, mostly Black and Puerto Rican students blocked firefighters from entering the administration building to douse a small fire, reportedly the fifth small blaze of the day.

In contrast to City College, where administrators negotiated with student activists, at Brooklyn College they turned to law enforcement to quell student protest. They got an injunction barring students from "congregating in or near buildings, creating loud or excessive noise, or employing, inciting or encouraging force or violence." Students fought the injunction with attorneys from the Emergency Civil Liberties Commission and the New York Civil Liberties Union, who argued that it was an unconstitutional restraint on freedom of speech and assembly. It should be noted that there were many white students who had been advocating and engaging in aggressive forms of protest—and this was well known to campus authorities. Indeed, some Brooklyn College officials, like administrators at many American colleges, saw radical whites, especially those in SDS, as more destructive than Black student activists. Some even viewed white radicals as instigating Black student revolt. Peck later testified before a U.S. Senate committee investigating campus riots.

Montana senator Lee Metcalf asked him, "So you think that SDS in spite of the fact that they were not part of this black revolt, spurred it on and encouraged it, and, using your phrase, masterminded it?" To which Peck replied, "All they could." He added that he did not think SDS had the same emotional commitment to "the cause of blacks" but used it to advance general social destruction. Interestingly, though, this worldview did not prevent Peck from targeting Black and Puerto Rican students—and no white students—for arrest that spring.[19]

Shortly before dawn on May 12, 1969, police officers raided the homes of seventeen Brooklyn College students, all of them either African American or Puerto Rican, including Orlando Pile and Askia Davis. They arrested the students and even arrested Pile's mother, Blanche Pile, for interference. Another two students were also indicted. Because they were college students with no criminal records, and they had strong family and community ties, the fifteen-thousand-dollar bail for each student was widely seen as excessive. The students spent four days at Riker's Island. They were each charged with eighteen felonies and five misdemeanors, including inciting riot and arson, which together carried a sentence of 228 years. The allegations had come from an undercover police informant who had infiltrated BLAC and befriended the students. "He looked the part," given his big Afro, dark skin, and beard, Askia Davis notes. "He had the rhetoric, but he was really a cop." In Pile's view, the allegations by the police informant were a form of retaliation: they represented the administration's attempt to thwart the Black student movement and block their demands to change Brooklyn College. The day after the raids, the prosecutor claimed to have found in various homes "a revolver, a sharp-edged spear and clubs," as well as batteries and gasoline, which he called "material used to manufacture firebombs."[20]

The eighteen-year-old Davis was a member of the Black Panther Party and had actually been named on the original warrant for the New York "Panther 21," but had been in California when the police made those arrests. "It was meant to be the Panther 22," he says, which likely explains the overwhelming force they used to arrest him that morning in May. He remembers his thoughts when he heard a knock on the door early that morning. "A young lady lived next door. I was basically trying to seduce her. She used to knock at my door; we used to tease and flirt, but nothing ever happened. So I get this knock at five o'clock in the morning, and I said, 'Wow, she finally gave in.'" Nine police officers came to make the arrest. Three came through the door. "They threw me to the floor; put a gun to my head, and cocked the trigger." When the officer finally pulled the gun back and saw the very youthful-looking Davis, he said, "God, you're nothing but a kid." They searched the house and found nothing unlawful. Riker's was a "rough experience," but it made him feel he could endure hardship and prevail. He believed that authorities were trying to punish and intimidate them for their activism.[21]

The media gave an inflammatory account. The *New York Post* reported that the students were in possession of "The Writings of Che Guevara," "Quotations from Mao Tse-tung," and a "typewritten document entitled 'Blueprint for Campus Revolt,'" which the district attorney said referred to the "strategy at San Francisco State College."[22] *New York Daily News* readers were given an over-the-top account designed to stoke fears of communism: "Brooklyn District Attorney Eugene Gold revealed that 122 detectives making pre-dawn arrests in four boroughs found inflammatory writings of Chinese and Cuban Communists."[23] This media frame exacerbated the already powerful stigma of criminal prosecution in the eyes of the broader public. But closer to home, the arrests backfired, generating greater support for BLAC from both the campus and community.

Black leaders in particular stepped up. "The black community really got together" to support us, Davis says. Attorneys George Wade and Ray Williams argued before Judge Dominic Rinaldi that the bail was punitive. Williams also pointed to the racial bias in the arrests, noting that "there were S.D.S. students involved but they were not brought in because they are white." Outraged at the assertion, the judge warned him against "using the courtroom as a vehicle for racist statements." But the Appellate Division ordered the bail reduced to sixty-five hundred dollars. U.S. Representative Shirley Chisholm, herself a Brooklyn College graduate, raised the bail money. She convinced Dr. Thomas W. Matthew, the president of the National Economic Growth and Reconstruction Organization, to put up his share of Interfaith Hospital, a drug treatment clinic in Queens, as collateral. And she got Reverend William A. Jones of Bethany Baptist to put up his church.[24] As it turns out, the case never went anywhere—the state never produced any evidence. After about a year of delay and negotiation, the attorneys and judge reached a deal in which the students accepted a short probationary period, and the charges were dismissed and the students' records ultimately expunged. The *Kingsman* editorialized that the probationary period "seems suspiciously like a move to repress dissent on campus, since the 19 are not guilty enough to be prosecuted."[25]

After the arrests and the stationing of one hundred police officers on campus, a large group of students and faculty went on strike. Their demands were: drop the charges against the "BC 19," implement the eighteen demands, and get the police off campus. Askia Davis says he didn't realize how much support they had from the majority white campus until this point. The *Kingsman* editorialized in support: "The 20 arrests on Tuesday morning were conducted in a manner that heaped disgrace on the American legal system and added to many students' hatred and distrust of the New York City Police." It demanded that the administration remove police from campus, reporting that an officer had arrested a student for spitting, which had led to a bloody clash.[26] The relentless pressure finally induced the college to make concessions, and President Peck and the faculty went on record urging the Board of Higher Education, the governing body of CUNY colleges, to enact a new open admissions policy. They passed a resolution urging the board "to offer a college education to every high school graduate in the city, particularly needy Negroes and Puerto Ricans."[27] Clearly, the students' efforts to bring the Black liberation movement to Brooklyn College had an effect. An even more epochal story unfolded in Manhattan.

Student activists at the City College of New York (CCNY), too, had engaged in a long series of escalating tactics before two hundred of them took over the buildings of south campus on April 22, 1969, and renamed it the "University of Harlem." This was preceded on April 16 with a boisterous march through campus by Black and Puerto Rican college and high school students and their left-wing white supporters, who chanted the popular Black Panther refrain: "The Revolution has come, time to pick up the gun." As at most colleges, the assassination of Martin Luther King Jr. sparked a new determination, even a sense of obligation, to accelerate the pace of change. "The movement really began in 1968," recalls south campus occupier Robert Feaster, who later took the name Sekou Sundiata.[28] The struggle at City was led by "the Black and Puerto Rican Student Community"—a name that richly signifies the politics of the era by emphasizing the collective over the individual and asserting a Black-brown partnership in a Black nationalist era that was moving toward "Third Worldism." The left-wing W.E.B. Du Bois Club also contributed to the formulation of the "five demands," having presented President Buell Gallagher in November 1968 with a petition of sixteen hundred signatures titled "End Racism at CCNY." This evidently motivated students of color to launch their own effort. "We were indignant," Sundiata says, "that the Du Bois Society was circulating those kinds of demands which really articulated our interests, and that we had not moved on them ourselves."[29]

City College, located in the heart of Harlem, was only 4 percent Black and 5 percent Puerto Rican.[30] As a CCNY professor put it, "There City College sits, smack dab in the middle of the largest Black community in the country, and only 9% of its daytime students are Black or Puerto Rican. And 5% of that 9% came through the SEEK program."[31] Like Brooklyn College, City's faculty and students were predominantly Jewish, a composition that reflected, in part, the legacy of anti-Semitic admissions and hiring practices at private universities. City College had developed a reputation as the proletarian Harvard, as a bastion of educational excellence for the sons and daughters of immigrants. The students relied on research by CUNY economics professor Alfred Conrad to ascertain the racial composition of area high schools, and as a result, they called for a student body that was 43 percent Black. "The racial composition of all entering classes should reflect the Black and Puerto Rican population of the New York City high schools," was the most controversial of the five demands. It envisioned an enormous change in enrollment and suggests that students had embraced a radically new conception of a public university's responsibility to its community. As the students put it, "We are committed to make this college more relevant to the community."[32] In some respects, though, this was an approach steeped in City College history. CCNY had been founded as a free college to serve the children of the poor and, from 1900 to 1925, had required only a high school diploma for entrance. A minimum grade average was then introduced, but open admissions returned for World War II veterans.[33] Kenneth Clark, a City College psychology professor, often reminded New Yorkers that the policy of open admissions "is as old as the history of the college itself. . . . We are not developing something new," he said; "we are returning to the historic purposes of the city colleges, the basic rationale upon which they were set up over 100 years ago, when the deprived groups were immigrants from southern and eastern Europe."[34]

Students in SEEK developed a distinct consciousness that helped forge the unity and discipline that were at the heart of successful Black student organizing. A series of rules differentiated SEEK students from others at City College and made them feel like outsiders: they were barred from playing on athletic teams, for example, and from participating in student government. As a result, the Onyx Society, the City College Black student organization originally formed in 1966, shifted away from a social focus toward a more political orientation. A "Committee of Ten" emerged within Onyx, and these students became the leaders of the south campus takeover in April. As on other campuses, these budding revolutionaries did not just pick up megaphones and shout slogans— they immersed themselves in the contemporary literature of Black radicalism. They read and debated Malcolm X, Frantz Fanon, Nathan Hare's *Black Anglo-Saxons,* Carmichael and Hamilton's *Black Power,* and Harold Cruse's *Crisis of the Negro Intellectual.*[35]

During the 1969 protest, three students played leading roles as negotiators: Charles Powell, who was also a member of the Black Panther Party, Serge Mullery, and Rick Reed, who had formerly worked with SNCC. Reed was reportedly "the visionary and the strategist." According to one student, he "had great insight and inspired the belief that we could change the admissions system." Henry Arce and Luis Reyes Rivera were key Puerto Rican student leaders. During the two-week occupation of south campus, Arce's mother organized the delivery of food from the community, and prominent politicians and activists visited "the University of Harlem," including Kathleen Cleaver, Betty Shabazz, Adam Clayton Powell Jr., and James Forman.[36] "Members of the community are constantly coming onto the campus to examine what we are doing and to give support," the Black and Puerto Rican Student Community (BPRSC) announced. These visitors sometimes joined student-led classes offering "political and social analysis of what is happening in this country."[37]

After admissions, the second-most controversial BPRSC demand was for a School for Black and Puerto Rican Studies. According to the students, the curriculum at City College offered "virtually nothing" on Africa or African Americans. In the words of Toni Cade, author of the groundbreaking feminist text *The Black Woman: An Anthology,* and a highly regarded mentor to the students, the English department clung to "the deeply entrenched notion that Anglo-Saxon literature is The Literature."[38] The leadership of SEEK professor Toni Cade is worth elaborating on, especially since the Black liberation movement from the late 1960s has been framed—and not without some merit—as a quest to restore Black manhood.[39] Still, Black women played critical roles in the campus uprisings. Cade penned an open letter to students encouraging them to seize control of their educational destinies. Steeped in the vernacular of the era, it offered both guidance and solidarity and conveyed the humanism propelling radical activism. It bears quoting at length. "Dear Bloods," she wrote, "There are two traditions within our culture that are worth looking at, for they tell us a great deal about our responses. One, we have been conditioned to turn off, short out, be cool; two, we have often been pushed to make something from nothing. The first response is a negative one. We did it, or do it, to survive surely— but at great cost to ourselves. We've learned how to bottle up anger, put our minds in a jar, wear a mask. The second is a creative urge. It too comes out of the need to survive. . . . Out of which bag do you dip?" she asked. "Something out of nothing is so much better than blowing a fuse," she advised. "On the assumption that all of you mumblers, grumblers, malcontents, workers, designers, etc. are serious about what you've been saying ('A real education—blah, blah, blah'), the Afro-American-Hispanic Studies Center is/was set up. Until it is fully operating, *the responsibility of getting that education rests with you in large part.* Jumping up and down, foaming at the mouth, rattling coffee-cups and other weaponry don't get it. If you are serious, set up a counter course in the Experimental College. If you are serious, contact each other." She closed with: "Serious, Miss Cade."[40]

Cade was not only an adviser to the students, but she also formulated and publicized a model for a Black and Hispanic studies center at City College. "At least 90% of the several hundred rebellions that have taken place on the American college campuses and in the American high schools in the last six years," she wrote in a campus newspaper, "were propelled by and revealed a gross dissatisfaction with the curriculum (its premises, its omissions, its presentations, its designers)." Struggles over knowledge and learning had moved to the forefront of Black activism. This essay was composed before the takeover of south campus, but Cade saw it coming: "We can safely assume that an explosion is imminent," she declared. "The students have already indicated that they are weary of being lied to, tired of playing games, damned if they'll be indoctrinated, programmed, ripped off any longer." Cade proposed that the center be "a course-offering agency, a research agency, a buttress, a skills bank, [and] a conference center." Doubtless the most controversial idea in Cade's proposal was for the center to be "controlled by Black and Latin students and faculty who will have the power to hire using their own standards, and to design courses considering their own needs." She appended a list of courses that the center might offer, including "American Justice and the Afro-American," "Negritude,"

"Revolution," and "Trends in Western Thought." Her eventual goal, which in light of the demographics of City College constituted a radical departure, was that "the Center would lead ultimately to a Black University."[41]

In February 1969, the college had hired Barbara Christian, a Caribbean-born literary scholar who would produce pioneering scholarship on Black women writers during her long career at Berkeley, and Wilfred Cartey, a Trinidadian-born literary scholar, to design a Black studies program. Both were also affiliated with Columbia University; Christian completed her doctorate there with honors in 1970. According to Christian, the call for a School for Black and Puerto Rican Studies was "a very controversial demand." Initially, she wrote, "the students were primarily concerned with their own culture—Black, African, Afro-American, West Indian, Puerto Rican culture." But the involvement of Asian American students in the struggle at City College encouraged them to broaden their vision. "The students then took a look at how many courses were offered on Latin America, how many courses on Asia. And there were very few." This desire to address the needs of all "minority" groups on campus induced Christian and Cartey to propose a School of Urban and Third World Studies, but the faculty senate rejected their proposal late that spring.[42] As we shall see, the college administration resisted the proposals designed by Black professors and moved instead to implement a very different vision.

Paradoxically, as the students were struggling to radically expand the size of CUNY colleges, the already existing SEEK program was slated for drastic cuts, a development that foreshadowed worrisome things to come. In his February 1969 budget proposal, Governor Nelson B. Rockefeller slashed SEEK funding. This sparked a spring mobilization on New York campuses, which all sent busloads of students to Albany to save SEEK. CCNY alone sent thirty-five buses. Still, despite their staunch support for SEEK, the BPRSC rejected paternalist aspects of its structure. Most bothersome was that SEEK counselors were required to be clinical psychologists, a requirement that helped make them mostly white. SEEK students felt this stigmatized them as "psychologically flawed." The only counselor of color was Betty Rawls, who became a strong ally and mentor to the student activists, and who participated in the spring negotiations with administrators. Thus, the BPRSC demanded "a voice for SEEK students in setting guidelines for the SEEK Program, including the hiring and firing of all personnel." And in their list of five demands, the students, like their counterparts in Brooklyn, stipulated that courses in Spanish language and Black and Puerto Rican history be required for all education majors.[43]

The response to the protest was sharply polarized. On the one hand, the students received considerable support from many Black and Puerto Rican New Yorkers, who provided the students occupying south campus with supplies, solidarity, and legal protection. These community members viewed the sit-in as part of the civil rights movement's quest for inclusion. But the students also faced substantial criticism and, they felt, misunderstanding. They were accused of lowering standards, supporting racial exclusion, and pushing an agenda that was more political than academic. In response to such criticism, the students issued press releases offering careful elaboration of their positions. They explained that, yes, white students could take courses in the School for Black and Puerto Rican studies; it was not a "racial" project, but one meant to teach and research the history and culture of "80% of the world's population." Moreover, "the school is not a vehicle for political indoctrination." It "will not have a watered down degree," they emphasized. Students had to meet all the regular requirements to graduate. And the admissions demand—to offer graduates of area high schools a proportionate place at City—"will not lower the standards of the college. Students would be given supportive services on the model of SEEK and would not be allowed to move on through the college unless they fulfilled the standards for graduation at CCNY."[44]

Many Jewish leaders in New York City vocally opposed the new Black and Puerto Rican radicalism, seeing it as an unwise rejection of time-honored liberal assimilation strategies and a possible conduit for anti-Zionism or even anti-Semitism. The years 1968 and 1969 saw many flashpoints of Black-Jewish conflict in New York City, as well as various efforts to articulate the source of tensions. The Black and Puerto Rican student struggles at City and Brooklyn Colleges took place in this context. "The rhetoric of the Black Power movement," wrote a New York rabbi, "has made Negroes less willing than the youngsters of previous ethnic groups to demonstrate the patience required for the laborious step-by-step ascent up the economic ladder. . . . The belief that special advantages are due him—now being impressed upon the young Negro by militants—is disastrous and should be exposed for the crippler it is. Jews, at least, had the advantage of knowing how difficult their advance would be and therefore plunged into the task of self-preparation with enormous self-sacrifice and without the self-delusion being instilled in young Negroes."[45] This kind of approach, which presumed to know the best interests of African Americans, and which failed to acknowledge the significance of skin color in comparing Black and Jewish experiences, was being roundly rejected by African Americans. SNCC activist Julius Lester offered this response to the rabbi: "I think that black people have destroyed the previous relationship which they had with the Jewish community, in which we were the victims of a kind of paternalism, which is only a benevolent racism. It is oppressive, no matter how gentle its touch. That old relationship has been destroyed and the stage is set now for a real relationship where *our* feelings, *our* view of America and how to operate has to be given serious consideration."[46]

Students leaders won support from the Black and Puerto Rican Faculty group and the integrated but predominately white Faculty for Action.[47] As white SEEK professor Fran Geteles remembers, the student activists were savvy organizers who understood that both groups had something to offer. Some historians of the civil rights movement have lamented that the rise of Black Power politics led to an emphasis on slogans and speeches at the expense of grassroots organizing.[48] But Geteles's memory complicates this interpretation. She feels that "the students were very smart politically. They adopted Black nationalist ideas but didn't behave in an exclusionary way. They were shrewd organizers."[49] A Brooklyn College professor had a similar recollection. Carlos Russell, an Afro-Panamanian educator and activist who directed SEEK before becoming dean of the School for Contemporary Studies at Brooklyn College, described Black student activists there as committed, idealistic, and skilled organizers.[50]

The BPRSC gained considerable support from white students, notwithstanding a visible and aggressive band of white opponents. SDS, the City College Commune, and the Du Bois Club organized white support. In a broadside, "The Stake of Whites in the Struggle," the latter group declared, "Right now, it is Black and Puerto Rican youth who are in the main fighting for this right—because it is they who have been most excluded. But, is it not in everyone's interest to fight for the right to go to college? Shouldn't white people join their black and Puerto Rican brothers and sisters in this fight and demand an education for all?" After the protest, southern civil rights leader Floyd McKissick praised this support as a shift from previous patterns: "This support can signify the beginning of a truly useful coalition—not the kind of coalition advocated by so many white labor leaders and their Black flunkies, the kind that leaves Blacks to rely on the decisions and leadership of whites, but

FIGURE 14. "Support the Five Demands" was the rallying cry for students at City
College of New York during the occupation of south campus in spring 1969.

the kind of coalition which is led by Blacks—especially when dealing
with issues which most directly affect the Black Community."[51]

After the seizure of south campus, President Buell G. Gallagher
closed the college and began an intense period of round-the-clock negotiations with student leaders. But an array of critics swung into action.
City College alumni held influential positions in the city, and many
clamored for a police response. Mayor John Lindsay's policy was to
bring in police only if requested to do so by the college president, and
Gallagher did not want a police raid. And Wilfred Cartey had stirred
his faculty colleagues with moving arguments against calling the police
to south campus, in favor of "conciliation with black students." Also
influencing administrators was CCNY's location in Harlem, an African
American neighborhood whose community leaders had aligned themselves with the students. Askia Davis thinks this is the main reason arrests were not made at City, but were made at Brooklyn College, which

is located in an area that was affluent and white.[52] A year earlier, when protesting students at Columbia University had taken over several buildings on the upper Manhattan campus, city police had evicted the Black and white students with different methods, in part because of the fear of a Black uprising in nearby Harlem. Police clobbered many of the white students at Columbia as they forcibly evicted them, while they arrested Black students without violence.[53]

The occupation of south campus at City College occurred shortly after a photo had circulated around the world, of heavily armed Black students at Cornell exiting a building after the administration had agreed to several of their demands. In the eyes of some, Cornell became Munich—and denunciations of liberal "capitulation" to threats of armed violence proliferated. Buell Gallagher took to the radio in New York City, declaring, "Both incidents [CCNY and Cornell] illustrate graphically the failure of student extremists to understand what a university stands for." At this juncture, Gallagher revealed his distance from Black students: "The student militants' rejection of personal accountability, regardless of whether their background is privileged or ghetto, stands at the heart of the campus revolution across the country. Tyranny, whether exercised by the majority, or a minority, is still tyranny." He also echoed a widely held view among college officials that student radicalism would strengthen conservatism. "With each forcible takeover, each ransacking of administration files, each disruption of classes for the majority of students, the hands of the ultraconservatives in the legislature are strengthened."[54] Yet at the same time, as Gallagher began negotiations with the students, he came to respect their sincerity and the seriousness of their mission. A week later he was asked to defend his decision not to call the police when he had called them several months earlier to quell a largely white antiwar protest. "The circumstances are not the same," he explained. "They were causing extensive damage . . . smoking pot and fornicating in public," but the Black and Puerto Rican students occupying south campus "are behaving in an orderly manner." And as he got to know Black and Puerto Rican student activists that spring, this view solidified.[55]

The upcoming fall election turned the CCNY sit-in into a citywide political controversy and foreshadowed the way in which racial backlash politics would dramatically shape electoral discourse in the ensuing decades. State Senator John J. Marchi, who was opposing the liberal Lindsay for the Republican nomination, attacked the mayor "for not taking swift police action" at City and other CUNY campuses.[56] Actually, there had been at least one police officer on south campus—an undercover agent, whom the students had discovered, interrogated, and released.[57] Another candidate took the matter to court. City Comptroller Mario Procaccino, who was seeking the Democratic nomination for mayor, obtained a Supreme Court injunction directing the college to open on May 5, precisely the point at which students and administrators believed they were making substantial progress. It is important to stress that there were many liberal administrators at CCNY and CUNY who favored negotiation rather than strong-arm tactics. Still, as ordered by the court, police opened the campus and occupied it for the rest of the term as a wave of fires, vandalism, and violent attacks on Black students followed. The protest leaders and their faculty supporters responded with a continued boycott of classes. And the college lost its president. Gallagher, who had been president for seventeen years, resigned on May 10.[58] He said that "politically motivated outside forces" had made it "impossible to carry on the process of reason and persuasion."[59] Indeed, that same day a *New York Daily News* editorial called for the House Internal Security Committee to probe charges that "Red Cuba and Red China are helping to finance some of the worst campus troublemakers." It called for a "Hayakawa for City College," referring to the authoritarian president of San Francisco State College who was willingly doing the bidding of conservative California politicians, most notably Governor Ronald Reagan. Their wish seemed to come true with the selection of Joseph Copeland, a sixty-one-year-old botanist, as acting president, whose commencement address equated the occupiers of south campus with the Ku Klux Klan, sparking a walkout by graduating Black and Puerto Rican students.[60]

More than sixty students walked out of the commencement ceremonies at Madison Square Garden about midway through Copeland's speech when, after denouncing the old and new left, he went on to assail "racial extremists, both white and black, who seek to impose a new apartheid or racial separatism on American society at a moment when for the first time in three centuries the promise and possibility of racial reconciliation have at last appeared on the horizon." Forces on the left, he said, "exploited every grievance, real and imaginary," in order "to create disorder and disruption." He garnered a combination of boos, hissing, and applause while the students departed. He moved on to pillory "racial quotas" declaring that "no real contributions can be made by lowering standards to the level of performance of the ghetto high schools." One young man replied to a query about why he had walked out: "Did you hear the speech? You had no choice."[61]

To be sure, many administrators at CCNY applauded the student movement. In May 1969 George Paster, the dean of students at City College, resigned in protest over what he viewed as the hidebound nature of academic institutions. "People who want to change such institutions," he said, "have to grab them by the scruff of the neck and yell: 'please listen to me' if they are ever to be heard. I honestly don't know any way you can break through the rigidity of the institution other than the way the blacks and Puerto Ricans have done it." He felt that students used force "to be heard not really to destroy." Moreover, in a point echoed by administrators at other campuses, Paster felt that, "once they had been heard, we sat down to some of the best and most productive discussions ever in the college—they have taught us so much."[62]

It was not just college administrators, alumni, political conservatives, or white ethnic politicians who found fault with the Black and Puerto Rican student movement. Several Black leaders did as well. These critics included many from the integrationist old guard, like Roy Wilkins, the longtime executive director of the NAACP, and social democrats, like Bayard Rustin, for whom the identity politics of Black Power was anathema. But since their target was Black nationalism as much as Black studies, they sometimes invoked an inaccurate or superficial conception of Black studies. "In their hurt pride in themselves, and in their outrage, they have called retreat from the tough and trying battle of a minority for dignity and equality," Wilkins said of student militants. "They don't call it retreat, of course. They have all sorts of fancy rationalizations for their course." Wilkins was particularly aghast at any proposal that seemed geared for Black students only, calling this "black Jim Crow studies" or "black academic separatism."[63] Bayard Rustin, a longtime civil rights activist and key adviser to Martin Luther King, echoed this concern over separatism and added two others. Black studies, he wrote, "must not be used for the purpose of image-building or to enable young black students to escape the challenges of the university by setting up a program of 'soul courses' that they can just play with and pass." And it must not become "subordinated to political and ideological goals" or used to "train cadres of ghetto organizers."[64]

But the BPRSC at City College also had important supporters among the citywide Black and Puerto Rican leadership. Louis Nunez, executive director of Aspira, a Puerto Rican educational advocacy organization, and an alumnus of City College, expressed his support for the five demands to the Board of Higher Education. City College, he argued, must do in the 1970s "what it did so well in the 1930s, namely, raise up from poverty, in one generation, an entire group." He endorsed open admissions, but cautioned that "CUNY cannot blandly assume that mere admittance meets the problem." The curriculum would have to be updated, faculty-to-student ratios reassessed, and the qualifications for faculty reconsidered.[65]

The student uprisings across the city induced the Board of Higher Education to accelerate and broaden an open admissions plan slated to begin in 1975. The original plan was to assign most high school graduates to community colleges rather than four-year, or senior, colleges, but student protest won a much larger number of slots at the senior colleges and moved up the launch date of the admissions plan to 1970. Of course, the students had not led the call for open admissions, but their support for quotas to increase the Black and Puerto Rican student population had inspired intense opposition. Allen Ballard, a Black CCNY professor, director of SEEK, and scholar of Black education, argued that, "by moving from a quota arrangement specifically designed to serve the needs of Black and Puerto Rican students to a position of open admissions, the board both diverted the thrust of the Black and Puerto Rican demands and gained a white middle class constituency for the program." Ballard, it should be noted, was the first Black director of SEEK, and he implemented the BPRSC demand to permit the hiring of social workers, rather than solely clinical psychologists, as SEEK counselors. Still, the impact of open admissions on Black and Puerto Rican educational opportunity was substantial. "I don't know, as of this writing," Ballard wrote in 1973, "whether open admissions will be a success or not. However, it has opened vistas for Black and Puerto Rican high school youth previously condemned to a life of poverty because their averages and SAT scores did meet the requirements of the City University of New York."[66] Indeed, the activism of 1968 and 1969 irrevocably altered the character and mission of the CUNY colleges. For their part, alumni saw open admissions as the death knell of a great university, and donations plunged.[67]

The impact of open admissions was stunning: thirty-five thousand freshmen entered CUNY campuses in 1970, a 75 percent increase from 1969. One-quarter of these entering students were Black or Latino. According to New York Post columnist Murray Kempton, "The proof is not in, but there are grounds for real hope that the deprived can compete. . . . For the first time, a student at Benjamin Franklin can believe it when his counselor tells him that, with work, he has a chance to go to college, and not just any college, but City College."[68] After open admissions, 75 percent of New York City high school graduates attended college, a rate well ahead of the national average. According to historian Conrad Dyer, two-thirds of these students would have been ineligible to attend college, even community college, under the old admissions standards. In 1975, five times as many Black and Puerto Rican students were enrolled in the senior colleges than in 1969. The Black community struggle for greater access to public higher education also created many new administrative positions for African Americans. Just as Charles Hurst became the first Black college president in Chicago during this time, Richard Trent achieved that status in New York in 1970, when he became president of the newly created Medgar Evers College, a four-year CUNY institution located in Bedford-Stuyvesant.[69]

The quest for Black studies encountered much greater difficulties. To the extent that there was a Black revolution on campus, it was often followed by a counterrevolution, an administrative attempt to contain or delimit the expansive vision of student activists and their faculty allies. This is precisely what happened at City College. Over the summer, the Board of Higher Education had rejected the demand to establish a separate school of Third World studies, but it authorized CUNY colleges to set up urban and ethnic studies departments. Without consulting the BPRSC or Black and Puerto Rican professors, including the two—Christian and Cartey—that City had hired to design such a program, acting CCNY president Joseph Copeland announced the creation of a new Urban and Ethnic Studies department and appointed Osborne E. Scott, a former Army chaplain and current vice president of the American Leprosy Missions, as chair.[70] Wilfred Cartey called the two-course department "an insult not only to the black and Puerto Rican community, but to City College itself." This move by a college president to grant a Black studies program and then turn around and contain or undermine it was not unique to City College. Most colleges around the country failed to finance or build the kinds of innovative, large, and comprehensive African American studies units that Black student activists and their faculty allies had envisioned. At City, this development was transparent, as Copeland had been hired as a revanchist president. His quest found blunt expression when he publicly called Professor Cartey "shiftless." Calling it an "insidious and malicious" remark, Cartey threatened a lawsuit, declaring, "I'm not seeking an apology. I'm seeking redress for a group." For his part, Copeland claimed to have "never associated that word in my understanding with any racial group." But this supposed naïveté is contradicted by his evident awareness of the

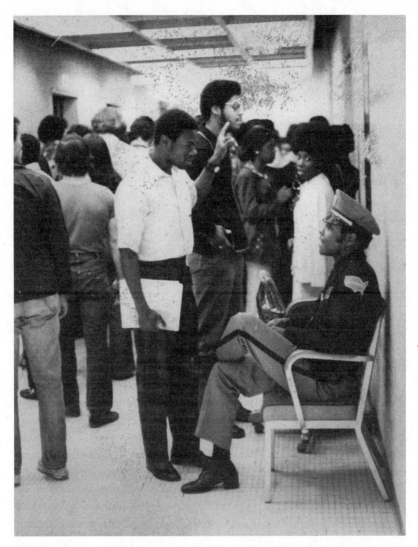

FIGURE 15. The new open admissions policy quickly changed the demographics of City College, making it better reflect the racial composition of local high schools.

connotations of the word in his original statement. "He's too goddamn shiftless—and you can use that word in your story there—shiftless," he had declared.[71]

Students at City College shunned the department, kept up a battle, and finally won a Black studies department three years later. In the fall of 1972, at the urging of a Black faculty and student panel, the college

made an offer of tenure to Leonard Jeffries, a 1971 CUNY PhD in political science who had been teaching Black studies at San Jose State College.[72] He served for more than two decades as chair before stepping
down as a result of controversy generated by a televised speech that
traded in generalizations and pandering—a speech that called whites
and Blacks, ice and sun people, respectively, and singled out Jews, from
the broader category of whites, as perpetrators of racism. As a rule, a
long-serving chair is not a sign of departmental vitality. Jeffries left the
academic research track early and became active in a grassroots circle
of Afrocentric educators and community members. In the context of
intense demand for Black studies scholars and limited supply, Jeffries
exemplified a phenomenon of graduate students and newly minted
PhDs hired into senior leadership roles very early in their academic
careers. But the arc of Black studies at CCNY is instructive: a comparative, expansive model was replaced by an administrative shell, and
what finally emerged was a unit known for narrow nationalism and
disconnected from either scholarship and research or a broader social
movement.

The tendency by many to credit—or blame—the City College protest
with the onset of open admissions has, along with the legacy of the criminal prosecution, worked to suppress an acknowledgement of the significance of the struggle at Brooklyn College. But the students there achieved
a great deal. "We were responsible for changing the climate of the campus," says Orlando Pile, now a physician.[73] After open admissions, the
number of Black and Puerto Rican students rose significantly, but as
Askia Davis acknowledges, "it wasn't just Blacks and Latinos who ben-
efited from open admissions—a lot of working-class whites had been
shut out too." Other reforms included the establishment of the Afro-
American Studies Institute and the Puerto Rican Studies Institute, which
later became departments; significant changes in required courses; and
more Black and Puerto Rican counselors.[74]

A significant, though controversial, outgrowth of the protest was the
creation in 1972 of a new division in the college called the School for
Contemporary Studies (SCS), whose mission was to be "present oriented, concerned primarily with the social problems that are engaging
our contemporary world." Faculty included Eli Messenger of the New
York Marxist School and the prominent political economist Sumner
Rosen. Until its demise in 1976, the school was in downtown Brooklyn,
quite a distance from the main campus, and it offered a unique field
studies requirement: students did internships in legal services agencies,

health service organizations, and penal institutions. "A special feature of the program," according to the SCS dean Carlos Russell, "will be an attempt to blend theory and practice towards the creation of a 'scholar-activist.'" As a two-year program, it also required students to have an additional major in another division of the college. As Dean Russell recalls, the program exemplified the call for relevance raised in the 1960s by bringing "the streets and classrooms together."[75]

But at least one student leader was "ambivalent." Askia Davis "was of two minds about" the School for Contemporary Studies. "I was anxious about it," he recalls. He saw the circumstances of its location "as putting Blacks and Latinos at this extension campus downtown and off the main campus." He felt this undercut their mission of reimagining Brooklyn College as a whole. "We were just beginning to transform the main campus," he notes, "and that was very, very important to us." The student activists debated these issues. They respected Russell but were not responsible for his hiring.[76]

An evaluation in 1976 found that "some students appear to have been profoundly affected by their experience in field study." But the report cast light on an ironic outcome of the student movement. The SCS, the evaluation committee felt, had been designed for the "bright, activist students of the late 1960s," but it had come to serve the "open-admissions students"—working-class Black, Puerto Rican, and white students whose educational needs were different. The students needed remediation and skills development, and they were "not being sufficiently prepared" at SCS for the transfer, after two years, to the main Brooklyn College campus in Midwood. The report called for more counseling and tutoring and a greater focus on writing and the development of academic skills. It lamented that Brooklyn College faculty seemed to view the SCS curriculum, faculty, and students as beneath the standards of the college, and it concluded that racism shaped their judgments. Evidently, a majority of the students at the SCS were Black, and whites on the main campus commonly referred to it as "the black school." "Midwood faculty should not describe the SCS as a dumping ground for unwanted students," the committee warned, "nor should they describe it as the 'black school' nor should they commit the serious educational error of cruelly and publicly pre-judging the ability of the School's students not on the basis of their ability or performance but merely on their attendance at the School." Adding to this problem were internal rifts between Russell and his faculty, and concerns about effective school leadership. The SCS did not survive the city's fiscal crisis.[77]

Critics of open admissions always remained, arguing that high admissions standards had made City and Brooklyn top schools. "Only at CUNY," a SEEK professor wryly observed, "were those standards viewed as fixed, immutable and exempt from social and political realities."[78] Albert H. Bowker, former chancellor of CUNY, thought racial resentment drove the attacks on open admissions. "There's been a lot of white flight from City College," he observed. "And most of the people who write about this are City College graduates who are mad."[79] In a fateful conjuncture, open admissions coincided with the New York City fiscal crisis of the 1970s, and the sharp drop in funding seemed to make the discourse of failure shrouding open admissions a self-fulfilling prophecy. The severe budget cuts climaxed in the "retrenchment of 1976," when the State of New York took over the City University of New York, laid off many faculty, and imposed tuition for the first time.[80] The case load of SEEK counselor Fran Geteles doubled from fifty to one hundred students. "Class sizes also grew sharply," she says, "which made it much harder to help students as before. Remedial classes had been no more than twenty; now some had forty students."[81]

At Brooklyn there was a similar surge in enrollments, and a failure to add the necessary resources and services for the new student body, prompting a high dropout rate. According to one estimate, in 1970, thirteen hundred students entered Brooklyn College who would not otherwise have been eligible. This included several hundred minority students in the older SEEK and EOP programs. But the majority of open-admission students hailed from the white working class. They were "not welcomed with open arms" but faced stigma. The tracking arising from the need for remediation was expected but reinforced their separation from the rest of the college. By 1974, a significant portion of the first open admissions class had dropped out, while the share of open admissions students in succeeding classes had grown to constitute one-half of the entering class. Then the fiscal crisis hit, sinking the whole experiment. Large numbers of remedial teachers lost their jobs, and some entrance requirements were reintroduced. "We have come full circle," a student said.[82]

As a result, an increasingly negative view of open admissions took root. One observer summed up the prevailing view by the early 1980s: it "shuffles its poor students through four years of over-crowded and under-taught classes—then pushes them out the door with a worthless diploma."[83] Still, those "worthless" diplomas brought thousands of Black and Puerto Rican graduates into the middle class. But the attacks took their toll. By 1990, some of the creators and proponents of open admissions were lamenting that the college had made such a radical change with too little resources and planning. Allen Ballard thinks CUNY should have implemented "a well articulated, gradually phased in, well funded operation aimed at a saveable number of Black and Puerto Rican students in the high schools." Former SEEK Professor Leslie Berger feels similarly: "It was almost criminal to let them come in and let them fail because of the lack of service. We knew what we needed. It was no mystery."[84] In 1998, Republican Mayor Rudolph Giuliani declared that "open enrollment is a failure," and the CUNY Board of Trustees replaced it with standardized tests for admissions and eliminated all remedial courses from the senior colleges. As a City College student wrote, "The avenue for education for many NY high school students has been closed."[85]

This discourse of failure obscures the fact that a generation of lawyers, civil servants, teachers, artists, and social workers in New York City got their start through open admissions, notwithstanding its severe underfunding and other flaws. Black and Puerto Rican college students in the late 1960s rejected market-driven approaches to higher education. They insisted upon the right of working-class African American and Puerto Ricans to receive the benefits of public higher education in New York City. As Barbara Christian put it in 1969, a "much overlooked factor is that City College is supported by taxes. And Black and Puerto Rican people pay taxes just like everybody else. Yet they are not in any way represented in the ethnic make-up of the College."[86]

Inspiring this generation was the conviction that seniors at poorly funded and poorly performing public high schools should not be punished for society's failure to provide high-quality secondary education for all, but rather, should be rewarded for their determination and desire to gain a college education. These student activists understood that college was critical to social mobility, especially since workers of color in New York City had already been hit hard by deindustrialization and automation.[87] It's important to appreciate that the struggle for affirmative action, open admissions, and Black and Third World studies was centered at public universities as much as, if not more than, at private ones. This was a struggle not of elites but of the children of migrants and immigrants. Even with the restoration of stricter admissions requirements and the increased tuition in the 1990s, CUNY campuses still felt the legacy of the 1960s. The student struggles brought an irrevocable change to urban higher education and opened doors that were difficult to entirely shut. A related but different kind of student movement was taking place at the same time on campuses of historically Black colleges and universities. All of these diverse campus struggles shared the fundamental goal of using higher education to advance the economic security and social status of African Americans in the United States.

CHAPTER 5

Toward a Black University

*Radicalism, Repression, and Reform at Historically
Black Colleges*

Black student protest at white colleges in the North and West garnered
extensive mainstream media coverage, yet most Black collegians in the
late 1960s still attended historically Black colleges and universities (HB-
CUs), and students on these campuses, too, were up in arms. But journalists gave these struggles scant attention, and historians have given
them even less. If the goal of the civil rights movement was to open the
doors of white universities to more Black students and faculty, why did
Black colleges become such volatile sites of struggle? As chapter 1 illustrates, part of the answer lies in the shift among youth away from the
discourse of integration toward a new politics of self-determination.
Black students wanted to save public Black institutions from being "integrated" into white-run universities, and to generally strengthen, upgrade, and modernize HBCUs, making them exemplars of Black self-
determination. Black colleges were vital institutions: even as emblems
of Jim Crow, they testified to the signal importance of education and
striving in Black life and culture since the nineteenth century. Moreover,
since most Black students in the late 1960s still attended Black colleges,
they became a very logical base for the student movement. In 1968,
150,000 Black students, or 61 percent of all Blacks enrolled in college,
attended HBCUs.[1] There were three main goals of the student movement on Black campuses: to increase Black consciousness, upgrade academics and improve the physical plant, and finally, expand student
participation in governance. Tragically, as the struggle escalated, stu-

dents on many campuses faced an onslaught of lethal violence by police forces.

This powerful, bottom-up push by students to modernize and transform Black colleges came at a time of intense policy focus on the desegregation of educational institutions. There was anxiety and concern about the future of Black colleges: would Black students shun them? Would courts and legislatures close them? Would integration be a one-way street? Would Black communities lose control over another set of educational institutions? In many respects, the student movement prefigured and encouraged the transition in federal education policy away from support for strict integration toward support for public Black colleges as part of a pluralist educational system. Black students were laying claim to Black colleges and struggling to reshape them for a new day. During the 1970s, a battle raged between the NAACP Legal Defense Fund and the presidents of historically Black colleges over the best way to achieve educational parity for Blacks in southern public higher education. HBCU leaders feared that the federal court decision *Adams v. Richardson,* directing states to dismantle race-based dual systems of public higher education, would spell the end of Black-controlled institutions. But the judge in *Adams* ruled that states could not close HBCUs to achieve parity. It turns out that *Adams* unlocked new funding that was used to improve rather than dismantle Black schools as states moved toward unitary systems. Student activism to save and improve historically Black colleges was an unheralded but critical factor in producing this outcome. In the late 1960s, as white colleges intensified recruitment of African Americans, enrollment figures in Black colleges began to decline; but they stabilized in the 1970s and rose in the 1980s.[2]

As we saw in the first chapter, the students at Howard University in Washington, D.C., were pivotal in launching the Black student movement. Their struggle intensified the following year, erupting in a major showdown with the administration that ushered in a season of change. Founded after the Civil War, Howard was considered among the best of Black colleges. In an unusual arrangement, Howard defines itself as private although it receives the bulk of its funding from appropriations by the United States Congress. When students returned to Howard in the fall of 1968, they noted some changes since the protests of the previous spring—they had the option of taking several new African and African American studies courses. But many students still hoped to see Howard made into a Black university and for students to be invested with greater power. Activists had won a big victory in spring elections, bringing into office strong supporters of what incoming student council president Lewis Myers called "the black agenda." QT Jackson, the new head of the student assembly, declared to a skeptical audience of faculty and administrators at the Opening Day ceremonies: "We intend to bring blackness to Howard University. Black brotherhood, Black unity, Black thought, and Black action."[3]

What did students and intellectuals mean by a Black university? Generally advocates meant either the establishment of a brand new entity, or the process by which Negro colleges would transform themselves for the post-Jim-Crow era. As Vincent Harding, historian at Spelman College, put it, "The search for the Black University is really a part of our larger search for a sense of direction and life in the new, black-oriented time that is upon us." In his view, a key challenge of the era was finding "pathways toward unity and solidarity, toward inner strength and communal wisdom." A Black university marked a decisive rejection of the view "promoted by Booker T. Washington" that higher education should prepare Black youth to live in world of white domination and control, and instead sought "to enter that stream of global anti-colonialism which refuses to educate young people primarily for the service of the colonizers." The overriding goal was to serve the Black community, whose needs, Harding and others insisted, were different from the needs of the white community. He called the quest a clear response to Frantz Fanon's challenge to "risk the creation of new institutions and new modes of thought on behalf of a new humanity." Rather than constitute a rejection of academic discipline, a Black university would, in Harding's view, make even greater demands for rigor and commitment from its students.[4] Sociology graduate student Gerald McWorter similarly saw a Black university as a prophetic institution that ought to be "focused on the Afro-American community." Blackness, he argued, "is an affirmation of an identity independent of the historical human evils of modern nation-states, and is closely tied to the emerging international identity of man in his struggle for a better life." The Black university must seek the greatest possible psychological and structural independence "from the oppressor" and replace "U.S. individualism with communalism."[5]

Some proponents saw a Black university as a more efficient alternative to the scattering of underfunded, understaffed Black studies units at white colleges; it would be a means to consolidate Black intellectual and pedagogical talent and maximize its influence. Vincent Harding promoted this view. More controversially, he urged Black students and faculty in the North to reject the lure of integration, which in his view was aiding in the destruction of Black colleges.[6] The quest to transform HBCUs would not be easy. The novelist John Oliver Killens had been a writer in residence at Fisk University in Nashville, where he dreamed of a Black "communiversity"—a place to unify Black people and bring them "home." "Human reconstruction is the goal of the black university," he wrote (echoing a common theme), in order "to rid the world of niggers." Killens conceded that the quest for a Black university at Fisk faced many challenges, including the board of trustees and white faculty—who, he said, might be liberal or radical but would likely envision "an Afro-American Berkeley" rather than a "W. E. B. DuBois University." But the most "insidious" group in opposition was "our own black brothers and sisters of the faculty," who feared white opposition and wanted Fisk to be "a finishing school for nice young ladies and gentlemen."[7]

It was not only Black radicals who saw Howard as a seedbed for revolutionary change. "The Black Revolution is upon us and it won't go away just because we ignore it or refuse to believe that its spokesmen mean what they say."[8] So declared retired Marine Corps counterinsurgency specialist Robert Corson, who served as a visiting professor in the economics department at Howard during the 1968–1969 year. In a remarkable encounter, Bernard Fall, a Howard professor who was doing research in South Vietnam, met Corson there and impressed upon him the great urgency of "the Black revolution" back home. Black students were on the precipice of revolution, Fall insisted, and stopping them would entail winning over their hearts and minds. When Professor Fall died from a mine explosion the very next day, Corson decided to investigate his admonition. After a friend in the Justice Department confirmed Fall's fears, Corson returned to the states and got himself hired at Howard.

When he arrived, administrators told him that student protest was linked to "a Communist plot." They were "petrified" of "black student power," Corson wrote, and they blamed the whole protest on a "sinister Communist conspiracy." The student demands were unreasonable, administrators complained to him, "and based on a Marxist view of shared authority in running a university." Moreover, "nonstudents were using Howard as a center for the distribution of 'black power' literature to other Negro colleges." This is the problem that Corson, the counterinsurgency specialist, came to solve. A classic cold war liberal, he wrote a book about his year at Howard and used it to make a plea for the greater integration of African Americans, particularly college graduates, in American life. In his view, "Black revolutionaries" had the power to lure Black college students into a violent revolutionary struggle unless white society changed its ways. He ended his book with an appeal to the nation: "To eliminate racism, make use of the full potential of the black minority, and avoid a black revolution—to bring about meaningful, positive, peaceful social change—is a task for all Americans."[9]

Student government leaders at Howard University took advantage of their control of student activity fees to host a five-day national conference in November called "Toward A Black University" (TABU). Two thousand people attended and heard Stokely Carmichael, Harold Cruse, and Ron Karenga exhort students to make their education "relevant to the total black community." Nathan Hare, who had been fired by Howard the previous summer, declined to attend. In his view, "unless every Howard student comes armed with a shotgun and Molotov cocktail they are defenseless against an Amos 'n' Andy administration." But the conference was intended for discussion not confrontation, and it featured seventy-five workshops analyzing every aspect of the Black university. "During those bright warm five days," a journalist wrote, "the Howard campus was full of dashikis, Afros, undercover FBI agents and revolutionary talk."[10]

Stokely Carmichael's two speeches attracted packed audiences. His keynote before two thousand people hammered home a message he had been telling students around the country: "You've got to quit talking and start acting."[11] And as he had just done at San Francisco State College, Carmichael openly and forcefully advocated armed struggle. "We are for revolutionary violence," he declared, adding: "The system has begun to recognize this and implemented counterrevolutionary violence." He insisted that being a revolutionary required violence. "In order to become a revolutionary," Carmichael said, "one must be willing to pick up the gun and kill for one's own people—not kill one's own people."[12] Several months later, the eminent scholar St. Clair Drake noted that Carmichael was going around "giving speeches promoting a kind of violence by students."[13] Given the intense federal surveillance of Black radicals, and the potential for "counterrevolutionary violence," as Carmichael put it, it is perhaps not very surprising that he soon relocated to the African nation of Guinea.

The Black arts movement had an empowering and inspiring relationship to the student movement—at Howard and all over the country. TABU featured performances by poet Amiri Baraka, actor Ossie Davis,

FIGURE 16. Greatly admired by black college students, Stokely Carmichael, a leader of the Student Non-Violent Coordinating Committee, spoke at colleges across the country in 1968 and 1969 and inspired students to engage in direct action protest.

poet Ted Joans, jazz drummer Max Roach, and jazz vocalist Abby Lincoln. An odd note at the conference was the presentation by Harold Cruse, author of *The Crisis of the Negro Intellectual,* a popular polemic known for its attack on virtually every major Black leader, past and present. Cruse abruptly stopped in the middle of his address before about seven hundred people and left the stage, citing illness. Student leader Lewis Myers recalls that Cruse had come in for a lot of criticism at the conference, and that he had a difficult time holding his own with either the academics or the young radicals. Still, Myers admired Cruse and felt he was misunderstood.[14]

The economist Robert S. Browne gave a paper, "Financing the Black University," that mixed practicality with a vision for far-reaching change. An underappreciated scholar and activist, Browne exemplified the idealism and commitment of young intellectuals in the movement. An early critic of the war in Vietnam, where he had worked for the U.S. government in the late 1950s, Browne later left his teaching position at Fairleigh Dickinson University to devote himself full time to building Black institutions. He founded and directed the Black Economic Research Center in Harlem, which published the important journal *Review of Black Political Economy;* he also established the Emergency Land Fund to save Black-owned land in the South, and the 21st Century Foundation to encourage and channel Black philanthropy to social justice and economic development projects in Black communities. At TABU Browne commended the student organizers of the conference. "In my travels around the country I have had indelibly impressed upon me the fervency with which today's young black college men and women are striving to discover new forms in which they can express their desire to play a meaningful role in building a new future for Afro-Americans." The "creation of a black university is perhaps the most promising means for realizing these objectives," he declared as he outlined a variety of forms such an initiative might take and offered innovative fundraising strategies. But he urged activists to be realistic about the touchy subject of funding. "We must be cautious in accepting money from others, to be sure," he said. "But money we must have if we are going to make notable improvements in our position. My recommendation would be to admit this unpalatable truth and to accept financing from accepted white sources, at least for our capital plant."[15]

To be sure, making Howard a Black university was not a universal quest among Howard students. Many wondered if this was even an appropriate mission for an institution of higher education, and others disagreed with Black nationalism. Some of these critics formed a group, Students for an Educational Institution, which opposed the push for a Black university. It is important to state that a sizeable cohort of more traditional or conservative students could be found on all Black college campuses. A Black university, this group argued, would not adequately prepare students to live in a diverse society, and some felt that overemphasizing racial consciousness might still creativity and undermine a broader collegiate training.[16] While the conferees were debating "how to make existing colleges more responsive to the Negro revolution," other Howard students worried that such a setting would ill prepare them to compete in the job market. "All right," conceded one young woman, Howard is "'bourgeois' and not 'revolutionary,' but what are they going to replace it with? Where are they going to get $50 million to even replace this school?"[17]

At the same time, the TABU conference strongly influenced the students in attendance, including Ewart Brown, a leader of the Howard protests in 1968 as well as 1969. He hoped that a Black university "would completely obliterate the Negro concept," by which he meant the concern for white authority and validation, which he felt was a constant presence.[18] In his view, a Black university did not have to exclude whites: "A black university is not a hatred school." However, he acknowledged that some students had a different view. Evidently, white reporters had been barred from the workshops, and white professors had been asked to leave, causing radio station WWDC to blast "discrimination at Howard."[19] The Bermuda-born Brown noted some of the excesses of Black nationalism but saw this as a charged moment in history, a stage in political development. Commenting on the recent expulsion of whites from meetings, he said, "Now obviously there is no merit whatsoever; no logical reason for anyone to go in and chase whites out of a building; but you see this is where we are." There are many reasons to hate white people, he observed. "But it's not constructive. The focus needs to be on black people, not white people."[20] Brown also thought that arming the masses was a bad idea.[21] For student council president Lewis Myers, the "conference was a turning point in black collegiate life and in black life. It was one of the major events of that time. I had never seen anything like it." He felt that TABU "solidified the black student movement." From 1966 to 1968, Black student activism had been emerging in various locations in isolation. But TABU brought a lot of people together. Moreover, according to Myers, who went on to become a leading civil rights attorney, the conference "shook Howard."[22]

The shaking began in earnest that winter. Early in 1969, protest erupted at Howard's professional schools, hardly typical locations of student unrest. These future lawyers, social workers, and doctors took over buildings and boycotted classes in an effort to upgrade a Howard education. And in keeping with the Black Power ethos of serving the people, students in all these divisions pressed administrators to make the curriculum and training more "relevant" to the needs of Black communities. In January students at the medical school began a boycott of anatomy classes.[23] According to Ewart Brown, the Howard anatomy department was not adequately preparing students for the national boards, and as a result, Howard students had low passing rates. No stranger to protest, Brown had occupied the administration building the previous spring as an undergraduate. He reported that, of the 106 students in his class, not a single one broke the boycott. Their target was department chair Montague Cobb, a pioneering African American anthropologist, prolific scholar, and later president of the NAACP. "He was a giant. A very talented man," recalls Brown. "In class he was an entertainer, a performer. Class was like a theater. He sometimes played the violin," Brown said. "Passing the board," however, "was a secondary concern."[24] After an eighteen-day boycott, the university announced that Cobb, who had been head of the department for twenty-one years, would not be reappointed as head after June. But following a faculty outcry, Howard offset the embarrassment by naming him a Distinguished Professor of Anatomy.[25]

In February, students at the Howard Law School began a boycott of classes and a week later seized the main building and chained the doors shut. Ironically, Patricia Roberts Harris had just been installed as the first female dean of the Law School, and she stepped into the job just as students escalated their tactics. Administrators had previously agreed to a series of demands, including a reduction in the semester hours required for graduation, the addition of courses more relevant to the practice of law in Black communities, extended hours at the library, and a new grading system. Showing how seriously they took their role in making change, the students occupied the building in order to win student participation in the committee charged with implementing these reforms.[26] According to Joseph Clair, president of the second-year law class, students wanted "a voice in the operation of this law school to make it more relevant to the students here and the communities to which we hope to return." The administration granted other demands but was adamant in not ceding such an elevated role in governance to the students. Faced with a court order to leave the building, the future lawyers departed. And so did Dean Harris. She resigned her position as dean after only one month, in protest over President James M. Nabrit Jr.'s failure to keep her and the law faculty involved in discussions with students over resolving the boycott, which continued until mid-March.[27]

In another illustration of the widespread nature of graduate and professional student discontent, students in the School of Social Work boycotted classes for more than a month later that semester. They wanted a greater role in hiring faculty and, like the other students in professional divisions, wanted to reshape Howard's educational mission and product. Student Arthur J. Cox, from the Bronx, explained, "Most of us, including the white students, came to Howard's Social Work School looking for that something extra that would help us be more effective in the black community."[28]

Dissent soon spread to the undergraduate college. The campus newspaper reprinted the previous year's demands and noted that a few had been met, but that the "underlying issue of POWER has been avoided." Students deserved a voice in running Howard, the student editors believed.[29] "And here at the 'Capstone of Negro Education,'" declared Ewart Brown, "there still is no Black Studies program."[30] Indeed, the professional school protests turned out to be a mere prelude for an even bigger convulsion in May, when militant students took over eight buildings and the faculty voted to close the campus. There was more student protest across the United States—strikes, building seizures, demonstrations—in May 1969 than ever before in American history, although it would escalate even further the following spring. A coordinating committee of graduates and undergraduates organized the May protests at Howard. Still, only about two hundred students, considerably fewer than the previous spring, participated in the occupations, but activists from the city joined in. Members of the Black United Front, several clergy, Marion Berry of the Student Non-Violent Coordinating Committee, and the ever-present Jimmy Garrett from Federal City College all gave support. "No longer do we conceive of Howard University as an educational community separate and distinct from the total black community," an activist insisted. "There is now a united black community of which a black university becomes the educational apparatus for defining black values and black goals."

The students hoped to dramatically reshape governance of the university, calling for an equal student say over faculty hiring and promotion and the participation of "community representatives" in such matters. They also wanted an increase in Black faculty. A sign on the anthropology-sociology building declared: This is a Black Struggle. And protesters called for the sociology department, whose faculty was predominantly white, to be "desegregated" to the point of having at least an equal balance of Blacks and whites. The support of off-campus

Black activists emboldened Howard students but also entailed the loss of some control. According to the press, youth from the community threw rocks at cars and set fires, which included a fire set at a building housing the Reserve Officer Training Corps. The nonstudent activists evidently took the lead in asking white journalists to leave a rally, and according to one account, "at least a half dozen Negroes carrying clubs observed the departure of white reporters and cameramen."[31] Babalola Cole, a lecturer in political science, praised the 1968 protest, calling it "well-organized and not destructive." The one in 1969, he felt, "was not bad but there were some unpleasant overtones."[32] The presence of outside activists in the occupied buildings reportedly paved the way for the faculty to endorse President Nabrit's resolution to "get rid of the revolutionaries."[33] Nabrit went on television and warned students to leave or face forcible removal. It would be the first time in Howard history that administrators had moved to arrest protesting students. Many students decided to exit, but others—students and nonstudents—stayed, and federal marshals moved in, arresting twenty and ending the three-day seizure.[34]

The administration successfully reopened the campus, but their subsequent behavior caused a federal judge to dismiss contempt charges against the twenty defendants. Evidently without consulting counsel, Howard officials purchased full-page advertisements in two major newspapers at the outset of criminal proceedings, providing the administration's account of the protests and their view of student culpability. Defense attorneys were outraged and the judge dumbfounded at such obvious interference: "The Court has concluded that in light of these circumstances which fall short of contempt it will nonetheless be difficult if not impossible to select an impartial jury for the remaining trials scheduled this month." The judge urged Howard officials to "make responsible use of the summer months to make genuine progress on the problems at hand" and recommended that students engage in "permissible forms of dissent" upon returning to campus in the fall.[35]

Since the Black Power era, Howard has continued to be regarded as a traditional university—conservative in many respects and certainly not exemplifying the idea of a Black university advanced in the late 1960s. Yet the student revolts that rocked Howard from 1966 to 1969 left a lasting legacy, and more strides were taken to fulfill the demands of students than is perhaps remembered or publicly commemorated. Ewart Brown, who later served as the premier of Bermuda and joined the Howard University Board of Trustees in 1990, believes his generation had an enduring effect on Howard. "Howard is a different place. Many of the directions it took were irreversible, such as making a commitment to be excellent as Howard University (not as the black Harvard); and a commitment to producing black professionals whose work could relieve some of the difficulties facing black people." The medical school, for example, "takes on diabetes, hypertension, and sickle cell projects and outreach. All of this," he feels, "is a result of the challenges of the late 1960s." In fact a Center for Sickle Cell Disease opened in 1971, followed by a new, spacious hospital in 1975.[36]

A Department of African American Studies was established at Howard, and the political scientist Russell Adams served as chair for more than thirty years. In 1970 Andrew Billingsley, a scholar closely associated with the Black studies movement, was named vice president for academic affairs and charged with reorganizing graduate studies and several professional schools. Billingsley helped bring many changes to Howard, including establishing an Institute for Urban Affairs and Research, which included a University Without Walls Program and a University Year for Action, which offered course credit for service projects in disadvantaged communities. Billingsley also helped launch new professional programs in business, human ecology, education, and telecommunications and several new PhD programs. He was recruited to serve as president of Morgan State University, in Baltimore, in 1975, and said one of the attractions "was a chance to build an urban university. That's what I came to do. The idea was to produce black leadership."[37]

It was not just urban, cosmopolitan Howard that was rocked by student unrest in this era. Serious student organizing and militant acts of protest became commonplace on historically Black college campuses large and small, public and private. Much of this activity, including even violent clashes, fell off the national media radar, especially because the spring of 1969 saw scores of elite universities—Cornell, Harvard, Berkeley, City College—overtaken by student protest. The Orangeburg Massacre had deeply affected Black college students, reminding them of the ever-present potential for police violence. For some, the April 1969 building occupation at Cornell, where Black students had armed themselves in anticipation of a white student assault and emerged unscathed, prompted a serious consideration of armed self-defense. On April 28, 1969, the very same month, seventy-five students at tiny Voorhees College, an Episcopalian college in Denmark, South Carolina, less than thirty miles from Orangeburg, took over the library-administration building. Fearing police aggression, they brought rifles.

They christened the college "the liberated Malcolm X University," plastering the walls with pictures of Malcolm X, as well as antiwar posters emblazoned with "No Vietcong ever called me nigger." They threw leaflets out the windows explaining that their weapons were solely for self-defense. "We aren't going to allow another Orangeburg," they boldly declared.[38] The students desired an Afro-American studies program, additional Black faculty, and greater collegiate involvement in the local community. Against the wishes of the president, the board of trustees acceded to political pressure and called in the National Guard. But quick-thinking faculty intervention helped defuse the crisis before the Guard arrived on campus. Physics professor Bernie Dingle convinced the students to leave the building. According to another faculty member, Dingle "persuaded the kids to come out and get on the bus and go to jail and put down their guns 'cause otherwise someone was going to get killed. And they followed him out and onto the bus."[39] No shots were fired, there was no damage, and no one was hurt, but thirty-six students were later arrested, and a large number suspended, at the insistence of the board of trustees. The president of Voorhees had granted amnesty to the students, but Governor Robert E. McNair insisted that an example must be set, and eight students were tried the following year. The college administration was predominantly Black, but it was subordinate to the board, which was predominantly white. The college was closed for the rest of the semester.[40]

Some of the Black faculty and administrators supported the students and recognized the need for reform. John Potts, the president of Voorhees, had actually reached an agreement with the students during the occupation, and later affirmed that he had not been under duress. He promised to organize a Black studies program and end compulsory class attendance after freshman year. In May, Bernie Dingle, an African American who served as chairman of the campus chapter of the American Association of University Professors, presented a petition on behalf of the association chapter supporting Potts for not wanting to call in law enforcement, and calling for the resignation of the chairman of the board for usurping administrative prerogatives.[41]

In February 1970, Voorhees abruptly announced that the contracts of Dingle and four other Black professors would not be renewed the following year. Even though Dingle had helped to peacefully end the protest of the previous spring, the college, in one colleague's view, seemed to suspect him of having caused it.[42] Students quickly mobilized a protest: they called for the removal of the Reverend J. Kenneth Morris, the white chairman of the board of trustees, and the rehiring of the five professors. "We cannot continually sit by," their statement read, "and watch black faculty who are concerned about our education get fired. We must take stands." The larger context was critical. Since 1965, there had been a sharp jump in the number of white faculty, who by 1970 were 60 percent of the faculty, adding to growing concerns about the fate of Black colleges in the post-Jim-Crow era. "We are determined to do whatever is necessary to see that Voorhees College meets the needs and aspirations of black people," declared student activist Alvin Evans. The head of the state chapter of the NAACP called Rev. Morris an "arrogant, paternalistic white" who once referred to Voorhees as "my hobby." Reflecting the approach of students at other HBCUs, the students at Voorhees also became advocates for the broader Black community. They called for higher wages for workers at the college and for Black participation in local governance. African Americans constituted 60 percent of the county, but there was not a single Black officeholder in city or county government. The campus Black Awareness Coordinating Committee organized a highly effective one-day campus boycott, but the next day, a Friday, the college responded by officially closing the campus and ordering all students to leave. In defiance, a group reported to be between sixty and two hundred students stayed on campus and conferred with local Black community leaders for support and guidance. An Urban League official said, "I've never seen a group of more nonviolent young people," but, fearing another armed takeover and the attendant negative publicity, the administration called the governor for assistance over the weekend, and he brought in a couple of hundred National Guardsmen. They smashed windows and broke down doors, but found no guns and turned up only two students, both leaders in student government, whom they arrested for trespassing before sealing off the campus.[43]

In their search, troops forced their way into a faculty member's home seeking out students. "Well, the troops did come about three o'clock in the morning," Robert Romer recalls. Romer was a white professor who was seen as sympathetic to the students' concerns. "It was cold, about the first of February, I think. There's a pounding on the door and I go down in my pajamas and there's a bunch of soldiers, with guns, with bayonets. And here's a guy with a bayonet pointed at my stomach. I still sort of have nightmares occasionally. It's the middle of the night, it's cold, I'm holding up my pajamas with the one hand, there's a bayonet at my stomach . . . and the sergeant says, 'We're going to search your house.' So I did what I was told to do by the ACLU, American Civil Liberties Union, I said, "I deny you permission to search the house." And then he says to his troops, 'Search the house, men.' And so I said again, "I refuse to give you permission to search my house.' And then I stood aside, I mean, what am I gonna do?" The administration closed the campus for a month, during which time everyone "was in a panic that this campus was going to disappear." After the school reopened, "everybody practically agreed not to talk about anything; just, cross your fingers and pray and hope we get to the end of May without anybody getting hurt."[44] In a letter to parents, a college administrator blamed "a small group of revolutionary militants on our campus" for the campus closure, whose goal, he alleged, was the destruction of Voorhees College.[45]

After closing the campus, the administration moved to immediately dismiss the five faculty members, alleging that their presence would incite students further. They even banned them from campus. The American Association of University Professors investigated and termed these actions unwarranted and "draconian," and deemed Dingle's dismissal a violation of due process and endorsed his reinstatement.[46] In July 1970 a jury convicted seven students from the 1969 protest for rioting, looting, and arson, and they were sentenced to eighteen months to two years at hard labor. In trials resulting from campus disturbances, there were sometimes disagreements between the more traditional attorneys and the more militant students. In the Voorhees case, Matthew Perry, a prominent civil rights lawyer who later became a federal judge, defended the students. One of those convicted, Alvin Evans, became a leader in a new national organization of Black students called SOBU, the Student Organization for Black Unity. The SOBU News Service opposed Perry's courtroom strategy, which was to minimize politicking and to stress that all of the defendants were from Denmark and had no police records. He advised against staging demonstrations or rallying support in the community. But after the convictions, the students felt that he "had failed to take into account the power of American racism." Voorhees, in SOBU's view, was a white-controlled college "run by racists in the name of the church." In the aftermath of the protests, SOBU felt that the administration tried to create an "apolitical climate" by purging the campus of militants, threatening to cut off financial aid, and promoting the fraternity system.[47] But at the same time, Episcopal Church leaders formed a task force to investigate overall conditions at the college, including curriculum and faculty hiring, and to make recommendations for reform. In an ironic development nearly four decades later, Cleveland Sellers, who had been shot in Orangeburg, became president of Voorhees College.

Voorhees might have narrowly averted bloodshed, but North Carolina A&T State University did not. This public college in Greensboro with four thousand students illustrates two important points about the student movement at HBCUs: they often had close connections to community-based civil rights struggles, and they faced a greater likelihood of police occupation and invasion than Black protesters on majority white campuses. We have seen this second point demonstrated at Orangeburg, Howard, Voorhees, and Texas Southern University, but the intensity and lethality of police crackdowns was increasing. As the Black student movement intensified in the South, so, too, did the police response. The shooting deaths of Black students at Jackson State College in Mississippi in 1970 are sometimes remembered alongside the killings that same year of white students at Kent State in Ohio, but they were part of a rising tide of lethal police assaults on Black college campuses.

It is useful to recall, as well, that police officers nationwide had highly negative attitudes toward students, African Americans, and radicals. The National Commission on the Causes and Prevention of Violence found "that student demonstrators and black militants arouse extreme hatred, fear, contempt and anger among the police." An observer with the President's Commission on Law Enforcement rode with police officers in three Northern cities and heard 72 percent of them express "considerable prejudice" against Black people. The 1968 report of the Kerner Commission included similar findings. One scholar warned, "When college administrators consider bringing in the police on campus, they must realize that they are bringing in an armed body of men who harbor powerful antagonisms against those with whom they are called upon to deal."[48]

Greensboro had been a center of civil rights activity throughout the 1960s and was at the forefront of Black Power activism in the South.[49] A cohort of young activists influenced by Malcolm X, dedicated to grassroots organizing, and in some cases funded by War on Poverty programs began to question the emphasis on integration and gradualism that, to them, seemed to deliver few gains. Nelson Johnson, Air Force veteran and student at North Carolina A&T, became a key campus and community leader. "North Carolina A&T was at the center of the movement," Johnson discovered when he enrolled there in 1965. Issues ranging from community control of schools to opposition to the Vietnam War inspired intense organizing. In 1968, Nelson Johnson helped to organize a mock funeral procession for the slain students in Orangeburg, in which the governor of South Carolina was burned in effigy. The demonstration was one of the largest in Greensboro history. By Johnson's senior year, the city was in the midst of a widespread Black student rebellion. There was one confrontation after another. In March 1969 cafeteria workers at A&T went on strike and twenty-five hundred students marched to the president's office in support.[50]

In May the refusal to honor the results of a high school election sparked a conflagration between Black students and city and state police. When the white school board overturned the election of an activist as president of the student council at all-Black Dudley High School, hundreds of students walked out. Police gassed and arrested rock-throwing students, beginning three days of siege. Angered over the school's usurpation of democracy and its heavy-handed response, Dudley students went to nearby North Carolina A&T for support, and soon hundreds of college students joined their protest. Coincidentally, the founding convention of a new national Black student group, the Student Organization for Black Unity, was taking place at A&T. Nelson Johnson stood on a table there and urged support for the Dudley students, an act that was later labeled an "incitement to riot," which landed him in jail.[51] The National Guard soon joined forces with the police, arresting and beating hundreds of students.

Students staged protests on the A&T campus, and police amassed in force after reports of sniper fire from a dormitory, Scott Hall. Despite the restive atmosphere, not all students were involved in activism. Late at night on Wednesday, May 21, Willie Grimes and a group of five or more friends were walking across campus en route to a nearby restaurant. Grimes was not an activist and had not been involved in the campus uprisings. His companions, whom investigators never consulted, reported that shots rang out from an automobile that "came out of nowhere" whose "lights came on at the last minute." The young men scrambled for cover, got up, and found Grimes lying unconscious. An FBI investigator said he was "very sure it was a stray bullet" that killed the sophomore, but said he was never able to determine where it came from. Students believed otherwise. Doctors declared Willie Grimes, a twenty-year-old from rural North Carolina, dead in the early morning hours of May 22, while the campus continued to explode, now in anger and mourning over the senseless killing. John Collins and Larry Kirby were with Grimes during the shooting and took him to the hospital. They returned to campus, where Collins remembers "a lot of fire all night long." He heard bullets flying from above as police teargassed the building. He and other students stayed close to the floor with wet towels over their heads as protection against the tear gas. Larry Kirby said "there was a lot of shooting from campus, from the dormitory" that night—so much so that he remembers a counselor getting on the loudspeaker "asking students to hold their fire so the police could withdraw."[52]

Early in the morning of May 23, there was an "ambush on Luther Street" in which five police officers and two students were shot, but all survived. The governor and military officials mobilized a massive response. The president of the college had announced the closing of the campus by the next evening, but unbeknownst to school officials, the governor ordered an earlier clearing of campus. A "combined ground and air offensive" descended upon A&T, featuring six hundred National Guardsman, a tank, several armed personnel carriers, an airplane and a helicopter, which dropped tear gas canisters onto Scott Hall, reportedly the source of persistent sniping. A journalist called it "the most massive armed assault ever made against an American university."[53] Around 6:45 in the morning, students were told to evacuate Scott Hall. Hundreds of infantryman from the Second Battalion surrounded the building, while a helicopter released "nausea gas." An airplane dropped canisters of smoke, reportedly to conceal the advance of National Guardsmen. Shots rang from the dorm, and soldiers "responded with a barrage of automatic rifle fire" and threw gas grenades into the building. The troops took out a hundred students from Scott Hall and two hundred more from other buildings. There was no gunfire, no resistance. They sent them to two state prisons, where they were fingerprinted and detained for the rest of the day. "It looked like war," a photojournalist for United Press International, said of the attack. Some were later charged with crimes, although no student was caught using or possessing a gun during the massive search and seizure. Guardsmen ransacked Scott Hall, destroying furniture and student belongings in the search for weapons.[54]

Nelson Johnson played a leading role in convincing the North Carolina State Advisory Committee of the United States Commission on Civil Rights to hold an "open meeting" in Greensboro in order to ascertain the causes of the "civil disturbances" and whether the response of law enforcement was excessive and racially motivated. Thirty-two people offered information at the two-day meeting that fall, although the North Carolina National Guard refused to participate. Issued in March, the report, *Trouble in Greensboro,* rebuked the school board and a range of community leaders for ignoring student discontent at Dudley and spurning efforts at negotiated solutions. "It is a sad commentary that the only group in the community who would take the Dudley students seriously were the students at A&T State University." The committee concluded that widespread racism in education, housing, and employment in the city of Greensboro was ultimately culpable for the May protests. They strongly condemned the conduct of the National Guard and the entire military offensive at A&T, finding that the president of the university should have been allowed to resolve the crisis. The committee rebuked the use of arms by students, but found that "more professional methods could have been used to subdue those few students who engaged in such activity." The Guard confiscated student property and inflicted widespread and costly damage in the dormitories, including smashing or shooting in 65 percent of the doors, when keys could have been used. The troops found only two weapons, underscoring, in the committee's view, that their response far exceeded the danger. "It is difficult to justify the lawlessness and disorder in which this operation was executed," they concluded.[55]

It is hard to know the impact of this report on local authorities, but it seems to have been ignored. In Nelson Johnson's view, "Greensboro's political elite trashed the report."[56] And tragically, ten years later, what became known as the Greensboro Massacre showed yet again the hostile gulf separating the police and grassroots activists.

Sadly, the death of Willie Grimes was only the first in a wave of police killings of college students over the next few years. The invasion of Cambodia by United States ground forces in April 1970 sparked a new wave of campus uprisings, leading to a nationwide student strike and the closure of scores of universities. At Ohio State in Columbus, antiwar protesters joined Black student activists—who had been pressing unsuccessfully for change ever since King's assassination two years before—for a campuswide student strike. For several days, city and state police and the National Guard unleashed a barrage of tear gas and live ammunition to put down the strike. At least seven people were shot, perhaps a hundred were injured and several hundred students were arrested. There were no deaths, but the use of shotguns stunned and outraged the campus community and finally pushed the administration to launch a Black studies program and increase Black student admissions.[57] This open warfare in Columbus has been largely forgotten, most likely because the National Guard unleashed even greater and more lethal violence on another Ohio campus only a couple of days later. On May 4, at Kent State University, the National Guard shot into a crowd of students, killing four and wounding nine, all white. Americans were appalled at the loss of life and this military-type assault on a college campus.

Still, police forces continued a season of violent suppression of dissent. On May 11 police killed six African American protesters in Augusta, Georgia. Four days later forty city and state police fired 140 shots into the windows of a women's dormitory at Jackson State College in Jackson, Mississippi, killing two African American students—one a junior at the college, the other a high schooler, and injuring twelve others. The police claimed to be responding to a sniper or rock thrower. The Jackson State students were protesting racism in the city, the war in Vietnam and Cambodia, and the Kent State murders. No one was ever held responsible for any of these deaths—the only result was the appointment of a Presidential Commission on Campus Unrest, which investigated both the Jackson and Kent State shootings. The commission, headed by former Pennsylvania governor William Scranton and known as the Scranton Commission, held public hearings over the summer, which aired intense anger at the war in Vietnam and blamed Nixon, and especially Vice President Spiro Agnew, for encouraging violence against students and other radicals.

Police violence against Black students put pressure on Black college administrators to condemn the government's actions. A group of students, faculty, and administrators at Atlanta University denounced the "terror directed against black people in the United States." It laid a share of the blame on divisive politicians who sought political advance by instigating racial resentment. "In the current era of systematic repression of black people, police authorities are wantonly shooting down black men, women, and children while elected officials, both national and local, by their outrageously false and inflammatory public utterances, fan the fires of hatred and bigotry." Citing, too, the police execution of Black Panther Party leaders in Chicago, the Atlanta University statement called this violence "genocide." "Victims of this oppression, wherever they may be, along with other men of goodwill, must join together to halt this brutal assault."[58] On May 20, 1970, a delegation of fifteen Black college presidents presented a forceful statement to President Nixon listing and lamenting the many injustices imposed on Black

Americans and denouncing Nixon policies of "law and order" and "benign neglect" for exacerbating white racism. "We wish to convey to you the disenchantment of blacks, especially black youth, with our society and with the Federal Government," they declared. They called for a shift away from militarism to domestic priorities; the appointment of "a black Deputy Attorney General of unquestioned commitment to civil liberties to be responsible for the investigation and recommendations for prosecutions for those responsible for the killings of unarmed citizens and to monitor the use of law enforcement assistance"; and a presidential conference with Black student leaders. "Black college students are their own best spokesmen," they declared. "A sense of their mood is crucial to understanding the urgency of greater responsiveness to the black community."[59]

J. Otis Cochran, the national chairman of the Black American Law Students Association, testified before the Scranton Commission and gave a blistering reproach to the Nixon administration and a powerful defense of student radicals. "No matter what personal culpability is eventually assigned to individual guardsmen and police or their commanding officers in the tragedies that occurred this spring," Cochran declared, "nothing should be allowed to divert blame from the truly guilty party—members of the Nixon/Agnew Administration whose crude attacks on dissenters created the climate of intolerance and repression that some people interpreted as a license to kill." In the period before public disclosure of the Federal Bureau of Investigation's Counterintelligence Program, or COINTELPRO, his testimony shows that activists were beginning to suspect that they had become targets of a government conspiracy. "We had already seen the Administration implicitly declare war on political dissent in this country—the pattern behind the various Black Panther raids and trials and the trial of the Chicago Eight was too clear to allow any other conclusion," Cochran told the commission. Finally, he explained the rise of radicalism as an understandable reaction to an unyielding society. "Black and white dissenters in this country did not adopt more radical views of protest by choice: it was only after repeated failures of the passive, nonviolent strategy identified with Martin Luther King Jr. that the dissenters were forced to adopt different theories of dissent," he declared. "Many advocates of violence, of course, remain, but in general the policy of 'black brinkmanship' has been tempered by caution, and uncontrolled or spontaneous violence spurned as an anachronism."[60]

James E. Cheek, who had succeeded James Nabrit as president of Howard, very briefly served as a special advisor to the president on campus affairs, along with Vanderbilt University chancellor Alexander Heard, and later wrote the paper "Black Institutions and Black Students." Tellingly, he opened by equating the mood of Black students with African Americans as a whole: "The frustration, anger, outrage, fears and anxieties of black students are expressive of the same feelings and emotions which exist among a large spectrum of the black population—'moderate' as well as 'militant.'" In an effort to reconcile integration with Black Power, he argued that the push for "civil rights" had given way to a quest for "social justice," which included an emphasis on Black pride, Black studies, and racial solidarity. But more crucially, it required "a fundamental redistribution of the nation's opportunities, rewards, benefits, and powers." He made a series of recommendations to Nixon, urging much stronger federal support for Black access to higher education and for historically Black institutions of higher education.[61] The Cheek memo had great effect. At the time, the Nixon administration was searching for a civil rights policy that would de-emphasize integration, but not appear too hostile to African Americans. Strengthening Black educational institutions offered a solution. According to scholar Dean Kotlowski, the Nixon administration "significantly enlarged federal aid to black colleges." After reading Cheek's memo, Nixon directed his staff to develop a plan of assistance, albeit with condescension: "It is vitally important to have Black colleges going strong . . . so that Blacks develop the capacity to run something themselves." As a bonus, the policy might cultivate a loyal Black leadership cadre. In Kotlowski's telling, Nixon saw the policy as "one way we can encourage the good Blacks" such as Cheek, who "seems willing to work with us." Regardless of his motives, Nixon's financial support of HBCUs dovetailed with a growing Black skepticism of white-designed integration plans and a new determination to preserve Black-controlled institutions.[62]

Many law enforcement agencies apparently ignored the Scranton Commission's many recommendations promoting nonlethal resolution of campus disputes. Violence flared again two years after Jackson State in a deadly police assault against student protesters at Southern University in Baton Rouge, an event that has been largely omitted from civil rights historiography and neglected in public memory of the movement. On November 16, 1972, a still-unidentified sheriff's deputy fired his shotgun at twenty-year-old Denver A. Smith and twenty-year-old

Leonard D. Brown, killing both. No one was ever charged or prosecuted for these slayings, nor did the victims' families prevail in civil law-
suits. Strikingly, Governor Edwin Edwards, and Sheriff Al Amiss of East
Baton Rouge, blamed students for the deaths, even though a commission
appointed by the Louisiana Attorney General would corroborate witness
testimony that shots had been fired without cause at unarmed, fleeing
students. What happened at Southern? Had members of the Black Panther Party or Republic of New Africa smuggled guns onto campus or
threatened to kill the college president, as the governor and other officials
told the media in the immediate aftermath of the deaths? These charges,
of course, helped to frame the story in the public eye, even though such
allegations had nothing to do with the killing of Brown and Smith.

Southern, like all public Black colleges in the segregated South, had
been underfunded, allotted inferior facilities, and politically controlled
by means of a conservative administration. The university was gov-
erned by the all-white State Board of Education. And separate was
never equal during Jim Crow, a pattern that persisted into the 1970s
and beyond. The 1972–1973 per-student expenditure at predominantly
white Louisiana State University was $2,325, while the figure for South-
ern was only $1,327.[63] In the early 1970s, recalls student leader Fred
Prejean, "the Louisiana legislature threatened to close Southern University" as part of the integration of public higher education in the
state. This "put a fear in us," he says. "We did not want to see that
happen." Notwithstanding the blatant funding disparity and other in-
equities, Prejean and other students were committed to Southern's preservation. Desegregation, in their view, should not mean the dismantling
of Black institutions, whatever their shortcomings. With twelve thousand
students on campuses in Baton Rouge, its main campus; Shreveport; and
New Orleans, Southern was the nation's largest public HBCU. Southern
students built a large movement on both campuses with the goal of preserving, improving, and transforming their college.

Born in Lafayette, Fred Prejean graduated from high school in 1964
and joined the civil rights struggle, working in the burgeoning con-
sumer cooperative movement and acquiring considerable experience
as a community organizer before entering college in 1970. He went to
Southern on a Eleanor Roosevelt Leadership Fellowship, funded by the
Ford Foundation, and used his organizing skills to help build a campus
movement. A small group of students in the psychology department
began meeting to discuss the inadequacies in their department, and the
group quickly expanded to cover many other departments. They orga-

nized student leaders from each department, who went out and canvassed the students in their departments to find out their particular needs and grievances. "Each department compiled a list of things that needed to be fixed," Prejean recounts. "They felt an ownership of the document." This formed the basis of the demands presented to G. Leon Netterville, Southern's president, that fall. They named their group Students United because it had the same initials as the university, a sign of their support for the institution they were endeavoring to reform.

The students' document of grievances began with a bold preface: "We, as 'students united,' find it necessary to exercise our duly possessed rights as Black men and women to abolish all conditions which threaten our existence. For too long we have been victims of constant neglect and administration censorship; for too long we have been denied a voice in the selection of those people who administer the functions of this University." With extraordinary range and detail, the students enumerated 197 specific complaints. They called for "more black awareness" in the curriculum, a greater student voice in administrative affairs, and the improvement of basic campus services, such as cafeteria food, medical services, and housing. Students complained that the mattresses in the dormitories were so old that it was preferable to sleep on the floor. Moreover, they accused the president of being authoritarian and insensitive to their needs and to the changing times.

In October 1972, Charles Waddell, the chair of the psychology department and a sympathetic figure to students resigned, blaming administration encroachment on his rights and responsibilities. This set off weeks of marches, boycotts, and sit-ins at the Baton Rouge and New Orleans campuses. On October 23, students presented Netterville with their demands. The scale of their protests indicates both deep-seated student discontent and remarkable organization and discipline. One thousand students marched to Louisiana's Board of Education and met with two assistant superintendents. Determined for action, they then marched to the capitol and met with the governor. On October 31, another large group of students marched on the administration building in Baton Rouge to see President Netterville. The governor dispatched the National Guard, but the students had already left by the time they arrived. In the meantime, students boycotted classes.[64]

Southern had a reputation during the civil rights era for expelling student activists and punishing dissent. "In spite of our efforts to promote nonviolent behavior," Fred Prejean says, "we were constantly harassed, threatened, and placed under surveillance by police." He faced "intense intimidation" in his effort to increase Black student rights. There were the phone calls. A woman professing to be student would phone Prejean in the middle of the night and try to maintain a conversation for a long time. He figured the goal was to interfere with his sleep and generally harass him. The woman would ramble, posing as a student, but did not seem to know much about the university. It was always a female caller, Prejean remembers. Police officers also followed him. Once, on a three-hour drive to Monroe, Louisiana, two state police cars followed him. One was in front and the other tailed him from behind, sandwiching him for the whole drive.[65]

On the New Orleans campus, the students staged their own boycott of classes and occupied the administration building for nine days, adding the demand that Vice President Emmett W. Bashful, a political scientist who headed the New Orleans campus, also resign. Governor Edwards told the press that he had been given information "by secretive, highly confidential means" that militant groups had smuggled weapons inside, so he assembled a force to retake the building. He ordered the students to leave, while 150 sheriff's deputies and state troopers converged on campus along with two helicopters and an armored truck. At the last minute, Bashful resigned, saying he hoped "to avoid violence and possible bloodshed." In retrospect his concerns appear highly justified, and with this partial victory the students left the building. The state declined to accept Bashful's resignation, however, and he would spend the next twenty years as chancellor.[66]

Back in Baton Rouge, administrators, faculty, and students were engaged in intense negotiations. But mysterious, destructive acts, whose perpetrators were never identified, also occurred. On November 7, an explosive device went off in a campus building, a fire destroyed the horticulture barn, and six Molotov cocktails were found in the vicinity. According to Fred Prejean, Students United was avowedly nonviolent, but there were men on campus with military experience, and radicals of many stripes. But they usually "followed us," he said, meaning the broader based student leadership. The next day, warrants were issued for the arrest of eight student leaders, and two were arrested. Yet at the same time, the negotiating teams were making progress and had reached agreement on many issues.[67] As the class boycott and demonstrations continued, President Netterville promised to announce amnesty for the arrested students, and administrators continued close communication with the sheriff's department. In an abrupt reversal, the promise of amnesty was withdrawn, and administrators ordered the arrest of Fred

Prejean and three other student leaders. At four o'clock in the morning on November 16, police officers came to Prejean's home and took him into custody. The university had secured injunctions barring him from campus, but Prejean had gone there many times to lead demonstrations. Why, he wondered, did they arrest him for criminal trespass on that morning and then hold him in jail all day long? His family had come immediately to post the bond.[68]

Upset when they learned the news, a large contingent of students went to President Netterville's office in the administration building to appeal for the students' release from jail. Netterville met with the students briefly, left to take a phone call, and never returned. The students stayed in his office while large numbers of students gathered outside. Claiming to have been alerted by an informant that the students were intending to seize the building, the governor had dispatched a state police tactical squad and about fifty-five sheriff's deputies to the campus and put a few hundred national guardsmen on alert. But the students insisted that they had no such plans: it was the university's actions that prompted their presence in the building that morning, not a planned protest.

Sheriff Al Amiss announced to the roughly two hundred students milling around the administration building that they had five minutes to disperse. Denver Smith's nineteen-year-old sister, Josephine, said later that many students could not hear what the police were saying because helicopters flying overhead drowned out their words. But in short order, the troops began firing volleys of tear gas into the crowd. Television film showed students Denver Smith and Leonard Brown running away from the administration building, fleeing the tear gas, when each was hit at virtually the same time.[69] Number 4 shotgun pellets in the head and arms killed the two young men. Neither student was an activist. Remarkably, Sheriff Amiss allowed officers to carry weapons of their choice to campus. In this time of great conflict, emotions, and upheaval, the sheriff permitted his men wide discretion in lethal weaponry. And on that day the officers "were equipped with a variety of ammunition, including tear gas shotgun shells, tear gas canisters, number 4 and 00 buckshot shells and high velocity rifle ammunition."[70]

Immediately after the shootings the governor and sheriff plastered the local and national media with denials of police shootings, and continuous efforts to blame students or "outside agitators" for the deaths. They exerted considerable energy in seeking to frame the story in this light. The governor claimed that "it was perfectly clear" that someone inside the building or in the crowd of students fired one or more smoke bombs at the police before they fired tear gas. In fact, a state investigation later revealed that no such thing happened; the students neither had nor used any weapons or incendiary devices. Television footage showed a sheriff's deputy fire a tear gas canister at a student who caught it, and tossed it back. It took authorities longer to identify the body of Leonard Brown, leading Governor Edwards to speculate that he was "an outsider." And in the next sentence he mentioned that members of the Black Panther Party and Republic of New Africa happened to be present in the state of Louisiana.[71]

At the same time, Edwin Edwards began to rationalize the killings as a regrettable but necessary reassertion of state power. "For two weeks I have withstood criticism that I have been too lenient with the students," he said, referring to the building occupation in New Orleans. What happened in Baton Rouge "is a clear example of what happens in a violent confrontation."[72] In an exchange with students who asked him if he valued property rights over human rights, the governor declared, "No. But I'll tell you what I do hold above human life, and this is lawfully constituted authority."[73] A controversial and outspoken figure in Louisiana politics, Edwards would serve four terms as governor, before being convicted of racketeering charges in 2001 and sentenced to ten years in prison. Formerly a member of Congress, Edwards had served on the House Internal Security Committee, which had investigated antiwar demonstrators in 1970. During testimony by the chief of police of Washington, D.C., Edwards asked why the police never discharged their weapons. "In some instances the use of force is clearly justified," Edwards declared. "Why do you carry guns if you seem to have a mental block against using them?"[74]

In the midst of campus despair, anger, and shock, President Netterville continued the crackdown. The day after the slayings, he fired two faculty members whom he accused of aiding student protesters. The only support professors ever gave, according to Prejean, was answering student questions and seeking to provide them with a measure of protection. Much like the governor's obsession with "outside agitators," the president's focus on faculty as the provocateurs, just like at Voorhees, denied the students' own agency and grievances. The faculty members, Joseph Johnson, chairman of the physics department, and George Baker, an assistant professor of engineering, sued the university in federal court with the aid of the National Education Association.[75] Students were alarmed at the police action, and several felt they had been set up for an intentional attack. Fred Prejean called the incident "a conspiracy on the part of the president of Southern University, Leon Netterville; the sheriff, Al Amiss, and the Governor of this state." Netterville held a press conference to deny the allegation that he had set up the students. One of the fired professors, George Baker, called the killings "the last dying gasp . . . of the white leadership downtown . . . to control the black community."[76]

Many expressed outrage at the deaths of the two young men. Two hundred students marched from LSU to the capitol, where they held a memorial service for the slain students. College presidents issued statements deploring the violence; students held demonstrations at Stanford, Boston College, University of California at Los Angeles, and many other campuses.[77] Still, this mourning and outrage was small and selective. The nation as a whole ignored the killings of Denver Smith and Leonard Brown. Southern soon joined Jackson State, North Carolina A&T, and Orangeburg in the roster of forgotten Black casualties of the civil rights era. Distrustful of the government's ability to conduct a fair and impartial investigation, African American activists from Louisiana and around the country organized a separate Black-led investigation of the slayings. Just a couple of days after the killings, the Black People's Committee of Inquiry was formed under the leadership of Haywood Burns, a civil rights attorney and founder of the National Conference of Black Lawyers, and D'Army Bailey, a sit-in leader expelled from Southern who had become a lawyer, and who was then a member of the city council in Berkeley, California.

As soon as he read about the shootings and the claim that students were culpable, D'Army Bailey called Murphy Bell, a prominent Black attorney in Baton Rouge who had represented Bailey in his Southern case a few years back. "Is there anything I can do?" he asked Bell, who encouraged him to come to Louisiana. He flew down and conferred with Bell and some students, and met with local Black attorneys Etta Kay Hearn, R. Judge Eames, and Robert Williams, and they decided to organize an inquiry. They had little faith in the criminal justice system of Louisiana. Bailey's next stop was New York, where Leslie Dunbar helped him secure five thousand dollars from the Field Foundation. "With that grant, I called various national figures to get involved in the hearing," including Haywood Burns, who became cochair, John Lewis, Owusu Sadauki, Walter Lee Bailey, and Ira Simmons, another city councilman in Berkeley.

The decision to convene an autonomous inquiry showed the widespread belief in entrenched racism in law enforcement, but it also demonstrated the Black freedom struggle's commitment to building democratic procedures in the South. James Wayne, a top Black aide to Governor Edwards, was D'Army Bailey's college friend, and he helped secure the noninterference of the governor. The attorneys secured a hall in the Black community, lined up witnesses, and hired a court reporter. The sheriff's office had not initiated an investigation immediately after the killings, so students had collected shotgun shells at the scene. In a surprise, the governor showed up at the hearing. "It was an extraordinary event," Bailey remembers, and there was extensive media coverage. "It was important. We were able to puncture the claim that it was student rambunctiousness that led to the killing of these two boys." Although no one was able to identify the shooter, "it was clear that it [the shots] came from the line of officers who were firing the tear gas." George Baker, one of the recently dismissed professors, testified that students were at all times willing to negotiate their demands. After the hearings, Bailey and Haywood Burns returned to Baton Rouge to write their report. They stayed up all night at a roadside motel going through the testimony. Nearly forty years later, he recalls the "discomfort being there in that atmosphere. We didn't publicize our arrival, but people knew. It was known that we were there."[78]

They issued the "Preliminary Findings of the Black People's Committee of Inquiry" at a press conference the next day. The report concluded that "students *did not throw nor fire* the first tear gas canister, and were not armed on November 16, 1972," and found fault with the administration's suppression of due process and student dissent on campus. The committee found the governor negligent and irresponsible in his "rush to erroneous judgment," and the sheriff "emotionally and professionally ill-equipped to cope with the situation at Southern University on November 16, 1972, to the point of a clear, demonstrative, and wanton disregard for human life." Moreover, the committee concluded that a sheriff's deputy or deputies "fired the fatal shots which claimed the lives of Denver Smith and Leonard Brown." At the press conference, Bailey and Burns also offered their opinion that authorities in Louisiana knew who pulled the trigger. "Our conclusion was that they could discern the identity and that some people knew." We "were trying to smoke them out," Bailey recalls. A federal grand jury later subpoenaed Bailey and asked him what made Haywood Burns and him think that the state knew the shooter's identity. "But we had no further information to provide. So that was the end of it." But the Black People's Committee was widely seen as crucial to ensuring a fairer state investigation.[79]

The same day that the Black People's Committee held its public hearings, the Louisiana attorney general's Special Commission of Inquiry on the Southern University Tragedy began its own, closed-door sessions. The twelve-member commission was half Black and half white, a notable degree of racial integration for an adjudicating body in a southern state. The report of the latter found fault with law enforcement and elected officials, and concluded that a single shot felled both young men, and that it most likely came from a sheriff's deputy. But they failed to identify the shooter and no one was ever indicted in the case.[80] Interestingly, the National Education Association conducted its own comprehensive inquiry into the violation of teacher and student rights at Southern. After receiving requests from local affiliates, the NEA set up a seven-member biracial commission chaired by the New York State commissioner of education.[81] Many national observers blamed President Netterville for bringing the police on campus. As the Chicago Defender noted, "The experience at Kent College and Jackson University, where student lives were sacrificed on the altar of conformity, should have taught the authorities at Southern University that school discipline when enforced through outside forces often has a tragic ending."[82] Indeed many questioned why the recommendations issued by the President's Commission on Campus Unrest had not been more widely adopted by college presidents. The president of the YMCA scolded President Nixon for not doing more to endorse the work of his own commission. "We wonder why the recommendations of that Commission have not been more forcefully supported by you," since they would "help to avoid such drastic confrontations."[83] The chaplains at the Atlanta University Center wired Governor Edwards and President Nixon, urging action. "Does not South Carolina State, Kent State and Jackson State Universities teach anything?" the clergy leaders implored. "Does the state always have to be found supporting and condoning wrongful actions on the part of its officials?"[84]

Like the police assault on the dormitory in Jackson State, which left two young people dead, the police killing of Denver Smith and Leonard Brown seemed to many to stir very little outrage, especially compared to the national outpouring of grief over the National Guard killings of four white students at Kent State in Ohio. An editorial in the Black Collegian criticized this double standard of remembrance and outrage. Several students had been killed at South Carolina State, Jackson State, and Texas Southern, the author declared.[85] "Yet no case has been reopened. Why are we not screaming about the injustice? Good God, we are being murdered, not just on the college campus, but everywhere, with the same lack of consideration and lack of law as during the days of lynching." The Kent State victims had been immortalized in a song by Neil Young. "Ask any kid on the street and he can sing it for you." Where were the tributes to the Black students, the writer demanded to know. In actuality, two performers did recognize the slain students at Jackson State and Southern in popular song: the Steve Miller Band recorded "Jackson-Kent Blues" and Gil Scott-Heron's "H20 Gate Blues" mentioned "Kent State, Jackson State, Southern Louisiana." But these were modest acknowledgements of an upsurge of violence that most Americans chose to forget.[86]

The shock over the slayings of the two young men, not to mention the remarkable amnesia that has surrounded this case ever since, has obscured the larger significance of the student movement at Southern University. Fred Prejean thinks student power pushed the idea of closing Southern off the Louisiana legislative agenda. "As a result of the protest, and demonstration of student strength and power, the legislature backed off of the merger and began to increase spending." Southern today is "totally different" from the campus of the early 1970s, he says. Federal and state financing helped upgrade the physical plant. There are "new buildings across campus." They refurbished the Law School, injected more funding, and attracted many white students. A journalist captured a critical dimension of the Black student movement, which this Black Power generation is rarely given credit for: "More and more nowadays, white Southerners are heard to say the black colleges should be closed permanently and the students sent to the integrated, predominantly white state universities. But more and more of the black students who attend schools like Southern are fighting to keep the black institutions because these colleges, they argue, are the best training grounds for black leaders. Do not close them the students say; just fire the old administrators and turn the colleges over to younger persons who are in step with black thinking."[87]

But notwithstanding the survival of Southern University, the murder of Smith and Brown left deep scars. "The killings had a traumatic effect on me," Prejean says. "I think of it everyday. It showed me an ugly reality." After the violence, Prejean had to fight to continue his education. Southern blocked him and five other student leaders from returning to campus in January 1973. Prejean had pled guilty to the criminal trespass charge at the urging of an attorney who had telephoned him out of the blue and identified himself as his counsel. This attorney refused to say who had hired him, and he made Prejean stay in the hallway during the court hearing. In turn, Southern used this criminal conviction to bar him from returning to campus. Prejean decided to sue, and James Gray, the first Black law professor at Louisiana State University, won the case. Prejean graduated from Southern University with a degree in accounting in 1974.[88]

The student movement of the 1960s and early 1970s brought meaningful changes to historically Black colleges. Even the administrators who often opposed the students' tactics were persuaded of the merits of their demands. According to a 1972 survey of Black college administrators, "70 per cent or more of the deans believed that the students' dissatisfactions with food service, dormitory facilities, dormitory regulations, absence of an organized program of black studies, instructional practices, lack of student participation in running the school, student personnel services, and social privileges were legitimate."[89] That's a high percentage and a long list. Students may not have achieved a Black university in its utopian form, but they helped make HBCUs better serve their needs. To a largely unappreciated extent, this upsurge transformed many aspects of Black college life, including, in the words of one administrator, "the codes of campus citizenship, relations among administrators, students and faculty members, decision-making process, student expectations, disciplinary procedures and other aspects of the college community."[90]

Moreover, students played a critical role in simply preserving public institutions of Black higher education after the demise of Jim Crow. This contribution in many ways deserves to stand as one of the most important achievements and legacies of the Black Power movement as a whole, yet it often goes unacknowledged. Preserving HBCUs, moreover, was a goal shared by both the "militant" students and the more conservative college presidents. Strikingly, despite this chapter in their history, historically Black colleges and universities retain a reputation for political quiescence and student conservatism. The police occupations and violence that engulfed many campuses, and the unprosecuted killings of so many students, likely contributed to this parallel legacy, stilling activism and engendering a certain forgetting.

CHAPTER 6

The Counterrevolution on Campus

Why Was Black Studies So Controversial?

The incorporation of Black studies in American higher education was a major goal of the Black student movement, but as we have seen from San Francisco State College, City College of New York, Northwestern University, and many other campuses, the promise to implement it was typically followed by another period of struggle. Whether it was because of hostility, clashing visions, budget cuts, indifference, or other challenges, the effort to institutionalize Black studies was long and difficult. To the extent that there was a "black revolution on campus," it was followed, in many instances, by a "counterrevolution," a determined effort to contain the more ambitious desires of students and intellectuals. This chapter explores critical challenges and points of contention during the early Black studies movement, with a particular focus on events at Harvard University. The struggle at Harvard concerned issues common to virtually every effort to institutionalize Black studies, although not all were as contentious or politicized as in Cambridge, Massachusetts, in the early 1970s. As St. Clair Drake dryly noted, "The 1968–73 period was a unique one in American academia."[1]

This chapter also examines the controversy and conflicts surrounding the meaning and mission of Black studies. Black studies was controversial among many, both inside and outside academe, for its intellectual ideas, shaped as they were by the swirling ideological currents of Black nationalism. Black studies was seen by many as an academically suspect, antiwhite, emotional intrusion into a landscape of rigor and reason. But rather than a movement of narrow nationalism and anti-intellectualism, as some critics charged, the early Black studies movement advanced ideas that have had significant influence in American and African American intellectual life. It emphasized interdisciplinary study, questioned notions of objectivity, destabilized metanarratives, and interrogated prevailing methodologies. Indeed, the capacious vision of most architects of Black studies is striking: they viewed it as an opportunity to create Black-controlled institutions and to assume greater authority over research in Black culture and history. At the same time, they saw African American studies as a means to transform American intellectual life more generally and, ultimately, some hoped, the status of Black people in society as a whole. While the early Black studies movement broke new ground, it was not, by any means, of one voice: there were spirited debates about the direction ahead and, indeed, the very definition and mission of the new discipline.

Because Black studies arrived like an explosion on the American scene, and because students brought it into being and then graduated, Black scholars had to move quickly to give it definition and shape. Many stressed the innovation and legitimacy of a "Black perspective" as a unifying principle—almost a methodology—for this new multi-disciplinary academic formation. A "Black perspective" not only answered critics who questioned the rationale for Black studies, but it also aimed to unmask the pretense of universalism in Euro-American intellectual thought and teaching. It is vital to underscore the overwhelmingly Eurocentric nature of the American college curricula and the extent to which white scholars argued that their theories and research had "universal" application. The Black studies movement forcefully pushed back against this claim and began a process that would open up space for other marginalized experiences, perspectives, and identities to find their own space in higher education.

Some critics of a "Black perspective" tended to see it as little more than racial essentialism. "There is no white truth or black truth or Aryan physics or Bolshevik biology," retorted white scholar Sidney Hook. For other skeptics, the notion of a Black perspective connoted a didactic mission aimed at molding Black minds into one view or a monolithic conception, which risked disguising the ideological heterogeneity among Black people. This was the objection voiced by historian Eugene Genovese. "There is no such thing as a black ideology or a black point of view," he declared. "Rather there are various black nationalist biases," and conservative and integrationist views too.[2]

Proponents of a Black perspective, however, anticipated these criticisms. Black intellectual production, from the nineteenth century through its professionalization in historically Black colleges, has been part of a cosmopolitan, humanist tradition,[3] but African American political and intellectual thought of the late 1960s and early 1970s is often flattened, caricatured and squeezed into a narrowly nationalist box. Indeed, there is much that belongs in that box, especially the pervasive patriarchy and homophobia. Yet the various articulations of a "Black perspective" that arose in these years of radical political struggle and upheaval were transnational, critical, and expansive. The foundational moment of modern Black studies bears out historian Manning Marable's assertion that "pluralism and diversity" are "at the heart of the Black intellectual tradition."[4] And this is true in spite of powerful countervailing pressures coming not only from political ferment but also from many people's perception of what a new academic enterprise entailed— the widespread sense that discipline-building required an authoritative move, that it demanded a unified theory of Black reality to justify the creation of Black studies.

The early Black studies movement produced a rich and voluminous outpouring of writings seeking to define its mission—many first appeared in the *Black Scholar,* the *Journal of Negro Education,* or the *Journal of Black Studies.* A sampling of these has since been anthologized, but many were also presented at the multitude of conferences, workshops, and gatherings and remain unpublished. At a California workshop, Lawrence Crouchett's presentation, "The 'Black Perspective': From *A* Black's Perspective" underscored the idea that an assertion of commonality did not preclude difference and individuality. A "'black perspective' simply means a way of perceiving an object, a situation, an issue or a problem as a black person—because of his unique experiences in the United States—would perceive it," he argued. This notion of "positionality" would in fact powerfully influence ethnic studies in the ensuing decades. Hardly rigid and essentialist, a Black perspective was in this view necessarily improvisational and creative: "These unique experiences cause black people to weigh things differently from the way others do. You must understand that black people are involved in a struggle to cause 'mainstream America' to relate to us as equal human beings. Therefore, black people must be defensive, sensitive, militant, suspicious, cautious, and committed to democracy. All this is part of our 'survival kit.' Conventional education has ignored the 'black perspective'; it was too anxious and committed to justifying the 'white perspective.' "[5]

According to its proponents, Black studies exposed not only the racial bias in Euro-American scholarship but also destabilized notions of scholarly objectivity, detachment, and universality that were the hallmarks of professional academic culture in the United States. Historian Vincent Harding wrote, "No longer is the black view accepted as one which is narrow compared to the white—or the universal—but it is considered a view far richer and humane, pressing us beyond the constructions of the white, conquering, west, moving us out into the true universe. . . . Blackness is perhaps a door to a far larger view of the world than white America has ever known." Black students, in Harding's view, were "no longer fooled by the special claims of the great universities to be the sources of wisdom, objectivity and truth."[6] In an essay exploring the distinction between *Black Studies* and *the Study of Black People,* Cédric Clark defined the former as "the research, practice, and teaching of a social science whose repertoire of concepts include as fundamental and essential those derived directly from the Black American cultural experience." He emphasized that Black studies challenged the epistemology and methodology of the social sciences. It "raises fundamental questions with regard to the 'objectivity' of social knowledge," and "despite efforts by [Peter] Berger, [Robert] Merton, and others, the relevance of epistemology . . . remains a relatively undeveloped area of American social science." Now, with the rise of Black studies, a social scientist's "unquestioned assumptions" will be "held up to a closer, more critical scrutiny than ever before."[7]

The Trinidadian scholar Basil Matthews, a professor at Talladega College, saw a Black perspective as part of the search for a new humanity. "Western social theory is assumed to be universal. But its applicability to black people and black experience is open to serious question," he asserted. He clarified, however, that the task of Black studies was not simply corrective. "It might appear," he wrote, "that the primary purpose of the new discipline is to correct and remedy the shortcomings of Western science. But such a view would reflect less than half the truth. The approach corrects and remedies precisely because it is different and regenerative in approach. The new approach is essentially a promise and an effort to positively and creatively advance the knowledge of the specifics of the black experience." The answer to white studies is not a narrow reaction "but black wisdom within the wider context of total humanity."[8]

Many scholars emphasized academe's omission of the experience of Black people and the transformative potential it thus carried. "The black perspective," wrote one scholar, "is desperately needed because American intellectualism has failed to deal adequately with the realities of the black presence in America." As education activist Preston Wilcox put it, "The old perspectives have assigned inhuman status to Blacks." The demand for a Black perspective represents a "broad condemnation of the integrity, adequacy and honesty of the US educational establishment." Common to this discourse was the idea that the affirmation of a racial particularity served as a springboard to a broader intellectual insurgency, or humanism. In a speech later published in book form as the *Challenge of Blackness,* Lerone Bennett defined *Blackness* as the search for universal truth. "We cannot think now because we have no intellectual instruments," he argued, "save those which were designed expressly to keep us from seeing. It is necessary for us to develop a new frame of reference, which transcends the limits of white concepts. We must abandon the partial frame of reference of our oppressors and create new concepts which will release our reality, which is also the reality of the overwhelming majority of men and women on this globe."[9]

For many, the idea of a Black perspective meant reclaiming scholarly debates about Black people from scholars who appeared disparaging and dismissive of Black life. There are white sociologists, Harvard's Ewart Guinier observed, "who examine the black experience with a concept that black people are a problem, that black culture does not exist or if it exists is a distorted and inferior imitation of American culture." In contrast, a Black point of view "says Black culture has been a viable means of survival for Black people. Black culture expresses the Black experience," and is neither "inferior nor superior to another culture."[10] Historian Vincent Harding saw the need to claim control as an assertion of Black people's dignity: "Black history is refusal to give over our lives, our creativity, our history, our future into the hands of white America, for they proved themselves totally inadequate and ultimately dangerous. So we demand hegemony over our institutions. We seek control of the telling of our story."[11] This "we" may appear monolithic, but many and divergent Black perspectives on the telling of the history of the African diaspora asserted themselves in these years.

Many theorists of a Black perspective were careful to articulate an expansive and critical vision. After visiting more than a hundred campuses in 1969, one scholar defined Black studies as "an attempt to create a humane and viable intellectual and ideological alternative to

Western cultural imperialism. By widening the narrow perspective of 'white studies,' black studies will force American intellectualism toward, not away from, attainment of the intellectual idea of encompassing the totality of human perspectives and experiences." In fact, Black studies would enable the academy to actually begin to do the comprehensive universal work that it had long claimed to do. This same scholar wrote, "Black studies is an attempt to return American intellectualism to its proper mission, namely, to conserve, to examine, to expand, and to communicate the scope of human experience as it exists and has existed." Moreover, acceptance of a Black perspective would legitimize other marginalized perspectives. This researcher wrote, "If interpreting reality from the Black perspective is a legitimate extension of intellectual endeavors, then so too must other long ignored perspectives be capable of shedding new light on the human experience. . . . For example, American intellectualism has a masculine bias which is as entrenched as its bias against non-Western people. At this moment we know far too little about the feminine perspective to be able to assess its potential impact. The best guess is that it will have a profound balancing effect on what has been an almost exclusively male-oriented vision of human reality." Imagine, too, "how the Native American perspective would alter the dominant view of the American West."[12]

Proponents of Black studies did not conceptualize it as an insular area of inquiry only of interest to black people, but as the opening salvo in major changes in the American academy. Armstead Robinson called Black studies "the cutting edge of a revolution in American education." "American intellectualism is on the verge of a new age," another scholar declared, "and Black studies is the forerunner of that new age." And doubtless in all seriousness, the sociologist Andrew Billingsley, who helped set up Black studies at Berkeley, called it "an instrument for the redemption of western society as we know it." In his view, "Black studies provides us with an opportunity to dream of things that never were and to ask why not. Black people have never controlled anything on these shores," he noted, and the new discipline offers a unique opportunity for African Americans to build something new.[13]

The young historian Armstead Robinson, who had organized an important symposium on Black studies at Yale University in 1968 as a graduate student, and who then went on to help develop several Black studies programs, conducted a survey of the field in 1969. In his view, Black studies provoked a crisis because it was exposing the fact that the education system in the United States upheld Western cultural imperialism. Black studies revealed that the rest of the curriculum constituted "white studies." With its mask of objectivity pulled off, what would "white studies" do now? "Black studies cannot be understood outside the context of a black revolution," he argued, because it "should involve you from the cradle to the grave. We have to create a totality of learning experiences for Black people which will make blackness automatic and avoid for the next generation of black children the kind of agonizing appraisals, anxieties and doubts that upset black people today."[14]

A dominant theme among Black studies proponents was its transformative potential and ability to illuminate larger truths about the United States. "Black history can give the American society unparalleled insights into the deficiencies of its own value system as carried out in practice," two white historians wrote. "Americans have, in a sense, built a nation upon the deception that they are a community of co-equal individuals participating co-equally in community affairs. Solid studies in Black history will put that illusion into perspective."[15] Darwin Turner echoed this view that Black studies could generate a more faithful alternative to the core myths of American life. "Reality and the official ideology of Americanism could not and cannot be reconciled," he argued, seeing in Black studies the potential to develop a new, more honest national narrative.[16] The historian Benjamin Quarles was of a generation of Black academicians who were more skeptical of the new idiom, but he still found much to approve. "The newer black history has a revolutionary potential," Quarles declared. "For blacks it is a new way to see themselves. For whites it furnishes a new version of American history, one that especially challenges our national sense of smugness and self-righteousness and our avowal of fair play. Beyond this the newer black history summons the entire historical guild—writers, teachers and learners—to higher levels of expectation and performance."[17]

In many respects, these idealistic visions for the new discipline of African American studies seem at a far remove from the rough-and-tumble political battles that propelled its birth. Black student activism may have won Black studies, but to many white academic elites, Black studies remained an oxymoron. Could a Black perspective produce valuable knowledge? Was there a Black intellectual tradition? Was there sufficient scholarship and imagination to justify a department of African American studies? For many white American intellectuals, the answer to all these questions was an unblinking no. Establishing the discipline in such an intellectual and political environment was a profound challenge, even with the many opportunities and concessions won in the late 1960s.

As at many other schools, the assassination of Dr. King propelled the creation of Black studies at Harvard. As a result of Black student agitation, a student-faculty committee under the chairmanship of economics professor Henry Rosovsky issued a report in January 1969 recommending the creation of a degree-granting program in Afro-American studies, a research center in Afro-American studies, a Black cultural center, improvement of the program in African studies, and a sharp increase in the number of Black graduate students. It was a strong affirmation of change that validated the many grievances of Black students at Harvard and endorsed their ideas for change. But it did make two recommendations that would become points of contention. The Rosovsky Report recommended that majors (or concentrators, at Harvard) in Afro-American studies also complete a second major, and that faculty in Black studies also hold appointments in other departments. Thus, decisions over faculty hiring and promotion would be made in concert with another department—and since every other department at Harvard was virtually all white, this granted those with a poor record in hiring African Americans, and little experience in Black subject matter, authority over faculty in Black studies. The rule requiring double majors also suggested that Black studies was not sufficiently developed or academically rigorous to stand alone as a major. But for the members of the Rosovsky Committee, this model was in many respects ideal because it brought a new, politicized area of study into the broader curriculum in a way that tethered it to the preexisting culture and norms of the college. It was the responsible, sensible choice, designed to affirm the high standards of the institution.[18]

Between January and April 1969, students in the Association of African and Afro-American Students at Harvard and Radcliffe (AFRO) conducted their own investigation into the best way to establish Black studies at Harvard, and came to a different conclusion. They concluded that a traditional department was the best means of ensuring stature, permanence, and greater autonomy over faculty selection. (Of course, there is no such thing as complete departmental autonomy in hiring and promotion, since the college and university must ratify such decisions.) Michael Thelwell, a founding member of the Department of Afro-American Studies at the University of Massachusetts, summed up this view when he noted that traditional departments "have, over the years, displayed no interest in incorporating the black experience, a black perspective, or even Negro faculty-members into their operations. What should now dispose us to trust them? And even if we should, how will they, after centuries of indifference, suddenly develop the competence and sensitivity which would enable them to do an acceptable job?"[19] Similarly, AFRO came to view the requirement for a double major as onerous and a result of a double standard.

Of course there were other issues roiling Harvard in the spring of 1969, and the struggle for Black studies got bound up with the antiwar movement, specifically the effort to abolish the Reserve Officer Training Corps program. Students for a Democratic Society led a takeover in April of University Hall, and when the administration called in the police to forcibly evict the students, it inflamed the campus and caused a majority of the student body to go on strike. The call for a Black studies department became one the demands. April was filled with intense, heated debates among students and faculty over the form and nature of Black studies.[20] Students Jeff Howard and Wesley Profit spoke at the April 17 meeting of the faculty, seeking to persuade them to support AFRO's vision for Black studies. "We're not here to intimidate you, to accuse you, or hopefully, to argue with you" Howard began in his remarks to the assembly, but in "a spirit of cooperation." He called their proposal "not a repudiation of the Rosovsky Report" but "a friendly amendment." That spring a standing committee comprised exclusively of faculty had begun to design an Afro-American studies program, and troubled by some of their decisions, AFRO proposed a formal role for students. Process, or the role of students, became an additional point of divergence between AFRO and the committee, although the students argued that their participation was faithful to the original intent of the Rosovsky Report. At the faculty meeting, Jeff Howard quoted the report's endorsement of students' participation, in light of their "high degree of interest, knowledge, and competence in this emerging and in some ways unique field of studies."

Henry Rosovsky spoke next, defended the current plan and process, and reminded the faculty that a double concentration was part of the original Rosovsky Report. But in a seeming concession, he noted, "It is possible that Afro-American studies will be a major on its own in the future." And then, in apparent contradiction to what the standing committee was in the midst of doing, he added that it was "best to let the incoming chairman set the lasting guidelines of the program." But he rejected student membership in the standing committee, because it would grant students a voice in the hiring of tenured faculty members.

At a follow-up meeting on April 22, the faculty voted in favor of AFRO's proposal, giving Afro-American studies departmental status, "offering a standard field of concentration," and adding six students to the standing committee, three to be chosen by AFRO and three by potential concentrators.[21] Clyde Lindsay, a student, hailed the faculty resolution. "I consider this a great victory for black students and for American education." But Rosovsky immediately resigned from the standing committee, saying such a major change in educational policy "should be studied carefully and considered in a calm atmosphere." Richard Musgrave, another economist, took his place as chair.[22]

Two points need to be added to this account of the department's origins. First, in his remarks to the faculty on April 17, Professor Rosovsky noted that the standing committee had already offered a tenured position to three distinguished scholars: two had declined and one was still weighing the offer; and it had offered visiting faculty positions to two other individuals, who had each turned them down. "To our knowledge," Rosovsky stated, "no one declined because he found fault with our program." After students had acquired voting rights on the standing committee, opponents of this development contended that it would obstruct hiring, since, in their view, no self-respecting scholar would submit to a review by undergraduates. Similarly, many faculty and administrators at Harvard and elsewhere came to believe that the departmental structure also thwarted hiring in Black studies, since in their view most scholars would naturally prefer affiliation with an established discipline. But it is important to note that the difficulty in hiring faculty at Harvard preceded both the addition of students to the standing committee and the turn to departmental status. As we have already seen and will examine further, there were numerous challenges in recruiting faculty to teach Black studies, regardless of its structure.[23]

Second, critics of the AFRO proposal subsequently promoted the notion that professors had voted for it under duress, in a pressure-filled atmosphere of student upheaval and rebellion. Exemplifying this portrayal, a story circulated that a Black student had come to the faculty meeting carrying a large knife. (It is perhaps relevant to recall that earlier that same month, an Associated Press photograph of Black student protesters at Cornell University carrying rifles and ammunition appeared on the covers of magazines and newspapers around the country.) The *Crimson* actually ran a photo of an unidentified Black male student walking on campus carrying a meat cleaver on the day of the faculty vote. But according to Wesley Profit, this student never spoke at the meeting, and faculty members never saw the knife. The young man—who hoped to speak at the faculty meeting—had a dramatic, preacher-like style and thought that, for better effect, in the middle of his remarks he would take out the hatchetlike knife and slam it into podium. But Profit, fellow leader Skip Griffin, and other students refused to allow him to bring the knife into the faculty meeting. Profit said they all understood the historic nature of the day—it was evidently the first time students ever addressed the faculty, and the meeting was being broadcast on the college radio station. There was no need for a hatchet! The disappointed student departed and was later photographed walking with his girlfriend on campus, still carrying the knife. The *Crimson* photo likely helped to convince many at Harvard that a student had actually come to the faculty meeting with a knife, presumably with a threatening intent.[24]

Still, despite the student strike and atmosphere of protest, faculty supporters of the resolution defended their vote, and the professors who worked with students on the standing committee expressed satisfaction with the process.[25] When Martin Kilson, an African American political scientist and member of the Rosovsky Committee, blamed the "political threats of the militant extremists" in AFRO for intimidating the faculty to allow a student role in organizing the department, Professor Jack Stein disagreed. He defended his vote, believing students had a legitimate concern over pedagogy and deserved the right to have a voice. In Kilson's view, "only persons of tested scholarly abilities and training should be involved in the organization and administration of black studies curricula." He found it galling that Harvard had allowed students to "*exercise scholarly authority*" over a "complex interdisciplinary field."[26] However, the new chair of the standing committee, Richard Musgrave, denied the rumor that people were spurning their job offers because of the presence of students on the committee. The heavy competition for the few specialists in the field accounted for their difficulties, he reported.[27] Nevertheless, the faculty's rejection of the Rosovsky plan in favor of AFRO's was deeply resented by many at Harvard, some of whom would continue to fight for their vision of Afro-American studies notwithstanding the 1969 defeat.

The demand for greater student rights and voice was in fact widespread on American campuses in these years—students were even demanding voting rights in the U.S. Department of Education.[28] So Harvard was hardly unique. Still, student leadership was particularly associated with Black studies for a simple reason. Students—not scholars—were responsible for the creation of Black studies programs. It is absolutely vital to appreciate this distinction if one wants to truly understand the contentious early years of Black studies. "Black studies programs came into existence not because of the efforts of scholars who detected the cavernous lacunae in the curriculum vis-à-vis the Afro-American experience," observed Tobe Johnson, a professor at Morehouse. "They came into existence primarily because of the pressures of black students and their white allies for a curriculum more relevant to that experience."[29] This is not to downplay the paramount significance of sympathetic faculty and administrators. But the fact remains that, at most places, a petition drive, sit-in, demonstration, or strike, or the threat of these, led to the creation of new courses.

Indeed, on many campuses, the faculty initially rebuffed student entreaties for Black-content courses. "The bedrock foundation for the emergence of contemporary Black studies was laid by Black urban, lower-class students as they tried to get better Black studies courses from traditional departments," noted education scholar Carlos Brossard.[30] Sadly, this group garnered very little credit for their founding role and faced a lot of criticism and scorn. As Carlene Young, a director of Black studies at UCLA, observed, "Black studies has been available to scholars for several generations." But "it was not until the Black consciousness movement of the 1960s forced the issue that Afro-Americans began to be afforded their rightful place in the annals of the history and development of American society."[31]

Harvard faced a question every campus faced. If students had demanded and won Black studies, who would give it form? Who would actually build the new departments and programs? The white faculty and administrators who had heretofore failed to integrate their faculties and curriculum? The one or two Black scholars who were on the faculty of the university, and who may or may not have been involved in the student push for Black studies? Or, would the Black students who had fought for it play a leading role in its implementation? Some people anticipated the student desire for involvement. "Since the black studies movement was initiated by black students rather than by teachers and educators," one scholar predicted, "it can be assumed that the former will try to exercise a quasi-proprietary influence on the future development of black studies programs."[32]

Students did not demand the same degree of involvement everywhere, and it was not controversial everywhere—but the students' sense of ownership over Black studies and their desire to be involved in forging it was common. At Stanford, for example, a committee of four Black students, three Black professors, and two white professors oversaw the first year in Afro-American studies.[33] Students at Wesleyan formed a committee to review all candidates applying for Afro-American studies positions.[34] In the prospectus for the Africana Studies and Research Center at Cornell, James Turner wrote that "students will participate significantly in the direction and development of the Center" and "will be involved in matters of policy, curriculum and faculty recruitment."[35]

But there was hardly consensus on student involvement. As at Harvard, some people saw student involvement in faculty affairs as a sign of academic weakness. Many scholars suspected that the student activists demanding Black studies were driven more by emotional and political considerations than intellectual interest, and worried that their commitment to the new units would prove ephemeral or that universities would use Black studies to reinvent "separate but equal" and thus shortchange Black students just as they were entering white universities in large numbers. The young historian John Blassingame applauded Black students for shining a light on discriminatory hiring practices, but worried that student preference for Black teachers would overlook knowledgeable whites and lead to the hiring of unqualified personnel. "Negro students ignore the possible crippling effects of hiring simply *any* black man," he asserted, although, to be fair, the evidence does not indicate that most students had such a simple yardstick of evaluation when rejecting whites and demanding Black professors. When Columbia University hired white historian Eric Foner to teach a course in Black history, for example, some Black students took the course and also picketed it, recognizing the white professor's qualifications, but viewing this as an advantageous opportunity to press Columbia to integrate the history department. And sure enough their protest contributed to the hiring of Nathan Huggins.[36]

Blassingame's biggest concern was what he saw as the immense political pressure emanating from students. "The threat to black intellectuals is real," he wrote. "Not only do the black students demand that the teachers in black studies be Negroes, they also want them to have the right shade of 'blackness.' In essence, this means that the black scholar must have the right ideological leanings. As some of us succumb to the persuasive arguments to hop on the treadmill and try to keep up with the mercurial changes in the black 'party line,'" he wrote, "serious scholarship is likely to suffer."[37] As the Black studies department at San Francisco State in 1969–1970 illustrates, students who were well organized and possessed of a clear political agenda for Black studies could be dogmatic and intimidating toward Black faculty. But in most schools, students did not seek to exert that level of ideological control.

One area of student participation in departmental governance that troubled many scholars was the questioning of job applicants about the race of their spouses. In their view, this illustrated the risk of students assuming professional roles without the appropriate professionalization. Fairly or not, with the ascendancy of Black nationalism, students often interpreted the marital affiliations of Black scholars (men, in the main) as a sign of their larger communal affiliation and orientation. An interracial couple did not exemplify the idea of Black people coming together that animated much of the Black Power movement, and some felt that marriages of Black men to white women, in particular, constituted a race-based rejection of African American women. But the introduction of this issue in the hiring process signaled, for many scholars, an inappropriate entry of ideology into a professional context. During an interview for a job in the Black studies department at Lehman College in the Bronx, a committee of students asked the historian William Seraille about the racial identity of his wife. He happens to be married to a Black woman, and he got the job, but he remembers his surprise at the question. Blassingame described a friend's different experience. "After being approved by the faculty, he went before the black students to prove his ideological fitness," Blassingame wrote. "When he opened up his remarks to them by pointing out that he had a white wife, the students rejected him. In spite of his qualifications he was not hired."[38] Mary Jane Hewitt, an administrator at UCLA in the late 1960s, recalls the hostility encountered by African American scholar Sylvester Whittaker, who served very briefly as the director of the Center for African American Studies. "His ex-wife was white," she says. "And all the ladies he dated were white, and this is why he marvels today at Claudia Mitchell-Kernan having been a successful director of that center for all those years with a white husband, when he thinks about how they crucified him because of his white wife and white girlfriends." Ron Karenga's "guys" she recalls, gave Whittaker a hard time.[39]

St. Clair Drake said that until 1967 the criticism he received for being married interracially came from whites, but then Black women began to question him. "At Roosevelt last year the Black Student Association wasn't having much to do with me," he noted, summing up the students' view of him this way: "The thing that is wrong with [Drake] is that he is a nigger that talks black and sleeps white." But

Drake criticized others for concealing from public knowledge the fact that they were sleeping with white women. In his view, he was at least honest and got married. Fifty-eight years old and a distinguished social scientist, Drake was one of the scholars that Harvard tried to hire to chair Afro-American studies, but he had already said yes to Stanford's same offer. When Harvard called, he said, "I felt like telling them, why didn't you ask me 20 years ago, when I really could have used the research facilities and support. But they wait until the kids are ready to burn the place down before they ask me."[40]

This leads to another major challenge and point of contestation in the early Black studies movement—who was qualified and willing to teach Black studies? It was not easy to staff the scores of new Black studies programs, centers, and departments that sprang up across the country in 1969 and the early 1970s. A couple of hundred campuses launched search committees for specialists in Black studies—all at the same time. After Martin Luther King's assassination, Charles Hamilton discovered, "black professors (preferably with PhDs) became one of the most sought after commodities on the market."[41] Black PhDs were the most in demand, but they were few in number. Of the thirteen thousand professional sociologists in 1970, for example, only eighty-five were Black.[42] According to a survey in 1970, fewer than 1 percent of PhD holders in the United States were Black, and most in this group were over age fifty-five.[43] Spelman historian Vincent Harding was committed to staying in the South and teaching Black students. "I have received in the past several years, you have no idea how many offers to come teach in the North. This is a time that schools that were not interested in black teachers five years ago will do anything to get them." He made a passionate attempt to convince Black students and scholars to resist the brain drain of HBCUs and stay in or move to the South.[44]

While still a graduate student at Northwestern in the late 1960s, John Bracey was flooded with job offers. Both he and James Turner, another Northwestern graduate student, joined African American studies programs before completing their doctorates, and their stories further illustrate the unusual or unconventional circumstances that often shaped hiring in the field. Turner became the first director of the Africana Studies and Research Center at Cornell University. A Black nationalist, he sought to recruit scholars of like mind and argued against "white-defined" academic qualifications. "They call them objective criteria, but these reflect colonial education," he felt. At Cornell, he argued for a hiring process where "there could be no judgment by whites, and no review mechanism of the hiring of Blacks at all. Our definition of the program meant, in the first instance, that Black people must hire each other."[45] John Bracey's hiring in the Department of Afro-American Studies at the University of Massachusetts in 1972 was the ironic result of an even more unpopular political philosophy. W.E.B. Du Bois had instructed that the executor of his estate, Herbert Aptheker, also an historian and member of the Communist Party, accompany the gift of his personal papers to the University of Massachusetts. But the state legislature balked at the prospect of hiring this openly communist scholar, though they remained interested in acquiring Du Bois's massive and highly valuable personal archive. Aptheker decided to take advantage of whatever leverage he might have and proposed that, in his place, the university add five additional faculty positions in Afro-American studies, one of which became Bracey's position.[46]

To be sure, not every young Black scholar who worked on African American subjects wanted to join a Black studies program. It is vital to remember that even though universities were designing new courses and programs, most academics did not regard the field as academically legitimate. Plus, many did not share the Black nationalist project of some of the field's founders. James Turner encountered this dilemma in hiring at Cornell. "The problem we have found is finding Black people who can understand that their whole notion of scholarship has been so shaped by white people that they can't see and think for themselves," he declared. "Too many of them really believe that the stuff we are talking about is a compromise of intellectual integrity. They look at us and say, 'I think you cats really want to discourage doing academic work.'" In Turner's opinion, "the real problem is not simply personnel, but personnel who are inclined towards a Black orientation and who won't blow the whole thing."[47]

Many young Black scholars likely questioned whether Black studies would even last, and may have viewed launching a career in the field as risky. On this reluctance by Black scholars, St. Clair Drake observed, "They want the security and prestige of being in a traditional department. Black studies might be a fad, and they'd be left out in the cold."[48] Norvel Smith, the Black president of Merritt College in Oakland, alma mater of Huey P. Newton and home of one of the first Black studies departments, saw a significant tension between the career aspirations of many Black scholars and the political sensibilities of radical Black youth. "A black faculty member," in his view, "likes to feel that his professional position is justified on a basis other than race, and he resents the encumbrances of black students. . . . In addition, many faculty members are turned off by the student rhetoric."[49] Charles Hamilton was inundated with job offers in the late 1960s; he chose not to join a Black studies program, deciding instead to join the political science faculty at Columbia University. While still a graduate student, Sterling Stuckey was invited to chair the new Department of African American Studies at Northwestern, but he declined and subsequently began his career in the history department. Jim Pitts, who also did his graduate work at Northwestern and later joined their sociology department, remembers the atmosphere in African American studies at Northwestern as "poisoned" and found the idea of working there unappealing.[50]

Sometimes, this scenario was reversed, and a Black scholar on the faculty regardless of scholarly expertise was tapped to teach African American studies. Robert Singleton, an assistant professor of industrial relations at the University of California, Los Angeles, was asked by students to head the new Center for Afro-American Studies. He thinks his efforts to restrain police—who were rounding up all Black males after the shooting deaths of two students who were leaders in the Black Panther Party on campus in January 1969—made the students like him. At the time, he felt he was not qualified—he had not yet completed his PhD—but he agreed to serve on an interim basis because he felt that the job needed to be done.[51]

As for the prospect of hiring whites, the general view in the early years, especially, is summed up by the white chairman of a Black studies planning committee at a large, urban university: "Our students do not say that no white professor can teach any aspect of Black studies, but that few are competent to do so, few have the right attitudes or knowledge, and most importantly, the typical 'liberal' professor" allows the interracial class to become a rap session. Our black students do *not* want to be in the position of finding either that they are guinea-pigs for class discussion or that they know more of the subject at hand than the instructor."[52] Overall, Black students voiced a strong preference for Black professors in Black studies courses, while Black scholars expressed more openness to the participation of qualified non-Black professors. An all-Black search committee at Fordham University in the Bronx hired the white historian Mark Naison in 1970. Naison felt he had been hired "not only because of my research on black history but because the program's founders saw teaching whites about African American history and culture as complementary to their mission of promoting black unity and empowerment." He became "an evangelist for black studies among white and Latino students," and found that "some black students resented what I was doing." But with the passage of time and large course enrollments, "the hostility dissipated" and Naison became integrated into the life of the program.[53]

Historian Clayborne Carson attributes his quick ascent from computer programmer to professor to, in part, the significance of race in the early Black studies movement and the desire by Black students to have Black professors in this burgeoning field. As an auditor of a "new course" at UCLA on the history of race in the United States, taught by white historian Gary Nash, he ended up leading a discussion section. This propelled Carson to enter graduate school in 1969, and two years later he became an acting assistant professor. "The professors who engineered my recruitment were responding to forceful Black student demands for an African American history course taught by a Black professor. My hiring followed an interview session with leaders of the Black Student Union and was made possible by an expedient decision to deny tenure to a non-Black professor, Ronald Takaki, the superb historian who taught UCLA's first African American history course." Carson regretted the racial politics in the hiring process and the denial of tenure to Takaki, a Hawaiian of Japanese descent, who went on to a distinguished career in Asian American studies at Berkeley, where he helped to launch the ethnic studies department. For his part, Carson was relieved to leave the political hothouse of UCLA for a position at Stanford, where he built a career as one of the nation's leading scholars of the civil rights movement.[54]

As Harvard's early attempts to hire in Afro-American studies show, the fact that many universities were competing for the same scholars, and that many Black PhDs shunned Black studies, made hiring difficult. Universities often turned to nontraditional sources of recruitment, which in turn served to reinforce the notion that Black studies was not a serious academic venture. John Blassingame, ever the gadfly, expressed sharp criticism of early Black studies instructors. Because of "their lack of commitment and the urgent demand," Blassingame wrote, "many colleges are hiring all manner of people to teach black-oriented courses, especially if they are black. Social workers, graduate students who have just embarked on their graduate careers, high school teachers, principals, and practically anyone who looks black or has mentioned Negroes in an article, book or seminar paper are hired to teach Afro-American courses." While clearly hyperbole, this statement does capture the sense of improvisation and scrambling by an unprepared academic establishment in the wake of a major nationwide movement victory. Sterling Stuckey, who assisted in recruiting candidates for the African American studies department at Northwestern, concedes that it was difficult to find qualified people and thinks they made a few inappropriate hires. And ultimately, there were instances where inappropriate instructors either intimidated administrators into promoting them, or preserved their jobs as a result of the low opinion or misunderstanding of the field held by many in academia. These early hiring decisions adversely affected some departments for decades and certainly influenced the broader image of the field.[55] Michael Thelwell offered a broader perspective. He noted the concern of many that colleges would set up "hastily manufactured and meaningless programs" taught by "semi-literate dashiki-clad demagogues with nothing to offer but a 'militant black rap.'" He had seen very few of these, although he acknowledged the risk. "It would be pointless to pretend that this danger does not exist in some small degree," he wrote, "but my impression of the basic good sense of this student generation, and their serious commitment and sense of responsibility to themselves and their community, reassures me that this tendency will be a short-lived one."[56]

As much as faculty supporters of Black studies wanted to be responsive to student demands, they also wanted quality programs, and many worried that an insufficient faculty supply would lead to a pattern of weak, understaffed programs that might cast the whole discipline in a bad light and put it in actual jeopardy. A few scholars proposed models to consolidate talent and guide the creation of the field in a more purposeful, coherent fashion. Vincent Harding called for a Commission for Black Education to plan and organize higher education for African Americans.[57] Expressing a popular idea, Melvin Drimmer argued for the development of a dozen or so centers for the teaching and study of Black history, and he envisioned Black colleges as the logical starting point.[58] Darwin Turner, the dean of the graduate school at North Carolina A&T, wanted both respectability and innovation in Black studies: "I am sufficiently traditional and black that I want to be certain that Afro-American studies programs are respectably staffed with a core of Ph.Ds. Otherwise the intellectual snobs of our campuses will cite the sparsity of them in the program to support their suspicion that Afro-American studies are designed for the dumb and disadvantaged, and good students may fear to become identified with a program stigmatized as intellectually inferior." But at the same time, Turner defended the view that a broader range of talent should be tapped for the college classroom. "I warn against the pompous pretense that a teacher cannot be used unless he has a master's or doctor's degree," he declared, figuring that "an organizer with ten years experience in the black ghetto could teach a course in sociology maybe better than someone whose research only came from libraries." He urged three solutions: finance and encourage Black students to attend graduate school; develop regional, cooperative Black studies centers; and utilize "those individuals who have a lot of practical experience but lack an advanced degree." This was already happening for creative writers and artists. "Ralph Ellison and Gwendolyn Brooks would be hired at almost any institution in the country," Turner noted.[59]

After losing St. Clair Drake to Stanford and being turned down by John Hope Franklin, who held a distinguished professorship at the University of Chicago and moreover had no interest in joining a department of Black studies, Harvard hired Ewart Guinier, a lawyer, former trade unionist, and longtime Black community leader, to chair the new Department of Afro-American Studies. As a nonacademic operating in an elite academic environment, Guinier called upon prominent scholars for counsel and advice, notably Charles Hamilton, Hollis Lynch, and especially Sterling Stuckey. But Guinier encountered enormous challenges in getting Harvard to fulfill its commitments to the department. As Hollis Lynch later observed, "The Harvard administration did not share Professor Guinier's grand ambition and design for his Department and certainly put many obstacles in the way of actualizing them."[60] The university succeeded in undermining or reversing key victories of 1969, including the student role in hiring, full faculty appointments, inclusion of African studies, and development of a research institute. Faculty and student leaders in Afro-American studies managed to preserve its departmental character, but the toll in demoralization and shrinkage was high.

A review of the department by internal and external scholars in 1972 provided the first occasion to trim its sails. By this point, the department had graduated its first class of fourteen concentrators—who were headed to law, business, and graduate schools. It had ten instructors, although Guinier remained the sole tenured professor, and offered a wide range of courses each semester in African and African American studies. Guinier had a global conception of Black studies, believing that it "should cover the history and culture of Black people from ancient times to the present," including "experiences in Africa and North America and the Caribbean."[61] The students, course offerings, and faculty

FIGURE 17. Lerone Bennett and Ewart Guinier, the first chair of the Department of Afro-American Studies at Harvard, converse at a conference of the Association for the Study of Afro-American Life and History.

were diverse, with white students generally comprising 40 to 60 percent of course enrollments. But nonetheless a portrait of a racially exclusive and philosophically separatist department was widely promoted. Political scientist Martin Kilson—the first tenured Black faculty member at Harvard—had served on the Rosovsky Committee and was a firm believer in the benefits of joint appointments, program status, and traditional faculty control for African American studies. He was severely disappointed in the April 1969 faculty decision and became a vocal critic of the department in the 1970s. He portrayed departmental status as "tragic" and argued that it made Black studies "academically and technically diffuse and disoriented," and put this generation of Black students at a disadvantage. "They will be dilettantes at best, and charlatans at worst," he warned.[62]

During the 1972 review of the department, Kilson circulated his "Memorandum on Direction of Reforms in Afro-American Studies Curriculum at Harvard University," which expressed his objections, especially the idea that students should not be able to major exclusively in

Afro-American studies. Aggressively seeking to shape the review, Kilson characterized the department as a hostile Black island in the erudite sea of Harvard. He assailed the inclusion of students on the executive committee, describing them as "black racialist—if not black racist—in outlook" and blaming them for the lack of white teachers, who in his view had a kind of right to be there. (And there actually had been white instructors in the department.) Kilson wanted "the rich talent of white scholars at Harvard" to be brought to bear on the struggling department, even suggesting, remarkably, Nathan Glazer and Daniel Patrick Moynihan, whose *Beyond the Melting Pot,* had questioned the vitality and contribution of Black American culture. Glazer and Moynihan were part of a generation of white "experts" whose scant encounter with Black history and culture had given rise to the Black studies movement.[63] Contacted by Harvard for his view of the Afro-American studies department's status, political scientist Ron Walters expressed concern about Martin Kilson's characterization of the department. Black studies did not politicize the university, he argued, "it was already politicized by a thousand issues more volatile than black studies." Moreover, in forming the department, "Harvard recognized that any legitimate black effort is controlled and developed by black people." Walters expressed frustration that Kilson would reduce this quest to "the dictates of a bunch of 'militants.'" It is "the desire of *those involved* in black studies whether they be militants or moderates," he declared, "to have an authentically black educational experience."[64]

Ewart Guinier felt that many influential people at Harvard wished to undo the faculty vote of April 1969, so the department produced its own self-evaluation as a means of ensuring that their perspective— many accomplishments despite weak university support—would get a public airing. Harvard graduate students Andrea Rushing and Wesley Profit helped put together "The First Three Years." It was released two days before the official review, and in Profit's view, it saved the department. "The report prevented the university from dismantling the department," he believes. He credits Guinier's seasoned organizing skills and willingness to fight back as essential to the survival of Afro-American studies as a department.[65]

The review committee, headed by federal judge Wade H. McCree Jr., found a middle ground between the department and its critics. The committee's report praised the dedication of the department's chair and concentrators, yet many of its recommendations undercut the department's vision. It urged Harvard to reaffirm its commitment to the department and to immediately hire at least two more senior faculty; recommended but did not require joint majors; suggested greater focus on Afro-Americans and less attention to African studies; dissolved the standing committee—which had been the vehicle for including students in faculty recruitment—but kept students on all other departmental committees; created a new interdepartmental faculty search committee; and urged creation of the delayed W.E.B. Du Bois Institute for Afro-American Research. It also recommended (but did not require) that joint appointments with other departments be used to facilitate faculty recruitment. The committee found that "one of the problems of attracting eminent black and white scholars to the Department is the fact that they have earned acceptance in 'conventional' disciplines at other institutions which they would not want to forsake by going into a department which appears to be 'on trial' and/or accorded second-class status by Harvard."[66]

In the aftermath of the review, the marginalization and isolation of the department intensified. The effort to assemble a stable tenure-track faculty remained a challenge, and it took several more years to hire the second tenured faculty member, the music scholar Eileen Southern, who was jointly appointed to the music department. The sociologist Orlando Patterson had joined the department as an assistant professor but later moved to sociology after an acrimonious falling out with Guinier. The department's first internal tenure candidate, Ephraim Issac, a specialist in African languages and a Harvard PhD, was denied tenure but won a settlement after it was discovered that the college had wrongfully instructed an external review committee that Issac had to be jointly appointed in order to get tenure.[67]

In the meantime, Professor Kilson escalated his criticism of the department and aimed his guns at Harvard's use of affirmative action in undergraduate admissions, which, like Afro-American studies, he saw as leading to an inferior Black presence at Harvard. Kilson used the words *militant* and *militancy* repeatedly in diagnosing this apparent problem. The effects of the "separatism and militancy" of the late 1960s, he insisted, "were having a disastrous impact on the academic achievement and intellectual growth of Negro students."[68] Kilson spent much of 1973 publicly disparaging the qualities and abilities of Black Harvard students and even took it upon himself to lobby for shift in admissions policy. In a lengthy memo to the university president and deans of the college, Kilson complained that many Black students admitted in the past six years lack a *"desire or capacity to acculturate to competi-*

tive academic and intellectual lifestyles" and urged a reconsideration of admissions criteria.[69] In yet another letter to Harvard administrators, he complained that "there are still too many black girls recruited into Radcliffe who are simply marginal intellectually; they are not really capable of or not really interested in superior intellectual and academic performance at an elite institution like Harvard."[70]

A series of articles in the *Harvard Bulletin* launched the public phase of his attack. He reiterated his concern that "the future quality of the Afro-American elites or professional classes is at stake" and alleged that the Afro-American studies department, "like others around the country, was created with scant concern for academic or intellectual standards." He questioned the competence of Black faculty and staff hired as a result of student protest—which included most Black faculty and staff at Harvard. He urged a move away from admitting "ghetto-type blacks" and toward favoring those possessed "of a strong preference for individualistic acculturation." Like some other traditionalist critics of the Black campus movement, Kilson sought to portray himself as its truest friend through his unabashed and fearless, and evidently lone, insistence on rigor. But the *Harvard Bulletin* researched some of Kilson's claims and reported that between 75 and 80 percent of Black students admitted in recent years "would not be categorized as disadvantaged," and found as well that "Black students from disadvantaged backgrounds do equivalent work to that done by middle-class blacks, in terms of rank list and grade-point averages."[71]

The *Bulletin* provided space for rebuttals, and a group of students answered with aplomb. They assailed the collective portrait of Black incompetence that Kilson had put forward. It is apparent, they argued, "that by making his generalizations, Kilson denies to Harvard blacks the very individuality which he accuses them of rejecting and which for himself he holds so dear. Blacks at Harvard are such a heterogeneous lot that only someone with the professor's lively imagination could even conceive of the kinds of collective attitudes with which he associates us." The students debunked his claims of lower Black qualifications by pointing to the (comparatively high) SAT scores of Black admits in the preceding five years. Much of their dispute mirrored larger debates about the meaning of Blackness in the aftermath of Black Power. For Kilson, "'black solidarity behavior' is a problem—an obstruction to high academic achievement and upward social mobility that must be eliminated before blacks can approach the nirvana of middle-class American society." The students rejected this view, saying, "He genuinely believes, it seems, that there is no significance in cultural blackness unless it apes or imitates white cultural norms every step of the way." They offered a strong defense of cultural pluralism and the mutually constituted nature of Black and American identities. But their chief intervention was in vigorously questioning the portrait he had painted of them—as provincial, anti-intellectual, and victims and purveyors of groupthink.[72]

Law professor Derrick Bell, too, offered a rebuttal, noting that Kilson had been sounding this alarm for several years. "Like a bawdy tune with lyrics one would dare not repeat in public," Bell wrote, clearly fed up, "'Martin's Melodies' sing almost gleefully of black intellectual unreadiness in terms so broadly indicting the race that no sophisticated white would dare repeat them, however much he might agree with their expressions. It is no surprise that University publications have given Kilson's statements so much space. One can almost see the advocates of meritocracy rejoicing each time Kilson takes aim at the shortcomings of blacks in academe. . . . It may be that Professor Kilson is trying to help black students by his repeated public attacks. But as every social scientist should know, oppressed minorities are burdened by doubts of self-worth. Public criticism by a member of that group (particularly one as eminent as Professor Kilson) that focuses on shortcomings and ignores positive values will be used by the majority to justify continuance rather than cessation of oppressive behavior."[73]

On another occasion when Bell rose to the defense of Black students after a series of public criticism by Kilson, he noted that the Black community at Harvard had tried for a long time to ignore "Kilson's vicious slanders." But Bell had come to worry that administrators might mistake their silence for support.[74] Kilson was persistent. He reprised the essays as "The Black Experience at Harvard," for the *New York Times Magazine* a few months later, and in the first sentence declared that Black students "have reached a crisis" created "in large measure by black separatism and militancy." The essay is filled with lament for the glory days of his college years, and alarm and despair over what he sees as Black intolerance and failure on campus. "Since 1971," he claimed without an illustration, "the pressures for conformity to black-solidarity behavior have been well-nigh overwhelming at Harvard." But more damaging was his assertion that "black-solidarity forces are distinctly anti-intellectual and antiachievement in orientation," citing as evidence student pride in participating in "community affairs" and "posturing 'Black power' in relation to political issues like Harvard's Gulf Oil investments in Africa."

After the *Times* essay, Ewart Guinier offered a series of forceful responses in various media. "What has made the situation at Harvard so sadly disturbing is that, while white antagonists of Afro-American studies have remained almost completely silent, one or two Negro professors . . . have engaged in an orgy of rage against us." He regretted waiting so long to answer the attacks and contended that it had interfered with faculty recruitment.[75] Subsequently, in what became a final public embarrassment and major campus conflict, and in defiance of the recommendations by several committees, the administration excluded the department and Guinier from the planning and creation of the Du Bois Institute, sparking an outpouring of criticism by Professor Guinier on the eve of his retirement. Henry Rosovsky was dean of the college, and Derek Bok was president. Guinier released a strongly worded nineteen-page statement in which he accused Bok and Rosovsky of undermining the department, and surrendering to "forces supporting white supremacy within Harvard." There had been no success in making joint appointments ever since the McCree committee had recommended it as a recruitment tool. Guinier had long opposed this strategy, saying it deterred those interested in African American studies, and noted that he found it "absurd" to grant such a leading role to departments with histories of racist scholarship and all-white hiring practices. Still, they had tried to hire John Blassingame jointly, but the history department had rejected him; and according to Guinier, when they tried to hire him exclusively in Afro-American studies the university failed to provide sufficient research funds. Bok and Rosovsky termed Guinier's words "intemperate" and countered that they were seeking to strengthen the department. Bok appointed Andrew Brimmer, a Black former member of the Federal Reserve, to head a panel charged with developing the Du Bois Institute.[76]

But the exclusion of the department from the planning process for the institute also galvanized students, leading the Du Bois Institute Student Coalition to conduct a sit-in at Massachusetts Hall. For his part, Guinier accused administrators of abandoning "any pretense of manners, of courtesy, or civility in relating the Afro-American Studies Department." Their intent, he insisted, was "to hold black people up to ridicule and humiliation and, finally, to isolate and pistol whip us into submission as the entire Harvard community watches. Once and for all," he declared, "they want to teach us a lesson, to show us our place."[77] As a result of these heated and widely publicized conflicts, lack of administrative support, and divergent views of how to develop

African American studies, the department at Harvard remained very small until the early 1990s. Given that the positive media attention paid to Black studies at Harvard in later years helped to raise the profile of the department and likely enhanced the stature of the discipline in academe more generally, one can imagine that the spate of negative stories penned by Kilson and others in the 1970s fueled a broader skepticism of, if not contempt for, African American studies in general.[78]

The Harvard story seemed to confirm a discourse of crisis in, even failure of, Black studies that permeated discussions and representations of the field in the 1970s. A headline in the *Wall Street Journal* blared: "Black Studies Founder as Student Interest Declines and Faculties Grow More Skeptical." The *Washington Post* announced: "Once Popular Black Studies Now Attracting Only a Handful of Students."[79] Black studies "is in deep trouble," declared the *Black Scholar* under the headline "Politics of the Attack on Black Studies," which at least reframed the character of the crisis. In that article, Robert Allen found that three hundred programs had closed in the early 1970s, a dramatic but inflated figure.[80] As the fate of open admissions at the City University of New York demonstrated, widespread budget cuts during the recession of the mid-1970s had a devastating effect on new programs. At a 1975 conference titled "The Future of Black Studies," with more than a hundred program directors in attendance, all but one reported financial cutbacks.[81] "To survive and succeed," one critic noted, "Black programs required the support of the very structures they were designed to counterpose. This basic contradiction was not properly analyzed, understood or confronted." As a result, the new units were underfunded, given low status, and marginalized, and predictably this negatively affected student perceptions.[82]

Challenges to the discipline's academic legitimacy were common throughout the 1970s and 1980s. Leaders in Black studies regularly complained about the lack of support and acceptance from administrators and colleagues and the seemingly unending quest to "prove" its legitimacy. Carlene Young wrote, "Afro-American studies have been forced to struggle against continual assaults on their limited resources and structural integrity while maintaining strong academic programs, highly qualified faculty, and good enrollments." Moreover, she lamented, "there are still too many in the Academy who resent the 'intrusion' and, as a consequence, agitate for the demise of Afro-American Studies."[83]

The Ford Foundation's relationship to African American studies illustrates how the desire for self-determination and African American intellectual leadership profoundly shaped the early Black studies movement. Ford began an association with Black studies in 1968 when it funded a high-profile conference at Yale University. The young radicals Nathan Hare, Ron Karenga, and Gerald McWorter debated professors David Brion Davis, Robert Ferris Thompson, and Martin Kilson, showcasing the generational and political cleavages and challenges in the early Black studies movement. Most people at Ford held a conservative or traditionalist view of Black studies' best path—much like Rosovsky's at Harvard—and urged this view in grant making. "I would not favor support for the notion that only Blacks can teach or understand this subject, and that therefore the Department of Black studies must be separately organized," a top official informed foundation president McGeorge Bundy. "I fear it will become a cultural war camp, marked by myth-making and collective self-deception."[84] As we have seen, many liberal leaders of this era conflated departmental status with a commitment to racial separatism and, as the quote further suggests, had deep reservations about the intellectual legitimacy of African American studies. Roger Wilkins, a young African American program officer, urged Bundy to include the "younger and angrier Black scholars" in the advisory process. But as Farah Griffin has shown, Bundy instead heeded the advice of Sir Arthur Lewis, a Princeton-trained, Caribbean-born economist, who urged support for programs that aspired to the same standards as the established disciplines, as well as support for the production of more Black PhDs.[85]

In 1969 Ford disbursed more than one million dollars to fourteen colleges, as well as to the Institute of the Black World, in order to help launch Black studies. A Ford-sponsored conference in Aspen, Colorado, in July 1970 dramatically illustrated the desire by Black scholars to assert control over the burgeoning field and to convey this stance to white philanthropists and scholars. Ford sponsored the Aspen conference in order to take stock of the new programs and examine, as one Ford official put it, "the intellectual underpinnings of black studies." To the Ford official's dismay, however, much of the discussion at Aspen focused instead on "questions of control and the political and ideological performance of black studies."[86] The conflict started before the conference had even begun, when Vincent Harding objected to the list of invitees—noting the absence of several key leaders in the Black studies movement and objecting to the inclusion of white scholars as "resource" people. "I thought the list of non-directors was a strange one," he wrote to historian Edgar Toppin, whom Ford had asked to chair the event. "In light of the current intellectual and political mood among black people, I did not understand why there was a need to have any white scholars present to participate in a discussion on the future of Black studies," Harding wrote. "And it seemed very insensitive to include two who had publicly expressed serious questions about whether black scholars ought to control the definition of the black experience."[87]

On the first day of the conference, Harding, Roscoe Brown, Andrew Billingsley, St. Clair Drake, and others issued a statement as the "Black Caucus of the Aspen Black Studies Seminar." "Of major concern to us is the fact that Black expertise and leadership did not have the major role in conceptualizing and organizing the conference," they wrote, calling Ford's approach "reminiscent of the paternalistic ways in which White America has habitually treated Blacks throughout American history." Billingsley followed with his own stinging statement to the Ford officials, whom he lauded for supporting Black education, but criticized in this case for adopting "American white ways of doing things." "We do not mean to impugn the motives of anybody associated with it, but we do mean to say, as strongly as we can, that the effect was damaging." He "recommended very strongly that this mistake not be repeated again."[88]

Ford interpreted the professors' protest as either political posturing or a rejection of integration. James Armsey, who as Ford's director of higher education in the 1960s had barred grants to segregated universities, prompting several private southern schools, like Duke, Emory, and Vanderbilt, to desegregate, answered with a speech defending the foundation. "You spent the first morning censuring the Ford Foundation in connection with this seminar," he began. The whole point of the conference, in his view, was for Ford grantees "to get together, compare notes, swap experiences, review problems, exchange learnings and consider plans for the future." Its success or failure, he claimed, depended on the participants. In his view, Ford organized the conference in response to the needs and desires of Black studies directors, although he conceded that they should have hired a Black-owned agency to organize the gathering. But then Armsey switched to offense. Referring to criticism of his opening night welcome, he said, "It was inevitable, I suppose, that my remarks would be considered either paternalistic or patronizing. . . . In the scheme of things today, there appears to be no way in which the conduct of a white person in my position can be considered open, above board, and honest." He accused the Black caucus of engaging in "repetitive catharsis," of going "through these rituals in part to remind the white man of his guilt." "That may be a useful purpose at times," he declared, "but through overuse it can become self-defeating. By these tactics, you are driving your real white allies into isolation and opposition." His final jab was the statement that the "only guilt" he felt in connection with Black studies was in relaxing "the normal standards of intellectual rigor in recommending grants."[89]

A program officer chimed in that he was "deeply disturbed at the separatist philosophy" of several participants at Aspen, singling out Harding and Billingsley. There was certainly a problem of translation at Aspen—as Ford officials took literally Armstead Robinson's statement that the Black studies movement "represents the death of integration as a vital political imperative for Blacks in this country." Ford was obviously not going to fund "the death of integration," but Robinson's longer comments make clear that he was referring to a redefinition of Black identity, not an abandonment of desegregation.[90]

The directors of Black studies programs at Aspen voiced support for Harding's and Billingsley's critiques—although Ford officials hinted that some among the old guard, notably George Kelsey and Benjamin Quarles, had misgivings. Nevertheless, they all expressed surprise and dismay to discover that Ford had no intention of continuing to fund collegiate Black studies programs. Ford claimed to have always viewed its grants to Black studies programs as temporary, but their loss had a significant, often unanticipated, impact.[91] Ford believed that universities should assume the role of funding their own academic programs, but it is also plausible that Ford was disinclined to renew robust support in the immediate aftermath of Aspen. In any event, Ford continued to offer funding to Black students in PhD programs, which it had begun in 1969. Ford's support for Black studies resumed and expanded in the 1980s and beyond, benefiting not only major research universities such as Berkeley, Cornell, Harvard, UCLA, and Madison but also the field's two major professional organizations: the National Council of Black Studies, and the Association for the Study of Afro-American Life and History (formerly the Association for the Study of Negro Life and History). Importantly, in the 1980s, Ford also expanded fellowships for underrepresented minorities, which have played a significant part in funding young Black scholars.[92]

In addition to external skepticism about the academic rigor or legitimacy of Black studies, internal debates arose about the role of political ideology and activism in Black studies. Would Black studies follow the political inspiration and aspirations of its student founders, or would it move in a more traditional academic direction? Could it meet the expectation of some of its student founders and advance the Black revolution? Some professors pushed back, even when they often supported the larger thrust of the Black student struggle. A student in one of St. Clair Drake's classes at Stanford once asked him why they were sitting around talking about problems instead of being out there solving them. Drake answered, "There are intellectual tasks and there are street tasks for the black revolution, and my temperament and the university environment are more suited for the intellectual tasks."[93] During a visit to the University of Illinois in Urbana, Charles Hamilton witnessed an exchange that captured the chasm between militant students and traditionally trained scholars. A student asked, "Is the purpose of this program to help the student really change the society? Are we going to use the technology of the society to overthrow it?" Another student chimed in: "Are we going to have a program that teaches us how to make a buck, or turn this society upside down?" The Black professor responded, "We are not going to set up a separate university. After all, we are Americans."[94]

Education scholar Reginald Wilson endorsed the political mission of Black studies in a speech at Wayne State University in 1971. Black studies "must be seen" as a "direct attack against the cultural imperialism of white scholarship and the deliberate oppression by white educational institutions of Black youth," he declared. Anticipating the later critique of multiculturalism as depoliticizing, he declared, "*I do not*, therefore, perceive of Black studies like any other ethnic studies: that is, providing more background information, resurrecting the history of a neglected minority, making the educational experience more relevant to a particular subculture, and instilling pride in the members of that subculture. All of these things are fine *and* necessary, but they are not enough." In the end, Wilson saw "the real role of Black studies as nothing less than the revolutionizing of the American educational experience," and felt that "Black educators must see the school as the center for community action and a resource for effecting social change."[95]

But as the incorporation of Black studies took root, many scholars developed a more nuanced view of the relation between academic work and politics and began to pull back from the intense battles between Black nationalists, Marxists, and integrationists that had roiled many campuses. Roscoe Brown, the first director of the Institute of African American Affairs at New York University, felt that the question of whether Black studies should have an ideological mission had been a "major stumbling block in the development and analysis of black studies programs." He rejected the notion that Black studies could exist outside politics, since Black studies itself had forced the recognition that intellectual production had ideological content. He argued instead that it should not "espouse a specific ideology" such as integration or Black nationalism.[96]

Carlos Brossard at the University of Pittsburgh reported "strong interpersonal warfare around ideological differences and national backgrounds of Blacks," and identified the main binaries as Marxists versus Black nationalists, reformers versus revolutionaries, or academic-focused institution-builders versus community-oriented activist-types. In many respects, these differences were "healthy" and often productive for the growth of the discipline, but in some instances, he offered, they also "came with acrimony." Some left-leaning scholars came to see the incidence of nonpublishing cultural nationalists serving long reigns as department chairs as a sign of the intentional marginalization of the field. Yet at the same time, Nathan Hare resigned from the *Black Scholar* in the mid-1970s, complaining that the journal had been taken over by "instant Marxists" and that Black nationalists were getting insufficient exposure.[97]

These ideological conflicts intruded into the new journals and professional organizations for the field. At a meeting of the African Heritage Studies Association at Wayne State in the 1970s, Gerald McWorter, a Marxist sociologist and activist, presented "a sharp polemic against" Stokely Carmichael and poet Haki Madhubuti. He remembers the session as so heated and jam-packed that other sessions at the conference were cancelled. In the morning, McWorter debated Madhubuti, and in the afternoon, he debated Carmichael. It was "very intense," McWorter, now Abdul Alkalimat, remembers, and "kept going all day long." In his view, the key political question was: "Is the battle we face a fight against racism or is the battle a fight against imperialism?"[98] Alkalimat did not shy from ideological confrontation. A couple of years later, he organized a Chicago-based Illinois Council for Black Studies, and when in 1982 Illinois hosted the annual conference of the National Council of Black Studies, and Alkalimat won election to its board, the nationalist-dominated body challenged the tally and ultimately succeeded in keeping him off. To many this appeared unfair, and according to Rhett Jones, many scholars "abandoned organized Black Studies entirely, others left the national organization—now viewed as nationalist controlled—and concentrated their energies at the state level or on individual African-American Studies units."[99] Many worried that instead of being enriched by this ideological fervor, the new discipline had been weakened.

Gradually, as the demands of incorporation into the academy became felt, and as the cohort who fought for Black studies either moved on or were pushed out, the sense that Black studies was serving broader Black communities and remained committed to a broader political mission began to fade. This was not true everywhere, and it was an uneven process. Public universities in California experienced this shift in the most wrenching and acute way, as student and scholar activists on so many campuses were barred from organizing Black and Third World studies units. An ex-student dramatized it this way: "When we left, Black studies lost its political edge. It was taken over by either poverty pimp-type hustlers, or straight traditional academic types. Either way, that's not what we fought for."[100]

Several activists came to see Black studies units as structured to quell student militancy, with chairs caught in the cross fire between disappointed, militant students and the administration. Armstead Robinson, a leader of the struggle at Yale, felt the programs that were created were "the subverted products of what Black students were trying to produce after Martin Luther King died."[101] In the early 1970s, a journalist found "most black studies programs in California have settled into an uneasy but working relationship in the academic world," but "in the process, black studies lost most of its most strident supporters, many of whom now brand the programs as 'meaningless.'" Former Howard and San Francisco State professor Nathan Hare became a leading proponent of the idea that Black studies had failed to fulfill its mission. "As it is typically taught, black studies is not particularly relevant," he said. "It has to relate to everyday life, but instead it's the same old abstract kind of learning." He felt it should "express the ideology, goals and thought of the black struggle."[102] An assessment of the field in 1971 found that "many programs which grew out of struggles for 'autonomy' and 'nation-building' have already been sucked back fully into the dominating university structures."[103]

Student activist Jack Daniels had coauthored the widely circulated "Black Paper for Black Studies" a seventy-page prospectus for a School for Black Studies at the University of Pittsburgh, which advocated a unit deeply connected to the Black community, Black liberation, and nation building. But a few years later, after becoming a professor, he felt that "the great debate" between scholarship and activism was "stretching black studies' internal fibers to the breaking point." The political origins of Black studies were necessary, Professor Daniels now declared, but they had become an "albatross and must be removed from the neck of Black Studies." He argued that the discipline would ultimately rise or fall based not on its activist merits or profile but on its ability to mark out new intellectual terrain and produce compelling scholarship. "Black studies is indeed one of the most significant challenges ever presented to American colleges and universities." The critical need was not for a master plan, or new theories, or greater ideological warfare, but "basic research." There "simply cannot be viable Black studies instruction or viable Black studies community programs until viable basic research furnishes the data for instruction and application." He said the shortage of faculty was real, but that the only response was to develop more. "New trails must be blazed. . . . Intellectual and spiritual giants have preceded us," he declared, "and we must heed their legacies." He advocated abandoning the ever present reactive stance—we all know the limitations of white scholarship, he said; now we must become the agenda setters, forget Moynihan, Glazer, and the like, and make ourselves the new experts.[104]

As they continued the effort to give meaning to Black studies, scholars also focused on institution building in order to ensure the field's survival. Documenting the rise of the field was part of this impulse. An influential early effort was Nick Aaron Ford's *Black Studies: Threat or Challenge*, published in 1973. His attention to white and Black campuses and selection of two-year community colleges, as well as elite four-year institutions, as case studies conveyed the breadth of the movement and its extensive national impact. He collected data on more than two hundred programs, identified seven major objectives for Black studies, and argued that it was a "threat" in that it challenged racist education and scholarship. Additionally, Ford's insistence on the long history of Black scholarship and his discussion of such pioneering scholars as historian and sociologist W.E.B. Du Bois, historian Carter G. Woodson, sociologist Charles E. Johnson, sociologist E. Franklin Frazier, historian Benjamin Quarles, philosopher Alain Locke, and others helped to raise awareness among a new generation that Black studies was by no means "new," and that it in fact rested on a few generations of Black scholarship.[105] Ford found that most instructors in Black studies programs were without rank or tenure, but another study ten years later found marked improvement in both indices.[106] Since its creation, there have been numerous efforts to measure the size of the emerging discipline, with varying estimates of the number of Black studies centers, programs, and departments. In 1974 *Black Scholar* editor and historian Robert L. Allen reported that the five hundred colleges that had provided full-scale Black studies programs three years earlier had dropped to two hundred. A survey of the field conducted in 1983 found that, "at its zenith, the number of programs and departments reached no more than 300 formally organized units."[107] A 1995 article declared the existence of seven hundred ethnic studies programs in the United States. Numerous other tabulations and surveys have been done and continue to pour forth.

A professional structure for African American studies was emerging, exemplified by the formation of the National Council of Black Studies (NCBS) in 1975. The NCBS originated from the efforts of faculty in North Carolina, under the leadership of Bertha Maxwell, a rare female leader in the early Black studies movement. They endeavored to form a national body and had a series of organizational meetings in Atlanta, Boulder, Columbus, and Princeton. Another stream of activity that ultimately flowed into the NCBS emerged from a group of Black studies directors who first met at a conference Rossyln, Virginia, in 1972 and subsequently formed their group into the National Africana Accreditation and Review Panel. The program for the first NCBS conference in 1977 showed the preoccupation in the early years with professionalization and gaining legitimacy, rather than scholarship, which was the focus of only one session at the weekend event. Other sessions at the conference were titled "The Case for and against the Standardization of Black Studies," "Evaluating Black Studies Programs: Establishing the Critical Ground Rules," and "Building a Black United Front: Black Studies and the Black Community." Illustrating the continuing male face of the field, the program listed seventy-two male speakers and sixteen women. In line with an emerging consensus among scholars, the NCBS took the official position that departmental status was the preferred structure for African American studies and urged other units "to establish the long-range goal of achieving departmental status." Indeed, more than twenty-five years later, the Afro-American studies program at Yale, which was often touted in the 1970s as a success compared to that of Harvard, achieved departmental status.[108]

Reflecting the new ethos of self-determination and racial solidarity, this period in U.S. history saw a rapid proliferation of Black professional organizations, and academia helped lead the way. Black caucuses formed in the traditional disciplines would play a major role in opening up opportunities and visibility for scholars of color. The National Conference of Black Political Scientists was formed in 1969 at Southern University, the largest public HBCU in the country. The Association of Black Sociologists was founded in 1970 as the Caucus of Black Sociologists. The Association of Black Psychologists was founded in San Francisco in 1968 and consists of professionals rather than academics, but its goals and ethos very much reflect the era's fusion of Black nationalist politics and professional commitments. The mission statement of the Association of Black Anthropologists, formed in 1970, continues to embody the transformative effects of Black studies movement. In 2010 the Association's Web site declared that the Association "will achieve its mission by ensuring that people studied by anthropologists are not only objects of study but active makers and/or participants in their own history. We intend to highlight situations of exploitation, oppression and discrimination. Further it is our objective to analyze and critique social science theories that misrepresent the reality of exploited groups while at the same time construct more adequate theories to interpret the dynamics of oppression." This mission expresses a strong critique of the history of anthropology in the United States and a reformulation of its mission.[109]

To be sure, the professional organization of Black scholars began well before the 1960s. The Association for the Study of Negro Life and History had been founded in 1915, and its *Journal of Negro History* and annual conferences greatly enhanced the development of scholarly collaboration and networking in the new discipline. Moreover, the College Language Association, an organization of Black college teachers of English and foreign languages, had been founded in 1937. A host of journals appeared in the 1970s to help anchor the field, including *The Black Scholar*, the *Western Journal of Black Studies*, and the *Journal of Black Studies*. These joined older journals from the long and thriving history of Black scholarship, such as the *Journal of Negro History*, *Phylon*, and the *Journal of Negro Education*. Throughout the 1970s and 1980s the *Journal of Negro Education* was indispensable to documenting the growth of Black studies and publishing a variety of perspectives on its organization and mission.

In sum, as the focus shifted from Black students to Black scholars in the making of African American studies, new styles, visions, and sensibilities took root. A cohort of Black faculty emerged after the building takeovers and sit-ins, and they fought to create Black studies in keeping with the vision, to some extent, of student activists. But it was not easy.

These scholars faced administrative opposition, student pressure, and professional obligations. Unexpectedly, the seemingly never-ending battle of incorporation absorbed and drained the political energies of Black studies faculty, distracting attention from community leadership and other types of political engagement that Black student leaders had once envisioned as central to the project. As the years passed, new political tensions and debates emerged within the professional orbit of Black studies as scholars sought to figure out the best way to ease the battles, gain resources and personnel, and most important, win respect and recognition.

CHAPTER 7

The Black Revolution
Off-Campus

The Black student and Black studies movements were enormously influential on American campuses, but to what extent did they affect Black
communities and the broader American society? The rhetoric of these
movements was suffused with promises to bridge the gap between town
and gown, but did their leaders follow through on these commitments?
The belief that knowledge of African and African American history and
culture would empower Black people and Black communities had
gained popularity in the late 1960s and shaped many activist initiatives.
Off-campus initiatives demonstrated the popularity of the idea that
Black-controlled education, such as television documentaries, community-
based schooling, or radical think tanks, would transform African American life. Moreover, in spite of its image of orthodoxy, Black nationalism gave rise to a range of perspectives and forms: international and
local, class conscious, and Afrocentric.

In a remarkable project that gave ordinary Americans access to the
Black history courses beginning to be offered on college campuses, Vincent Harding, William Strickland, and John Henrik Clarke organized
the production of a televised series of lectures called *Black Heritage:
A History of Afro-Americans*. These men personally bridged the gap
between scholarship and activism, as all were educators who became
actively involved in the Black liberation struggle. A specialist in African
American history and close coworker of Martin Luther King Jr.,
Harding chaired the history department at Spelman College in Atlanta.

FIGURE 18. Legendary Harlem historian John Henrik Clarke.

A self-educated intellectual and legend in Harlem, Dr. Clarke dedicated his life to reversing racist depictions of Africa and served as the first chairman of the Department of Black and Puerto Rican Studies at Hunter College in Manhattan. A veteran of the northern student movement, Bill Strickland later taught political science in the Department of Afro-American Studies at the University of Massachusetts. He and Harding were also founders of the Institute of the Black World, in Atlanta in 1969, described later in this chapter.

A series of 108 thirty-minute lectures that ran for eighteen weeks, *Black Heritage* began with Dr. Clarke lecturing on ancient African civilizations and concluded with Dr. Harding and James Forman discussing the relation of the African American freedom struggle to the formerly colonized nations of Africa, Asia, and Latin America. A distinguished roster of scholars, including St. Clair Drake, Benjamin Quarles, Horace Mann Bond, Sterling Stuckey, Toni Cade, Edgar Toppin, Lerone Bennett, C. Eric Lincoln, James Shenton, Robert Browne, and Gerald McWorter, offered lectures on wide-ranging aspects of Black life, labor, culture, and politics mostly, but not exclusively, in the United States. Mirroring a college semester, the series began on WCBS-TV in January 1969 and concluded in May, airing six days a week. The broadcast times posed a challenge for workaday audiences in this era before the advent of television recording devices. Even the *New York Times* television critic deemed the 9 A.M. slot "inconvenient" and the 7:30 slot on Saturday mornings "insulting." But untold thousands of viewers managed to watch the series and loved it. In the opening telecast, Harding, whom the *Times* critic described as "almost hypnotic because of the passion and commitment he brought to his subject," spoke "on the importance of Negroes' understanding their past if they are to cope with their present and shape their future." "For a white viewer," the critic wrote, "Professor Harding effortlessly achieved his central point. His lecture was indeed a new perspective on history and an exciting one at that."[1] Interestingly, the program's name meant that mainstream publications such as the *Times* would have to print nomenclature other than "Negro" on a fairly regular basis.

Hundreds of viewers sent letters or postcards expressing their feelings about the show or asking for a copy of its syllabus, the availability of which Vincent Harding had announced. Probably owing to the show's broadcast time, many letters came from housewives and retirees. As early as January, an official at WCBS wrote to Harding: "This program has prompted quite a response—such as transcript requests, favorable comments, requests for time change, etc." Some letters were from crotchety white viewers, but most were from admirers. The president of the Black student organization at New York University wrote to the university's president asking him to purchase the entire series for use in the classroom, and copied Vincent Harding. The boxer Archie Moore wrote to Harding: "I think you're the greatest teacher I ever heard on Black history." "Every day since you began the lecture series on Black Heritage," wrote John Rosenthal, a teacher at Trenton Central High School in New Jersey, "we have been watching your program. We are using it as part of our class work on Black history." The manager of a television station in Hartford, Connecticut, wanted to run it there. "Let me support in the strongest possible terms the broadcasting of this series in our area," he wrote, testifying to the show's high quality. "The programs thus far have been extremely interesting, and the entire series promises to be lively as well as informative. I am sure they will be of considerable appeal."[2]

In Vincent Harding's view the program's greatest contribution "was showing these beautiful, gifted human beings" to the world. *Black Heritage* "opened up to the country, to the academy and the non-academy, the human resources that were available for the telling of the story of the African American community. . . . A lot of people were very moved by this, especially in the Black community." Another benefit was more professional. Many leading scholars had expressed doubt that it would be possible to establish African American studies at the graduate level, claiming there was insufficient scholarly material. In Harding's view, "These folks provide testimony to the fact that this was not true."[3]

Nonetheless, the series quickly became enmeshed in two political struggles, one material and the other ideological. The first had to do with behind-the-scenes personnel. This era saw the rise of Black public affairs television shows—programs like *Say Brother, Soul, Black Journal, Black Perspective,* and *Like It Is*—which surfaced nationally in the wake of urban uprisings, the criticism of journalistic practices by the Kerner Commission, and mandates by the Federal Communications Commission.[4] In addition to diversifying the airwaves and bringing Black perspectives to television content, the creators of these shows hoped they would integrate television workplaces as well. Harding and his colleagues wanted *Black Heritage* to have Black workers behind the camera, Black spectators in the screening audiences, and Black publicists spreading the word; but as it turned out, this vision entailed a fight. On January 2, Harding, Clarke, and Strickland issued a "Statement of the Black Members of the Advisory Committee of *Black Heritage*" to Columbia University and WCBS-TV. Like the students on their campuses, the professors issued a series of demands, including a call for a Black cameraman for every lecture and the retention of a Black-owned public relations firm, and vowed production would be halted until the demands were met. And a few days later, they were.[5] Over the summer, eighty-three CBS affiliates picked up *Black Heritage,* including WBBM in Chicago, which aired it at six in the morning. The press announcement illustrated the success of the protest as it emphasized that the show was written, presented, and produced by Black people, and listed various behind-the-scenes positions staffed by Black talent, including those of stage manager, producer, visual researcher, and set designer.[6]

Black Heritage showcased the many intellectual and political perspectives that inspired and shaped the Black studies movement: Pan-Africanist, Black nationalist, Marxist, and liberal traditionalist, among others.[7] These perspectives were deeply rooted in African American scholarship, as, for example, the many turns in the life and letters of W.E.B. Du Bois illustrates. But such rich and diverse perspectives were likely new to a general American audience. The views in *Black Heritage* complicated, for example, Gunnar Myrdal's more optimistic portrayal of America's creed, found in his best-selling 1944 expose of racial inequality, the *American Dilemma*. Moreover, the series did not portray a triumphalist narrative of race relations with seemingly inexorable progress, as the State Department's cold war cultural programs were wont to do.[8] *Black Heritage* emphasized instead the centrality of racism and slavery to the United States; but even more important, it highlighted the many forms of African American resistance and cultural creativity and resilience.

Ever since the Black studies movement had begun in earnest in the 1960s, integrationist leader Roy Wilkins had resisted it, and *Black Heritage* raised his ire. In a vituperative attack first sent to the president of CBS and later printed in the *New York Times*, Wilkins, the executive director of the National Association for the Advancement of Colored People, assailed the show for trying to foist one viewpoint, "that of the so-called Black Revolution—upon viewers and the nation." Decrying the attention to the Marcus Garvey movement, which Wilkins termed "non-history" intended to suit "the present-day propagandists for Black Separatism," he was especially piqued at what he felt was scant attention to the history of his own organization. To a degree, Wilkins was right that scholars had often failed to acknowledge the many contributions of the NAACP, especially the branches, but still, the NAACP and Wilkins were more regularly consulted by government leaders, and more frequently praised in the mainstream media, than any other Black American leaders, making his strident response and attempt to block the distribution of the series all the more troubling. The prospect of CBS marketing the series to schools was, in Wilkins's view, "catastrophic" and "appalling." "If CBS participates further in what is far more of a sinister masquerade than has been indicated in this letter," he warned ominously, "it cannot escape culpability—regardless of the smoothness of its rationalization—for a share in the inevitable and highly destructive confusions and conflicts in our future national life."[9]

In a response published in the *New York Times,* John Henrik Clarke reminded readers that "we promised to take a bold new look at the impact of African people on world history." Clarke's tone was much more restrained; still, he endeavored to correct what he saw as errors and misrepresentations in Wilkins's description of *Black Heritage.* He defended the program's attention to Garveyism, Malcolm X, and other Black nationalists and highlighted the distinguished scholarship and intellectual diversity of the many lecturers. "The show was directed, produced and coordinated by Afro-American personnel," he emphasized, wishing Wilkins had acknowledged this. It "represented for the first time, black people being responsible for the content and production of an entire television series."[10] In retrospect, Wilkins's alarmist predictions clearly come across as exaggerated. How do we make sense of such a reaction from a prominent African American leader to such a highly acclaimed show? As already noted, Wilkins saw the rise of Black studies, fairly or not, as a threat to the NAACP's long support for educational integration. Additionally, perhaps the elder statesman was feeling pushed aside. One result of the domestic anticommunist movement had been to suppress more radical Black voices and elevate the NAACP as the exclusive political voice for Black America. This arrangement had begun to unravel during the rise of direct-action protest in the South and continued to unravel in the 1960s. By 1969, Wilkins was losing the battle to maintain exclusive control over the racial narrative in the United States, and new, younger voices in the NAACP had also emerged, offering more supportive words to the Black student movement and its many achievements.

Black Heritage powerfully illustrates that the quest for Black intellectual authority did not produce a monolithic Black perspective, notwithstanding Wilkins's characterization. But this diversity did not yet include gender or sexuality. A handful of women appeared in the series, including Toni Cade, Barbara Ann Teer, Joanne Grant, and Betty Shabazz, but the lecturers were overwhelmingly male. References to the experiences of Black women are included in many of the lectures, but African American women's history, literature, and culture as categories of their own are not. In many respects, the series illuminates the state of the field on the eve of Black feminism, before many of its insights and approaches had arisen to powerfully reshape scholarship. But to be sure, the omission also reflects the choice of many Black male scholars to cultivate an intellectual movement led largely by men.

A nice contrast emerged at Ohio State University in the 1970s, where for several years a Black woman, Mary Ann Williams, an associate professor of theater and communications in the Black studies department, hosted a weekly television show called AFROMATION, as well as a weekly radio show, *The Black Studies Broadcast Journal.* Both were aired on the campus station WOSU, and a few of the radio shows were aired by National Public Radio. The shows featured leading Black political, intellectual, and cultural figures in the region and the nation, and showcased the works of prominent Black artists and entertainers. They brought together the Black arts movement and Black studies movement, as well as urban political struggles of the 1970s.[11] Mary Ann Williams was not the only Black studies educator to use the public airwaves to promote broader transmission of Black thought and culture. Tuskegee airman and Bronx Community College president Roscoe Brown ran a radio program out of the Institute of African American Affairs at New York University and hosted several Black public affairs television programs in New York over many decades.

Other initiatives in this era also asserted and publicized Black intellectual and cultural achievements. The Black studies movement made this possible, even necessary. In 1969, fifty leading Black scholars, writers, and artists founded the Black Academy of Arts and Letters with a three-year grant from the Twenty-First Century Foundation, a pioneering Black philanthropy established by the visionary economist Robert S. Browne. They declared themselves in the tradition of the venerable turn-of-the-century American Negro Academy. During its short, roughly four-year life span, the officers and inductees of the BAAL constituted a who's who of Black America. Founders included Romare Bearden, John Henrik Clarke, Ossie Davis, Duke Ellington, John Hope Franklin, Benjamin Mays, John Killens, Martin Kilson, Sidney Poitier, Frederick O'Neal, Charles Wesley, Charles White, Lawrence Reddick, Gordon Parks, Lloyd Richards, Jean Hutson, Arna Bontemps, Lerone Bennett, St. Clair Drake, Alex Haley, and Paul Robeson. Its first president, the historian C. Eric Lincoln, described its mission as fostering "the arts and letters of black people" and securing "public recognition of their achievements by blacks and whites." Exemplifying the ideals of institution building, self-determination, and pride in Black culture, the BAAL, according to Lincoln, "is concrete evidence that black people . . . achieve at high levels."[12]

In his founding address, "The Excellence of Soul," Lincoln said the BAAL "exists as a symbol of the love and concern we have for our children. I intend no cheap and shallow ethnocentric rhetoric when I say that we are a great people." The American public, and specifically the academy, he insisted, should recognize the full range of Black contributions to the history of the United States. "In the long span of Black history in America, were there only Douglass, Washington and King? To name a hundred chairs for Martin Luther King is to be contemptuous of the people King gave his life to have recognized. Why are there no Charles Drew or Daniel Hale Williams chairs in medicine? Why no E. Franklin Frazier or Charles S. Johnson chairs in sociology? When will there be a Lewis Latimer chair in physics? When will we have Langston Hughes fellowships? Ira Aldridge fellowships? Augusta Savage fellowships? Granville Woods fellowships?"[13]

Beginning in 1970, the BAAL hosted annual award ceremonies that served to promote intergenerational affinity among Black artists and scholars at a time when the radicalization of Black politics and culture had raised tensions. The awards also embraced intellectual and artistic icons who had been targets of government persecution during the McCarthy era. Prominent radicals were honored in a way that would have been impossible even a decade earlier. At the 1970 ceremony hosted by Harry Belafonte at a downtown hotel, the BAAL enrolled W.E.B. Du Bois, Carter G. Woodson, and Henry O. Tanner in its Hall of Fame. Woodson was a Harvard-trained historian who founded the Association for the Study of Negro Life and History (later renamed the Association for the Study of Afro-American Life and History), the *Journal of Negro History,* and Black History Week. In his acceptance speech for Woodson, the current president of the Association for the Study of Negro Life and History announced that the name would soon be changed from *Negro* to *Black.* Sadie Tanner Mossell, the first African American woman to earn a PhD in the United States, accepted the award in behalf of her uncle, the renowned painter Henry Tanner. Du Bois was the dean of Black intellectuals, the first Black recipient of a PhD from Harvard, and a founder of the NAACP who moved to the left and was prosecuted by the U.S. government in 1950 for being an agent of a foreign power after he circulated the Stockholm Peace Appeal. He was acquitted, but in growing disillusion he formally joined the Communist Party and emigrated to Ghana, where he passed away in 1963.[14]

For their contribution to arts and letters, the BAAL gave awards to Lena Horne and C.L.R. James, who had both suffered under McCarthyism. A Trinidadian-born journalist, novelist, historian, anticolonial agitator, and Marxist theorist, James was deported as a foreign-born subversive in the 1950s. Black college students came to know him as the author of the landmark *The Black Jacobins: Toussaint L'Ouverture and the San Domingo Revolution,* an account of the Haitian Revolution. Many radical thinkers or activists from other countries had been barred from entering the United States since the 1950s, but the easing of these restrictions by the late 1960s and early 1970s, and the creation of academic positions as a result of the emergence of Black studies programs, enabled many overseas intellectuals and activists to work and speak in the United States. James was able to return to the United States to teach at Northwestern and Federal City College. The BAAL also gave an award to Paul Robeson for his "outstanding contribution" to the Black experience. Robeson would pass away in 1976. At one time he had been one of the most famous Americans in the world. A revered athlete, actor, activist, and singer, his move to labor-based radicalism and support for communist positions cost him his career, fame, and fortune. Paul Robeson Jr. accepted on behalf of his father, and the press release declared: "The bestowing of the award by the Black Academy to his father marked the lifting of the curtain of silence which had been dropped around Robeson by major communication media following his strong position on the Korean war and other issues facing black people."[15]

Despite the BAAL's attempt to overcome the legacy of the anticommunist crusade, the government did not cooperate. Shirley Graham Du Bois had been invited to accept the award for her late spouse. She still resided in Ghana and had become a Ghanaian citizen. The State Department actually issued her a visa, but the Justice Department blocked it, claiming she belonged to thirty subversive organizations. The BAAL organized an all-out effort to get the visa and strategically gained the support of prominent liberals Roy Wilkins and Charlie Rangel. They prevailed, and Graham Du Bois was permitted to return to the United States and accept the award for her husband. The BAAL successfully pushed the Justice Department to reverse its stance. While she was in the country, Graham Du Bois visited the University of Massachusetts and spoke as a guest of the W.E.B. Du Bois Department of Afro-American Studies.[16]

In recognition of younger artists, Diana Sands and Leroi Jones were given awards. Jones, soon to change his name to Amiri Baraka, challenged the Black academy to embrace liberation for Black people everywhere and to challenge the "art for art's sake" notion. In the keynote address, Mayor Richard Hatcher of Gary, Indiana, declared: "When we say Black culture, we are not talking about a culture which is racist and reactionary, which seals off Black society from the rest of the nation, which glorifies in separatism or wants to return to Africa. We are talking about a culture which encourages, develops, subsidizes and pays attention to itself, which takes pride in its color and its past, which rids itself of self-hate and self-doubt, which does not mirror and ape a white society, especially the worst of it. When we struggle to liberate ourselves, we have the opportunity to liberate all America."[17]

The second banquet in 1971 showed the continuing growth of the Black Academy and its ideals. More than a thousand people attended the ceremony at the Waldorf Astoria, which was hosted by Ossie Davis and filmed by a cable television channel. Frederick Douglass, Ira Aldridge, and George Washington Williams were inducted into the Hall of Fame. Fred Weaver, the great-grandson of Douglass, and Major Ira Aldrige, the great-grandson of Aldridge, accepted the awards. Katherine Dunham, Gwendolyn Brooks, and Duke Ellington were honored for their lifelong contributions to arts and letters. Four writers each won five hundred dollars, including Mari Evans, a Black-arts-movement poet and author of the highly acclaimed book *I Am a Black Woman;* and the historian Franklin Knight, for his book *Slave Society in Cuba.* George Jackson, an activist prison inmate who had been slain a month earlier in the San Quentin prison, won for distinguished nonfiction for *Soledad Brother.* His mother, Mrs. Georgia Jackson, accepted in his behalf.[18] The BAAL appears to have dissolved within a couple of years, but its efforts to formally bestow Black recognition on Black literary, artistic, and scholarly achievement was an important sign of the broader impact of the Black studies and Black arts movements.

A movement to create independent Black institutions, mostly primary schools, arose during the Black Power era alongside the Black studies movement. The goal of these schools was to create Black educational independence and self-determination in an Africa-centered framework and to shape and cultivate the next generation of leaders. Many of these educational initiatives did not survive the 1970s, but a few continued for decades, most notably the Institute of Positive Education/ New Concept School in Chicago, founded by Carol Lee and Haki Madhubuti. More recently, several independent Black institutions have become publicly funded charter schools. One remarkable project, the Nairobi Schools, was launched in East Palo Alto, California, and spanned from preschool to junior college. It was the only independent Black school system in the United States. It enters our story because

Nairobi included a college—which was in many ways a by-product of the Black student movement—and because the whole project was sustained by the same educational milieu that inspired Black studies. The Nairobi school system originated in local activists' disaffection with integration, and it later expanded after the expulsions of protesting Black and Mexican American students from nearby high schools and colleges. It embodied the Black nationalist fervor and movement energy of the era.

"We are pioneering a brand-new way for black folks," said founder Gertrude Wilks.[19] East Palo Alto was an unincorporated community across the freeway from Palo Alto, the affluent home of Stanford University. By the late 1960s, it had become predominantly African American, and activists sponsored a ballot referendum in 1968 to change the town's name to Nairobi, but it failed. Still, a vibrant independent Black schooling movement proudly carried this name of the Kenyan capital, and East Palo Alto would become an emblem of the quest for Black self-determination throughout the 1970s and beyond. Community activist Gertrude Wilks and educators Mary and Bob Hoover were founders of Nairobi. Wilks's daughter had encountered racial slurs and threats of violence in a Palo Alto school, so Wilks's decision to begin an alternative school, literally in her home, stemmed from a mother's desire to protect her child from hostility and ensure that she was nurtured in the classroom. For the Hoovers, the impetus was more philosophical and political. Bob Hoover was a former activist with the Student Non-Violent Coordinating Committee who ran the College Readiness Program at the College of San Mateo, a public two-year school. Mary Hoover was a language specialist who developed an innovative adult literacy curriculum, as well as culturally affirming educational materials for African American children. Her work would infuse the curriculum at Nairobi.

Activists in East Palo Alto were influenced by the critique of integration advanced by SNCC, especially by Stokely Carmichael. In the mid-1960s, Carmichael came to town and attended a meeting of education activists who were discussing strategies to integrate the local high schools. At the end of the meeting, Bob Hoover recalls, Stokely finally spoke. "I don't understand," he began, "why you would be working this hard to send your children's minds to be educated by people who have oppressed you for four hundred years." And "It just hit me," says Hoover, who had been operating in the civil rights mainstream: "we need to be educating our own children."[20] In the aftermath, many leaders in

East Palo Alto began to shift their focus away from integration and toward gaining independence and control of both the schools and the local governance structures.

Founded in 1966, the Nairobi Schools evolved into an elementary school, high school, and two-year college by 1969. Incorporating both volunteer teachers and, eventually, a paid staff, the Nairobi Schools educated five hundred students five days a week for a decade. "The college students taught high school students, and the high school students taught the little ones in the park," Wilks remembers. In addition to the impetus to develop Black-controlled institutions, there was a strong desire to create upper schools to educate politically active youth who had been expelled or suspended from mainstream schools. The first students in Nairobi High School were the ones "catching all kinds of hell" in the regular schools. They were "either going to jail, being kicked out of school, or being harassed by teachers, administration, white students, and everybody else." George Murray, the former Black Panther minister of education and San Francisco State strike leader, who had entered Stanford as a graduate student after his release from jail, was the first principal of Nairobi High School. He recruited several Stanford students as teachers and "molded that staff into one beautifully functioning unit." There were twenty-five students the first year, and two graduates entered Pitzer, one of the Claremont Colleges in California.[21]

Robert Hoover founded and became president of Nairobi College in 1969 after having been fired from San Mateo Junior College. "We had a sit-in inside the administration building and closed it down. A number of our kids got arrested and went to jail. They fired me," he says, and another professor in the College Readiness Program resigned. "When we left, most of the students left" as well, becoming the basis for the student body at Nairobi College.[22] Other independent Black institutions, notably Malcolm X Liberation University in Durham, North Carolina, and Jimmy Garrett's Center for Black Education in Washington, D.C., also attracted students and teachers who had been expelled from college because of their movement activism, or who had voluntarily left. Nairobi College began with 120 students and twenty-five faculty volunteers teaching math, English, history, electronics, journalism, political science, and Swahili. "A mixture of the routine and the radical," one observer noted.[23]

According to Hoover, the "curriculum was a collective effort" that emphasized the importance of developing leadership and having control over your own destiny. Stanford graduate student and future literary scholar Robert O'Meally taught a course at Nairobi. Dr. Mary Hoover, who later taught at Howard and advised the Oakland School District on the use of Ebonics, created Nairobi's English department. "To this day," Bob Hoover contends, "some of the best vehicles for teaching people to read and write were developed at Nairobi College."[24] Like other Black educational institutions, Nairobi adopted rituals that celebrated both African and African American culture and history. School holidays included Nigerian Independence Day on October 1, the founding of the Black Panther Party on October 17, Rosa Parks's resistance to segregation on December 1, Ghanaian Independence on March 6, and Malcolm X's birthday on May 19. Of course, Kwanzaa was celebrated from December 25 to January 1.[25]

Nairobi strove to institutionalize the ethic of student involvement and governance that animated the campus revolts. Just as the incorporation of student rights in the founding of Malcolm X College in Chicago showed, Black student activists fully shared in the generational challenges and youth assertions of the era. According to Bob Hoover, "The students really run the school." They interviewed and hired staff and sat on the board of directors.[26] Also on the board were citizens of East Palo Alto; and cementing the exchange, Nairobi students had work-study jobs in the community. In this way, the college developed an interlocking relationship with town leaders. After a couple of years as president of Nairobi College, Hoover turned it over to Donald Smothers, a twenty-six-year-old graduate of San Francisco State, who had been one of Hoover's students at the College of San Mateo. In fact, eight faculty or staff at Nairobi College had once been part of the College Readiness Program at the College of San Mateo, testifying to the strong bonds Hoover had cultivated with the original cohort of Nairobi student-founders.[27]

As the ideal of self-determination took root, the relationship between Black initiatives and white funding and control was increasingly scrutinized. As we have seen, the Black studies directors' conference at Aspen, which was sponsored by the Ford Foundation, gave rise to fierce debates about the role of white funding for Black studies. While the founders of Nairobi desired autonomy from white control, they did not necessarily reject white money—as long as they could spend it as they saw fit. There were two sources of financial support in the 1970s that helped to enable Nairobi's longevity and success: a white heiress and the federal government. A member of the Colgate family had supported the College Readiness Program at the College of San Mateo, and Hoover and his colleague Jean Wirth approached her to help launch Nairobi. She wrote a check for $30,000 that same day and agreed to contribute $120,000 overall for the first year of operations. "That's what got us started. A wealthy lady who wanted to help." Her contribution helped finance teacher salaries. That first pledge continued for the next decade. We "got Colgate money the whole time," Hoover said, a "$30,000 check every quarter," a rather stunning example of corporate-derived wealth redirected to Black community empowerment.[28]

When they were at San Mateo, Wirth and Hoover had designed a highly successful minority student recruitment and retention program, which they had been called upon to replicate at colleges in California and across the country. "As a result of our work, we had a lot of contact with the Department of Education"; and because of this, recalls Hoover, "we were able to get them to agree to provide financial aid to Nairobi College for the first year, even though we were not accredited." Even better, "this arrangement lasted the life of the college."[29] Nairobi students received a combination of federal funding, grants, and loans, including Equal Opportunity Grants, National Defense Student Loans, a work-study program, Talent Search, and Student Special Services, helping to explain the longevity of an independent Black school located in a cash-strapped working-class community.[30] In addition, the college's reputation and track record enabled Hoover to forge productive relationships with nearby colleges and universities. Stanford permitted Nairobi students to use its library and other campus facilities. San Jose State College and the Irvine and Berkeley campuses of University of California agreed to accept transfer students from Nairobi. And many students went on to study at Stanford University. "We were able to get them to agree to take our students even though we were not accredited." Nairobi administrators told the colleges "not to grant credit for their first semester, to wait and see if they could do the work," and they agreed.[31]

In contrast to the largely Black student population at the elementary and high schools, Nairobi college was a "Third World college," reflecting the mix of Black and Mexican American students who had attended Hoover's College Readiness Program at San Mateo. While signaling a genuine effort to forge unity among people of color, Third Worldism existed in some tension with the simultaneous current of Black cultural nationalism, and the Black and Chicano students soon went separate ways. The few whites involved in the early years of Nairobi, mostly as teachers, left too. In 1970, Nairobi activists opened a second campus, designed for Chicano students, in Redwood City, called Venceremos. It included courses on the Mexican revolution, Latin American politics, and people's theater, but the college closed after four years, in part because of lower support in the Mexican American community.[32] "We weren't ready for it," Hoover felt. "The leadership of the two communities was not together. Coalitions between peoples of color are still important," he insisted in 1972, "but the problems are not going to be solved anytime soon. Meanwhile, we have to remember our first priority [is] the [Black] community."[33]

Nairobi exemplified the manner in which the Black consciousness movement infused campus and community through the twin vehicles of education and the arts. The college was located in a majority Black community where the Black studies and Black arts movements flowered together. East Palo Alto in the 1960s and 1970s was the center of an independent Black political, economic, cultural, and educational movement. Nairobi ran many summer programs involving hundreds of children, many of whom ended up going to Nairobi College and pursuing careers in education. "We had a huge impact on the community," says Hoover. Nairobi became a magnet for Black people around the country who shared its philosophy, which focused on developing leaders in an Afrocentric framework. Every year while he remained in the United States, Stokely Carmichael visited Nairobi. "Stokely never got the credit I thought he was due," remarked Hoover, who called him "one of the most brilliant people I've ever met." The writer Alex Haley spent a month at Nairobi, giving lectures about the process of writing his novel *Roots*. An African dance troupe spent six months as artists-in-residence and performed all over California. Nairobi had an extraordinary choir. Many guest speakers came through, and local scholars gave Nairobi special attention. St. Clair Drake, the prominent sociologist and pioneer of African diaspora studies, was the first chair of the Department of African and African American Studies at Stanford. He spoke at Nairobi often, and Hoover would also take groups of children to visit him on campus, where he "told incredible stories." "I love St. Clair Drake," Hoover recalls, expressing an admiration shared by many in this generation.[34]

Nairobi was part of a small, nationwide, independent Black schooling movement inspired by ideologies of Pan-Africanism, nation building, and African communalism. The independent educational movement (in addition to some Black studies departments) became a leading location for the flowering of Black cultural nationalism in the 1970s, which articulated itself through conferences, journals, and other writings. Two conferences in 1970 helped to define the mission of independent Black institutions (IBIs); one took place on the West Coast, at Nairobi, and the other on the East Coast, at Uhuru Sasa School in Brooklyn. The conferences defined the mission of IBIs in three parts: "The IBI should project the concept of communalism, decolonization, humanism, harmony between the individual and his environment"; second, the IBI "should try to mold an individual with a new African personality," and third, the IBI should "teach subjects that relate to Black Nation building." In a sign of how far this vision could travel from the liberal arts world of academic Black studies, appropriate nation-building skills included plumbing, carpentry, engineering, first aid, and farming. A cohort of Black student radicals took the call for "relevance" in this pragmatic direction, rejecting the liberal arts orientation of Black studies and, in some instances, moving abroad to help build new African nation-states. In addition, the IBI mission reflected the impulse in Black nationalism toward personal renewal and rejection of the oppressive frameworks of a racist society. Yet at the same time, the search for an African personality or a Black nation gave rise, in some instances, to a mystical, patriarchal, or authoritarian turn.[35]

Hoover and other Nairobi leaders tended to emphasize the practical aims of their larger ideological mission. They made "a clear distinction between the nuts–and-bolts work of building self-sufficient communities and the theoretical abstractions of nation-building in the grand design," one observer noted in 1972. "A separate black country inside this country is not a real option," said Hoover, "but black communities are. They are a reality." Explaining Nairobi's approach, Hoover elaborated: "We're trying to rescue people, to give them direction, to bring back skills and expertise to our community. All the rhetoric about revolution, about change—it's no good if you don't know what you're after, and if a lot of talk is all you've got, you're not going anywhere."[36]

Owing to funding challenges, Nairobi College shut its doors in 1981. Like *Black Heritage,* it is a little-known but significant outgrowth of the Black student movement and helped to reshape racial identity and consciousness beyond the college campus. The Black studies movement influenced Black communities and American educational, political, cultural, and social life in unexpected ways. One such way was the rise of African American intellectuals as a source of assertive, highly visible race leadership. This was by no means new, as the decadeslong leadership of W. E. B. Du Bois and many others attests. But intellectuals had been somewhat eclipsed by the broad introduction of many new sources of leadership in the long civil rights era. The creation of Black studies units helped give greater status and authority, as well as more employment, to Black intellectuals. Moreover, the campus movement itself highlighted the political and public roles of scholars and academe more generally.

A group of activist Black intellectuals in Atlanta created the Institute of the Black World (IBW) in 1969. The IBW provided direction to the early Black studies movement and sought to promote radical Black intellectuals as broader race leaders and political advocates. The institute began as a series of conversations in 1967 between Morehouse literary scholar Stephen Henderson and Spelman historian Vincent Harding (of *Black Heritage* fame) in response to student demands that Negro colleges become more Black-oriented. They imagined the prospect of a W.E.B. Du Bois Institute for Advanced Afro-American Studies, perhaps at the Atlanta University Center, as a way to revive the activist intellectual tradition of Du Bois and strongly assert global consciousness in the rising Black studies movement. Joining Henderson and Harding in planning the activities and mission of the proposed institute were Gerald McWorter (later Abdul Alkalimat), A.B. Spelman, Council Taylor, and William Strickland.

McWorter—a graduate student in sociology at the University of Chicago, and an activist with both the Chicago Friends of SNCC and the Organization of Black American Culture—had grown up around "the Negro history movement and the Communist Party movement" in Chicago. One aunt, Eleanor Rye, was a leading activist in the Communist Party, and another, Thelma Wheaton Kirkpatrick, was one of the founders of the Du Sable Museum of African American History and Culture.[37] McWorter taught a course at Spelman and took part in a building takeover at Morehouse during a meeting of the board of trustees. "Black Unity in the Atlanta University Center" was the credo of student activists, and they envisioned transforming its five colleges into "the Martin Luther King University." Alkalimat was later "run out of Atlanta" for his role in the student protest.[38]

The assassination of Martin Luther King Jr. devastated the Atlanta community yet galvanized a new level of political mobilization and response. When Coretta Scott King approached Harding, a close friend and ally of Dr. King, to participate in a proposed King Memorial Center, he suggested housing the institute there. She was enthusiastic, and the institute began its career as part of the King Memorial Center. The desired affiliation with the colleges of Atlanta University never happened, and this prodded a search for a new name. According to Harding, their intention in choosing the name *Institute of the Black World* was to convey a focus on Black people globally, a rejection of individualism for collective struggle, and a commitment to gather not just academics but Black activists and artists as well.

The institute aspired to exert significant influence on the development of Black studies. It began with several assumptions: that the field was "still being born," that defining it was "a task and challenge for black people in America and elsewhere," that it should not be bound by traditional academic disciplines, and that "serious building" would take years, not weeks or months.[39] As one of its first events, the IBW hosted a Black Studies Directors' Seminar in November 1969, which attracted the heads of thirty-five programs from around the country. It "brought together people fighting the white academy from all over the country," Harding recalls. For the participants, it was like "coming home, refueling," a place to gain "understanding of the commonalities and differences" of their experiences. Lerone Bennett, whose recent article in *Ebony* highlighting the racism of Abraham Lincoln sparked intense debate, led off with a speech, "The Quest for Blackness," which called upon those gathered to "abandon the partial frame of reference of our oppressors and create new concepts which will release our reality, which is also the reality of the overwhelming majority of men and women on the globe."[40]

Other speakers reinforced this call for Black intellectual self-determination. For Bill Strickland, Black scholars had the obligation to "present an intellectual defense of the black community" and reverse the emphasis on black pathology and failure popularized in some white-authored texts—what he termed "the diseases of Jensenism, Styronism, Moynihanism." Armstead Robinson offered a critical appraisal of "white studies" and "western cultural imperialism" disguised as universalism, while Basil Matthews elaborated a multilayered definition of a "Black perspective," which he argued was at the heart of their intervention.[41] In Harding's view, the IBW's efforts in the early years of the Black studies movement emphasized three points that shaped debates as the field emerged, that Black studies units should be interdisciplinary, approach Black people in an international context, and connect to a broader community. He said they were constantly asking Black studies directors: "What is (your unit's) connection to the community?"[42]

The IBW hosted scholars in residence who taught seminars, conducted individual research, and participated in collective research projects of the institute, an initiative that a hundred-thousand-dollar Ford Foundation grant helped make possible. Ford described the IBW as "a small assem-

FIGURE 19. Two giants of Black scholarship: Vincent Harding and St. Clair Drake at a summer research symposium at the IBW in 1971.

bly of intellectuals who seek, through research and reflection, to define, elaborate and interpret the black experience."[43] In the fall of 1969, Lerone Bennett, Sterling Stuckey, Joyce Ladner, and William Strickland joined Harding and Henderson as research fellows. Ladner was the lone female in an enterprise that tended to elevate male voices and leadership throughout its duration. Harding acknowledges that, before he left in 1974, the institute did not take up the issue of Black feminism, and that women were more often present as staff members and community allies than as scholars.[44] The IBW welcomed radical, foreign-born scholars and in some instances help them get through the McCarthy-era immigration restrictions, which had previously made entry into the United States difficult. C.L.R James, the Trinidadian scholar, and Walter Rodney, the Guyanese historian and radical organizer, spent considerable time at the IBW. Jamaican historian Robert Hill, a specialist on Marcus Garvey and the Garvey movement internationally, was a fellow for two years and a key political theorist at the institute. The West Indian intellectuals brought a greater openness toward Marxism and

FIGURE 20. William Strickland, left, who brought sharp political analysis to the work of the IBW, and Walter Rodney, right, radical activist and author of the foundational text *How Europe Underdeveloped Africa.*

class analysis than was then prevalent among American-born Black intellectuals and activists. But the political crosscurrents moved in many directions: Stokely Carmichael and Walter Rodney helped bring ideas of Black Power, popular in the United States, to the Caribbean and West Indian communities in Canada. It is important to underscore that, at its inception, the Black studies movement in the United States embraced the study of the African diaspora, not just Black America, and embraced the insights and scholarship of Black scholars from around the world. And importantly, at the zenith of Black nationalism, the IBW helped to make these connections, and this worldliness, possible and concrete.

As the institute's mission and orbit of scholars and activists became clear, some King family members and friends expressed concern that the project was too Black-oriented. "Some among the King family and co-workers had not entered into the spirit of Black consciousness, the Black identity movement," recalls Harding.[45] Evidently, an invitation by

Harding to Stokely Carmichael to speak under IBW auspices at More-house in April 1970 "offended" members of the King Memorial Foundation Board.[46] Carmichael had popularized the idea of Black Power, a turn in the movement that Dr. King had lamented even as he remained in conversation and solidarity with Carmichael. And, as always, there were fund-raising concerns, which also had forestalled a formal affiliation with Atlanta University. In the summer of 1969 the board of directors of the King Memorial Center pressured the IBW to dismiss Alkalimat and Spelman from the summer project owing to their participation in the student "lock-in" at Morehouse.[47]

A year later, the board undertook an official review of the institute and raised three objections: that the IBW avoided the concept of non-violence; that it focused on the Black world rather than the life of Dr. King; and that it was committed to having only Black researchers.[48] The Federal Bureau of Investigation monitored this schism through a source who opposed the political activism of the IBW staff and Harding's approach to Black history.[49] Harding had often emphasized that "our most central purpose" was to work "as fully as we can towards Black control over the definition of the Black experience." "Our vision of America," Harding wrote in a report intended for the King Memorial Center's board, "leads us to believe that black people must be the vanguard for change if there is to be any hope for anyone." The opposition to Harding was sufficiently strong that the IBW left the King Memorial Center in the summer of 1970 and became independent.[50]

In the early 1970s the IBW shifted its focus somewhat toward political analysis. According to historian Manning Marable, who also passed through the IBW, "Hundreds of black intellectuals worked at the IBW offices or with its staff, from historian Mary Berry, formerly the head of the Education division of HEW, to former Communist Party member Harry Haywood."[51] While initially associated with the ideas generated in the Black Power upsurge of the late 1960s, the IBW came to embody a more far-reaching and class conscious Black radicalism. In a 1969 lecture, Harding defined "the movement from Negro to Black history as being parallel on political lines to the movement from integration into a call for decolonization and liberation."[52] In many respects, this description captures the expansive, but decidedly internationalist and radical, politics of the IBW. Vincent Harding left the IBW in 1974, and Howard Dodson assumed the directorship. Dodson first came to the IBW as a graduate student from Berkeley, where he had gone after having been inspired to study history after watching *Black Heritage*. Berkeley scholar Andrew Billingsley organized a contingent of graduate students, including Dodson, to join him for a year of research at the IBW, but after Billingsley was offered a position at Berkeley as dean, he stayed. Dodson nevertheless went to Atlanta, and it profoundly influenced his career trajectory.

The Federal Bureau of Investigation and other state and federal agencies had been subjecting Black activists and organizations to surveillance, harassment, disruption, and even assassination during the civil rights and Black liberation movements. As we have seen, the Black student movement had become a target of COINTELPRO, and through the IBW the radical Black studies movement became a target as well. Special agents routinely sent reports on IBW activities to Washington yet never alleged illegal behavior. One report noted that the IBW criticized the government but advocated working within the system "as opposed to violent revolutionary means."[53] Funding from the Ford Foundation during the first couple of years had enabled the IBW to operate as a research center and host visiting fellows. But according to Howard Dodson, the FBI began to interfere and the funding came to an end.[54] Funding was an ever-present dilemma for African American activists seeking any measure of autonomy in institution building, and the loss of funds dealt a major blow. Ironically, just as FBI repression was affecting his own organization, IBW associate Bill Strickland devoted considerable energy to documenting and publicizing government repression of Black radicals and the Black liberation movement as a whole.[55]

In 1975 the IBW faced an all-out assault. The office was burglarized three times—Harding called it "the Watergate type burglary of our office" because files were removed and searched.[56] An anti-Castro group claimed credit for the first two burglaries.[57] At that time, an IBW staff member headed the pro-Castro Venceremos Brigade in Atlanta. Moreover, staff members were subjected to dozens of harassing and threatening phone calls and letters, both at home and work. One letter described a twenty-five-thousand-dollar contract to a Cuban exile to kill the staff member's wife, while another letter to the office said, "We will blow mother fucking buildings up we mean business, You have until mid-April, Niggers will not rule America." Howard Dodson requested an FBI investigation, but they declined, saying the local police department could handle it.[58] The IBW staff suspected they had become targets of a broader campaign: their phones were tapped and the Internal Revenue Service audited the whole staff. Dodson urged the Congressional Black Caucus to investigate. "Black people are under attack throughout the nation," Harding noted.[59] The repression was devastating, but the dedicated group in Atlanta held on the best they could. The IBW survived for a few more years and continued to do significant educational work, but with a much-reduced budget and smaller staff.

In its heyday, the IBW offered a unique gathering space for a national network of Black scholars, activists, artists, and political leaders, and a model of Black intellectual life that was rooted in local struggles yet shaped by a global consciousness. The repression of the more radical and insurgent voices in the Black student–Black studies movements, whether through arrest, expulsion, dismissal, harassment, denial of funding, or other means, removed or silenced many of these people and their perspectives. In some cases this encouraged the growth of a narrower cultural nationalism, or more typically, the repression simply left a void.

It was not only scholars and intellectuals who endeavored to carry the campus struggle into the broader Black community. Many students graduated (or dropped out) of college and joined the movement full time. They emerged in the immediate post-Jim-Crow era, when antidiscrimination laws had been passed but poverty and racism continued, and activists faced new challenges in deciding how to define the continuing problem of inequality, frame the struggle, and maintain the momentum of the civil rights movement. Paradoxically, the 1970s bore the scars of COINTELPRO and continuing police repression of activists, yet gave rise to a new generation of radical organizations, which identified with a broad ideological spectrum, from Pan-Africanist to Marxist-Leninist. The youth who had been drawn to Malcolm X and Stokely Carmichael and the ideas of Black Power continued on a journey that took them in a range of ideological directions. They grappled with the growing class stratification of Black America and debated the continuing relevance and effectiveness of Black nationalism. According to Manning Marable, "Most of these early ideological debates occurred in an open and tolerant spirit," in part because many activists "were veterans of the Civil Rights movement and knew each other well." The quest for Black unity kept ideological cleavages in check and motivated cultural nationalists and Marxist-Leninists to work together in new organizations such as the African Liberation Support Committee and the Student Organization for Black Unity.[60] Black students graduated and left campus struggles behind, but they did not leave activism behind. For many, the student movement was the critical seedtime for decades of activism and community and civic leadership.

Nelson Johnson of Greensboro, North Carolina, exemplifies this journey. He gained renown during his college days as a community activist and student government leader at the historically Black North Carolina A&T. But Johnson was also a leading figure in the broader Greensboro community, involving himself in numerous struggles focused on housing, jobs, and education. He was at the founding convention, held at A&T in May 1969, of the Student Organization for Black Unity (SOBU, which became YOBU, the Youth Organization for Black Unity about a year later). SOBU's founding occurred amid widespread discontent among Black youth in Greensboro and dramatic political mobilization across the city's Black community. This local ferment made a powerful impression on the students who had gathered there from around the country, such as Edward Whitfield from Cornell (he was one of the armed student leaders photographed exiting Straight Hall after a protest in April 1969) and Mark Smith, a Harvard student involved in setting up the Department of Afro-American Studies.

Johnson was designated the first chairman of SOBU, and Smith, who had dropped out of Harvard to organize in the South, served as vice chairman. Cleveland Sellers, the former SNCC leader who had been shot in Orangeburg in 1968, became active in SOBU as he awaited trial for inciting a riot—the police riot, otherwise known as the Orangeburg Massacre. Indeed, he was not the only SOBU activist facing such a charge. During SOBU's first year, Johnson focused on staying out of jail, especially since his wife, Joyce, was pregnant with their first child. But he was tried, convicted, and given a long sentence for inciting a riot during the Dudley-A&T protests, even though the North Carolina State Advisory Committee to the U.S. Civil Rights Commission had just praised the A&T students for coming to the aid of the beleaguered Dudley students. Moreover, with blatant prejudice, the legislature hastily changed sentencing guidelines to lengthen Johnson's sentence. But Black leaders in Greensboro pushed back and successfully appealed to the governor for clemency, and Johnson was released after serving two months.

SOBU wanted to channel the activist energy of Black students into the community and organize on the grassroots level, as SNCC had done. But times had changed. "When the decade of the 1970s opened," Johnson recalls, "I had very little historical perspective. I thought the sixties were normal, and that we would continue to build ever bigger mass movements for social change."[61] In Mark Smith's view, SOBU "adopted the philosophy that the way to organize people was in doing things with them, or for them, rather than the Alinsky-type model of finding an enemy and mobilizing around them."[62] Because de jure segregation had been defeated, he felt, they no longer faced a clear target such as disenfranchisement or whites-only establishments. Complicating SOBU's relationship to local communities was its ideology of Pan-Africanism. "Pan-Africanism was the dominant ideology within SOBU and YOBU," according to Johnson. "It holds that the liberation of blacks in America is impossible without first liberating Africa, black people are a world community without national or class differences, and the enemy is white people—all white people."[63] Much of this new interest in Africa came from supporting contemporary struggles against white settler regimes in South Africa and Zimbabwe and Portuguese colonial rule in Angola, Guinea-Bissau, and Mozambique. SOBU's newspaper was called the *African World* and gave extensive coverage to current events in Africa as well as solidarity efforts in the diaspora. In fact many SOBU leaders played key roles in making the first African Liberation Day parade in 1972 a major success.

SOBU promoted a seemingly paradoxical blend of revolutionary analysis and concrete, practical training. According to Mark Smith, Pan-Africanism "had a self-help component to it, which resulted in people doing schools, clinics, and farms. Malcolm X Liberation University was training people to repair tractors that they were going to go to Tanzania to work on, and that kind of stuff."[64] Yet SOBU wanted to transform African American students into revolutionaries. They complained that most Black students spent too much time "rapping," while "our enemy continues to build underground police stations, ship and store nerve gas[,] . . . build detention centers, expand economic control of African resources, manipulate and start wars (Nigerian civil war) and enslave Africans (Southern Africa)." SOBU advocated the development of technical skills to help defeat European colonial and imperial powers and rebuild the African world. *"Pan-Africanism is not an idea to think about,"* they declared. *"It is work that needs to be done."*[65]

SOBU focused considerable attention on supporting independent Black schools, particularly the Center for Black Education, which had been organized by Jimmy Garrett, Federal City College students, and former SNCC activists in Washington, D.C.; and Malcolm X Liberation University, in Greensboro, which had begun its life in Durham as a result of efforts by former Duke students and a charismatic activist from Milwaukee, Howard Fuller. (Fuller soon changed his name to Owusu Sadauki.) SOBU continued the effort to make Black colleges "black in fact." And some in SOBU developed a critique of Black studies in majority white institutions as "a pacification plan." "The goal of Black studies," one SOBU theorist argued, "is to take some of the best minds in the Black community and make them dependent and addicted to the colonizer's system." In response, SOBU and some others advocated "Africanization" of Black people, and complete educational autonomy.[66]

SOBU sometimes advanced a simplistic political analysis. For example, one SOBU statement declared that it was futile to distinguish between the Irish and Jews, southerners and northerners. "Foxes and wolves are kith and kin," it said. There was "one world-wide European family." And on the other side, SOBU declared that the "goals of African people are one and the same," even as many young African American radicals were encountering intense divisions within anticolonial struggles.[67] Moreover, the emphasis on rejecting the "West" and cultivating new African value systems that pervaded Black nationalist discourse in these years, especially in the IBI movement, sometimes expressed itself in homophobic and patriarchal forms. Howard Fuller/Owusu Sadauki gave the keynote speech at a SOBU conference in South Carolina, where students had spent several days studying and debating Pan-Africanism. According to a participant, Sadauki "expressed the need for students to change their life styles, value systems and ambitions, to overcome the drugs, the apathy, the miscegenation, women's liberation, homosexuality and the egos." Sadauki gave voice to the social conservatism and the rejection of white women as romantic or sexual partners found in much Black nationalist thought.[68]

In 1971 Sadauki went on a transformative journey in southern Africa that included a visit with the resistance group FRELIMO, of Mozambique, and returned with a new perspective on the character of imperialism. Encounters with liberation leaders and struggles in Africa, many of which were explicitly socialist, especially in Mozambique, Guinea-Bissau, South Africa, and Angola, encouraged many African American nationalists to reconsider their antipathy toward socialism. At the same time, the Chinese Communist Party's support of Black American nationalists, most famously Robert F. Williams, as well as Fidel Castro's and the Cuban nation's extensive human and material support for anticolonial struggles, caused many African Americans to reexamine the seemingly knee-jerk rejection of socialist thought and practice as "European." Anticolonial leader and theorist Amilcar Cabral, from Guinea-Bissau, was particularly influential. On a visit to the United States,

Cabral urged African Americans to unite with others in the United States—including progressive whites—to fight imperialism. "This was a real challenge to us," Nelson Johnson later recalled, "because we thought white people *as a whole* were the enemy. Here was our hero, an African revolutionary leader, telling us to unite with whites."[69]

As a result, ideological convulsion swept many Black radical organizations in the early to mid-1970s. Several prominent Black nationalist leaders moved to Maoism or Marxist-Leninism, most notably Amiri Baraka, of the Congress of African Peoples, and Sadauki, a leader of the African Liberation Support Committee. Many simply endeavored to integrate a more systematic class analysis into their critique of racism. Ironically, this new openness to Marxism, which had been generated in part by interactions with African radicals, encouraged a growing skepticism of the relevance of Pan-Africanism to the lives of poor and working-class African Americans. SOBU/YOBU was deeply influenced by these ideological struggles, and intense debates unfolded on the pages of their newspaper, the *African World*. "Our movement toward Marxism," Nelson Johnson recalls, "was really via Africa."[70] It was important to Johnson and others in SOBU that their turn to the left not be understood as an affiliation with the white working-class. Rather, it was driven by a concern for, and identification with, the Black working-class.

It turns out that SOBU/YOBU activists had already been finding it difficult to practice what they preached. "Some of us were deeply involved in community issues before we became Pan-Africanists," notes Mark Smith. "We soon learned to leave our Pan-Africanism at home, because attempts to superimpose it on the real struggles of the masses met with confusion and rejection."[71] According to Nelson Johnson, "One of the early critics of pan-Africanism was Sandi Neely," a Bennett College graduate who later married Smith. The two of them organized a study group and tried to encourage a new direction, which Johnson initially rejected. "I was still a dyed-in-the-wool black nationalist. I had trained myself never to smile at white folks. I thought Mark and Sandi were being taken in by whites."[72] Smith remembers, "What led me and a lot of other people away from Pan-Africanism was its inability to connect up, either an explanatory framework or an action path, with the conditions that people felt in their lives. . . . Trying to explain to people in Jackson what 'We are an African people' has to do with the minimum wage gets to be real hard." Smith drove around Mississippi with Stokely Carmichael in 1970 or 1971 visiting some of SNCC's old battlegrounds. "People turned out to see him because he was a legend," Smith recalls, but they were "baffled about what all this meant." Carmichael spoke of Nkrumah and Africa, and "people were saying, 'I remember Stokely and them fondly, but what does this have to do with anything?' And I remember thinking the same thing myself, and I'm with the guy."[73]

The rise of feminism was another important ideological development of the early 1970s, one that influenced veterans of the Black student movement. The following chapter narrates this story more fully, but the effects of the women's movement were felt in SOBU/YOBU. Sandi Neely and Joyce Nelson "led the struggle against women's oppression, against the feudal traditions of pan-Africanism, and against male chauvinism," Nelson Johnson remembers. "They fought against the political belittlement of women, criticized those men who ran around on their wives or girlfriends, and pushed for women to be promoted into leadership positions." According to Johnson, "Sandi and Joyce teamed up to even challenge me on this male stuff." And he credits Neely with getting women into leadership positions in the organization.[74]

Many YOBU members took jobs in textile mills in order to help build pro-union sentiment and unite Black and white workers, but YOBU as an organization soon dissolved. Mark Smith returned to Harvard to finish his undergraduate degree and eventually went to medical school. Nelson Johnson, Sandi (Neely) Smith, and others stayed in the mill. "I had studied Marxism and was increasingly persuaded that we were challenged to unite black and white workers," Johnson reflects. "The principal industry in this town and in this region was the textile industry. So, a number of us who were in an all-black formation went into the textile mill . . . to build unity between black and white workers."[75] Johnson and others from YOBU, as well as activists from the African Liberation Support Committee, including Owusu Sadauki, built a new organization called the Revolutionary Workers League that established chapters in New York, Washington, Houston, and San Francisco.

About a year later, in 1975 or 1976, the league dissolved after its leaders voted to merge with the Workers Viewpoint Organization (WVO), a mostly Asian American group based in New York that was committed to building a new Communist Party. Johnson calls this "one of the most difficult periods of my life. It pitted me against my close friend and mentor, Owusu Sadauki."[76] After a ten-year sojourn as a radical organizer in North Carolina, Sadauki returned to Milwaukee, changed his name back to Howard Fuller, and began working with conservative foundations to promote the use of public funds to finance the private education of Black children. Johnson, for his part, moved fully into multiracial labor organizing. The North Carolina WVO contingent attracted large numbers of Black textile workers in support of the union and began to have an impact. But a rejuvenated Ku Klux Klan took note of their successes. There had been Klan rallies in the region aimed at interracial working-class organizing, so the WVO decided to hold a anti-Klan rally at a public housing project in Greensboro.

A caravan of armed Klansmen and neo-Nazis had been given the details of the WVO demonstration by a Greensboro police officer, who operated as an undercover Klansman, but the police department never informed the WVO of these hostile, armed forces. On the day of the rally, November 3, 1979, police were nowhere in sight as the Klansmen and neo-Nazis opened fire on the protesters, killing five and wounding many. Nelson Johnson was stabbed. Sandi Smith was killed. Bill Sampson, the key organizer in the textile plant was also killed. Jim Waller was killed. Cesar Cauce, who organized workers at Duke University, and Mike Nathan, a physician, were also killed that day. White juries in both the state and federal criminal trials voted to acquit. No one was ever convicted for the loss of life in what became known as the Greensboro Massacre. The media, moreover, blamed the communist activists for the deaths of their comrades. In 1985 a civil jury did award several hundred thousand dollars to some of the survivors, but the explosion of right-wing violence and failure to win criminal convictions were traumatic for Johnson, his comrades, and the wider community.[77]

More than two decades later, community leaders developed the Greensboro Truth and Reconciliation Commission in an effort to promote a fuller understanding of who was responsible for the killings, and a fuller understanding of the WVO, which had renamed itself the Communist Worker's Party shortly before that fateful day. The "communist" label was used to demonize the victims and ultimately deny them justice. "I actually am a peaceful and generous person," but "somehow in the public's mind I turned out to be a total monster," Johnson observes. "How did this happen" he asks, "when I was just trying to help poor folk and unite black and white folk, and I turn out to be seen as this kind of monster?" Not long after the massacre, Johnson found solace and solidarity in the church. "I ended up going to churches because people treated me kindly there," he notes. "A good hug was very meaningful to me then." After receiving a master's in divinity, Rev. Johnson founded the Faith Community Church. He has continued his commitment to social justice activism, especially labor organizing, but expresses it in a different register, as leader of the Beloved Community Center in Greensboro.[78]

In many respects, Nelson Johnson's efforts to radically transform the racial and class hierarchies of the modern South, and his subsequent encounter with violent repression, exemplifies the arc of the more militant Black student movement in the region. As we have seen, protesting students at many historically Black colleges faced police invasions resulting in considerable gunfire, many injuries, incarcerations, and several student deaths. The region's political elites moved forcefully when students, in their own brash and imperfect ways, tried to stake a claim to southern institutions and reshape them in more democratic and inclusive ways. The violent crackdowns sent a message that further change would come at great cost. For the Black students in the region who entered college in the aftermath of this traumatic period, seeking reform through mainstream professions and means must have appeared to be the only option.

The off-campus legacies of the Black student and Black studies movements illustrate the formation and evolution of an African American–influenced, activist public sphere in the 1970s. This was a significant by-product of the civil rights movement, and an important precursor to subsequent civic and educational iterations of multiculturalism. The effects of the Black freedom struggle were broad and diffuse, ranging from a change in public-affairs television broadcasting to community-based educational initiatives. Yet while students involved in the various efforts to bring the energy of the Black student and Black studies movements to the broader community—whether at Nairobi, through *Black Heritage,* in SOBU, or at the Institute of the Black World—were making their mark and grappling with internal debates and encountering various challenges, Black studies on campus was struggling to gain permanence and acquire legitimacy.

CHAPTER 8

What Happened to Black Studies?

After the creation of African American studies units, educators engaged in fierce debates about the field's academic mission and definition. The stakes were high, since in the eyes of many, legitimacy, status, and recognition in the academy hung in the balance. Many critics, both internal and external to Black studies, criticized it on two interrelated grounds: they claimed that it lacked curricular coherence, and that by not having a single methodology it failed to meet the definition of a discipline. As a result, many educators in the early Black studies movement pursued a two-pronged quest: for a standardized curriculum and an original, authoritative methodology. At the same time, many scholars in the Black studies movement questioned whether either of these pursuits was desirable or even attainable. In other words, while some scholars have insisted that African American studies must devise its own unique research methodology, others contend that as a multidiscipline, or interdisciplinary discipline, its strength lies in incorporating multiple, diverse methodologies. In a similar vein, while some have argued for a standardized curriculum, others argue that higher education is better served by dynamism and innovation. I argue that, in the final analysis, the discipline's acceptance in academe, to the extent that it has gained acceptance, has come from the production of influential scholarship and the development of new conceptual approaches that have influenced other disciplines. Pioneering scholarship and influential intellectual innovations, rather than a standardized pedagogy or methodology, have been the route to influence and stature in American intellectual life.

A tension between authority and freedom animates these debates. As late as 2000, an article in the *Chronicle of Higher Education* reinforced the idea that multiple perspectives and methodologies had retarded the progress of African American studies. The author criticizes the diverse character of African American studies courses at different universities. "The Ohio State class is chronological with a literary bent," she writes. "Duke's take: cultural studies. The Penn course filters everything through a W.E.B. Du Bois lens, and N.Y.U. combines pan-Africanism with urban studies." Of course, this sampling reflects the range one would find in the departments of history, sociology, or English at these same universities. But the author stresses disarray. "There's a reason 30 years after the discipline developed that people still wonder whether the black-studies curriculum represents a coherent subject or a smorgasbord," she concludes. In this view, the discipline's strengths—"eclectic, expansive, experimental curricula"—are also its weaknesses.[1]

James B. Stewart, a former president of the National Council of Black Studies, shares this anxiety about disarray. In his view: "We do everything—the diaspora, sex, history, language, economics, race." Yet he seems oblivious to the fact that each of these areas has been vital terrain for research innovation. "We don't have a paradigm," he laments. "That is why we don't make progress." If achieving this unified paradigm is the measure of progress, then Stewart, judging forty years of African American studies, must see little. Longtime Black studies educator Abdul Alkalimat shares Stewart's view that "standardization means the discipline exists."[2] Arthur Lewin, a professor of Black and Hispanic studies at Baruch College, agrees that Black studies lacks "a coherently stated rationale," a consequence, in his view, of having "burst full-blown upon the academic scene a generation ago."[3] Critics of African American studies often echo this view. Stanford scholar Shelby Steele calls African American studies "a bogus concept from the beginning because it was an idea grounded in politics, not in a particular methodology. These programs are dying of their own inertia because they've had 30 or 40 years to show us a serious academic program, and they've failed."[4] This view recalls that of Harvard political scientist Martin Kilson, that African American studies did not merit departmental status because it lacked its own unique methodology.

Much of the 1970s was spent formulating ways to standardize course content in African American studies across universities. For some, this impulse flowed from a view that greater cohesion in courses would better promote the social and political mission of the field. For others, standardizing the core curriculum signified professionalism and held the promise of elevating the reputation of the field. In a 1975 proposal, "Consortium for the Development of Black Studies Curriculum," Gerald McWorter (Abdul Alkalimat) noted with concern that "a uniform scholarly curriculum and pedagogy have yet to emerge and be accepted." This was particularly significant because "the heart of Black Studies is its curricular and pedagogical approach to the unique problems that it faces." Moreover, "the need for a model curriculum is growing because there exists considerable variation from campus to campus."[5] In 1980 the National Council of Black Studies adopted a model core curriculum, enshrining history, cultural studies, and social and behavioral studies as the three primary content areas for the field, and this tripartite approach continues to characterize the way many departments approach hiring and curricular development.

Assisting the effort to standardize teaching—especially for introductory courses—was the emergence in the 1980s of two popular textbooks. Abdul Alkalimat and his colleagues at "the People's College" published *Introduction to Afro-American Studies,* which included extensive discussion of Marxism, Pan-Africanism, and Black nationalism, while Ron Karenga's *Introduction to Black Studies* projected his cultural nationalist worldview known as Kawaida as a model for Black studies pedagogy. Many African American studies programs utilized these textbooks in the classroom. Yet these books—emerging in the midst of the field's incorporation, and penned by ideological partisans—bore witness to contradictory trends: both texts emphasized ideological positions that had waned, at least among intellectuals. Showing a fairly rapid move away from Black nationalism as a paradigm for the field, a 1980 survey of ten major Black studies programs found that only two identified Black nationalism as their "ideological rubric," while the other eight emphasized ideological diversity and rejected becoming "narrowly entrenched in any ideology." In the view of these eight programs, "a vibrant faculty dialogue is seen as a major stimulus" in the philosophical evolution of the field.[6]

In addition to seeking an authoritative curriculum, some sought to create a new methodology for the discipline. Scholars and teachers influenced by Afrocentrism have been among the most consistent advocates of creating a distinctive methodology. A school of thought within the larger universe of Black studies, Afrocentrism captured significant media attention in the 1990s. A variant of a long tradition of Black intellectualism focused on marking the achievements of African civilizations prior to European contact, contemporary Afrocentrism attracts a coterie of educators who often exist in an uneasy relationship with major scholarly developments in the discipline. Afrocentrism is most famously associated with Temple University professor Molefi Asante. Lamenting what he saw as "the absence of a comprehensive philosophical position" at the founding of African American studies, Asante developed "Afrocentricity," which stresses the need to recover and "center" African knowledge systems. In his view, this is "the only way you can approach African American studies."[7] Interestingly, the Black student movement was intensely engaged with contemporary struggles and riveted by Black Power, but it was not particularly focused on ancient Africa. There were exceptions: Askia Toure taught such a course at the Experimental College at San Francisco State; but as a rule, the students' Black nationalism was political as much as cultural, and as interested in contemporary struggles in the African diaspora as in Egyptian achievements.

In Black historiography, there is a long and rich tradition of countering the distortion of African culture and history produced by European writers, and of vindicating the achievements of African civilizations prior to colonialism.[8] The earliest Black history writing frequently held up Egyptian and Ethiopian history to refute notions of Black inferiority, argue against slavery, and imagine a different future for Black people in the United States and around the world.[9] By J.A. Rogers, John Henrik Clarke, Carter G. Woodson, William Hansberry, and others, this scholarship was vital to the struggle against white supremacy and very influential in Black communities. In some respects the Marxist Guyanese scholar and transnational activist Walter Rodney continued in this tradition with his landmark 1973 text, *How Europe Underdeveloped Africa*, which detailed the long economic exploitation of the continent and offered a framework for understanding contemporary underdevelopment. For many audiences today, the term *Afrocentric* simply signifies the rejection of Eurocentric approaches or paradigms, and Asante has described his goal as "the emancipation of African knowledge and people from the hegemonic ideology of white racial domination."[10] And he sometimes asserts that what Afrocentricity entails is simply an emphasis on African agency. But the stress on Black agency arguably characterizes all of Black studies. As noted earlier, the articulation and defense of a "Black perspective" defined the field from its inception. Rather, Asante advocates a particular version of Afrocentrism, or as he and others variously term it, Afrocentricity, Africentricity, or Africology. "Afrocentricity," he declared in one of his many texts devoted to defining the term, "is the ideological centerpiece of human regeneration, systematizing our history and experience with our own culture at the core of existence. In its epistemic dimensions it is also a methodology for discovering the truth about intercultural communication."[11]

The inclination to look for insights in the African past, hoping to escape or resolve the legacies of colonialism and enslavement, is fundamental to the approach of leading proponents of Afrocentricity. One of Asante's students, Greg Carr, now a professor of African American studies at Howard University, endeavors to draw upon "deep Africana thought" and the traditions of "classical and medieval Africa" to address the needs of Black people in contemporary society. A key mission of African American studies, Carr believes, is to reconnect "narratives of African identity to the contemporary era."[12] Maulana Karenga, founder of the US organization in Los Angeles, who coauthored the *Handbook of Black Studies* with Asante, believes that "the fundamental point of departure for African American studies or Black studies is an ongoing dialogue with African culture. That is, continuously asking it questions and seeking from it answers to the fundamental questions of humankind."[13]

Asante has undertaken extraordinary efforts to develop African American studies along Afrocentric lines, founding the important *Journal of Black Studies,* as well as the first PhD program in African American studies at Temple University, in 1988. He has been tireless in asserting and claiming influence. "I have written more books than any other African American scholar," he said in 1994. "I have written 36 books." As of 2009, that number had risen to seventy, and his followers often refer to this as "Asantian" literature.[14] Afrocentric students and educators convene at the Cheikh Anta Diop annual conferences sponsored by the Diopian Institute for Scholarly Advancement in Philadelphia. Afrocentric thinkers have also played significant roles in shaping the National Council of Black Studies and its annual conferences.[15]

While Asante and others insist that Afrocentricity is the field's most appropriate methodology, it has struggled to gain traction in Black studies and has inspired considerable criticism from within the discipline.

Critics have offered various objections, notably that Afrocentricity reinforces troubling discourses and hierarchies, falls short as an actual research methodology, and lacks engagement with the actual history and culture of Africa. A common concern is that it rejects the hybrid nature of African American genealogy, culture, and identities, and—ironically, in light of its focus on agency—slights the Black contribution to the making of the New World. Scholar Tricia Rose agrees with Greg Carr that an important African intellectual tradition preceded European contact, but in her view scholars must confront the transformations wrought by processes of enslavement and colonialism. "We are in the West, in the so-called New World," she contends, and should "examine the circumstances we are in, examine the hybridities that have emerged from it."[16]

As Melba Boyd puts it, "In the Afrocentric haste to discard all things European or American they have also discarded that which is uniquely Afro-American." Moreover, echoing another widely shared critique, Boyd notes, "What the Afrocentrists fail to realize, in their quest to claim civilization, is that our struggle, fundamentally and above all else, is for freedom for the common people. We do not desire to be the "new" aristocracy. Monarchies were not democracies. We aspire to a new society that does not worship royalty, racial hierarchies, gold, corporate power, or any other manifestation that demeans the human spirit."[17] Literary scholar Joyce A. Joyce echoes this criticism. "Ironically," she observes, "some Black nationalists and hardened Afrocentrists share superiority complexes and desire for power (disguised as agency) with the very hegemony they allegedly oppose." For Joyce, Black studies is "a creative change agent" conceived "as an intellectual discipline to deconstruct the injustices rooted in a disrespect for cultural differences."[18]

Similarly, Erskine Peters finds that Asante's *Kemet, Afrocentricity and Knowledge* problematically asserts that "all African societies find Kemet (ancient Egypt) a common source for intellectual and political ideas." Peters objects to this "imperialist logic" and finds it "dangerously like the erroneous historical paradigm which argues that European culture brought civilization to the rest of the globe." Moreover, he argues that Asante's theory had jumped ahead of his research, noting that "one comes away from Asante simply not having learned very much about African values."[19] Other scholars have objected to the definition of race "as some kind of innate biological bond" advanced in Afrocentric writings, as well as the portrayal of culture, which, historian Barbara Ransby argues, is "equally erroneous. . . . Culture is not something fixed, static, and ahistorical" but is "dynamic and constantly in flux." "Afrocentrists who look back and romanticize a fixed moment in the history of ancient Egypt as the source of our salvation from our current dilemmas," Ransby argues, "fail to fully appreciate this fact."[20] Likewise, Perry Hall argues that Afrocentrism promotes "a static view of culture and history. . . . For Blacks to discover who they were is important, but only part of discovering who they are, who they can be and where they can go."[21]

Afrocentricity has arguably had more influence in community-based pedagogy, cultural programming, and heritage tours than in the production of research. This is best exemplified by the influence of Kawaida, a worldview formulated by Maulana Karenga as a means of promoting self-determination, unity, economic cooperation, and creativity in Black American communities. Influential in some early Black studies programs, Kawaida's biggest influence by far has been its offshoot, the Afrocentric holiday Kwanzaa—which, falling in the school vacation week after Christmas, has spawned some of the most well-attended public programming at cultural institutions around the country. Afrocentricity has a didactic dimension that emphasizes the need to "recover" and "restore" lost value systems, ways of knowing, and cultural traditions more generally. The Association for the Study of Classical African Civilizations—an organization founded by Chicagoan Jacob Carruthers, a longtime professor at the Center for Inner City Studies at Northeastern Illinois University—embraces this mission, which tends to distinguish it from more academic African American studies. Reflecting the mix of education, cosmology, and ritual that characterizes many grassroots expressions of Afrocentrism, the Association promotes spiritual development, the veneration of African ancestors, the application of ancient Nile Valley culture in contemporary life, and holistic approaches to healthy living.[22] As a result of this more didactic and spiritual orientation and the coincident incorporation of Black studies into the academy, a wider chasm than had existed during earlier eras has developed between Afrocentric teachers and writers and more mainstream African American studies scholars.

Still, Afrocentricity's forceful critique of European "civilization," its emphasis on Black achievement, and its mistrust of white-led education have strong resonance. And context is crucial. The continuing assault on Black humanity in post-Jim-Crow America is central to its appeal.

Afrocentricity gained visibility in the 1990s, a time when journalists, sociologists, and politicians promoted narratives of inner-city drug use, rampant criminality, and family breakdown. These narratives appeared to indict individual behaviors yet suggested a communal failure, all the while ignoring the post-civil-rights history of urban disinvestment, regressive taxation, massive job loss, and aggressive policing targeted particularly at young men of color.

Whether it is Afrocentricity or something else, most scholars in Black studies reject the effort to impose a single methodology, seeing it as unrealistic and stifling. Rhett Jones, cofounder and longtime chair of the Department of Africana Studies at Brown University, was an early critic of the "one size fits all" approach to the discipline. "In its early years, Black studies wasted considerable human, intellectual, and material resources in battles over finding the master plan for the study of Black people," he argues. Similarly, he feels that "much energy was also wasted on responding to the charge by America's Eurocentric, racist disciplines that Black studies had no methodology of its own. Neither did the Eurocentrists. And they still don't. . . . Historians are no more agreed on methodology or theory than are anthropologists, sociologists or philosophers."[23] In contrast to those who see pluralism in Black studies as a weakness, Jones believes that this characteristic has been vital to the development and staying power of the field. Pluralism was "a credit to black studies" he observes, as "its founders realized there could be no master plan as to how the discipline should serve black Americans."[24]

Historian Francille Rusan Wilson similarly resists the effort to impose a single approach. "There's not one way to be black or to study black people," she asserts. "The discipline is quite alive," in her view, "and the differences indicate that."[25] Political scientist Floyd Hayes concurs, stating, "One must ask whether there should be conformity to a model curriculum and a single theoretical or ideological orientation in African American studies." Hayes believes it is important to cultivate "a more flexible and innovative atmosphere" so that "African American studies can continue to grow and develop."[26] Reacting to criticism of the eclectic philosophies in early Black studies, philosopher Angela Davis observes that it was "precisely the lack of unitary theoretical definition during those early years" which made the field so "intellectually exciting." In her view, it was fruitless to imagine transcending the very real contradictions and disagreements in the early Black studies movement.[27]

While the significance of teaching to the rise of Black studies in the United States cannot be minimized or discounted, ultimately it has been the quality of research and scholarship that has fueled the development and stature of African American studies within academia. Despite persistent portrayals of Black studies as intellectually barren and steeped in racial essentialism, scholars in the field have produced work that has broadly influenced academic scholarship. It is beyond the scope of this book to catalogue and assess the groundbreaking works by literary theorists, sociologists, anthropologists, philosophers, historians, and others in the broad field of African American and diaspora studies that were published in the 1970s and 1980s. Scholars such as Robert L. Harris, Vincent Harding, Sterling Stuckey, Joyce Ladner, Henry Louis Gates, Darlene Clark Hine, Mary Helen Washington, Robert Stepto, John Blassingame, Mary Frances Berry, Andrew Billingsley, and Ronald Walters, among scores of others, continued the long tradition of Black scholarly innovation. However, this point needs to be stressed: a Black scholarly tradition did not begin with the creation of Black studies programs, but these programs provided a new infrastructure and incentive for its growth and development.

One important example of scholarly innovation in Black studies was the rise of diaspora studies. Defining the scope and subject of Black studies was a point of contestation in the early years of academic incorporation. Despite the efforts of university administrators to confine the field to the United States, a persistent desire to encompass the global African diaspora ultimately spawned considerable conceptual innovation and scholarly productivity.[28] Black studies scholars have from the movement's inception been international in their origins and much more diverse than the Black American population as a whole, which in the late 1960s was overwhelmingly U.S. born. Notwithstanding the nomenclature of their university unit, many scholars in Black studies have embraced Pan-Africanism, the Black World, or the African diaspora as a guiding paradigm for teaching and scholarship.

As illustrated in the case studies throughout this book, the Black nationalism of this student generation was internationalist; the Black Panther Party saw itself as part of a global upsurge. Nineteen-sixties Black nationalism was forged amid rising critiques of the U.S. war in Vietnam and in explicit identification with, and admiration for, leaders of African liberation struggles and new nation-states. Two leading icons for this generation—Muhammad Ali and Malcolm X—exemplify this twin thrust. Both embraced their African origins, traveled extensively on the continent, and criticized U.S. efforts to suppress Black diasporic affiliations and anti-imperialist stances. Related to the turn toward Black Power, or variations thereof, was the decisive break from cold war strictures that had narrowed the terms of dissent in the United States. Activists challenged the idea of "American exceptionalism," which had worked both to deny the centrality of racism in the United States and to sever earlier transnational alliances and identifications.

This internationalist Black consciousness continued, even accelerated, in the 1970s. The early Black studies movement coincided with major anticolonial struggles in Angola, Mozambique, and Guinea-Bissau; struggles against white settler regimes in southern Africa; and a widening African solidarity movement among Black American radicals. According to St. Clair Drake, "The country was deeply mired in the Vietnam War but many black youth were much more interested in how the war against Portugal was going in Mozambique, Angola and Guinea-Bissau than in the war in Vietnam." In his view, it was critical to understand that *"the modern Black studies movement emerged within this international context."*[29]

As a result, it was fairly common to find Pan-African in a program's name or in its course offerings. At Lehman College in New York City, remembers Charlotte Morgan-Cato, "the rallying cry 'Portuguese wine is African Blood' was well-known among the students as we regularly hosted African scholars, Black nationalist leaders, radical public intellectuals and local political leaders who espoused the Pan-African cause."[30] According to Drake, "Newly organized Black studies programs contributed to the raising of consciousness with regard to Africa between 1970 and 1974, and to the emergence of the group that organized a very effective lobby," the African Liberation Support Committee.[31] The committee organized annual African Liberation Day demonstrations and played a leading role in planning the Sixth Pan-African Congress in Tanzania. Many in the African Liberation Support Committee orbit, including Owusu Sadauki/Howard Fuller, Nelson Johnson, Abdul Alkalimat, Jimmy Garrett, C.L.R. James, James Turner, Lerone Bennett, and Haki Madhubuti—were deeply connected to the Black student and Black studies movements. The strong activist commitment to African solidarity by scholars in the early Black studies movement concretely and dramatically illustrates the field's international focus. The defeat of Portugal in 1974 brought to a close one chapter in the long career of U.S.-based Pan-Africanism. The struggles against apartheid, white rule in Zimbabwe, and the South African occupation of Namibia continued, but the African Liberation Support Committee disbanded in the ideological conflict between Marxists and Black nationalists. Additionally, Morgan-Cato, at Lehman College, felt that "student interest in the movement of international liberation" was also cut short in the mid-1970s as a result of fiscal crisis, retrenchment, and shifts in student outlooks and priorities.[32]

Still, a global consciousness in Black studies was not simply a product of solidarity struggles in the postwar era. It has marked Black historical writing ever since its origins in the nineteenth century. As many studies of Black historiography have shown, writers from the early nineteenth century forward have been invested in rewriting the Western distortion of African peoples and societies, as well as keenly interested in erecting a powerful counterdiscourse to the statelessness, dispersal, subjugation, and dehumanization of Africans in diaspora. W.E.B. Du Bois is most famously associated with this effort, but its practitioners are numerous.[33] In addition, the most important Black community institutions—notably churches and newspapers—paid attention to the African diaspora. Until McCarthy-era repression undermined African American anticolonial organizations and networks, major Black newspapers, especially the *Chicago Defender* and *Pittsburgh Courier,* gave extensive coverage to developments in Africa and the Caribbean.[34]

Although the Black studies movement is often thought of as resolutely U.S.-based, many of its early scholars tried to persuade universities and funders to connect formally the study of continental Africa, the Caribbean, and the United States. There was widespread agreement that the typical American curriculum had "ignored the African heritage of African Americans, characterizing them as having begun their existence in North America as a tabula rasa—blank slates to be imprinted with Euro-American Culture." This was a difficult battle, in part because African studies had been programmatically established after World War II as a result of cold war pressures to develop knowledge about an area of the world that the United States viewed as part of Soviet strategic designs. These programs, in the words of historian Robert L. Harris, "had no real link to Black people in the New World." African studies "became wedded to a modernization theory that measured African societies by Western standards. African history, culture and politics were explored more within the context of the colonial powers than with any attention to African cultural continuities in the Western Hemisphere."

In contrast, according to Harris, Black American intellectuals had long resisted this "compartmentalization of knowledge about Black people."[35]

The Black studies movement unleashed a salvo against the colonial paradigm, but faced resistance from administrators and faculty in African studies. White scholars, many of whom objected to the focus on identity and politics in Black studies, dominated African studies programs in the United States. When Afro-American studies began at Boston University, its director, Adelaide Hill, wanted to forge ties with the already existing African studies program. "The problem of the relationship of the two areas has agonized both faculties," she reported. "Some Africanists," she found, "do not see a relationship between what they are doing and the new Black American emphasis." In the end, the two units agreed that there are "common and autonomous zones between the two areas." Similarly, Harvard's Department of Afro-American Studies sought to include African studies under its purview, but met administrative resistance, in part because the department was seen as too political and too influenced by Black nationalism.[36]

American-born sociologist St. Clair Drake labored his entire academic career to promote the study of the Africa diaspora in all its scope and complexity. He often reminded his audiences that "the first African Studies programs were at Fisk and Lincoln, but these received no grants from the foundations," in contrast to the white-run African studies programs at elite universities that were lavishly funded during the cold war era. The push by some scholars in the Black studies movement to unify the two fields produced tensions. The Africanists "fear the political impulse associated with Afro-American Studies and the possibility of the lowering of standards," Drake found, and "in their effort to maintain their own preserves" sometimes shifted from undergraduate to graduate education. At Drake's Roosevelt University, however, African and African American studies were taught together.[37]

Never a monolith, Black studies has given rise to varying conceptions of diaspora. In 1969 Drake proposed a summer institute in Jamaica. "This location serves to emphasize one of the objectives of the institute, that of teaching Negro history and culture in its cosmopolitan pan-African and South Atlantic context," he noted. The workshop intended to emphasize "cultural continuity" between Africa and "the black diaspora" in South, Central, and North America. "The institute will be concerned with the cultural, historical, and political connections between Africa, the United States, and the Caribbean," Drake wrote.[38] In contrast, at a seminar of Black studies directors, the director of Princeton's program advanced several rationales for a global approach, including illustrating diversity in Black life. His framework, which emphasized difference as much as commonality, shows the varied approaches to the study of diaspora that have always marked the discipline. "The black experience varies geographically and culturally and therefore falls within the study of comparative racial and ethnic relations," he argued. "There is a common denominator in being black," he felt, "but race is a lesser factor in the definition of the person in some situations. For example, in the Caribbean area generally, class is more definitive of who a person is than race. In the United States the opposite is the case."[39]

The early Black studies movement was unable to immediately achieve the goal of encompassing African studies.[40] Nonetheless, courses in Afro-American studies departments often extended beyond American borders. A 1980 examination of ten major programs found that all of them "encompass the Diaspora in their scope," and that all "address their curricular attention in some measure to Africa" even while putting most emphasis on the experience of Black people in the United States.[41] The Program in Afro-American Studies at Brown pioneered coursework in the African diaspora beginning in the 1970s at the initiative of Ghanaian scholar Anani Dzidzienyo.[42] In a 1977–1978 survey of Black studies programs, Drake found that "all give some attention to the implications of an African origin for Black people in the New World, and increasingly a "diaspora" frame of reference focuses some attention upon the Caribbean and Latin America for comparison with the United States."[43] When Roscoe Brown was appointed to direct the new Institute of African American Affairs at New York University, he announced that "the term 'Afro-American' will include our Black brothers from the various parts of the Caribbean, such as Haiti, Puerto Rico, the West Indies, the Virgin Islands, and other Caribbean peoples who are of African descent." His attention to "brothers" and omission of "sisters"— certainly ironic in light of the stress on subjectivity and identity in the Black studies movement—was common in these years before feminist assertion dramatically affected language and consciousness. Still, Brown put resources behind this pledge, convening a yearlong seminar in 1971–1972 on the Black experience in the Caribbean and South America.[44]

The Center for African and African American Studies at the University of Michigan at Ann Arbor was an important exception to this early failure to formally include African studies under the rubric of Black studies. At its founding in 1970, Niara Sudarkasa, a professor of anthropology and future director of the center, "ensured the new center would deal not only with African American experience, but also with sub-Saharan Africa itself." Godfrey Uzoigwe, an Africanist at Ann Arbor, noted, "CAAS is one of the few black studies programs in which the comparative emphasis was built into its structure from the beginning."[45]

Yet other avenues for forging networks and affinities among scholars of Africa and the diaspora emerged, most notably the African Heritage Studies Association, which was founded in 1969 after John Henrik Clarke and others led a protest at the annual convention of the African Studies Association (ASA) in Montreal. Black scholars of Africa had long felt marginalized in the ASA and had been pressing for greater Black leadership in the organization and for the ASA to play a more active and progressive role in influencing American policy toward Africa. In Montreal, the Black Caucus of the ASA declared the Association "fundamentally invalid and illegitimate" and even "injurious to the welfare of African people." It assailed the group's scholarship, leadership, and affiliations. "This organization which purports to study Africa has never done so," the caucus declared, "and has in fact studied the colonial heritage of Africa." They condemned "the intellectual arrogance of white people, which has perpetuated and legitimized a kind of academic colonialism and has distorted the definition of the nature of cultural life and social organization of African peoples."[46]

A major point of conflict was the demand for "racial parity" within the ASA, with an equal number of board seats designated for whites and blacks. Several radical whites, like Immanuel Wallerstein, supported the Black Caucus, but most white Africanists objected to many or most of their demands. As John Henrik Clarke recalled, the white Africanists "resented the projection of an African people as a world people with a common cause and a common destiny. More than anything else they resented the Afro-Americans being linked with the Africans in Africa." In Clarke's view, the white Africanist scholars possessed the sense of dominion and paternalism that had been generated by European colonialism and Western imperialism more generally. "Africa to them was a kind of ethnic plantation over which they reigned and explained to the world." The conflict at Montreal gave rise to the African Heritage Studies Association (AHSA), which in the early 1970s, prior to the creation of the National Council of Black Studies, served as an annual gathering and institutional network for Black studies scholars. Dr. Clarke, its founding president, defined the AHSA as "committed to the preservation, interpretation, and creative presentation of the historical and cultural heritage of African people" throughout the world. "We interpret African history from a Pan-Africanist perspective that defines all black people as an African people," he insisted. "We do not accept the arbitrary lines of geographical demarcations that were created to reflect colonialist spheres of influence."[47]

The meetings of the AHSA reflected the various currents of Black nationalism in the 1970s, as well as the continuing interest in "relevance," or contemporary policy and political issues. The 1978 conference in New York illustrates these concerns and the global character of the AHSA. Most of the presenters were university scholars, but also on panels were the Nigerian ambassador, the African National Congress representative to the United States, and several attorneys and filmmakers. Politics and culture dominated points of discussion at the conference. Session titles included U.S. Foreign Policy in Southern Africa; Blacks in American Politics; Caribbean Nation Building; The Military in Post-Independence Africa; Forum on Southern Africa; A Decade of Assessment of Black Studies; Black Artists in America; Caribbean Literature; Black Men, Black Women and the Black Family; Affirmative Action and Social Change; Integrating Black Music into the Curriculum; and Legacy of Colonialism.[48] Notwithstanding what the Association's name might convey, the conferences of the African Heritage Studies Association during the 1970s were contemporary in emphasis, and they strongly demonstrated the interest of the Black studies community in the United States in African liberation struggles and new nation-states. Yet, like the ASA from which it had bolted, the AHSA remained predominantly male and seemingly oblivious to the rising tide of feminism. On this score, its Black nationalism offered a circumscribed vision of postcolonial change, protecting male leadership prerogatives and forgoing discussions of alternative visions of postcolonial leadership and liberation.

Notwithstanding efforts by administrators or others to limit the scope of African American studies to the United States, these early efforts to formally include Africa as well as the diaspora in Black studies departments and professional organizations ultimately bore fruit. Four decades later it became increasingly common to encounter Departments of African and African American Studies or Departments of Africana Studies, which explicitly take Africa, the United States, the Caribbean, and Latin America as their subject. Campuses as diverse as the University of Illinois, Dartmouth College, the University of Minnesota, Duke University, Harvard University, Pennsylvania State University, the University of Kansas, Stanford University, the University of Texas, and Arizona State University join together African and African American studies. Of course, the limitations of budgets and faculty size may interfere with fully realizing the promise of interdisciplinary, truly global coverage. And to be sure, there continue to be significant challenges in integrating African and African diasporic studies in the same units, as well as tensions and divergences between Africanist and African Americanist scholars. The process of defining African diaspora studies, indeed of defining blackness, is ongoing and the subject of lively debate. But the crucial point is that the Black studies movement ultimately achieved a degree of success in undoing the colonialist compartmentalization of research and knowledge that had insisted on severing African studies from African American studies.

In addition to diaspora, another development in the Black studies movement that generated innovative research and helped to propel the discipline forward in the midst of an ongoing discursive climate of "crisis" was the rise of Black feminism and its influence in both Black studies and academia more generally. Black feminist scholars insisted on the need to move beyond a monolithic focus on the racialized subject and take into account interconnected, and multiple, subjectivities and oppressions. They argued for the significance of gender, but also brought heightened attention to class and sexuality, an interpretive move that influenced other disciplines in addition to Black studies. However, this outcome was by no means easy or assured. Black women intellectuals had to wage a fight to legitimate their perspective, and they often encountered withering criticism from male—and sometimes female—scholars in their effort to cultivate a feminist revision of the Black studies movement. According to Rhett Jones, a Brown University Africana Studies professor, "Our discipline also failed to address Black women's issues," which he feels is "surprising in a field claiming to take a new perspective on scholarship."[49] Many Black women have argued that this failure flowed from the male chauvinist, homophobic tenor of the nationalist 1960s. "The truth of it is," Toni Cade reflects, "a whole lot of organizations back then in the sixties floundered, fell apart, and wasted a lot of resources in the process, due in large measure to male ego, male whim, and macho theatre. That story needs to be told."[50]

Many scholars of modern Black feminism have characterized its emergence as a reaction, on the one hand, to the sexism of the Black

Power movement, and on the other hand, to the racism in the white women's movement and broader U.S. society. But more recently, historians have argued that the racial identity politics of the Black Power movement were a generative influence for the rise of gender identity politics in Black feminist organizing and assertion.[51] Both perspectives provide useful insight on developments in the Black student and Black studies movements. These movements had blithely embraced male leadership and conventional gender roles, but at the same time, they had also encouraged not only critical consciousness, self-affirmation, and a group-based identity but also individual empowerment and personal agency. And all these phenomena stimulated the rise of Black feminism(s) and, later, Black women's studies.

The publication of the landmark text *The Black Woman* by Toni Cade in 1970 opened a period of growth, questioning, and assertion in Black women's activist, literary, cultural, and academic organizing. Notably, the paperback appeared at a time when the major media characterized feminism as a white woman's movement of little relevance or concern for Black women, and when the majority of Black men and women readily agreed with this assessment. In these years, white feminist activists evinced little awareness of, or interest in, the particular experiences or needs of women of color. Moreover, the ethos and political strategy of the Black Power era was indisputably race first. Widely recognized as a writer and literary figure, Cade was also a leader in the Black studies movement, having advised protesting students while a professor at City College and designed an innovative plan for a Black studies department there. The *Black Woman* was an eclectic volume of activist writing, and it featured three essays by Cade. In one she denounced conventional gender roles for what she described as their debilitating impact on the movement. Instead of trying to prove one's manhood or womanhood, she asks, in a creative turn, why not just seek "blackhood"? In response to critics who might call patriarchy a white system, she cautions that "we have not been immune to the conditioning; we are just as jammed in the rigid confines of those basically oppressive socially contrived roles. For if a woman is tough, she is a rough mamma, a strident bitch, a ball breaker, a castrator. And if a man is at all sensitive, tender, spiritual, he's a faggot." The worst part was the effect of such thinking on a liberation movement. She called it "a dangerous trend" to "program Sapphire out of her 'evil' ways into a cover-up, shut-up, lay-back-and-be-cool obedience role."[52]

Her essay "The Pill: Genocide or Liberation?" frankly explored the tensions and debates between Black men and woman over contraception in light of the long history of reproductive abuse and theories of Black genetic inferiority, on the one hand, and patriarchy and conservative sexual norms on the other. The Nation of Islam, for its part, denied a woman's right to control reproduction. Leader Elijah Muhammad famously said a "woman is man's field to produce his nation."[53] Still, Cade's advocacy of a Black woman's right to reproductive self-determination was resolute. Her essay exemplifies the kinds of discussions that feminists were committed to having and the kinds of topics they insisted were political. Yet Cade entered a political minefield.

A striking feature of Black studies units when they first formed on hundreds of campuses was their male character—although, to be sure, every academic discipline was overwhelmingly male in the early 1970s. A 1968 survey of doctoral and professional degrees conferred by Black institutions found an extraordinary gender gap: 91 percent of the degrees were awarded to Black men, and 9 percent to Black women.[54] This translated into a stark gender disparity on collegiate faculties. At the University of Pittsburgh in 1972, for example, 8 percent of the professional staff was Black, and of this group just 14 percent were women. Among the white professionals, the presence of women was, at 17 percent, slightly higher, but this number too showed the disproportionate male presence in academe. The distinctions were sharpest in the upper ranks. White males filled half of the associate and full professor positions at the university; Black men held 31 percent of them, white females 19 percent, while Black women held just 3 percent of these higher paying, more prestigious positions. In the University of Pittsburgh's Black studies department, only three women numbered among the seventeen faculty members.[55] As one observer noted, this large differential reflected broader social patterns, as signified dramatically in a 1971 *Ebony* tabulation of the nation's one hundred leading Black Americans, which listed only nine women.[56]

When asked in the 1990s whether women in the early Black studies movement had been given their due, Mary Jane Hewitt, who had directed various affirmative action programs at UCLA, responded, "Well, there weren't that many opportunities, given or offered, for black women to do much of anything." In "the late sixties," she explained, "there weren't that many women around, very few, and certainly not in top positions."[57] To be sure, this scenario was changing, as women of all backgrounds began to enter the academic profession in greater numbers. But the small numbers of Black women scholars and administrators in the academy encountered marginalization, consternation, and resistance.

Constance M. Carroll, a Black woman who later served as a college president, wrote in 1972: "Black women in higher education are isolated, underutilized, and often demoralized." Denied the same opportunities for mobility and networking, they faced numerous challenges and obstacles. "Black women have had very few models or champions to encourage and assist them in their development," Carroll wrote. "Black women have had to develop themselves on their own, with no help from whites or Black men, in order to 'make it' in academic institutions. This has taken its toll on Black women," she found, "in all areas of life and work."[58]

It is important to note that Black women scholars raised critical questions about the male character of the Black studies movement from its inception. At a 1969 conference of Black studies directors, Lillian Anthony from the University of Minnesota remarked that some faculty at her institution said, "We don't need a woman," after her name had been put forth by the search committee. "I am very much concerned about the Black woman's role in Afro-American studies departments or Black studies departments," she said. "I think it negates much of who we really are, and when men participate in that kind of deliberation, they are also negating themselves."[59]

The passage of the Education Amendments Act in 1972, prohibiting discrimination in federally funded institutions of higher education, and an investigation by the Department of Health, Education and Welfare of several hundred universities for noncompliance with federal guidelines regarding equal treatment of minorities and women, raised expectations, awareness, and discussion about hiring practices in academe. Universities had to submit written affirmative action plans in 1972 specifying their goals and timetables for achieving equal treatment of women and minorities. Many Black women feared that unless they asserted themselves, Black men and white women would be the prime beneficiaries of affirmative action policies. While some people claimed that Black women had an advantage, as their hiring would do "double duty" and fulfill a race and gender mandate, Black women knew the more likely outcome was their falling through the cracks. This legal/employment/policy circumstance encouraged Black women to define the uniqueness of their status in American life and to emphasize their commonalities as well as differences with the positions of Black men and white women.

The early to mid-1970s saw the appearance of courses, campus lectures, and programming devoted to Black women, including what was reportedly the first class on Black women writers, taught by Alice

Walker at the University of Massachusetts in Boston in 1973.[60] At the University of California, Los Angeles, a group of Black women students, faculty, and staff came together as the Black Women's Research Committee and launched a petition campaign demanding that "the university become more sensitive to the needs of black women on campus, and demonstrate that sensitivity via immediate action" in creating courses, lectures, and programming focusing on the Black woman. They "were appalled at the lack of programming for black women at UCLA" and noted that there had never been any courses anywhere in the university focusing on Black women.[61] In May 1973, the Black Women's Research Committee, in conjunction with the Center for Afro-American Studies, held the first Black Women's Spring Forum, a monthlong series of panels and lectures titled "Images of Black Womanhood." The primary objective of the forum was "to present an exhaustive, in-depth exploration delineating the recurring philosophical themes contributing to the development of Black womanhood in the United States." Titles of the panels and lectures included: Women in Africa, Women in America, Black Women in the Media, Black Women in Theater Arts, Black Women in Law/Politics, and Black Women at UCLA. In 1977, Toni Cade delivered the keynote address at a Black Women's Conference at the Institute of the Black World. This Atlanta-based think tank had been founded in 1969 as a bastion of mostly male scholars, who for many years generated complex analyses of the politics of race and class in the United States. By decade's end, the IBW, too, was feeling the impact of Black women's demands for a voice in Black activist and intellectual programming.[62]

An outpouring of Black feminist organizations, manifestoes, cultural production, literary anthologies, and polemical writing marked the 1970s, helping to set the stage for a new generation of academic scholarship in Black women's studies. The National Black Feminist Organization was formed in 1973, and in 1977 the Combahee River Collective boldly asserted the importance of a Black lesbian perspective amid the widespread disavowal of the Black lesbian experience in the Black liberation movement. In 1981 Bell Hooks published *Ain't I a Woman: Black Women and Feminism*, followed in 1982 by the landmark anthology *But Some of Us Are Brave: All the Women Are White, All the Blacks Are Men: Black Women's Studies*, edited by Gloria T. Hull, Patricia Bell Scott, and Barbara Smith. Hull and Smith's introduction called out the racism in the women's studies movement, and sexism and homophobia in the Black studies movement. "Only a feminist, pro-woman perspective that acknowledges the reality of sexual oppression in the lives of Black women, as well as the oppression of race and class, will make Black Women's Studies the transformer of consciousness it needs to be."[63] The rise of Black feminism strongly influenced the rise of Black women's studies, yet it is important to recall that the two are not synonymous. Not every scholar of Black women necessarily subscribes to the radical politics of Black feminism or produces scholarship in a feminist idiom.

By the 1980s a new generation of Black women scholars, especially in the humanities, insisted on gender as a category of analysis and began to place Black women at the center of their research. An examination of the emergence of the first generation of Black women scholars after the creation of Black studies illuminates Black studies' highly gendered landscape, as well as the various triggers for the cultivation of Black women's studies. Historian Sharon Harley underwent a political awakening as a student in the late 1960s: wearing an Afro, leading her college's small Black student organization, selling copies of the Black Panther Party newspaper, reading poetry from the Black arts movement, and attending the Congress of Afrikan Peoples in Atlanta. "Nothing to that point," she recalls, "approximated the euphoria I experienced at the Atlanta event." Close to three thousand participants attended sessions in Atlanta. But Black Power was complex and contradictory. Harley may or may not have attended the workshop on Black women, but the coordinator, Amina Baraka, began by quoting the cultural nationalist activist Ron Karenga: "What makes a woman appealing is femininity and she can't be feminine without being submissive." Baraka advised women to submit to their "natural roles," learn to cook better and improve their personal hygiene. Apparently, Black women's bodies needed to be disciplined, improved, and strikingly, made cleaner.[64] Still, as Harley's story illustrates, the Black Power movement was important in shaping the consciousness of a future feminist historian. Harley also considered herself a leftist and studied at Antioch College with veteran labor and civil rights activists Jack O'Dell and Bob Rhodes, who had also exposed graduate students in Chicago to Marxist theories of political economy in Saturday classes at the Communiversity on the city's south side.[65]

As part of a cohort of graduate students at Howard in the 1970s who would publish pioneering work in Black women's history, Harley had a vibrant and supportive graduate education but quickly encountered racial and gender exclusions in the profession. At conferences of the Association for the Study of Afro-American Life and History, the American Historical Association, and Organization of American Historians, she found few sessions that focused on women. Owing to this neglect of women's and specifically Black women's history, Harley and fellow graduate student Rosalyn Terborg-Penn found a niche in the new Berkshire Conference of Women Historians, and in the Racine Conference on Women organized by the white historian Gerda Lerner. A postwar Communist, Lerner was a pioneer in both Black and white women's history and published the important documentary collection *Black Women in White America* in 1972. "Although Lerner was the major force behind integrating black women into the profession and the scholarship of history," Harley still found that "the field at-large effectively made black women invisible or insignificant." She eventually concluded that only through the concerted agency of Black women historians would a new scholarship emerge. This was a critically important insight. "I was part of a movement of early black women historians who understood that our effort to encourage white women historians to adopt a more inclusive women's historical discourse was too laborious and that we had better do something about it on our own." As graduate students, Harley and Terborg-Penn coedited a groundbreaking volume, *The Afro-American Woman: Struggles and Images,* published in 1978, which featured essays by young scholars who would go on to be leading researchers in African American women's history.[66]

Rosalyn Terborg-Penn's scholarship has transformed scholarly views on Black women in the suffrage movement, but it took nearly twenty years to get her book published, not only because of the heavier teaching load at an HBCU, but also, more significantly, because of the effects of racism and sexism in academe and the publishing world. Entering graduate school in 1972, Terborg was the first person in Howard's history department to declare a dissertation topic in Black women's history. "I would have an uphill struggle," she wrote, "because I had to convince the faculty that black women's experience was viable." One professor called her topic "Mickey Mouse" and urged her to study something serious, such as Eleanor Roosevelt. In the professional circuit, she encountered white women historians who challenged her findings of racial discrimination in the suffrage movement, and Black male scholars who argued that "women's history was feminism and that it distracted us from the struggle to legitimize black studies." Terborg-Penn recalls that she and several of her Black female colleagues "noted this phenomenon—racism from white feminist scholars and sexism from black nationalist male scholars—and we tried to develop strategies to overcome the prejudice we discerned." In response, she and historian Elizabeth Parker began a series of conversations among colleagues across the country, which culminated in the formation of the Association of Black Women Historians in 1981. Terborg-Penn still struggled to find a publisher for her manuscript. One editor wanted her to give more attention to white women in the suffrage movement, but Indiana University Press, in a series under the direction of Darlene Clark Hine, a pioneering scholar of Black women's history, finally published the highly anticipated *African American Women and the Struggle for the Vote, 1850–1920* in 1998.[67]

Black women scholars had to struggle against the white male academy, as well as with condescension and opposition from within Black studies, simply to justify research on African American women. In writing her pathbreaking study of enslaved women, *Ar'n't I a Woman?* Deborah Gray White faced numerous hurdles. Many white historians criticized her for using the WPA slave narratives rather than traditional plantation sources, which of course were authored by slaveholders. But White was also challenging the core gender politics of Black nationalist scholarship, and she suffered retaliation. Her chair in African American studies at the University of Wisconsin, Milwaukee, made a contemptuous remark about her work and, she later learned, failed to support her bid for tenure. Evidently he was displeased that she had declined to perform the role of "official hospitality hostess" when their department hosted a meeting of the National Council of Black Studies. As a commentator on a panel discussing a book on Black nationalism and slavery, White endured twenty minutes of "an unrestrained verbal thrashing, the likes of which no scholar should have to endure," for merely suggesting that an examination of women and gender would have enriched the analysis.[68] These experiences show how the patriarchal politics of Black nationalism circumscribed the intellectual potential of the new discipline. Deborah Gray White, Darlene Clark Hine, Rosalyn Terborg-Penn, Sharon Harley, and many other Black women scholars have all been instrumental not only in redefining the fields of history and African American studies but also in doing the difficult and bruising breakthrough work that has helped the discipline of Black studies come closer to achieving an inclusive counterhegemonic vision.

By the 1980s, male scholars in African American studies were feeling the effects of Black feminism and Black women's scholarship more generally, and a few began to rethink their own research and pedagogy. At the University of Massachusetts in Amherst, John Bracey participated in a two-year faculty seminar on the differences, similarities, and underlying assumptions between Black studies and women's studies, and he later developed three new courses devoted to Black women's history.[69] Teaching a course in Black women's history in the Black studies department at Ohio State prompted Manning Marable to publish the essay "Groundings with My Sisters: Patriarchy and the Exploitation of Black Women" in 1983. "Black social history as it has been written to date has been profoundly patriarchal," Marable concluded. "The sexist critical framework of American white history has been accepted by Black male scholars."[70]

In Marable's view, this serious problem required that Black male intellectuals and activists engage in a rigorous retraining and rethinking. "Black male liberationists must relearn their own history," he argued, "by grounding themselves all the time in the wisdom of their sisters." While the essay's brief overview of history illustrates Black women's oppression and resistance, and shows the prevalence of patriarchal gender roles in Black nationalist movements, Marable was also intent upon emphasizing a counter-Black-male feminist tradition. He highlighted especially the vigorous advocacy for women's suffrage and equality by both Frederick Douglass and W.E.B. Du Bois.[71] Rhett Jones later argued that "Black studies was miraculously rescued by Womanist scholars of both genders, various races, and not—as some would have it—by those copycatting white feminists." This view perhaps spreads the credit too thin, as particular recognition is due Black female intellectuals, but his framing of the new scholarship as a rescue is instructive.[72]

The emergence of scholarship in African diaspora studies and Black women's studies, to take just two examples, exemplifies a critical point about the recent history of African American studies: on balance, its stature in the academy has rested on the production of innovative and influential scholarship. The quest for curricular standardization and a single authoritative Black studies methodology has generated interesting debates and useful materials, yet tellingly, neither ever seems to have been achieved, and still the discipline develops and moves forward.

The early Black studies movement opened a broader space for subaltern discourses in academia than many of its founders initially expected. The Black student movement and the rise of Black studies inspired a push by other marginalized groups for representation in research and teaching, including Asian Americans, Native Americans, Latinos and Latinas, all women, and gays and lesbians. As one scholar put it, "Just as the larger Black liberation movement has catalyzed activity against various facets of oppression, Black studies has given rise to calls by other groups—Puerto Ricans, Mexican Americans, Asian Americans, Native Americans, white ethnics, women and gays among them—for scholastic treatment of their experiences."[73] This is an extremely important legacy of the early Black studies movement. Yet, at the same time, Black studies has had a vexed relationship to these other developments, and a particularly fraught relationship with ethnic studies. On the one hand, Black studies has been an inspiration and fellow traveler to Asian American and Latino studies, yet on the other hand it's a wary coethnic and questioning ally. Since it was in the vanguard of the campus struggle, Black studies generated an image of power and clout in the eyes of many Latino and Asian American activists, yet Black people, especially in the housing and employment markets and certainly in the criminal legal system, have often felt vulnerable, even expendable, in relation to other nonwhite ethnic groups.

Ethnic studies first emerged in California and New York in the late 1960s. Typically, Asian American, Mexican American, or Puerto Rican students joined campus revolts launched by Black students, and made their own demands for curricular inclusion. Administrators in California often sought to group Asian, Latino, and African American studies together as ethnic studies. Sometimes this term arose following unsuccessful efforts to constitute a separate college of Third World studies. The shift in terminology itself reflects a process of rising administrative design and control. Sometimes, as at Los Angeles and San Diego, Black student leaders welcomed such joint efforts, but at other campuses the proponents of Black studies objected to unified consolidation. This was most famously true at Berkeley, where the original demand for a Third World college was ultimately incorporated into the university as the Department of Ethnic Studies, which Black studies faculty seceded from in the mid-1970s. They desired autonomy.

The scholar Alan Colon argued that grouping these diverse units together under ethnic studies "while clearly providing the chance for comparative study, would tend to make for conflicting agendas in program content to the disadvantage of all. No racial or ethnic studies program," he believed, "should lose sight of its specific intellectual-cognitive goals and tasks for the sake of a tenuous universal ethnic studies program unity." He stressed the pitfalls of having to compete for scarce resources, a view that was particularly widespread in the cash-strapped 1970s. "To introduce the element of racial-ethnic groups competing for diminishing resources under the same administrative umbrella has no positive advantage and may be viewed in some instances as a central administrative tactic to divide and conquer in some institutions hostile to Black studies." Yet this chronicler ended by advising that "possibilities for inter-racial and inter-ethnic cooperation in other projects on and off campus" should be "explored, nourished and actualized."[74] An assessment of the field conducted in 1994 for the Ford Foundation conveyed a continuing ambivalence. "In the coming years," Valerie Smith and Robert O'Meally predict, "The question of where African American studies will stand in relation to ethnic studies and revamped American studies programs will be prominent and difficult." They urge supporting collaborations but caution that many in Black studies fear losing ground unless its visibility and autonomy are preserved. In the words of a Black studies scholar, "When people say 'ethnic' they don't usually mean Blacks."[75]

At most institutions, ethnic studies arose after African American studies and has been incorporated separately into the academy. Yet, on many other campuses, especially those with smaller student-of-color populations, African American studies is grouped together with Asian, Latino, and Native American units to form a single ethnic studies programs. The newer programs, such as many Asian American studies programs established in the Midwest and East Coast in the 1990s, face the numerous challenges of being small, understaffed, and intellectually marginalized or misunderstood.[76] Still, it seems that when the questions of turf, existence, and administrative form are settled, the possibilities for greater intellectual discussion and collaboration along the lines of comparative race and diaspora can develop. A cutting-edge infrastructure for interdisciplinary, transnational ethnic studies has begun to emerge, including journals such as *Social Text, American Quarterly, Small Axe,* and *Ethnic and Racial Studies,* as well as numerous conferences. These collaborations and conceptual innovations have exerted a powerful intellectual influence in African American studies and ethnic studies in the twenty-first century.

In the early 1970s, many skeptics of various political persuasions had questioned whether African American studies would have longevity in colleges and universities. Some more conservative scholars predicted that its lack of intellectual reputation and overly political orientation would consign it to a short life, while many Black scholars questioned whether the academy would ever truly incorporate an intellectual insurgency led and defined by Black people. As we have seen, many of the more radical, expansive, community-connected visions for Black studies were defeated before they even had a chance to get off the ground. Moreover, the United States has a diverse and localized system of higher education, and many colleges and universities traversed this era relatively untouched by the Black studies movement. But despite numerous obstacles and challenges, African American studies has not only survived but also grown to have international stature and presence.[77] Crucially, despite ongoing rumors of its demise, African American studies continues to attract intellectuals who have produced the scholarly innovations and breakthroughs that have helped bring longevity to the discipline.

Reflections on the Movement and Its Legacy

The Black liberation movement did not unravel after the murder of Martin Luther King Jr., but grew and irrevocably changed the landscape of American higher education. The Black student and Black studies movements were forceful continuations of the overall Black freedom struggle, yet they have been comparatively forgotten or severed from the longer civil rights narrative. Why the amnesia? Perhaps it is not surprising that challenges to the status quo are quickly buried or discredited in popular narratives. Indeed, the Black student movement grew to encompass wide-ranging critiques of American society—from militarism to racial oppression, and it united a broad spectrum of African American, Latino, white, and Asian American liberals and radicals. Perhaps the censorship has been internally generated as well: maybe the students' confrontational rhetoric and tactics complicated their inclusion in the pantheon of civil rights heroes. Needless to say, vandalizing cars, planting small bombs, and calling administrators "motherfuckers" does not conform to the politics of respectability. Nevertheless, a budding scholarship, as well as the widespread campus commemorations of the fortieth anniversary of student strikes and Black studies programs, has begun to alter our understanding of the complexity of the late 1960s and the broad reach of the long civil rights movement.

The student activists of the late 1960s believed they could change society. They translated Black Power theories into concrete gains, producing, arguably, the most important and lasting movement victories of the late 1960s. Many of the ideas articulated by Malcolm X and Stokely Carmichael, such as gaining control over public institutions located in Black communities; reclaiming and revaluing Black people's African heritage; identifying with global anticolonial struggles; and throwing off the psychological shackles of self-hatred and internalized racism were all seriously and vigorously pursued by Black students and intellectuals on campuses across the country. The effects were profound. From open admissions to affirmative action and the rise of Black cultural centers and Black studies, the fruits of student protest permanently changed American higher education. Moreover, demands for Latino, Asian American, and women's studies soon followed, adding further dimensions to the opening up of collegiate and intellectual life and culture in the United States.

An unappreciated outcome of the Black student movement is the extent to which it enabled urban Black communities to make successful claims on local universities. Malcolm X College in Chicago, with its increase in Black faculty and administrators and its strong embrace of a mission to serve the needs of working-class Black Chicagoans, is a perfect example, but it was not unique. Community or junior colleges in scores of cities from Detroit to Los Angeles to Washington, D.C., underwent similar transformations and redefined missions, playing a vital role in both Black access to higher education and the opening up of professional and administrative opportunities in major urban institutions. San Francisco State, for all the harshness of the poststrike crackdown against strike leaders, became an important site of multiracial employment and educational opportunity in the Bay Area.

The quest for open admissions or large-scale entry of Black and Latino high school graduates into publicly funded urban colleges constituted a social leveling that challenged the more traditionally hierarchical college culture. And perhaps unsurprisingly, this effort spawned a forceful backlash, especially in New York City, with its storied history of immigrant success at City and Brooklyn Colleges. But what has been largely forgotten in the intense effort to overturn open admissions and restore the competitiveness of four-year public colleges is how white these institutions were in the late 1960s. While some may have viewed this as an appropriate exclusivity, many Black and Latino families saw it as blatantly exclusionary. And as city residents and taxpayers, they made a powerful push to make these institutions better serve their needs. A great tragedy is that open admissions got under way on the eve of the severe municipal fiscal crisis of the early 1970s. Funding for public universities was slashed just as their student populations shot up, and one by-product—the schools' greater reliance upon tuition to meet costs—has subsequently made higher education much more expensive for the contemporary working class and their children.

On the one hand, *The Black Revolution on Campus* is a fitting culmination to a narrative of civil rights reform that begins with *Brown*. The struggle to increase Black access to higher education is an affirmation of the long-standing conceptual links between education, opportunity, citizenship, and mobility in American ideology. African American college and university attendance and graduation rates rose as a result of this struggle. The Black student movement, in the context of the overall Black freedom struggle, successfully pressured institutions of higher education to place much greater emphasis and importance on Black college and university attendance and graduation. For a while at least, this appeared to become national policy, and the effects were significant. The opening up of greater educational opportunities for African Americans contributed to the growth and reconfiguration of the Black middle class in the 1970s and 1980s. Moreover, "diversity," in these years, was more than cosmetic: it signified a redistribution of resources. It meant opening up opportunities for people heretofore excluded, and this included not only African Americans but also other socially and economically marginalized minorities, such as Puerto Ricans, Mexican Americans, and Chinese Americans. In other words, affirmative action did not signal the pursuit of heterogeneity for the sake of heterogeneity, or diversity for the educational benefit of the white majority. Other students of color in these years had their own long histories of discrimination and struggle in the United States. The Latino and Asian American students who joined the radical campus movement were not part of the new wave of immigrants who came in enormous numbers to the United States in the decades following the 1965 congressional immigration reform. Rather, they were descendants of earlier histories of American labor recruitment, westward continental expansion, and overseas colonization.

On the other hand, *The Black Revolution on Campus* is a narrative of African Americans reconnecting with global struggles against imperialism and colonialism. The constricted definition of patriotism promulgated during the cold war had demanded a silencing of Black American support for anticolonial and antiwar struggles. Beginning with the Truman Doctrine of 1947, domestic civil rights struggles had been forcibly separated from broader anti-imperial struggles.[1] But the uprisings of the late 1960s changed everything. A global perspective by African American activists began to return as the civil rights movement intensified and radicalized, and as the war in Vietnam pulled increasing numbers of African Americans and other young men into the U.S. military. Not every Black student activist moved from campus Black Power to solidarity work for the Angolan or Zimbabwean independence struggles. But many did, and when the antiapartheid movement arose in the United States in the 1970s and 1980s it built on this foundation and drew many African American students and intellectuals.[2] The rise of African diaspora studies as part of the Black studies movement reflects this shift from the narrow Americanist thinking of the cold war era to a much broader and more critical global consciousness. Moreover, as the end of legal Jim Crow served to strengthen Black American citizenship and national affiliation, African American studies came to be a unique and generative space for debates over the meaning of national belonging versus the long history of diaspora consciousness and activist strategies.

This study offers a fresh appraisal of Black political thought during the Black Power era. It was a time of intense ideological fervor among young activists. The rising currents of Black nationalism galvanized this generation and inspired considerable grassroots organizing. Some were drawn to cultural nationalism, while others identified with a leftist analysis. Rather than remaining frozen in time, Black radicalism grew and evolved to incorporate new directions. Ideas in *The Autobiography of Malcolm X* and *Black Power: The Politics of Black Liberation* greatly inspired young people as they endeavored to redefine Black American identity and reshape American colleges. They succeeded in bringing a Black perspective to the entire process of integration, forcing administrators and faculty to hear their views and accommodate their cultural interests and aspirations. Students embraced many core tenets of Black nationalism, yet in many instances their Black nationalism was decidedly anti-imperialist and internationalist, owing certainly but not exclusively to the influence of the Black Panther Party and rising critiques of the Vietnam War. In some contexts, especially where there was a significant Asian American and Latino student population, this internationalism was articulated as Third Worldist, and in other contexts as Pan-Africanist. The students' evolving consciousness was shaped by experiences gained through alliances with Puerto Rican and Mexican American student struggles. Sometimes it was forged in study groups, where students read and debated a wide variety of texts. Moreover, as the 1960s gave way to the 1970s, Black feminism arose to dramatically influence the Black studies movement and Black radicalism in general. Black nationalism, in short, was subject to critique and reappraisal, and out of this process African American activists went in a variety of directions, joining labor, human rights, reparations, educational, environmental, prisoner rights, antiwar, and other social justice movements.

Scholars, including historians of the civil rights and Black Power eras, have neglected the rich history of historically Black colleges. In a narrative that diverges from the dominant story of school integration, African Americans strove forcefully to preserve the public Black college system in the 1970s. While still underfunded, and in some cases in acute crisis, HBCUs continue to serve a vital social and educational function, especially as affirmative action and other gains of the civil rights era have come under attack. The students' struggle put the quest for self-determination to test and helped to preserve important institutions that have shaped African American life and culture in the United States since the nineteenth century.

The Black Revolution on Campus reinforces the dialectic of reform and repression found in many accounts of the decline of the Black freedom struggle but suggests a wider swath of repression. Black student unions sometimes became targets of police surveillance and infiltration. Many campuses endured police invasions, and many experienced large numbers of student arrests and trials. For example, twenty-seven unarmed students at a state college in California were tried on seventy felony counts of conspiracy, assault, kidnapping, false imprisonment, robbery, and burglary in 1968 for occupying the president's office for four hours.[3] The police violence and shooting deaths at many Black colleges in the South sent a powerful message. Student protest was met with overwhelming state violence. Black lives were expendable, and white officers could kill with impunity. Considered singly, these episodes can appear disconnected, but together they demonstrate that it was not only Black Panthers or rioting youth who were targets of heavy-handed law enforcement in this era; upwardly mobile college students were, too. Still, it is important to acknowledge that the Orangeburg Massacre, in particular, helped to catalyze and give shape to a national Black student movement, which achieved many victories. Orangeburg may have been forgotten by many across the nation and whitewashed by South Carolina officialdom, but Black college students never forgot it and were inspired by the tragedy to intensify their own campus struggles.

Campus radicals of the late 1960s are often portrayed as either idealistic collegians who eventually settled down to adult lives of affluence,
professional ambition, and retreat from radicalism, or as irresponsible,
wild-eyed youth whose brash acts inspired police crackdowns and then
the rise of the right. The first scenario may be commercially appealing
and the second provides a useful scapegoat, but both are misleading
portraits of student activists, particularly Black student activists. Many
individuals suffered reprisals or repression, which permanently altered
their lives. This is especially true for those at San Francisco State, North
Carolina A&T, Brooklyn College, Southern University, and all the other
campuses where students endured police invasion, expulsion, harassment, or arrest. Fred Prejean was profoundly affected by the murders of
Denver Smith and Leonard Brown at Southern University in East Baton
Rouge. Many veterans of the San Francisco State strike have lived with
the legacy of that epochal struggle in very personal ways. Nathan Hare
never returned to academia after his dismissal by Hayakawa and had to
switch careers. George Murray, Black Panther leader and aspiring English professor, left political activism behind after the strike and has
pastored a church in Oakland ever since. SNCC activist Cleveland Sellers was shot in the back in Orangeburg and unjustly prosecuted, but
today he is president of Voorhees College in Denmark, South Carolina.
In 2002, his son Bakari T. Sellers was elected to the state legislature,
where he pursued a reckoning with the Orangeburg Massacre. Activists
Howard Fuller and Nelson Johnson went through intense ideological
passages yet remain active community leaders, in Milwaukee and Greensboro, respectively.

To be sure, for many people, the late 1960s marked the high point of
their activism, "the golden years" as one student leader put it. But for
many, many others, those tumultuous college years were the beginning
of a lifetime of activism, public service, or political and legal advocacy.
Danny Glover, an actor and San Francisco State strike leader, exemplifies
the enduring commitment to social justice by many of this generation.
Moreover, the range of Glover's political interests, spanning education,
labor, human rights, and especially antiracism and anti-imperialism, reflects the expansive Black radicalism of the Bay Area.[4] Other veterans of
the San Francisco State strike followed a similar trajectory, notably Hari
Dillon, whose Vanguard Public Foundation made grants to social justice
initiatives around the country for three decades.

Many student activists went to law school. In an ironic outcome,
given the Black Power critique of civil rights lawyers, many student

activists themselves became civil rights lawyers. But their lawyering style and philosophy were deeply affected by the social justice movements of their youth. Northwestern graduate Victor Goode served as director of the National Conference of Black Lawyers and joined the faculty of the City University of New York Law School, a school designed to foster public interest lawyering. Malcolm X College graduate Stan Willis has become a leading human rights lawyer in Chicago, founding Black People Against Torture and fighting for justice for the scores of African American survivors of a twenty-year police torture ring in Chicago. Charles M. Powell Jr., a student leader at City College, became a civil rights lawyer after being urged by then state senator Basil A. Paterson to go to law school. "I realized my role in life was not just about making money but about helping people survive and get what they deserve," he remarked on the thirtieth anniversary of the occupation of south campus.[5] Eva Jefferson Paterson of Northwestern worked with the Lawyers Committee for Human Rights for decades before founding her own organization, the Equal Justice Society in San Francisco. Howard student leader Lew Myers, who in 1969 believed that "black students were the best hope to save this country,"[6] graduated from Rutgers Law School and launched a career as a civil rights lawyer in Chicago, where he has represented, among others, the national Rainbow PUSH Coalition and Louis Farrakhan. D'Army Bailey, who led the Black People's Committee of Inquiry at Southern, served as a public defender and a judge in Tennessee and helped found the National Civil Rights Museum in Memphis, which stands on the site of the demolished Lorraine Motel.

When Ramona Tascoe entered San Francisco State College in 1967, she "intended to go to law school and become president of the United States." A triple major, she worked her way through college in the medical office of the legendary Carlton Goodlett, a physician, civil rights activist, and newspaper publisher. One day, Goodlett and his medical partner, who happened to head the local NAACP, asked her, "Why law?" and she responded, "Why not?" In unison, they replied, "Because you'd be one hell of a doctor." As a result, she turned down Stanford Law School and applied to medical school. With the revolution cresting in the Bay Area, Tascoe began to view medical school "as a safe place to hide." She was afraid to die, she said, and had begun "to see that leaders who were passionate and had a lot of capacity faced a risk of being killed." However, the University of California, San Francisco, School of

Medicine twice rejected her—unfortunately they judged phenomena unrelated to the practice of medicine. Her Afro was evidently too big. "We do not need anyone looking like Angela Davis coming to UCSF," they told her. She was finally admitted and has practiced medicine in Oakland for decades; more recently, she brought medical relief to Haiti following the earthquake of 2010.[7]

Many student activists entered the field of education or joined the academy, including Black studies. John Bracey and James Turner played vital roles in both the student movement and the Black studies movement. Bracey joined the faculty of the University of Massachusetts, Amherst, in 1972, where he taught African American history and helped develop a PhD program in African American studies. He and his colleagues assisted efforts to build Black studies programs at neighboring colleges, making western Massachusetts a surprising center of the movement. Turner played a leading role in the African Heritage Studies Association and brought a Pan-Africanist philosophy to the Africana Studies and Research Center at Cornell. Askia Davis, a Brooklyn College student leader and former Black Panther, built a career at the New York City Board of Education, serving as senior assistant to several chancellors. Northwestern student activist Wayne Watson has served as chancellor of Chicago City Colleges and president of Chicago State University. Abdul Alkalimat has pioneered "eblack studies" and is committed to bringing Black studies fully into the digital era.

This book demonstrates a complex origin story of African American studies in the academy. African American studies took root in historically Black colleges early in the twentieth century but was somewhat eclipsed by the long fight for integration in the postwar era. A clamor for it arose in the latter half of the 1960s at every type of college in the country—Black, white, public, private, two-year, four-year, and liberal arts—and at research universities. Students demanded it; on many campuses they helped to create it, and they rightly deserve credit for its beginnings. But then the narrative gets more complicated. On some campuses, students continued to stay vitally involved in forging the character and mission of Black studies programs. But on others, student activists passed the baton to administrators and professors, and as the overall Black liberation movement declined, the political mission of Black studies was not always embraced with the same perspective or fervor. The sense of its political potential tended to shift from a hope for broader social transformation and Black community empowerment to a narrower intellectual or academic transformation. To be sure, an intellectual transformation is no small thing, but the point is that many student activists had envisioned a more dramatic, even revolutionary, potential for Black studies. And as well, this view may have been a miscalculation. Indeed, many student activists graduated and went on to medical and law school, or organized in factories and Black communities, or journeyed overseas to help build new African nation-states, and began to see the terrain of struggle as necessarily broader than the campus.

The faculty who labored to incorporate African American studies into permanent programs, centers, departments, and even distinct colleges had a distinguished scholarly and literary tradition upon which to build. Frederick Douglass, St. Clair Drake, W.E.B. Du Bois, Carter G. Woodson, Horace Cayton, Ida B. Wells, Richard Wright, Ralph Ellison, Lorraine Hansberry, Abram Harris, Ralph Bunche, Oliver Cox, and many others could have easily wound up on a course syllabus. (Although a big problem in early Black studies courses was that much of this material was out of print.) Moreover, important scholarship continued to be produced by historians, sociologists, anthropologists, literary scholars, political scientists, and other academics during the 1970s and beyond. But during the first decade and beyond, Black studies programs did not always succeed in attracting research-active, professionally ambitious scholars, in large part because the fledgling discipline faced the challenge of winning institutional legitimacy and respect. In addition, some Black scholars sought to steer clear of the seeming politicization of African American studies and its association with Black nationalism.

Still, a wide-ranging group of Black artists, writers, educators, and activists rose to the occasion and helped to create African American studies departments, centers, and programs. And for these builders of the field, its links to the student movement, or Black radicalism or nationalism more generally, was a source of pride rather than lament. This feeling was mostly true of the first cohort of faculty hired to teach Black studies at San Francisco State. James Turner instilled this ethos in the Africana Center at Cornell. Michael Thelwell helped to build a department at the University of Massachusetts, Amherst, with a dynamic faculty composed of activists from the Black liberation movement, including John Bracey, William Strickland, and Ernest Allen. At Harvard, Ewart Guinier brought deep experience in labor and community organizing to his role as the chair of an embattled department. He may not have been an academic, and that likely put him at a disadvantage in navigating the rarified terrain of Harvard, but he did understand a political fight and he staunchly defended the department's integrity and mission.

In the short term, the Black studies movement fulfilled the students' goal of bridging the gap between campus and community, but ultimately its greatest impact has been in humanities and social science scholarship and in undergraduate, and increasingly graduate, education. Within the academy, Black studies has been judged by its contribution to scholarship and research innovation. In the early years, its accomplishments in these areas were widely questioned—indeed, answering skepticism about the scholarly legitimacy of Black studies consumed considerable energy in the discipline's first twenty years. Nonetheless, Black studies has ushered in a transformation of graduate training and knowledge production in the United States, putting categories of race and, ultimately, gender, class, sexuality, and ethnicity at the center of intellectual analysis across disciplines. Moreover, its emphasis on experiential learning is now considered a normal part of higher education. And it has modeled a diasporic and transnational orientation increasingly adopted in American studies and long a part of ethnic studies.

The hiring and promotion of Black faculty in departments other than African American studies, however, remains a slow process. The persistently low percentage of Black faculty at predominantly white universities, especially at elite ones, is the most powerful illustration of the limits to change in the American academy. Moreover, despite the many positive changes achieved through activism and policy reform, conservatives began organizing to reverse many of these gains almost immediately, especially open admissions and affirmative action in admissions. That story is beyond the scope of this study, but the conservative backlash against taking race into account in order to achieve a diverse student body has achieved considerable success in courts, legislatures, public opinion, and ballot initiatives.[8]

Perhaps we should revisit the insights of student leaders in the late 1960s to find our way out of this backlash, which, combined with soaring educational costs, has put higher education out of reach for so many or subjected them to extraordinary indebtedness. Black student activists and their allies insisted that higher education was a right not a privilege. They insisted that government make higher education available and affordable to all who sought it. Thus, they argued that public universities should be robustly supported by tax dollars. They rejected the market-driven approach that dominates the contemporary landscape of higher education, and viewed the discourse of merit as laden with disguised class and race privilege—a critique with continuing validity. Here, the students pushed the civil rights movement beyond a quest for equal opportunity in the current system, into a quest for much wider opportunity in a transformed system. And as with so many other struggles in the civil rights era, this one offered benefits not only to Black students but also to a much more diverse group of working-class youth.

Notes

INTRODUCTION

1. Cecil Williams, interview transcript, n.d., and Ron Dellums, interview transcript, n.d., Series 57, Box 13, Records of the National Commission on the Causes and Prevention of Violence, Lyndon B. Johnson Presidential Library, University of Texas, Austin; student quote from "Black Studies versus White Studies: 1969—a Year of Profound Identity Crisis for American Education," author unknown, c. 1969, Institute of the Black World Papers (hereafter IBW Papers), Box: Black studies: Aspen conference, Schomburg Center for Research in Black Culture, New York Public Library (hereafter Schomburg Center).

2. The few case studies of the Black student movement include Wayne Glasker, *Black Students in the Ivory Tower: African American Student Activism at the University of Pennsylvania, 1967–1990* (Amherst: University of Massachusetts Press, 2002); Joy Ann Williamson, *Black Power on Campus: University of Illinois, 1965–1975* (Urbana: University of Illinois Press, 2003); and Stefan Bradley, *Harlem vs. Columbia University: Black Student Power in the Late 1960s* (Urbana: University of Illinois Press, 2009). A sociological analysis of the institutional response to crisis is Fabio Rojas, *From Black Power to Black Studies: How a Radical Social Movement Became an Academic Discipline* (Baltimore: Johns Hopkins University Press, 2007).

3. St. Claire Drake, "What Happened to Black Studies?" *New York University Educational Quarterly* 10, no. 3 (Spring 1979): 15.

4. Census figures reported in New York State Black Studies Conference, *Conference on Black Studies* (Albany: New York State Education Department, 1978), 13.

5. There is a large scholarship on Black Power. See for example William Van Deburg, *New Day in Babylon: The Black Power Movement and American Culture* (Chicago: University of Chicago Press, 1992); Gerald Horne, *Fire This Time: The Watts Uprising and the 1960s* (Cambridge, MA: Da Capo Press, 1997); Robert Self, *American Babylon: Race and the Struggle for Postwar Oakland* (Princeton, NJ: Princeton University Press, 2004); Matthew Countryman, *Up South: Civil Rights and Black Power in Philadelphia* (Philadelphia: University of Pennsylvania Press, 2006); and Peniel Joseph, *Waiting till the Midnight Hour: A Narrative History of Black Power in America* (New York: Henry Holt, 2007).

6. See for example Donna Murch, *Living for the City: Migration, Education and the Rise of the Black Panther Party in Oakland, CA* (Chapel Hill: University of North Carolina Press, 2010).

7. A third group that sought to organize students was the Revolutionary Action Movement, an obscure, mostly underground network active in several northern cities for a short time in the 1960s. Its efforts are more difficult to document and verify. See an account by a former RAM leader: Muhammad Ahmad, *We Will Return in the Whirlwind: Black Radical Organizations, 1960–1975* (Chicago: Charles H. Kerr, 2007).

8. A remarkable number of participants and observers wrote books about the strike, including student journalists, a government commission, faculty members, and a fired president of the college. See chapter 2 for the citations. For more recent accounts that differ from mine, see Rojas, *From Black Power to Black Studies;* and Noliwe Rooks, *White Money/Black Power: The Surprising History of African American Studies* (Boston: Beacon Press, 2006).

9. Robert L. Allen, "Politics of the Attack on Black Studies," *Black Scholar* 6 (September 1974): 2.

CHAPTER 1. "MOVING TOWARD BLACKNESS"

1. Bennett Johnson, interview by author, Chicago, December 12, 2005. Dr. Du Bois made this comment at a forum organized by Johnson at the University of California, Los Angeles, c. 1955.

2. J. Anthony Lukas, "The Negro Student at an Integrated College," *New York Times,* June 3, 1968.

3. Richard J. Margolis, "The Two Nations at Wesleyan University," *New York Times,* January 18, 1970.

4. George Henderson, *Race and the University: A Memoir* (Norman: University of Oklahoma Press, 2010), 60.

5. Monteith, Coar, and Malone, quoted from "1968 + 40: The Black Student Movement and Its Legacy," November 1, 2008, Center for African American History, Northwestern University, Evanston, IL.

6. Francie Latour, "The Basis of Our Ethos," *Wellesley* 92, no. 3 (Spring 2008): 24.

7. Malcolm X, quoted from "A Summing Up: Louis Lomax interviews Malcolm X," 1963, Teaching American History, http://teachingamericanhistory.org/library/index.asp?document=539, accessed October 15, 2010.

8. Paul E. Wisdom and Kenneth A. Shaw, "Black Challenge to Higher Education," *Educational Record* (American Council on Education) (Fall 1969), IBW Papers, Box: Black studies: Aspen conference, Schomburg Center.

9. Daniel H. Perlstein, *Justice, Justice: School Politics and the Eclipse of Liberalism* (New York: Peter Lang, 2004), 141–142.

10. David E. Rosenbaum, "Study Finds State Universities Lag in Enrollment of Negroes," *New York Times,* May 18, 1969.

11. Latour, "The Basis of Our Ethos," 25.

12. Ramona Tascoe, telephone interview by author, December 3, 2009.

13. Wesley Profit, telephone interview by author, July 28, 2005.

14. Denmark and Dempsey quoted in "What Happened?" in the audio recording "Columbia: 1968 + 40," April 25, 2008, Columbia 1968 Web site, www.columbia1968.com/conference/, accessed December 12, 2011. See also John Kifner, "Columbia's Radicals Hold a Bittersweet Reunion," *New York Times,* April 28, 2008.

15. Charles V. Hamilton, "They Demand Relevance: Black Students Protest, 1968–1969" (unpublished manuscript, c. 1971), 15, copy in author's possession.

16. Carol Oliver, "Separatism and Black Consciousness," *Emphasis: Daily Northwestern Magazine,* February 14, 1969, copy in author's possession.

17. "Black Studies versus White Studies: 1969—a Year of Profound identity Crisis for American Education," author unknown, c. 1969, IBW Papers, Box: Black studies: Aspen conference, Schomburg Center.

18. Lukas, "The Negro Student."

19. Latour, "The Basis of Our Ethos," 25.

20. Nan Robertson, "The Student Scene: A Feeling of Powerlessness Provokes Anger among Militants," *New York Times,* November 20, 1967.

21. Hamilton, "They Demand Relevance," 28, 41.

22. Ibid., 19.

23. Ibid., 31–32, emphasis in the original.

24. Gael Graham, *Young Activists: American High School Students in the Age of Protest* (DeKalb: Northern Illinois University Press, 2006), 59–61.

25. Hamilton, "They Demand Relevance," 42–43.

26. For Williams, see Timothy Tyson, *Radio Free Dixie: Robert F. Williams and the Roots of Black Power* (Chapel Hill: University of North Carolina Press, 1999).

27. Henderson, *Race and the University,* 37.

28. *Black Heritage,* Episode 12–100, transcript, n.d., John Henrik Clarke Papers, Box 12, Folder 31, Schomburg Center.

29. Hamilton, "They Demand Relevance," 40.

30. Ibid., 34.

31. Henderson, *Race and the University,* 40.

32. Graham, *Young Activists,* 60.

33. Ibid., 59.

34. Lukas, "The Negro Student"; Durward Long, "Black Protest," in *Protest! Student Activism in America,* ed. Julian Foster and Durward Long (New York: William Morrow, 1969), 466.

35. Darlene Clark Hine, "Becoming a Black Woman's Historian," in *Living Histories: Black Women Historians in the Ivory Tower*, ed., Deborah Gray White (Chapel Hill: University of North Carolina Press, 2008), 47–49.

36. Deborah Gray White, "My History in History," in *Living Histories: Black Women Historians in the Ivory Tower*, ed. White (Chapel Hill: University of North Carolina Press, 2008), 88.

37. Hamilton, "They Demand Relevance," 66–67, emphasis in the original.

38. Lukas, "The Negro Student."

39. Hamilton, "They Demand Relevance," 38–39.

40. Sally Avery Bermanzohn, *Through Survivors' Eyes: From the Sixties to the Greensboro Massacre* (Nashville, TN: Vanderbilt University Press, 2003), 76.

41. Long, "Black Protest," 474; Denmark, quoted from audio recording "Columbia: 1968+40."

42. Hamilton, "They Demand Relevance," 75.

43. Charles Ogletree, "Brown Babies at Stanford in the Early 1970s," *Journal of Blacks in Higher Education* (Summer 2004): 82.

44. Hamilton, "They Demand Relevance," 75.

45. Ibid., 70.

46. Darwin T. Turner, "The Center for African Afro-American Studies at North Carolina Agricultural and Technical State University," *Journal of Negro Education* 39, no. 3 (Summer 1970): 221–22.

47. *Hilltop* (Howard University), April 26, 1968, microfilm, Howard University Library, Washington, DC (hereafter HUL).

48. Linda Housch, quoted from *Black Heritage*, Episode 12–100, transcript.

49. Blair Justice, *Violence in the City* (Fort Worth: Texas Christian University Press, 1969), 43, 50.

50. NAACP, "NAACP to Defend Four Accused TSU Students," press release, June 10, 1967, NAACP Papers, Part 28, Series B, microfilm reel 10, Schomburg Center.

51. John Morsell to Attorney General Ramsey Clark, May 18, 1967, NAACP Papers, Part 28, Series B, microfilm reel 10, Schomburg Center.

52. Justice, *Violence in the City*, 40–46.

53. See Jack Bass and Jack Nelson, *The Orangeburg Massacre* (Macon, GA: Mercer University Press, 1970); and Cleveland Sellers, *The River of No Return: The Autobiography of a Black Militant and the Life and Death of SNCC* (New York: William Morrow, 1973). Twenty-five years later, Sellers received an official pardon.

54. Bermanzohn, *Through Survivors' Eyes*, 77; Karanja Keita Carroll and Itibari M. Zulu, "Dr. William M. King Interviewed: National Council of Black Studies Founding Member," *Journal of Pan African Studies* 3, no. 1 (September 2009): 24. See chapter 3 for a discussion of a mock funeral march on the west side of Chicago protesting the massacre.

55. *In loco parentis* refers to the university's legal assumption of parental authority over students who had not yet reached the age of adulthood, which in this period commenced at age twenty-one. Colleges imposed a vast array of rules relating to personal freedom, notably to prevent sexual interaction among males and females. There tended to be stricter regulation of female conduct.

56. Lawrence B. de Graaf, "Howard: The Evolution of a Black Student Revolt," *Protest! Student Activism in America,* ed. Julian Foster and Durward Long (New York: William Morrow, 1969), 321.

57. Ibid., 320–321.

58. Charles Hamilton, "The Place of the Black College in the Human Rights Struggle," *Negro Digest* 16, no. 11 (September 1967): 6–7, italics in the original.

59. Graaf, "Howard," 326.

60. *Hilltop,* September 15, 1967, microfilm, HUL.

61. Nathan Hare, interviewed by Robert Wright, November 17, 1968, transcript, 17, Ralph Bunche Civil Rights Documentation Project (hereafter Bunche Project), Moorland-Spingarn Collection, HUL.

62. *Hilltop,* editorial, September 22, 1967, microfilm, HUL.

63. Michael Harris, interviewed by Robert Martin, June 25, 1968, transcript, 11, 26, 33, Bunche Project, HUL.

64. Graaf, "Howard," 332.

65. *Hilltop,* March 8, 1968, microfilm, HUL.

66. Sara Slack, "Howard Students Mar Charter Day," *New York Amsterdam News,* March 16, 1968.

67. Courtland Cox, Marvin Holloway, and Charlie Cobb, "Occupation of a Building Brings New Dimensions" *Hilltop,* March 29, 1968, microfilm, HUL.

68. *Hilltop,* March 22 and 29, 1968, microfilm, HUL.

69. Graaf, "Howard," 235; *Hilltop,* March 29, 1968, microfilm, HUL.

70. *Hilltop,* March 19, 1968, microfilm, HUL.

71. Adrienne Manns, interview, August 1968, transcript, 35–37, 40, 45, Bunche Project, HUL.

72. George Gent, "TV: Negro Students Bare Resentment," *New York Times,* May 7, 1968.

73. Graaf, "Howard," 319; *Hilltop,* March 29, 1968, microfilm, HUL.

74. "Tuskegee Students Boycott Classes over Grievances," *New York Times,* March 26; "Tuskegee Students Lock in Trustees," *New York Times,* April 8, 1968.

75. Sara Slack, "The Rebellion in Our Colleges," *New York Amsterdam News,* May 18, 1968, 1.

76. Ibid. Wellesley agreed to add twenty more Black students for the fall, if they were found to be "qualified." "We will not lower our standards," an administrator declared.

77. For the California Master Plan for education, see Peter Shapiro and William Barlow, *An End to Silence: The San Francisco State College Student Movement in the 1960s* (New York: Bobbs-Merrill, 1971).

78. Harry Edwards, *The Revolt of the Black Athlete* (New York: Macmillan, 1969).

79. An important exception is the recent study by Donna Murch, *Living for the City: Education, Migration and the Rise of the Black Panther Party in Oakland, California* (Chapel Hill: University of North Carolina Press, 2010).

80. Alan Colon, "Black Studies: Historical Background, Modern Origins, and Development Priorities for the Early Twenty First Century," *Western Journal of Black Studies* 27, no. 3 (Fall 2003): 150.

81. Long, "Black Protest," 474; "Black Studies Gaining Shaky Niche on Campus," *Los Angeles Times,* May 7, 1972.

82. Jack McCurdy, "Afro-American Teacher Credential Approved," *Los Angeles Times,* October 11, 1968, 3; Charles Hamilton, "They Demand Relevance," 100–101; Soul Students Advisory Council, "Position Paper on Black Studies," n.d., IBW Papers, Survey of Black Studies Programs, Box 3, "Merritt College" Folder, Schomburg Center. See also Murch, *Living for the City,* 111–116.

83. Murch, *Living for the City,* 100.

CHAPTER 2. "A REVOLUTION IS BEGINNING"

1. The strike deserves a book-length, rather than chapter-length, treatment. See the many accounts penned by participants or observers: William H. Orrick Jr., *Shut It Down! A College in Crisis: San Francisco State College, October 1968–April 1969* (Washington, DC: National Commission on the Causes and Prevention of Violence, 1969); Robert Smith, Richard Axen, and Devere Pentony, *By Any Means Necessary: The Revolutionary Struggle at San Francisco State* (San Francisco: Jossey-Bass, 1970); Dikran Karaguezian, *Blow It Up! The Black Student Revolt at San Francisco State and the Emergence of Dr. Hayakawa* (Boston: Gambit, 1971); and William Barlow and Peter Shapiro, *An End to Silence: The San Francisco State College Student Movement in the '60s* (New York: Pegasus, 1971). These recent scholarly accounts differ somewhat from mine: Fabio Rojas, *From Black Power to Black Studies: How a Radical Social Movement Became an Academic Discipline* (Baltimore: Johns Hopkins University Press, 2007); and Noliwe Rooks, *White Money/Black Power: The Surprising History of African American Studies* (Boston: Beacon Press, 2006).

2. Bernard Stringer, telephone interview by author, October 22, 2009.

3. Jimmy Garrett, interview by author, Berkeley, California, August 9, 2005.

4. Jimmy Garrett, interview transcript, n.d., Records of the National Commission on the Causes and Prevention of Violence, Series 57, Box 13, Lyndon B. Johnson Presidential Library, University of Texas (hereafter LBJ); Garrett, interview by author.

5. Barlow and Shapiro, *An End to Silence,* 91.

6. George Murray, interview by author, Oakland, California, August 11, 2005.

7. Jerry Varnado, interview by author, San Francisco, August 12, 2005.

8. Karaguezian, *Blow It Up!* 9.

9. Hari Dillon, telephone interview by author, January 10, 2010.

10. Karaguezian, *Blow It Up!* 40–41; Garrett, interview, LBJ.

11. "Black Studies Curriculum 1968," in Strike Collection, BSU Folder, Special Collections, San Francisco State University, San Francisco (hereafter SFSU); Ramona Tascoe, telephone interview by author, December 3, 2009.

12. Joyce A. Joyce, *Black Studies as Human Studies: Critical Essays and Interviews* (Albany: State University of New York Press, 2005), 154–157.

13. It is vital to recognize that the Black studies movement of the late 1960s was but one phase in a long history of Black scholarship and letters, whose roots date to abolitionism.

14. Barlow and Shapiro, *An End to Silence*, 127; Varnado, interview; Orrick, *Shut It Down!* 115.

15. Garrett, interview by author.

16. Ibid.; John Summerskill, *President Seven* (New York: World Publishing, 1971).

17. Garrett, interview, LBJ; Nathan Hare, interview transcript, n.d., Box 13, LBJ; Barlow and Shapiro, *An End to Silence*, 135; see Orrick, *Shut It Down!*, appendix, for a copy of Hare's proposal.

18. Garrett later said that Hare "always credits me or discredits me with being the founder of Black studies. And I always credit him or discredit him with making it happen." Garrett, interview by author.

19. John Bunzel, "Black Studies at San Francisco State," *Public Interest* 13 (Fall 1968).

20. Smith, Axen, and Pentony, *By Any Means Necessary*, 141.

21. Ron Dellums, interview transcript, Box 13, LBJ.

22. "Lee," interview transcript, Box 13, LBJ.

23. Hare, interview, LBJ.

24. Hannibal Williams, interview transcript, Box 13, LBJ

25. Orrick, *Shut It Down!* 75.

26. State of California, Assembly, Select Committee on Campus Disturbances, *Report of the Select Committee on Campus Disturbances*, [May 1969], 160, Strike Collection, Folder: Select Committee on Campus Disturbances.

27. Clarence Thomas, telephone interview by author, January 18, 2010.

28. Barlow and Shapiro, *An End to Silence*, 112; Murray, interview; Thomas, telephone interview; Karaguezian, *Blow It Up!* 36–37; Dillon, telephone interview.

29. But the BSU, which had already persuaded the college to raise the number of EOP slots to 427 for the fall, did not formally join the SDS/TWLF protest. To the dismay of the BSU, however, the college fell short of its pledge, admitting only 300 students. The student body at SFSC that fall was 76 percent white, 5.3 percent Black, 2.3 percent Mexican American, and 8 percent "Oriental." Orrick, *Shut It Down!* 74; Dillon, telephone interview.

30. Orrick, *Shut It Down!* 28.

31. Barlow and Shapiro, *An End to Silence*, 186.

32. "SFS Footnotes," January 20, 1969, Box 12, LBJ.

33. Garrett, interview by author.

34. Karaguezian, *Blow It Up!* 68–83.

35. Smith, Axen, and Pentony, *By Any Means Necessary*, 133–135.

36. Karaguezian, *Blow It Up!* 83.

37. Smith, Axen, and Pentony, *By Any Means Necessary*, 122.

38. Tascoe, telephone interview.

39. Barlow and Shapiro, *An End to Silence*, 28; Karaguezian, *Blow It Up!* 37.

40. *Black Panther*, November 16, 1968, 13; Smith, Axen, and Pentony, *By Any Means Necessary*, 157; Orrick, *Shut It Down!* 33.

41. Karaguezian, *Blow It Up!* 87.

42. Ibid., 35.

43. Ibid., 38–39.

44. Ibid., 92.

45. Hare, interview, LBJ.

46. Nathan Hare, telephone interview by author, September 5, 2005; Orrick, *Shut It Down!*, appendix; Nathan Hare, "SFS BSU Demands," *Black Panther*, January 25, 1969.

47. Earl Caldwell, "Student Strikers on Coast Are Firm," *New York Times*, December 9, 1968.

48. Stokely Carmichael, speech transcript, Box 13, LBJ. College administrators evidently taped the speech surreptitiously.

49. Bennie Stewart, speech transcript, Box 13, LBJ. College administrators evidently taped the speech surreptitiously. See Robert Taber, *The War of the Flea: A Study of Guerrilla Warfare Theory and Practice* (New York: L. Stuart, 1965).

50. Dillon, telephone interview; Tascoe, telephone interview.

51. In order to protect the central committee from a mass arrest, only six members were allowed on campus each day, and each member had to prepare two students to take over his duties in the event of an arrest. Varnado, interview.

52. Tascoe, telephone interview.

53. Ibid.

54. Varnado, interview.

55. Dillon, telephone interview.

56. Tascoe, telephone interview.

57. Ibid.

58. Varnado, interview.

59. Karaguezian, *Blow It Up!* 115–116.

60. "Human Rights: Not Political Privileges," *Open Process*, January 22, 1969, Box 12, LBJ.

61. See San Francisco Bay Area Television Archive, San Francisco State University, www.library.sfsu.edu/about/collections/sfbatv/index.php.

62. Karaguezian, *Blow It Up!* 44–47; John Levin, notes from a talk, in author's possession, n.d.; John Levin, telephone interview by author, December 7, 2009.

63. Levin, notes from a talk; Levin, telephone interview.

64. Orrick, *Shut It Down!* 104.

65. Karaguezian, *Blow It Up!* 119.

66. KPIX, *Eye on the Bay News*, November 25, 1968, Bay Area Television Archive, SFSU, http://diva.sfsu.edu/collections/sfbatv/bundles/187260; Smith, Axen, and Pentony, *By Any Means Necessary*, 97.

67. Orrick, *Shut It Down!* 55.

68. Joseph White, telephone interview by author, December 9, 2009.

69. Wallace Turner, "Police Disperse a Campus Crowd," *New York Times*, December 5, 1968; Dillon, telephone interview.

70. Daryl E. Lembke, "3 Strike Leaders at S.F. State Seized by Police," *Los Angeles Times*, December 12, 1968; Smith, Axen and Pentony, *By Any Means Necessary*, 224.

71. Orrick, *Shut It Down!* 2.

72. *Wall Street Journal,* February 13, 1969, Box 10, LBJ.
73. John James Oliver, interview transcript, Box 13, LBJ.
74. Dellums, interview.
75. Brown, interview; Tom Fleming, "Hayakawa Rebuffs Community," *Sun Reporter,* December 7, 1968, 3.
76. Dr. Wesley Johnson, interview transcript, Box 13, LBJ.
77. Samuel Jackson, interview transcript, Box 13, LBJ; "Mediators Meet at S.F. State," *San Francisco Chronicle,* December 20, 1968; Karaguezian, *Blow It Up!* 180.
78. Orrick, *Shut It Down!* 125; Willie Brown, interview transcript, Box 13, LBJ.
79. Williams, interview.
80. Reginald Major, interview transcript, Box 13, LBJ.
81. Orrick, *Shut It Down!* 56.
82. Ibid., 38; Karaguezian, *Blow It Up!* 113.
83. *Wall Street Journal,* February 13, 1969, Box 10, LBJ; Smith, Axen, and Pentony, *By Any Means Necessary,* 303.
84. Tascoe, telephone interview.
85. Varnado, interview.
86. Orrick, *Shut It Down!* 131.
87. Jackson, interview transcript.
88. Letters, Social Protest Collection, Box 23, Folder 55, Bancroft Library, University of California, Berkeley; Howard Finberg, ed., *Crisis at San Francisco State,* San Francisco, 1969, pamphlet, Social Protest Collection, Box 24, Folder 9, Bancroft Library.
89. San Francisco State College, *Campus Communications Newsletter,* January 15, 1969, Strike Collection, Don Scoble File, SFSU.
90. *Wall Street Journal,* February 13, 1969, Box 10, LBJ.
91. Walter Riley, interview by author, May 8, 2010, Oak Park, Illinois.
92. Gary Hawkins, Local 1352, AFT, "Memorandum," November 5, 1968, Box 23, Folder 54, Social Protest Collection, Bancroft Library, University of California, Berkeley; Local 1352, AFT Flyer, Box 23, Folder 54, Social Protest Collection; *The Partisan* (official strike bulletin), February 2, 1969, Box 23, Folder 54, Social Protest Collection; Thomas, telephone interview.
93. For a recent study, see Jeffrey Haas, *The Assassination of Fred Hampton: How the FBI and Chicago Police Murdered a Black Panther* (Chicago: Lawrence Hill Books, 2009).
94. See an account by a former FBI agent: M. Wesley Swearingen, *FBI Secrets* (Boston: South End Press, 1995), 82. There is considerable writing on the Black Panther Party. For two accounts of the UCLA shootings, see Elaine Brown, *A Taste of Power: A Black Woman's Story* (New York: Pantheon Books, 1993); and Scot Brown, *Fighting for Us: Maulana Karenga, the us Organization and Black Cultural Nationalism* (New York: New York University Press, 2003).
95. Mary Jane Hewitt, oral history conducted by Elston L. Carr, July 8, 1997, transcript, 65, UCLA Oral History Program, Center for African American Studies Library, UCLA; Virgil P. Roberts, oral history conducted by Elston

L. Carr, August 26, 1996, transcript, 42, UCLA Oral History Program, Center for African American Studies Library, UCLA.

96. Roberts, oral history, 42.

97. Maulana (Ron) Karenga, oral history conducted by Elston L. Carr, 1996–1999, transcript, 96, UCLA Oral History Program, Center for African American Studies Library, UCLA.

98. Roberts, interview, 45.

99. Hewitt, interview, 81.

100. Roberts, interview, 58.

101. *Daily Bruin,* September 30, 1969, vertical file, Center for African American Studies Library, UCLA; Scot Brown, *Fighting for Us;* Karenga, interview, 209.

102. Murray, interview.

103. *San Francisco Chronicle,* February 22, 1969, Box 10, LBJ.

104. Murray, interview.

105. Carleton Goodlett, interview transcript, Box 13, LBJ.

106. Dellums, interview.

107. Tascoe, telephone interview; White quoted in Eric Anthony Joseph, "Mandate for Diversity: A Comparative Analysis of the Black Studies Movement at San Francisco State University and the Afrikan-American Experience at Biola University" (EdD diss., Biola University, La Mirada, CA, 1994), 164, 170; White, telephone interview.

108. Tascoe, telephone interview

109. Leroy Goodwin, quoted in *Black Fire,* May 3, 1969, Strike Collection, Black Fire Folder, SFSU; Dillon, telephone interview.

110. Dillon, telephone interview; *KTVU News,* 1969–2007, Bay Area Television Archives, SFSU, http://diva.sfsu.edu/collections/sfbatv/bundles/187238, accessed April 2010.

111. Murray, interview.

112. Dillon, telephone interview.

113. Varnado, interview.

114. "Remembering the Strike," *SF State Magazine,* www.sfsu.edu/~sfsumag /archive/fall_08/strike.html.

115. Barlow and Shapiro, *An End to Silence,* 309; Karaguezian, *Blow It Up!* 194.

116. State of California, Assembly, Select Committee on Campus Disturbances, *Report of the Select Committee on Campus Disturbances,* 157.

117. *Black Fire,* November 6, 1969, Strike Collection, SFSU.

118. Willie L. Brown Jr., "Minority Report," in *Report of the Select Committee on Campus Disturbances,* by State of California, Assembly, Select Committee on Campus Disturbances, [May 1969], 160, Strike Collection, Folder: Select Committee on Campus Disturbances.

119. White, telephone interview; Urban Whittaker, "Open Letter," *On the Record,* November 10, 1969, Strike Collection, BSU Folder, SFSU.

120. Thomas, telephone interview.

121. Ibid.

122. Joseph, "Mandate for Diversity," 184–185.
123. Hare, interview by author.
124. Daryl Lembke, "SF State College Black Studies Department," *Los Angeles Times*, November 9, 1969.
125. Wallace Turner, "Black Issue Hits Hayakawa Again," *New York Times*, December 24, 1969, 30; Daryl Lembke, "SF State's Black Studies Still in Grip of Chaos," *Los Angeles Times*, August 10, 1970, 3.
126. *Phoenix*, April 30, 1970, Strike Collection, BSU folder, SFSU; Thomas, telephone interview.
127. "Black Studies Gaining Shaky Niche on Campus," *Los Angeles Times*, May 7, 1972.
128. "Ex-Sen. Hayakawa Dies," *Los Angeles Times*, February 28, 1992, 1.
129. "Black Studies Gaining Shaky Niche on Campus."
130. Stringer, telephone interview.
131. Hari Dillon, "We Did Not Struggle in Vain," 1988, transcript of speech, Strike Collection, 20th Anniversary Folder, Special Collections, SFSU.
132. Murray, interview.
133. Goodlett, interview.
134. White, telephone interview.

CHAPTER 3. "A TURBULENT ERA OF TRANSITION"

1. Bennett Johnson, interview by author, Chicago, December 12, 2005.
2. See especially Harry Edwards, *Revolt of the Black Athlete* (New York: Free Press, 1969).
3. "NU 1968: An Observance of an Era," a video by Cherilyn Wright and Barbara Parkins, May 18, 1991, copy in author's possession.
4. Sandra Hill, Sandra Malone, and Kathryn Ogletree, quoted from "1968+40: The Black Student Movement at Northwestern and Its Legacy," October 31–November 1, 2008, Center for African American History, Northwestern University, Evanston, IL (hereafter "1968+40: The Black Student Movement at Northwestern").
5. "NU 1968."
6. Ibid.
7. Michael Smith, quoted from "1968+40: The Black Student Movement at Northwestern."
8. John Bracey, interview by author, New York, July 6, 2005.
9. Ibid.
10. "Black and White at Northwestern University," *Integrated Education*, 6, no. 3 (May–June 1968): 33–48.
11. John Bracey, quoted from "1968+40: The Black Student Movement at Northwestern."
12. John Bracey, telephone interview by author, July 8, 2005.
13. Remarks at "1968+40: The Black Student Movement at Northwestern."
14. Eva Jefferson Paterson, letter to author, November 28, 2010.

15. Bracey, telephone interview by author, July 8, 2005. The radio show aired on WCFL, known as "The Voice of Labor" and owned for decades by the Chicago Federation of Labor.

16. Payson S. Wild, "Memorandum Concerning the Black Students' Seizure of the University Business Office, 619 Clark Street, on the Morning of May 3, 1968," June 30, 1987, Black Student Protest II, April–May 1968 Folder, University Archives, Northwestern University, Evanston, IL (hereafter UA, NU).

17. Lucius Gregg, remarks from "1968 + 40: The Black Student Movement at Northwestern."

18. Bracey, interview, July 6, 2005.

19. Gregg, remarks from "1968 + 40."

20. Open Letter by Richard C. Christian, president, Northwestern University Alumni Association, September 1968, Black Student Protest II, April–May 1968 Folder, UA, NU.

21. "Agreement between Afro-American Student Union and FMO and a Committee Representing the Northwestern University Administration," May 4, 1968, NAACP Papers, 1993 accession, Box 178, Library of Congress, Washington, DC.

22. Helen Welker to editor, Chicago Daily News, May 7, 1968, Black Student Protest II, April–May 1968 Folder, UA, NU.

23. "A Sad Day for Northwestern," editorial, Chicago Tribune, May 6, 1968, Black Student Protest II, April–May 1968 Folder, UA, NU. According to John Bracey, the students were able to persuade the publisher of the Tribune, who sat on the board of trustees of Northwestern, to issue an apology for the inaccuracies and distortions in the editorial. Bracey, interview,

24. "Change at Northwestern," editorial, Chicago Daily News, May 7, 1968, Black Student Protest II, April–May 1968 Folder, UA, NU.

25. "Black and White at Northwestern University," 33–48.

26. Gregg, remarks from "1968 + 40."

27. "N.U. Gets $75,000 Pledge," Chicago Tribune, May 22, 1968; "N.U. Gets Funds from Five Companies," Chicago Tribune, September 1, 1968."

28. John Higginson, quoted from "1968 + 40: The Black Student Movement at Northwestern."

29. "A Turning Point," Daily Northwestern, May 3, 1988, Black Student Protest II, April–May 1968 Folder, UA, NU.

30. "Black and White at Northwestern University," 44.

31. Jimmy Garrett, interview by author, Berkeley, CA, August 9, 2005.

32. "The Conflict over Black Studies," Daily Northwestern, December 1, 1972; "II. The Afro-American Program," n.d., CAS/African American Studies Department Box, "General" Folder, UA, NU.

33. John Higginson, "Afroamerican Studies Program: Where Does It Go from Here?" Emphasis: Daily Northwestern Magazine, February 14, 1969, copy in author's possession; Milton Gardner, "Northwestern and Its Myth of Black Studies," Daily Northwestern, January 16, 1970; "To Be Presented to the College of Arts and Sciences on Thursday, January 22, 1970," unsigned resolu-

tion, Payson Wild Papers, Series 5/1, Box 1, African American Studies Folder, UA, NU.

34. Committee on Afro-American Studies to Dean Laurence Nobles, November 2, 1970, Weinberg College of Arts and Sciences Collection, African American Studies Department Folder, UA, NU.

35. Payson Wild to Freddye L. Hill, acting chairman, Education Committee, c. July 1971, Payson Wild Papers, Series 5/1, Box 1, African American Studies Folder, UA, NU.

36. Sterling Stuckey, interview by author, Chicago, October 23, 2009.

37. Ibid., June 19, 2008.

38. Lerone Bennett to Lawrence Nobles, acting dean of the College of Arts and Sciences, Northwestern University, February 17, 1972, personal papers of Lerone Bennett; Lerone Bennett, interview by author, Chicago, September 25, 2008.

39. "Rumblings Plague Afro Studies Department," *Chicago Metro News*, December 23, 1972, CAS/African American Studies Department Box, "General" Folder, UA, NU.

40. "Students in Battle over Black Studies," *Chicago Defender*, December 30, 1972; "The Conflict over Black Studies"; Stuckey, interview; Robert Hill, telephone interview by author, April 19, 2010.

41. Robert Hill, telephone interview; Carol Rudisell, telephone interview by author, April 7, 2010; Freddye Hill, telephone interview by author, April 6, 2010; "FMO Ends Black Studies boycott," *Daily Northwestern*, January 9, 1974, copy in author's possession; "Stuckey Urges Blacks to Unite," *Daily Northwestern*, October 1, 1973, CAS, Records of the Dean, Box 36, Folder 8, UA, NU.

42. Jan Carew, "African American Studies at Northwestern: A Position Paper," n.d. [circa 1973], CAS/African American Studies Department Box, "General" Folder, UA, NU.

43. "African American Studies: A Deep NU Legacy," *Daily Northwestern*, October 10, 1986.

44. Standish Willis, interview by author, Chicago, June 13, 2006; Henry English, interview by author, Chicago, August 16, 2007.

45. Willis, interview.

46. Charles Webb, "Getting Ourselves Together," *Phoenix*, Standish Willis personal collection, copy in author's possession.

47. English, interview.

48. Willis, interview; English, interview.

49. Willis, interview.

50. George E. Lewis, *A Power Stronger Than Itself: The AACM and American Experimental Music* (Chicago: University of Chicago Press, 2008), 166, 168. In a depressing coda to this era of activism, Black pride, and cultural flowering, the theater was later taken over by the criminal organization known as the El Rukns, and it became known as "the Fort" after their leader, now incarcerated, Jeff Fort. Willis, interview.

51. Willis, interview.

52. Frank de la Cerna, acting chairman, Black Student Congress, to "Brothers and Sisters," October 1968, Standish Willis personal collection, copy in author's possession.

53. Willie Calvin, "What Black Students Want," *Phoenix*, c. 1968, Standish Willis personal collection, copy in author's possession.

54. Willis, interview.

55. English, interview; Willis, interview.

56. "Distributed by the Student Senate to Students of Crane College, May 8, 1968," Standish Willis personal collection.

57. Memorandum from Ad Hoc Committee on Student Demands to All Faculty and Students, May 31, 1968, Standish Willis personal collection; English, interview.

58. Willis, interview.

59. Commission on Institutions of Higher Education of the North Central Association of Colleges and Secondary Schools, "Report for Malcolm X College," May 24, 1971, 2, in Photograph Collection, "Charles Hurst" Folder, offices of the *Chicago Defender*, Chicago.

60. Ibid., 3.

61. *Student Handbook, 1970–1971*, Standish Willis personal collection.

62. English, interview.

63. Alex Poinsett, "The Mastermind of Malcolm X College," *Ebony*, March 1970, 30.

64. Willis, interview.

65. "Malcolm X," *Jet*, June 18, 1970.

66. Commission on Institutions of Higher Education of the North Central Association of Colleges and Secondary Schools, "Report for Malcolm X College," 7–12.

67. Willis, interview.

68. Ibid.; Robert Rhodes, interview by author, Chicago, August 9, 2009.

69. Adam Green, *Selling the Race: Culture, Community, and Black Chicago, 1940–1955* (Chicago: University of Chicago Press, 2009).

CHAPTER 4. "BROOKLYN COLLEGE BELONGS TO US"

1. "CUNY contains the largest number of Black and Latino scholars ever to attend a single university in the history of the United States. The importance of CUNY as a source of opportunity for non-white students and their communities is highlighted by the fact that CUNY traditionally awards the largest number of Master's degrees to Black and Latino students of any institution in America. Last year CUNY conferred 1,011 Master's degrees to Black and Latino students, while the State University of New York ('SUNY') awarded only 233." Ronald B. McGuire, "The Struggle at CUNY: Open Admissions and Civil Rights," 1992, http://slamherstory.wordpress.com/2009/09/28/the-struggle-at-cuny-by-ron -mcguire/, accessed December 15, 2011.

2. Much has been written about open admissions; see for example David E. Lavin et al., *Right Versus Privilege: The Open Admissions Experiment at the City University of New York* (New York: Free Press, 1981). But scholars of the

civil rights and Black power movements have neglected or ignored it. For examples, see Harvard Sitkoff, *The Struggle for Black Equality: 1954–1992* (New York: Hill and Wang, 1993); and Peniel E. Joseph, *Waiting 'Till the Midnight Hour: A Narrative History of Black Power in America* (New York: Henry Holt, 2006).

3. According to professor of psychology Kenneth Clark, the idea for SEEK and open admissions first emerged in a series of breakfast meetings with himself; CUNY chancellor Albert Bowker; Gus Rosenberg, the president of the Board of Higher Education, and Ray Jones, the African American leader of Tammany Hall. Clark said the four quickly agreed upon the injustice of "a policy and practice of free tuition in the city colleges when the most economically deprived groups were being denied the benefits of free higher education." Kenneth B. Clark, "The Advantages and Disadvantages of Open Admissions—and Some History," in *Open Admissions: The Pros and Cons* (Washington, DC: Council for Basic Education, 1972), 45. In contrast, former CCNY professor and administrator Allen B. Ballard called SEEK "my idea" and reportedly wrote up the plan for it in 1964–1965. See Ballard, *Breaking Jericho's Walls* (Albany: State University of New York Press, 2011), 216–217.

4. According to Conrad M. Dyer, CUNY's motive in authorizing open admissions was "to appease an explosive urban youth population." Dyer, "Protest and the Politics of Open Admissions: The Impact of the Black and Puerto Rican Students' Community (of City College)" (PhD diss., City University of New York, 1990), 193.

5. Bart Meyers, "Radical Struggle for Open Admissions at CUNY," *Kingsman*, February 27, 1976; in 1968, 192 Black students entered as part of the new Educational Opportunity Program. Others came through SEEK, which by early 1969 comprised 470 students. Another new 1968 initiative was the "One Hundred Scholars" program, where the top 100 graduates of each high school were automatically admitted to college. Forty-five of these students chose Brooklyn College. Still, according to one student who entered that year, Black enrollment in the liberal arts college was only 1 percent. Barnard Collier, "Police Break Up Sit-In in Brooklyn at College Office," *New York Times*, May 21, 1968, 1; Duncan Pardue to Franklin Williams, February 5, 1969, IBW Papers, Box: Survey of Black Studies Programs, Folder: Brooklyn College, Schomburg Center.

6. United States Congress, Senate Committee on Government Operations, Permanent Subcommittee on Investigations, *Riots, Civil and Criminal Disorders*, 91st Cong. 1st sess. (Washington, DC: Government Printing Office, 1969), 5193.

7. Meyers, "Radical Struggle for Open Admissions at CUNY."

8. Duncan Pardue to Franklin Williams, February 5, 1969.

9. Askia Davis, interview by author, New York City, July 19, 2005.

10. Orlando Pile, telephone interview by author, June 30, 2005; Davis, interview; the president said he "deplored racism but procedures of academic freedom must be maintained." Only the Board of Higher Education, he said, could take action on specific evidence of racism. Meyers, "Radical Struggle for Open Admissions at CUNY."

11. Students at City College advocated for admitting Black and Puerto Rican students in proportion to their presence in local high schools. They also called for access for poor whites as well, and said they should constitute 20 percent of the freshmen class, reflecting their presence in the local high school population.

12. At City College, SEEK professor Fran Geteles said that the students there "were very sensitive to the issues of underpreparedness and were not asking for indiscriminate entrance." Frances Geteles, telephone interview by author, August 29, 2007. Conrad Dyer found that many former student activists reiterated this point in interviews. See Dyer, "Protest and the Politics of Open Admissions," 103.

13. United States Congress, Senate Committee on Government Operations, Permanent Subcommittee on Investigations, Riots, Civil and Criminal Disorders, 5197–5199.

14. Pile, interview.

15. Ibid.

16. Kingsman, April 23, 1969, special edition.

17. Meyers, "Radical Struggle for Open Admissions at CUNY."

18. Ibid; Murray Schumach, "Vandals Disturb Brooklyn Campus," New York Times, May 1, 1969.

19. United States Congress, Senate Committee on Government Operations, Permanent Subcommittee on Investigations, Riots, Civil and Criminal Disorders, 5203.

20. Emanuel Perlmutter, "20 Indicted in Brooklyn College Arson," New York Times, May 14, 1969; Kingsman, May 12, 1969, special edition; Davis, interview; Pile, interview.

21. Davis, interview.

22. New York Post, May 13, 1969, Five Demands Conflict Collection, Box 2, University Archives and Special Collections, City College of New York (hereafter CCNY).

23. New York Daily News, May 14, 1969, Five Demands Conflict Collection, Box 2, CCNY.

24. Perlmutter, "20 Indicted in Brooklyn College Arson"; Kingsman, May 16, 1969; Davis, interview. Ironically, Dr. Matthews also went to jail in 1969—for refusing to pay federal income tax. An outspoken advocate of self-help and Black capitalism, Matthews, the first Black neurosurgeon in the United States, said he gave his taxes to his organization, National Economic Growth and Reconstruction Organization, rather than pay for welfare programs. President Nixon commuted the six-month sentence after sixty-nine days. New York Times, April 2, 1973.

25. "BC 19 Get Probation," Kingsman, February 27, and Kingsman, March 6, 1970; Judge Rinaldi said the indictments would be dismissed after six months "if they behaved." Things didn't turn out as well for the prosecutor or the judge. In 1983 Eugene Gold, who was Brooklyn district attorney from 1968 to 1981, admitted to "unlawful sexual fondling" of a ten-year-old girl—the daughter of an Alabama prosecutor—in a Nashville hotel room during a convention of district attorneys. And Judge Dominic Rinaldi was suspended from the bench after

being indicted for perjury in 1973, although a jury later acquitted him. See "Gold Gets Probation in Fondling of Child; Agrees to Treatment," *New York Times*, October 21, 1983; and "Dominic Rinaldi Dies: A Retired Justice," *New York Times*, November 27, 1983.

26. "STRIKE!" editorial, *Kingsman*, May 12, 1969.

27. United States Congress, Senate Committee on Government Operations, Permanent Subcommittee on Investigations, *Riots, Civil and Criminal Disorders*, 5191.

28. Transcript of interview with Sekou Sundiata, formerly Robert Feaster, n.d., Legacy of Struggle Collection, Box 1, CCNY.

29. "Chronology of a Crisis," n.d., Legacy of Struggle Collection, Box 1, CCNY; Sundiata, interview.

30. These statistics describe 1967. Dyer, "Protest and the Politics of Open Admissions," 64. This was the first official ethnic census conducted at CUNY schools.

31. Barbara Christian, "City College Saga, Part 2: Dual Admissions," *Inside and Outside the Plaza*, n.d., reprinted from *Harlem News*, June 1969, Legacy of Struggle Collection, Box 2, CCNY.

32. Black and Puerto Rican Student Community, "The Black and Puerto Rican Student Community to the Faculty and Students of City College," press release, April 26, 1969, Five Demands Conflict Collection, Box 4, CCNY. Conrad's spouse, the writer Adrienne Rich, also taught at CCNY and was a supporter of the student activists. Geteles, telephone interview by author.

33. Christian, "City College Saga, Part 2."

34. Clark, "The Advantages and Disadvantages of Open Admissions," 47.

35. Dyer, "Protest and the Politics of Open Admissions," 84.

36. Ibid., 117–120.

37. "The Black and Puerto Rican Student Community to the Faculty and Students of City College."

38. Dyer, "Protest and the Politics of Open Admissions," 98; Toni Cade, "Realizing the Dream of the Black University," *Observation Post* (City College), February 14, 1969, Martha Weisman Papers, Open Admissions Folder, CCNY.

39. See for example Steve Estes, *I Am a Man!: Race, Manhood and the Civil Rights Movement* (Chapel Hill: University of North Carolina Press, 2005).

40. Miss Cade to Dear Bloods, n.d., Five Demands Conflict Collection, Public Relations Folder, CCNY.

41. Cade, "Realizing the Dream of the Black University."

42. Barbara Christian, "City College Saga: Lesson in Democracy," *Inside and Outside the Plaza*, August–September 1969, Legacy of Struggle Collection, Box 2, CCNY.

43. Alecia Edwards-Sibley, "The Five Demands," *The Paper*, April 2002, Martha Weisman Papers, Strike of 1969 Folder, CCNY.

44. Black and Puerto Rican Student Community, "Queries and Answers on Demands #1 and #4," May 28, 1969, Five Demands Conflict Collection, Box 7, CCNY.

45. Rabbi Jay Kaufman, "Thou Shalt Surely Rebuke Thy Neighbor," in *Black Anti-Semitism and Jewish Racism,* ed. Nat Hentoff (New York: Richard Baron, 1969), 55, 74.

46. Julius Lester, "A Response," in *Black Anti-Semitism and Jewish Racism,* ed. Nat Hentoff (New York: Richard Baron, 1969), 235.

47. There was some overlap—Betty Rawls and Barbara Christian were in both groups. Geteles, telephone interview.

48. See Clayborne Carson, *In Struggle: SNCC and the Black Awakening of the 1960s* (Cambridge, MA: Harvard University Press, 1981).

49. Geteles, telephone interview.

50. Carlos Russell, interview by author, New York City, June 11, 2005.

51. "The Stake of Whites in the Struggle," Box 16, Five Demands Conflict, CCNY; Floyd McKissick, "CUNY's Quota System," *New York Amsterdam News,* June 14, 1969.

52. Meyers, "Radical Struggle for Open Admissions at CUNY"; "Notes and Comment," Talk of the Town, *New Yorker,* May 3, 1969, in Legacy of Struggle Collection, Box 1, CCNY; Davis, interview.

53. For more on Columbia see Stefan Bradley, *Harlem v. Columbia University: Black Student Power in the Late 1960s* (Urbana: University of Illinois Press, 2009).

54. WCBS transcript, "Campus Disruption—II," April 23, 1969, Five Demands Conflict Collection, Public Relations Folder, CCNY.

55. *New York Post,* April 30, 1969, Five Demands Conflict Collection, Box 1, CCNY.

56. Schumach, "Vandals Disturb Brooklyn Campus."

57. Transcript of film (unfinished), Legacy of Struggle Collection, Box 2, CCNY.

58. Meyers, "Radical Struggle for Open Admissions at CUNY."

59. *New York Post,* May 10, 1969, Five Conflict Collection, Box 1, CCNY.

60. *Daily News,* editorial, May 10, 1969, Five Conflict Collection, Box 1, CCNY; *New York Post,* June 13, 1969, Five Conflict Collection, Box 1, CCNY.

61. Sylvan Fox, "60 From C.C.N.Y. Quit Graduation," *New York Times,* June 13, 1969.

62. "Dean Quitting CCNY Post Tells Why," *New York Post,* May 28, 1969.

63. Roy Wilkins, "The Case against Separatism: 'Black Jim Crow,'" *Black Studies: Myths and Realities* (New York: A. Philip Randolph Institute, 1969), 38–39.

64. Bayard Rustin, introduction to *Black Studies: Myths and Realities,* 6–7.

65. Louis Nunez to Board of Higher Education, May 1, 1969, Five Demands Conflict Collection, Public Relations Folder, CCNY.

66. Allen B. Ballard, *The Education of Black Folk: The Afro-American Struggle for Knowledge in White America* (New York: Harper and Row, 1973), 127, 141.

67. "Fortieth Open Admissions Anniversary," *Third Rail* (CUNY, College of Staten Island) (Spring 2009): 6.

68. Murray Kempton, "Fog over City College—II," *New York Post,* May 28, 1969.

69. Dyer, "Protest and the Politics of Open Admissions," 176.

70. "Urban and Ethnic Studies Dept. Created," *The Campus,* September 2, 1969, Martha Weisman Papers, Open Admissions Folder, CCNY.

71. "A Negro Professor at C.C.N.Y. Charges Slander," *New York Times,* September 20, 1969.

72. Students at Berkeley paid attention to events at CCNY because they shared an administrator, Albert Bowker. See BSU flyer, September 26, 1972, Social Protest Collection, Box 18, Folder 9, Bancroft Library, University of California, Berkeley.

73. Dr. Pile graduated in 1972, attended medical school at Rutgers University, and did his internship and residency at Martin Luther King Jr./Drew Medical Center in Los Angeles. Askia Davis is an administrator for the New York public school system. He has served as special assistant to three chancellors.

74. Davis, interview; Pile, interview.

75. Russell, interview; Memorandum, n.d., Box: Information Files, #91–021; Folder: BC—Schools—School for Contemporary Studies, Special Collections, Brooklyn College, Brooklyn, New York, University Archives; "Contemporary Studies Head Seeks New Values," *Kingsman,* October 15, 1971.

76. Davis, interview.

77. Russell, interview; "Report of the Committee to Evaluate the School for Contemporary Studies at Brooklyn College," March 1976, Box: Information Files, #91–021; Folder: BC—Schools—School for Contemporary Studies, Special Collections, Brooklyn College.

78. Ed Quinn and Leonard Kriegal, "How the Dream Was Deferred," *The Nation,* April 7, 1984, 412–414.

79. Albert H. Bowker, oral history conducted by Harriet Niathon, September 6, 1991, Regional Oral History Office, Bancroft Library, University of California, Berkeley.

80. Martha Weisman, "Legacy of Student Activism at the City College," April 21, 1989, Legacy of Struggle Collection, Box 1, CCNY.

81. Geteles, telephone interview.

82. Laird Cummings and Nanette Funk, "The Closing Door of Open Admissions," *Kingsman,* February 20, 1976.

83. Frank Rich, quoted in Quinn and Kriegal, "How the Dream Was Deferred," 412.

84. Dyer, "Protest and the Politics of Open Admissions," 184.

85. *Closing the Door: The Fight for a College Education,* a film by Ellie Bernstein, c. 1999, CCNY; Kelechi Onwuchekwa, "The Truth behind Open Admissions," *The Paper,* April 2002, Martha Weisman Papers, CCNY.

86. Christian, "City College Saga, Part 2."

87. See Martha Biondi, *To Stand and Fight: The Struggle for Civil Rights in Postwar New York City* (Cambridge, MA: Harvard University Press, 2003).

CHAPTER 5. TOWARD A BLACK UNIVERSITY

1. William R. Corson, *Promise or Peril: The Black College Student in America* (New York: Norton, 1970), 40.

2. See John Egerton, "*Adams v. Richardson:* Can Separate Be Equal?" *Change* 6, no. 10 (Winter 1974–1975): 29–39, www.jstor.org/stable/40176648; Julian B. Roebuck and Komanduri S. Murty, *Historically Black Colleges and Universities: Their Place in American Higher Education* (Westport, CT: Praeger, 1993).

3. *Hilltop* (Howard University), October 11, 1968, microfilm, HUL.

4. Vincent Harding, "Toward the Black University," *Ebony,* August 1970, 156.

5. Gerald McWorter, "The Nature and Needs of the Black University," *Negro Digest,* March 1968.

6. Vincent Harding, "New Creations or Familiar Death? An Open Letter to Black Students in the North," *Negro Digest,* March 1968.

7. John Oliver Killens, "The Artist and the Black University," *Black Scholar* 1, no. 1 (November 1969): 65, 64.

8. Corson, *Promise or Peril,* 120.

9. Ibid., 15, 21, 31, and 169.

10. George B. Davis, "The Howard University Conference," *Negro Digest,* March 1969.

11. Thomas A. Johnson, "Howard Students Discuss Reforms," *New York Times,* November 15, 1968, www.proquest.com.turing.library.northwestern.edu /, accessed May 12, 2006.

12. *Hilltop,* November 15, 1968, microfilm, HUL.

13. St. Clair Drake, interview by Robert Martin, July 28, 1969, transcript, Bunche Project, Moorland-Spingarn Collection, HUL.

14. *Hilltop,* November 22, 1968, microfilm, HUL; Lewis Myers Jr., interview by author, Chicago, June 29, 2006.

15. Robert S. Browne, "Financing the Black University" (paper presented at Howard University, November 13–17, 1968), Robert Browne Papers, Box 16, Folder 9, Schomburg Center.

16. *Hilltop,* October 11, 1968, microfilm, HUL.

17. Thomas A. Johnson, "Negro Students Seek Relevance," *New York Times,* November 18, 1968, www.proquest.com.turing.library.northwestern.edu/, ac cessed May 12, 2006.

18. Ewart Brown, "The Black University," in *The University and the Revolution,* ed. Gary R. Weaver and James H. Weaver (New York: Prentice-Hall, 1969), 147.

19. Davis, "The Howard University Conference."

20. Brown, "The Black University," 147.

21. Ewart Brown, interview by Robert Martin, September 14, 1968, transcript, Bunche Project, Moorland-Spingarn Collection, HUL.

22. Myers, interview.

23. *Hilltop,* February 14, 1969, microfilm, HUL.

24. Ewart Brown, telephone interview by author, July 17, 2006.

25. Leslie M. Rankin-Hill and Michael L. Blakey, "W. Montague Cobb (1904–1990): Physical Anthropologist, Anatomist, Activist," *American Anthropologist* 96 (1994): 74–96, www.aaanet.org/gad/history/084cobb.pdf, 13–14.

26. "Howard Students Seize Law School," *New York Times,* February 19, 1969, 34.

27. "Howard Students Yield," *New York Times,* February 20, 1969, 35; *Hilltop,* February 28, 1969, and *Hilltop,* March 14, 1969, microfilm, HUL.

28. C. Gerald Fraser, "Boycotting Students at Howard Threaten an Injunction," *New York Times,* May 13, 1969, 31; "Students to Negotiate to End Class Boycott," *Washington Afro-American,* April 26, 1969.

29. *Hilltop,* editorial, March 14, 1969, microfilm, HUL.

30. "What's Behind Black Student Unrest?" *Washington Afro-American,* February 15, 1969.

31. Bea A. Franklin, "Howard U. Closed Down after Campus Seizures," *New York Times,* May 8, 1969, 43; "Chaos Strikes Howard University," *Washington Afro-American,* May 10, 1969.

32. Babalola Cole, interview by Allen Coleman, November 20, 1970, transcript, Bunche Project, Moorland-Spingarn Collection, HUL.

33. "Howard U. Closed Down after Campus Seizures."

34. C. Gerald Fraser, "Howard Students Refuse to Relinquish Buildings," *New York Times,* May 9, 1969, 29; C. Gerald Fraser, "20 Arrested at Howard as Campus Siege Ends," *New York Times,* May 10, 1969, 14; Myers, interview.

35. *In Re Anderson,* 306 F. Supp. 712 (1969), United States District Court District of Columbia, June 20, 1969.

36. Brown, interview.

37. Charles V. Flowers, "Morgan State's Besieged President," *Baltimore Sun Magazine,* November 30, 1980, St. Clair Drake Papers (hereafter Drake Papers), Box 5, Folder 16, Schomburg Center.

38. "Negroes Besiege Carolina Campus," *New York Times,* April 29, 1969, 27.

39. "Robert Romer—1969/1970: Protests and State Troops at Voorhees College," www.americancenturies.mass.edu/centapp/oh/story.do?shortName =romer1969, accessed June 10, 2010.

40. *African World* (Student Organization for Black Unity), July 23, 1972, periodical contained in The Black Power Movement, Part I (microfilm collection), ed. Komozi Woodard, University Publications of America, reel 7.

41. "Armed Black Students," *New York Post,* April 30, 1969; "Academic Freedom and Tenure: Voorhees College (South Carolina)," *American Association of University Professors Bulletin,* 60, no. 1 (March 1974), 87, www.jstor .org/stable/40224708, accessed June 10, 2010.

42. See "Robert Romer—1969/1970."

43. *African World,* July 23, 1972; *Organization for Black Unity* (Harvard), March 24, 1970, newsletter, Ewart Guinier Papers (hereafter Guinier Papers), Box 45, Folder 5, Schomburg Center; "Carolina Negro College, Shut in Protests," *New York Times,* March 2, 1970.

44. "Robert Romer—1969/1970."

45. "Academic Freedom and Tenure," 84.

46. Ibid., 83.

47. *African World*, July 23, 1972.

48. Rodney Stark, "Protest+Police=Riot," in *Black Power and Student Rebellion*, ed. James McEvoy and Abraham Miller (Belmont, CA: Wadsworth, 1969), 172–173.

49. See William H. Chafe, *Civilities and Civil Rights: Greensboro, North Carolina, and the Black Struggle for Freedom* (New York: Oxford University Press, 1981).

50. Sally Avery Bermanzohn, *Through Survivors' Eyes: From the Sixties to the Greensboro Massacre* (Nashville, TN: Vanderbilt University Press, 2003), 67, 75, 90.

51. Signe Waller, *Love and Revolution: A Political Memoir: People's History of the Greensboro Massacre, Its Setting and Aftermath* (Lanham, MD: Rowman and Littlefield, 2002), 49.

52. Amy Dominello, "1969 Shooting at N.C. A & T," *Greensboro News-Record*, http://mm.news-record.com/legacy/indepth/06/williegrimes/grimes.html, accessed June 5, 2010.

53. "North Carolina A&T," *Village Voice* (New York), May 29, 1969.

54. Ibid.; "Collegians Driven Out by Gunfire," *Hartford Courant*, May 24, 1969.

55. North Carolina State Advisory Committee, *Trouble in Greensboro: A Report of an Open Meeting Concerning Disturbances at Dudley High School and North Carolina A&T State University* (N.p., Advisory Committee, March 1970), 6, 14, William Chafe Oral History Collection, Duke University, available on-line at Civil Rights Greensboro, http://library.uncg.edu/dp/crg/item.aspx?i=38, accessed June 16, 2010.

56. Bermanzohn, *Through Survivors' Eyes*, 92.

57. "7 Shot, Guard Called In Ohio State U Riot," *New York Times*, April 30, 1970, 1; Jerry M. Flint, "New Clash Erupts at Ohio State University," *New York Times*, May 1, 1970, 1.

58. "Atlanta University Position Paper on Racism and Violence in the United States," May 25, 1970, IBW Papers, Box: Black Studies Programs, Folder: Atlanta University, Schomburg Center.

59. "Black College Presidents Demand Action," *Integrated Education* 8 (July–August 1970): 13–14.

60. J. Otis Cochran, quoted from a transcript of testimony, n.d., Robert Finch Papers, in the Richard Nixon Papers, White House Central Files, Staff Member and Office Files, Box 27, National Archives, College Park, MD.

61. James E. Cheek, "Black Institutions and Black Students," *Integrated Education* 8 (November–December 1970): 16–20.

62. Dean Kotlowski, *Nixon's Civil Rights: Politics, Principle and Policy* (Cambridge, MA: Harvard University Press, 2001), 153–154.

63. Fred Prejean, transcript of remarks, Smith-Brown Memorial Service, Southern University, Baton Rouge, LA, November 16, 1992, in author's possession.

64. "Louisiana Blacks Disrupt Colleges," *New York Times*, November 5, 1972, 35.

65. Fred Prejean, transcript of remarks, Smith-Brown Memorial Service; Fred Prejean, telephone interview by author, June 30, 2010.

66. "Louisiana Governor Orders Eviction of Students," *New York Times*, November 9, 1972; "Confrontation in the South," *New York Times*, November 12, 1972.

67. "Ex-Professor Calls Slaying of SU Blacks 'White Plot,'" *Chicago Defender*, November 28, 1972, 20.

68. Prejean, interview.

69. Martin Waldron, "Louisiana Hints Error in Killings," *New York Times*, November 18, 1972, 77.

70. Louisiana, Attorney General, *Report of the Attorney General's Special Commission of Inquiry on the Southern University Tragedy of November 16, 1972* (Baton Rouge: Attorney General, State of Louisiana, 1973).

71. Martin Waldron, "2 Die in Clash with Police on Baton Rouge Campus," *New York Times*, November 17, 1972, 97; and Paul Delaney, "Southern Ousts 2 Professors," *New York Times*, November 20, 1972, 77; Louisiana, Attorney General, *Report of the Attorney General's Special Commission of Inquiry*.

72. Waldron, "2 Die in Clash With Police on Baton Rouge Campus."

73. "Black Colleges in Crisis," *Daily Challenge*, January 29, 1973, Guinier Papers, Box 47, Folder 8, Schomburg Center.

74. Ibid.

75. "Fired Profs Strike at Netterville," *Chicago Defender*, December 7, 1972, 12.

76. "Louisiana Hints Error in Killings"; "Southern Ousts 2 Professors"; "Ex-Professor Calls Slaying of SU Blacks 'White Plot.'"

77. "Scattered Demonstrations Score Killing of 2 on Southern Campus," *New York Times*, November 18, 1972, 22.

78. D'Army Bailey, telephone interview by author, July 1, 2010; Paul Delaney, "Southern U. Students Restive as 2 Inquiries Open," *New York Times*, November 28, 1972, 39.

79. "Preliminary Findings of the Black People's Committee of Inquiry," November 29, 1972, Fred Prejean personal collection, copy in author's possession, emphasis in the original; Bailey, interview.

80. Louisiana, Attorney General, *Report of the Attorney General's Special Commission of Inquiry.*

81. National Education Association, press release, March 14, 1973, Guinier Papers, Box 47, Folder 8, Schomburg Center.

82. "An Avoidable Tragedy," editorial, *Chicago Daily Defender*, November 25, 1972.

83. Mrs. Robert W. Claytor to the President, December 8, 1972, Robert Finch Papers, in the Richard Nixon Papers, White House Central Files, Subject Files, Human Rights, Box 37, National Archives, College Park, MD.

84. The Chaplains of Atlanta University Center, Rev. Julia McClain Walker, and others to President Nixon, Governor Edwards, November 22, 1972, Robert

Finch Papers, in the Richard Nixon Papers, White House Central Files, Subject Files, Human Rights, Box 37, National Archives, College Park, MD.

85. Several commentators in this period also referred to student deaths at Texas Southern, where a 1967 police assault had wounded students and killed a police officer.

86. "The Greater Outrage," *Black Collegian,* September–October 1973.

87. Fred Prejean, transcript of remarks, Smith-Brown Memorial Service; Prejean, interview; Roy Reed, "Two Dead—It Was a Predictable Tragedy," *New York Times,* November 19, 1972, E4.

88. Prejean, interview.

89. E. C. Harrison, "Student Unrest on the Black College Campus," *Journal of Negro Education* 41, no. 2 (Spring 1972): 114.

90. Ibid., 113.

CHAPTER 6. THE COUNTERREVOLUTION ON CAMPUS

1. St. Clair Drake, "The Black Studies Movement and the Stanford Response: Reflections," September 1974, Drake Papers, Box 93, Stanford BSU Folder, Schomburg Center.

2. Eugene Genovese, "Black Studies: Trouble Ahead," in *New Perspectives on Black Studies,* ed. John Blassingame (Urbana: University of Illinois Press, 1971), 107.

3. See especially Stephen G. Hall, *A Faithful Account of the Race: African American Historical Writing in Nineteenth Century America* (Chapel Hill: University of North Carolina Press, 2009).

4. Manning Marable, *Beyond Black and White: Transforming African American Politics* (New York: Verso, 1995), 115.

5. Larry Crouchett, "The 'Black Perspective': From *A* Black's Perspective," October 4, 1969, Drake Papers, Box 50, Cedric X Folder, Schomburg Center.

6. Vincent Harding, "Black Students and the Impossible Revolution," *Ebony,* August 1969, 144.

7. Cedric C. Clark, "Black Studies and the Study of Black People," October 4, 1969, pp. 1, 4, Drake Papers, Box 50, Cedric X Folder, Schomburg Center.

8. Basil Matthews, "Philosophical Basis of Black Studies," unpublished paper, n.d., Guinier Papers, Box 5, Folder 9, Schomburg Center.

9. "Black Studies versus White Studies: 1969—a Year of Profound Identity Crisis for American Education," 207-page manuscript, c. 1969, in IBW Papers, Box: Black Studies: conference papers and essays, Aspen conference, Schomburg Center (sadly, the author of this extraordinary document is unknown. I hypothesize that it is the late Armstead Robinson, but I am unable to confirm this); Preston Wilcox, "The Black University: A Movement or an Institution," IBW Papers, Black Studies Box, Aspen Binder 3, Schomburg Center; Lerone Bennett, quoted in transcript of "Black Studies Directors' Seminar: Panel Presentations, 7, 8, 9, November 1969," p. 197, Institute of the Black World, Atlanta, Georgia, IBW Papers, Box: Black Studies Directors' Seminar, Schomburg Center.

10. Ewart Guinier, interview by Norman Scott, July 26, 1972, transcript, Guinier Papers, Box 18, Folder 1, Schomburg Center.

11. Vincent Harding, *Beyond Chaos: Black History and the Search for a New Land* (1970), pamphlet, IBW Papers, Black Studies Box, Aspen Binder 3, Schomburg Center.

12. "Black Studies versus White Studies: 1969.

13. Robinson and Billingsley, quoted in transcript of "Black Studies Directors' Seminar."

14. Armstead Robinson, "Report on the Condition of Black Studies" (presented at the "Black Studies Directors' Seminar: Panel Presentations," November 7–9, 1969, Institute of the Black World, Atlanta, Georgia), Drake Papers, Box 50, Schomburg Center.

15. Joanna Schneider and Robert Zangrando, "Black History in the College Curriculum," *Rocky Mountain Social Science Journal* (1969), in IBW Papers, Binder vol. 3, Black Studies Box, Schomburg Center.

16. Darwin T. Turner, "A Black Teacher's Thoughts on Black Studies," transcript of speech at Black Studies Directors' Conference, July 1970, Aspen, CO, IBW Papers, Binder vol. 3, Black Studies Seminar, Aspen Box, Schomburg Center.

17. Benjamin Quarles, "History and Education" (speech to the Black Academy of Arts and Letters, September 19, 1970), IBW Papers, Box 9, Harding Files, Schomburg Center.

18. Harvard University News Office, "Afro-American and African Studies," press release, January 22, 1969, Guinier Papers, Box 22, Folder 6, Schomburg Center.

19. Michael Thelwell, "Black Studies: A Political Perspective," *Massachusetts Review* (1970).

20. Lawrence E. Eichel, Kenneth W. Jost, Robert D. Luskin, and Richard M. Neustadt, *The Harvard Strike* (New York: Houghton Mifflin, 1970).

21. "Minutes, Special Meeting of the Faculty of Arts and Sciences, Harvard University," April 17, 1969, Guinier Papers, Box 22, Folder 6; Copy of the resolution, April 22, 1969, Guinier Papers, Box 22, Folder 6, Schomburg Center.

22. Robert Reinhold, "Key Aide Scores Vote at Harvard," *New York Times*, April 24, 1969, www.proquest.com.turing.library.northwestern.edu/, accessed July 23, 2006.

23. Henry Rosovsky, quoted in "Minutes, Special Meeting of the Faculty of Arts and Sciences, Harvard University."

24. Wesley Profit, telephone interview by author, July 28, 2005. For example, English professor Alan Heimart, who spoke in favor of the resolution and was sympathetic to the students, later told a graduate student that a student had come to the meeting with a knife. Arnold Rampersad, conversation with author, May, 13, 2005, Stanford, California.

25. A student member of the committee, Myles Link, remembers that the students "were very engaged" in the process but were not of one mind. He recalls that there was "a lot of tension" in the meetings, in part because faculty were not used to working with students. Myles Link, telephone interview by author, November 15, 2010. Based on minutes of standing committee meetings, there was a simultaneous commitment to rigor, as well as flexibility and innovation, in the establishment of the department. Generally, the students supported

more urgency and open-mindedness in hiring, while faculty hewed to time-honored criteria. For example, in one meeting, a student said, "It was important to get somebody on board soon because we are dealing with a limited quantity," while a professor "saw it as a situation in which the supply is expanding" and so would consider it "unfortunate to make a premature appointment." Standing committee meeting minutes, May 19, 1969, Myles Link personal collection, copy in author's possession.

26. Martin Kilson, "Reflections on Structure and Content in Black Studies," *Journal of Black Studies* (March 1973): 300, emphasis in the original.

27. *Harvard Crimson*, October 22, 1969; William Trombley, "Harvard Black Studies Face Slow Start," *Los Angeles Times*, September 14, 1969, Guinier Papers, Box 22, Folder 9, Schomburg Center.

28. Fred M. Hechinger, "Students to Gain a Voice in U.S. Education Policy," *New York Times*, June 1, 1969, www.proquest.com.turing.library.northwestern .edu/, accessed May, 12, 2006.

29. Tobe Johnson, "Black Studies: Their Origin, Present State, and Prospects," (1969): 315 (journal title unclear), IBW Papers, Black Studies Box, Aspen Conference Binder, vol. 3, Schomburg Center.

30. Carlos A. Brossard, "Classifying Black Studies Programs," *Journal of Negro Education* 53, no. 3 (Summer 1984): 281.

31. Carlene Young, "The Struggle and Dream of Black Studies," *Journal of Negro Education*, 53, no. 3 (Summer 1984): 370.

32. Johnson, "Black Studies," 315.

33. Academy for Educational Development, *Black Studies: How It Works at Ten Universities* (New York: Academy for Educational Development, 1971).

34. "Proposal for an Afro-American Institute," March 3, 1969, IBW Papers, Box 5, Wesleyan Folder, Schomburg Center.

35. James Turner, "An Approach to Black Studies: Concept and Plan of the Africana Studies and Research Center," n.d., Black Economic Research Center Papers (hereafter BERC Papers), Box 22, Folder 4, Schomburg Center.

36. John Blassingame, "Black Studies: An Intellectual Crisis," *The Black Studies Debate*, ed. James M. Rosser and Jacob U. Gordon (Lawrence: University of Kansas, Division of Continuing Education, 1974), 72–73; Eric Foner, conversation with author, November 2010.

37. Blassingame, "Black Studies," 74.

38. William Seraille, conversation with author, New York City, 2005; Blassingame, "Black Studies," 74.

39. Mary Jane Hewitt, interview by Elston L. Carr, 1997–1999, transcript, 74, UCLA Oral History Project, Center for African American Studies Library, UCLA.

40. St. Clair Drake, interview by Robert Martin, July 28, 1969, transcript, 69, Bunche Project; "Black Studies Aim to Change Things," *New York Times*, May 15, 1969.

41. Charles Hamilton, "They Demand Relevance: Black Student Protest," (unpublished manuscript, c. 1971), 24, in author's possession.

42. Pat Ryan, "Black Academy Review," Spring 1970, IBW Papers, Binder vol. 3, Schomburg Center.

43. Ford Foundation, *A Survey of Black American Doctorates* (New York: Ford Foundation, 1970), in Institute of African-American Affairs Papers (hereafter IAAA Papers), Box 16, University Archives, New York University.

44. Barbara Campbell, "Why Should We Celebrate the 4th of July?" *New York Times,* March 23, 1969; Vincent Harding, "New Creation or Familiar Death: An Open Letter to Black Students in the North," reprint from *Negro Digest,* March 1969, Drake Papers, Box 49, Folder 27, Schomburg Center.

45. James Turner, "Cornell: A Case Study," in bound transcript "Black Studies Directors' Seminar, November 7–9, 1969, Atlanta," IBW Papers, Black Studies Directors' Seminar Box, Schomburg Center.

46. John Bracey, interview by author, New York, July 6, 2005.

47. Turner, "Cornell."

48. "Black Studies Aim to Change Things," *New York Times,* May 15, 1969.

49. Ibid.

50. Hamilton, conversation with author, March 2008, Chicago; Sterling Stuckey, interview by author, Chicago, June 19, 2008; Jim Pitts, telephone conversation with author, July 20, 2008.

51. Robert Singleton, interview by Elston L. Carr, Oral History Project, UCLA, 1999, Library, Center for African American History, UCLA.

52. Donald B. Easum, "The Call for Black Studies," Department of State, Foreign Service Institute, Summer Seminar, May 1969, IBW Papers, Aspen material, Binder vol. 3, Schomburg Center.

53. Mark D. Naison, "A 'White Boy' in African-American Studies," *Chronicle of Higher Education,* May 3, 2002.

54. Clayborne Carson, "The Critical Path: A Scholar in Struggle," *Souls* 4, no. 2 (Spring 2002): 33–34.

55. Blassingame, "Black Studies," 73; Stuckey, interview. Armstead Robinson's portrayal of Black studies instructors was often biting: they constituted "a new category of academic pimps and hustlers, both black and white." "Brothers are trucking Black studies," he wrote, because it brought "a rapid scaling up of personal status, academic rank and professional income." See Robinson, "Report on the Condition of Black Studies."

56. Thelwell, "Black Studies."

57. Vincent Harding, "The Relationship of Black Studies to Black Higher Education," transcript of speech at Black Studies Directors' Conference, July 1970, Aspen, CO, IBW Papers, Conferences Box, Aspen Folder, Schomburg Center.

58. Melvin Drimmer, "Teaching Black History in America: What Are the Problems?" *Journal of Negro Education* (1968), compiled in IBW Papers, binder vol. 2, Black Studies Seminar, Aspen Box, Schomburg Center.

59. Turner, "A Black Teacher's Thoughts on Black Studies."

60. Hollis Lynch, "Ewart Guinier," memorial statement, n.d., Guinier Papers, Box 2, Folder 7, Schomburg Center.

61. Guinier, interview.

62. Kilson, "Reflections on Structure and Content in Black Studies," 303. This essay originated as a speech given in 1971.

63. "Afro-Am Isolation Imminent Unless Department Integrates," *Harvard Independent*, January 6–12, 1972, Guinier Papers, Box 23, Folder 5, Schomburg Center.

64. Ronald Walters to Walter Leonard, December 21, 1971, BERC Papers, Box 17, Folder 11, Schomburg Center, emphasis in the original.

65. Profit, telephone interview; Department of Afro-American Studies, Harvard University, "The First Three Years," October 16, 1972, Guinier Papers, Box 23, Folder 11, Schomburg Center.

66. Harvard University, *Report of the Committee to Review the Department of Afro-American Studies* (Cambridge, MA, October 1972), bulletin, copy in author's possession.

67. "A Statement of the Afro-American Studies Department on Tenure and the Ephraim Isaac Case," October 29, 1975, in National Council of Black Studies Papers, Box 1, Folder 10, Schomburg Center; Profit, telephone interview.

68. Martin Kilson, "Blacks at Harvard: Solutions and Prospects," *Harvard Bulletin*, June 1973, 31, Guinier Papers, Box 36, Folder 1, Schomburg Center.

69. Martin Kilson, "Memorandum on Situation of Negro Students at Harvard College," January 10, 1973, Guinier Papers, Box 36, Folder 2, Schomburg Center, emphasis in the original.

70. Derrick Bell, "Why Does Kilson Do It?" *Harvard Bulletin*, June 1973, Guinier Papers, Box 36, Folder 4, Schomburg Center.

71. Kilson, "Blacks at Harvard"; and "Admissions: Some Questions of Policy," *Harvard Bulletin*, June 1973.

72. Eddie Williams Jr., "Professor Kilson's Contentions: A Reply," *Harvard Bulletin*, June 1973.

73. Bell, "Why Does Kilson Do It?"

74. Derrick Bell, letter to *Harvard Crimson*, n.d., Guinier Papers, Box 45, Folder 4, Schomburg Center.

75. Ewart Guinier, "Draft Report on 1973–1974 Academic Year," Guinier Papers, Box 24, Folder 2, Schomburg Center.

76. *Harvard Crimson*, October 2, 1974, Guinier Papers, Box 33, Folder 8, Schomburg Center; Peter Kihss, "Black Studies Feud Erupts at Harvard," *New York Times*, March 10, 1975, 26.

77. "Black Studies at Harvard," *The Word*, January 1976, Guinier Papers, Box 45, Folder 4, Schomburg Center.

78. Years later, Kilson blamed Bok and Rosovsky for not supporting the Department of Afro-American Studies. "The Harvard administration under President Derek Bok in the 1970–90 era was as financially indifferent as it could possibly be to the faculty development needs" of the department "without appearing fully opposed to its very existence." Moreover, he later learned from department chair Nathan Huggins that Rosovsky "exerted little pressure with the Bok administration on behalf of faculty development for Afro-American studies." Martin Kilson, "Afro-American Studies at Harvard," in *A Companion*

to African American Studies, ed. Lewis R. Gordon and Jane Anna Gordon (Malden, MA: Blackwell, 2006), 67.

79. Joann Lublin, "Black Studies Founder," *Wall Street Journal,* April 18, 1974, Vertical file, Black Studies Folder, University Archive, Wayne State University, Detroit; B.D. Colen, "Once Popular Black Studies," *Washington Post,* October 2, 1973, IAAA Papers, Box 18, University Archives, New York University.

80. Robert L. Allen, "Politics of the Attack on Black Studies," *Black Scholar* 6 (September 1974): 5.

81. "The Future of Black Studies in American Higher Education," *New York University Report,* February 12, 1975, IAAA Papers, Box 18, University Archives, New York University.

82. James McGinnis, "Towards a New Beginning: Crisis and Contradiction in Black Studies," *Black World,* March 1973.

83. Young, "The Struggle and Dream of Black Studies," 370.

84. Farah Jasmine Griffin, introduction [2006] to *Inclusive Scholarship: Developing Black Studies in the United States; A 25th Anniversary Retrospective of Ford Foundation Grant Making, 1982–2007* (New York: Ford Foundation, 2007), xiii.

85. Griffin, introduction, xiv.

86. John Scanlon, "Seminar on Afro-American Studies," memorandum, August 5, 1970, Ford Foundation Papers, Grant 70–188, reel 1657, Ford Foundation, New York.

87. Vincent Harding to Edgar Toppin, July 1, 1970, Ford Foundation Papers, Grant 70–188, reel 1657.

88. "Some Concerns of the Black Caucus at the Aspen Black Studies Seminar," Ford Foundation Papers, Grant 70–188, reel 1657, Ford Foundation, New York; "Comments by Dr. Andrew Billingsley," Black Studies Seminar, July 19–25, 1970, Ford Foundation Papers, Grant 70–188, reel 1657.

89. "Remarks by James W. Armsey to the Seminar," Black Studies Seminar, July 19–25, 1970, Ford Foundation Papers, Grant 70–188, reel 1657.

90. Scanlon, "Seminar on Afro-American Studies."

91. Roscoe Brown reported that his department had to make do with 20–25 percent less money after the expiration of the Ford grant. *NYU Report,* February 12, 1975, IAAA Papers, Box 18, University Archives, New York University.

92. Farah Jasmine Griffin, "An Introduction to the Huggins Report," *Inclusive Scholarship,* 7–8. Scholars differ on the influence of the Ford Foundation on the development of Black studies. Noliwe Rooks argues that their preference for programs rather than departments had a decisive impact, while Fabio Rojas notes the relatively small early financial involvement of Ford, finding this insufficient to exert much long-range influence. See Rooks, *White Money/Black Power: The Surprising History of African American Studies* (Boston: Beacon Press, 2006); and Rojas, *From Black Power to Black Studies: How a Radical Social Movement Became an Academic Discipline* (Baltimore, MD: Johns Hopkins University Press, 2007).

93. St. Clair Drake, quoted in "Black Is . . . for Credit," *Newsweek,* October 20, 1969.

94. Charles Hamilton, "They Demand Relevance: Black Student Protest," (unpublished manuscript, 1968–1969), 104, in author's possession.

95. R. Wilson, "Perspectives in Black Studies" (speech to Second Annual Ethnic Conference, Wayne State University, May 20, 1971), vertical file, Center for Black Studies Folder, University Archives, Wayne State University, Detroit, emphasis in the original.

96. Roscoe Brown, "Black Studies, a Year Later" (unpublished manuscript, Fall 1970), IAAA Papers, Box 18, University Archives, New York University.

97. Carlos Brossard, "Classifying Black Studies Programs," *Journal of Negro Education* 53, no. 3 (Summer 1984): 286; "Black Journals Reflect Shift from Racialism," *New York Times*, April 27, 1975.

98. Abdul Alkalimat, interview by author, Urbana, IL, March 31, 2006.

99. Rhett Jones, "Dreams, Nightmares and Realities: Afro-American Studies at Brown University, 1969–1986," in *A Companion to African American Studies*, ed. Jane Gordon and Lewis Gordon (Malden, MA: Blackwell, 2006), 41.

100. Center for Black Studies, University of Santa Barbara, *Educational Reform and Revolutionary Struggle: The Continuing Fight for Black Studies*, 1977, in Drake Papers, Box 50, Schomburg Center.

101. Armstead Robinson, "Black Studies and Black Students," Black Studies Seminar, Aspen, July 1970, Ford Foundation Papers, Grant 70–188, reel 1657, Ford Foundation, New York.

102. "Black Studies Gaining Shaky Niche on Campus," *Los Angeles Times*, May 7, 1972.

103. Institute of the Black World, "Notes on the Struggle for Black Higher Education," working or position paper, June 1971, IBW Papers, Black Agenda Box, Schomburg Center.

104. Jack L. Daniel, "Black Studies at the Crossroads: What Must Be Done and Why" (speech delivered at the American Association of Behavioral and Social Studies Annual Meeting, February 1975), in IAAA Papers, Box 18, University Archives, New York University.

105. Nick Aaron Ford, *Black Studies: Threat or Challenge?* (Port Washington, NY: Kennikat Press, 1973).

106. Alan King Colon, "A Critical Review of Black Studies Programs" (PhD diss., Stanford University, 1980), 112.

107. Carlos Brossard, "Classifying Black Studies Programs," *Journal of Negro Education* 53, no. 3 (Summer 1984): 280.

108. Joseph J. Russell, "Strides toward Organization," n.d., National Council of Black Studies Papers, Box 1, Folder 2, Schomburg Center; "Black Studies Accreditation Council Formed," press release, January 4, 1973, Guinier Papers, Box 20, Folder 1, Schomburg Center; Program, National Council for Black Studies, First Annual Convention, February 16–19, 1977, Columbus Ohio, BERC Papers, Box 17, Folder 11, Schomburg Center; Young, "The Struggle and Dream of Black Studies," 372.

109. See James E. Conyers, "The Association of Black Sociologists: A Descriptive Account from an Insider," *American Sociologist* 23, no. 1 (Spring 1992): 49–55; and the Web site of the Association of Black Anthropologists, www.aaanet.org/sections/aba/htdocs/About2.html, accessed July 28, 2011.

CHAPTER 7. THE BLACK REVOLUTION OFF-CAMPUS

1. Jack Gould, "TV: WCBS Introduces Promising 'Black Heritage,'" *New York Times*, January 7, 1969.

2. Audrey Gibson, WCBS-TV, to Vincent Harding, January 17, 1969; Winston Duckett to James Hester, January 21, 1969; Archie Moore to Vincent Harding, June 12, 1969; John Rosenthal to Vincent Harding, March 25, 1969; David Hauser, General Manager, WTIC, to Dear Sir, January 14, 1969, all in IBW Papers, Vincent Harding material, Box 7, Schomburg Center.

3. Vincent Harding, telephone interview by author, May 12, 2010.

4. See Devorah Heitner, "Black Power TV: A Cultural History of Black Public Affairs Television" (PhD diss., Northwestern University, 2007).

5. Vincent Harding et al., "Statement of the Black Members of the Advisory Committee of Black Heritage," January 2, 1969; "Memorandum of Understanding," January 8, 1969, both in IBW Papers, Vincent Harding material, Box 7, Schomburg Center.

6. "Black Heritage Series Feature CBS WBBM," *Chicago Daily Defender*, June 10, 1969, www.proquest.com.turing.library.northwestern.edu/, accessed May 5, 2010.

7. The series is stored at the Schomburg Center for Research in Black Culture, New York Public Library.

8. See Penny M. Von Eschen, *Race against Empire: Black Americans and Anticolonialism, 1935–1957* (Ithaca, NY: Cornell University Press, 1997).

9. Roy Wilkins, "Not the Real Black Experience," *New York Times*, June 15, 1969, www.proquest.com.turing.library.northwestern.edu/, accessed October 12, 2007.

10. John Henrik Clarke, "We See Ourselves in New Ways," letter to the editor, *New York Times*, June 15, 1969, www.proquest.com.turing.library.northwestern.edu/, accessed October 12, 2007.

11. Alan King Colon, "A Critical Review of Black Studies Programs" (PhD diss., Stanford University, 1980).

12. Twenty-First Century Fund, press release, March 27, 1969, and newsletter, March 1969, IBW Papers, Vincent Harding material, Box 9, Schomburg Center.

13. C. Eric Lincoln, "The Excellence of Soul," March 27, 1969, IBW Papers, Vincent Harding material, Box 9, Schomburg Center.

14. BAAL Confidential newsletter, May 29, 1970, IBW Papers, Vincent Harding material, Box 9, Schomburg Center.

15. BAAL press release, September 4, 1970; "First Annual Meeting of the Black Academy of Arts and Letters," n.d., IBW Papers, Vincent Harding material, Box 9, Schomburg Center.

16. "Ask Visa for Mrs. DuBois," *New York Amsterdam News*, May 9, 1970, 43; BAAL press release.

17. "First Annual Meeting of the Black Academy of Arts and Letters."

18. Simon Anekwe, "Academy Honors Black Arts," *New York Amsterdam News*, September 25, 1971, A!.

19. Jack Slater, "Learning Is an All-Black Thing," *Ebony*, September 1971, 89.

20. Robert Hoover, interview by author, Palo Alto, CA, August 11, 2005.

21. Robert Hoover, "Meeting Community Needs," in *The Minority Student on Campus*, ed. Robert A. Altman and Patricia O. Snyder (Berkeley, CA: Center for Research and Development, 1970), 194.

22. Hoover, interview.

23. John Egerton, "Success Comes to Nairobi College," *Change* 4, no. 4 (May 1972): 26, www.jstor.org/pss/40161453, accessed May 4, 2010.

24. Hoover, interview.

25. "Fall 1970 Course Offerings," IBW Papers, Box: Black Studies Programs, Folder: Nairobi College, Schomburg Center.

26. Hoover, "Meeting Community Needs," 195.

27. Egerton, "Success Comes to Nairobi College," 26.

28. Hoover, interview.

29. Ibid.

30. Egerton, "Success Comes to Nairobi College," 26.

31. Hoover, interview.

32. Hoover, "Meeting Community Needs," 195.

33. Egerton, "Success Comes to Nairobi College," 26.

34. Hoover, interview.

35. "To Set Up an Independent Black School," *Imani*, August–September 1971, IAAA Papers, Box 16, University Archives, New York University.

36. Egerton, "Success Comes to Nairobi College," 27.

37. Abdul Alkalimat, interview by author, Urbana, IL, March 31, 2006.

38. Ibid.

39. "Institute of the Black World: Basic Assumptions," May 1969, IBW Papers, Box: Black Studies Programs, Folder: An Approach to Black Studies, Schomburg Center.

40. Harding, telephone interview; Lerone Bennett, "The Quest for Black-ness," presented at the "Black Studies Directors' Seminar: Panel Presentations, 7, 8, 9, November 1969," Institute of the Black World, Atlanta, Georgia, IBW Papers, Box: Black Studies Directors' Seminar, Schomburg Center.

41. Strickland, Robinson, and Matthews, quoted from "Black Studies Directors' Seminar: Panel Presentations, 7, 8, 9 November 1969," Institute of the Black World, Atlanta, Georgia, IBW Papers, Box: Black Studies Directors' Seminar, Schomburg Center. Strickland referred to Arthur Jenson, who argued the genetic inferiority of Black people; William Styron, the white author of *The Confessions of Nat Turner*, a novel about the leader of a slave uprising whose portrait many Black nationalists disliked; and Daniel Patrick Moynihan, author of *The Negro Family: A Case for National Action*, which focused on the rising number of female-headed families. His inclusion on this list is ironic since many Black nationalists shared his concern over the supposedly skewed gender roles in Black America.

42. Harding, telephone interview.

43. Ford Foundation, press release, December 29, 1969, IBW Papers, Vincent Harding Material, Box 9, Schomburg Center.

44. Vincent Harding, telephone interview.

45. Ibid.

46. Special Agent in Charge, Atlanta, to the Director, July 23, 1970, IBW Papers, Box: FBI File, Schomburg Center.

47. Council Taylor to John Henrik Clarke, June 2, 1969, John Henrik Clarke Papers, Box 35, Folder 31, Schomburg Center.

48. Stephen Ward, "Scholarship in the Context of Struggle: Activist Intellectuals, the Institute of the Black World (IBW), and the Contours of Black Power Radicalism," *Black Scholar* 31 (2001): 50.

49. Special Agent in Charge, Atlanta, to the Director, February 12, 1970, IBW Papers, Box: FBI File, Schomburg Center.

50. "Report of the Staff of the Institute of the Black World," to Executive Committee of the Governing Council, IBW, May 11, 1970; and Vincent Harding, "Towards a Black Agenda," May 1, 1970, both in Drake Papers, Box 49, Folder 28, Schomburg Center.

51. Manning Marable, *Blackwater: Historical Studies in Race, Class Consciousness and Revolution* (Boulder: University Press of Colorado, 1993), 102.

52. Yvette Klein, "Prof. Harding Speaks in King Series," *Kingsman*, December 12, 1969, microfilm, Archives and Special Collections, Brooklyn College, Brooklyn, New York.

53. FBI Atlanta Office, Report on IBW April 4, 1972 to April 7, 1972, IBW Papers, Box: FBI File, Schomburg Center.

54. Howard Dodson to author, June 25, 2005, New York City.

55. See material in IBW Papers, Strickland Material, Box 11, Schomburg Center.

56. Vincent Harding to "Dear Friends," March 28, 1975, John Henrik Clarke Papers, Box 35, Folder 31, Schomburg Center.

57. IBW, press release, April 18, 1975, IBW Papers, Box: IBW under Attack, Schomburg Center.

58. Howard Dodson to U.S. Attorney General Edward Levi, August 8, 1975, IBW Papers, Box: FBI File, Schomburg Center.

59. "Black Research Group Target of Threats and Theft," *Muhammad Speaks,* April 25, 1975, IBW Papers, Box: IBW under Attack, Schomburg Center.

60. Marable, *Blackwater,* 104–105.

61. Sally Avery Bermanzohn, *Through Survivors' Eyes: From the Sixties to the Greensboro Massacre* (Vanderbilt, TN: Nashville University Press, 2003), 100.

62. Mark Smith, interview by author, Oakland, CA, August 10, 2005.

63. Bermanzohn, *Through Survivors' Eyes,* 105.

64. Smith, interview.

65. SOBU-OBU, "The Role of the Black Student through Revolution," 1970, Guinier Papers, Box 45, Folder 5, Schomburg Center, emphasis in the original. OBU was a chapter at Harvard.

66. "Critique of a Colonizing Program," n.d., Guinier Papers, Box 45, Folder 5, Schomburg Center.

67. "SOBU Statement on the Tenth Year Commemoration of the Sharpeville Massacre," March 21, 1970, Guinier Papers, Box 45, Folder 5, Schomburg Center.

68. "Students' Role in the Struggle," newspaper clipping, circa May 1971, Guinier Papers, Box 45, Folder 5, Schomburg Center.

69. Bermanzohn, *Through Survivors' Eyes*, 121.

70. Signe Waller, *Love and Revolution: A Political Memoir* (Lanham, MD: Rowman and Littlefield, 2002), 54–55.

71. Marable, *Blackwater*, 109. Marable contends as well that "many nationalists moved in the opposite direction," including Chicago's Haki Madhubuti, who, he claims, redoubled his suspicion that Black leftists were white-inspired disruptors of the movement, and that all whites were racists.

72. Bermanzohn, *Through Survivors' Eyes*, 122.

73. Smith, interview.

74. Bermanzohn, *Through Survivors' Eyes*, 111.

75. Nelson Johnson, interview by C. Otto Scharmer, June 3, 2009, "Transforming Capitalism," http://tc.presencing.com/posts/nelson-johnson-interview, accessed June 9, 2010.

76. Bermanzohn, *Through Survivors' Eyes*, 132.

77. See Waller, *Love and Revolution*; Bermanzohn, *Through Survivors' Eyes*.

78. Johnson, interview.

CHAPTER 8. WHAT HAPPENED TO BLACK STUDIES?

1. Alison Schneider, "Black Studies 101: Introductory Courses Reflect a Field Still Defining Itself," *Chronicle of Higher Education*, May 19, 2000.

2. Ibid.

3. Arthur Lewin, "Towards a Grand Theory of Black Studies: An Attempt to Discern the Dynamics and the Direction of the Discipline," *Western Journal of Black Studies* 25, no. 2 (Summer 2001): 76.

4. Chanel Lee, "Black to the Future: Where Does African American Studies Go From Here?" *Village Voice*, Educational Supplement, Fall 2005.

5. Gerald A. McWorter, Black Studies Program, University of Illinois at Chicago Circle, "A Proposal," August 1975, CAS Dean's Records, Box 36, Folder 13, University Archive, Northwestern University, Evanston, IL.

6. Abdul Alkalimat and Associates, *Introduction to Afro-American Studies* (Chicago: Twenty First Century Books and Publications, 1984–2009), www.eblackstudies.org; Maulana Karenga, *Introduction to Black Studies* (Los Angeles: University of Sankore Press, 1982); Alan King Colon, "A Critical Review of Black Studies Programs" (PhD diss., Stanford, 1980), 120.

7. Mary Christine Philip, "Of Black Studies: Pondering Strategies for the Future," *Black Issues in Higher Education*, December 29, 1994.

8. See for example the diverse work of John Henrik Clarke, Chancellor Williams, J.A. Rogers, W.E.B. Du Bois, Frank Snowden, and William Leo Hansberry.

9. See for example Stephen G. Hall, *A Faithful Account of the Race: African American Historical Writing in Nineteenth Century America* (Chapel Hill: University of North Carolina Press, 2009); and Maghan Keita, *Race and the Writing of History: Riddling the Sphinx* (New York: Oxford University Press, 2000).

10. Molefi Asante, "A Discourse on Black Studies: Liberating the Study of African People in the Western Academy," *Journal of Black Studies*, 36, no. 5 (May 2006): 646–662.

11. Molefi Asante, "The Ideological Significance of Afrocentricity in Intercultural Communication," *Journal of Black Studies* 14, no. 1 (September 1983): 7, www.jstor.org/stable/2784027.

12. Carr, quoted from "40th Anniversary of African American Studies in Academia," *The Tavis Smiley Show,* original air date, September 18, 2009, Public Radio International, http://thetavissmileyshow.com/100108_index.html.

13. Maulana Karenga, "Black Studies: A Critical Reassessment," *Race and Reason* 4 (1997–1998): 41.

14. Mary-Christine Phillip, "Of Black Studies: Pondering Strategies for the Future," *Black Issues in Higher Education,* December 29, 1994, 15; Ronald Roach, "Despite Struggles, Pioneering Black Studies Department Presses Forward," *Diverse Issues in Higher Education,* December 10, 2009, http://diverse education.com/article/13259/.

15. Roach, "Despite Struggles Pioneering Black Studies Department Presses Forward."

16. Rose, quoted from "40th Anniversary of African American Studies in Academia," *The Tavis Smiley Show.*

17. Melba Joyce Boyd, "Afrocentrics, Afro-Elitists and Afro-Eccentrics: The Polarization of Black Studies since the Student Struggles of the Sixties," in *Dispatches from the Ivory Tower,* ed. Manning Marable (New York: Columbia University Press, 2000), 207.

18. Joyce A. Joyce, *Black Studies as Human Studies* (Albany: State University of New York Press, 2005), 11, 9.

19. Erskine Peters, "Afrocentricity: Problems of Method and Nomenclature," *The African American Studies Reader,* ed. Nathaniel Norment Jr. (Durham, NC: Carolina Academic Press, 2001), 567, 568.

20. Barbara Ransby, "Afrocentrism and Cultural Nationalism," in *Dispatches from the Ivory Tower,* ed. Manning Marable (New York: Columbia University Press, 2000), 219.

21. Perry A. Hall, "Beyond Afrocentrism: Alternatives for African American Studies," *Africana Studies: Philosophical Perspectives and Theoretical Paradigms,* ed. Dolores P. Aldridge and E. Lincoln James (Pullman: Washington State University Press, 2007), 236.

22. "Renewing the Speeches of Those Who Heard: Intergenerational Exchanges, Good Speech, and Intellectual Warfare for the African Mind," Association for the Study of Classical African Civilizations, Program, March 4–6, 2010, Columbia, SC. See http://ascac.org/blog/conferences-events/ for subsequent programs and events; accessed December 15, 2011.

23. Rhett Jones, "Black Studies Failures and 'First Negroes,'" *Black Issues in Higher Education,* October 20, 1994, 16.

24. Rhett Jones, "The Lasting Contributions of African American Studies," *Journal of Blacks in Higher Education* 6 (Winter 1994–1995): 92.

25. Alison Schneider, "Black Studies 101: Introductory Courses Reflect a Field Still Defining Itself," *Chronicle of Higher Education,* May 19, 2000.

26. Floyd V. Hayes, "Preface to Instructors," in *Turbulent Voyage: Readings in African American Studies,* ed. Hayes (San Diego: Collegiate Press, 2000), xxxvi.

27. Angela Davis, speech at the Center for African American Studies, UCLA, March 24, 1995, printed in *CAAS Report*, vol. 16 (November 1, 2000), "CAAS: 25th anniversary" Folder, ephemera, University Archives, University of California, Los Angeles.

28. A global focus had long characterized Black history writing in the United States. See Robin Kelley's "'But a Local Phase of a World Problem': Black History's Global Vision, 1883–1950," *Journal of American History* 86, no. 3 (December 1999): 3.

29. St. Clair Drake, "Black Studies and Global Perspectives: An Essay," *Journal of Negro Education,* 53, no. 3 (Summer 1984): 231, emphasis in the original.

30. Charlotte Morgan-Cato, "A Retrospective View," in *A Companion to African American Studies,* ed. Lewis R. Gordon and Jane Anna Gordon (Malden, MA: Blackwell, 2006), 56.

31. Drake, "Black Studies and Global Perspectives," 231.

32. For the African Liberation Support Committee and ideological conflicts within the Black liberation movement, see Ronald Walters, *Pan-Africanism in the African Diaspora: An Analysis of Modern Afrocentric Political Movements* (Detroit: Wayne State University Press, 1997); and Fanon Che-Wilkins, "'In the Belly of the Beast': Black Power, Anti-imperialism, and the African Liberation Support Committee, 1968–1975" (PhD diss., New York University, 2001); Morgan-Cato, "A Retrospective View," 56.

33. See Kelley, "But a Local Phase of a World Problem."

34. See especially Penny M. Von Eschen, *Race against Empire: Black Americans and Anticolonialism, 1935–1957* (Ithaca, NY: Cornell University Press, 1997).

35. Robert L. Harris, "The Intellectual and Institutional Development of Africana Studies," in *Three Essays: Black Studies in the United States* (New York: Ford Foundation, 1990), reprinted in *Inclusive Scholarship: Developing Black Studies in the United States; A 25th Anniversary Retrospective of Ford Foundation Grant Making, 1982–2007* (New York: Ford Foundation, 2007), 95, 94.

36. Sylvester Whittaker, "Role of and Relationship between African, Caribbean, and Afro-American Studies," transcript, July 22, 1970, Black Studies Seminar, Aspen, Ford Foundation Papers, Grant 70–188, reel 1657.

37. Ibid.

38. St. Clair Drake, "Roosevelt University," IBW Papers, Box 3, Black Studies Survey Folder, Schomburg Center.

39. Whittaker, "Role of and Relationship between African, Caribbean, and Afro-American Studies."

40. One exception was the creation of Africana studies at Cornell, which included the study of Africa and the diaspora.

41. Colon, "A Critical Review of Black Studies Programs," 121, 96.

42. Rhett Jones, "Dreams, Nightmares and Realities: Afro-American Studies at Brown University, 1969–1986," in *A Companion to African American Studies,* ed. Lewis R. Gordon and Jane Anna Gordon (Malden, MA: Blackwell, 2006), 48.

43. St. Clair Drake, "What Happened to Black Studies?" *New York University Education Quarterly* 3 (Spring 1979).

44. Roscoe Brown, "Background Information on the IAAA," October 1969, IAAA Papers, Box 15, University Archives, New York University.

45. James Tobin, "When Doors Were Chained on State Street," *LSA Magazine*, Fall 2010, 7.

46. "Background: The African Heritage Studies Association," *Black World* (July 1970): 21.

47. John Henrik Clarke, "The African Heritage Studies Association: Some Notes on the Conflict with the African Studies Association and the Fight to Reclaim African History," *Issue: A Quarterly Journal of Africanist Opinion* 6 (Fall 1976): 8, 11.

48. African Heritage Association, Annual Conference, New York, April 20–23, 1978, Preliminary Program, BERC Papers, Box 13, Folder 9, Schomburg Center.

49. Jones, "Black Studies Failures and 'First Negroes,' " 16.

50. Toni Cade Bambara and Claudia Tate, eds., *Black Women Writers at Work* (New York: Continuum, 1983), 37.

51. For scholarship along these lines, see Stephen Ward, "Third World Women's Alliance: Black Feminist Radicalism and Black Power Politics," in *Black Power Movement*, ed. Peniel Joseph (New York: Routledge, 2006); and Jennifer Nelson, *Women of Color and the Reproductive Rights Movement* (New York: New York University Press, 2003).

52. Toni Cade Bambara, "On the Issue of Roles," in *The Black Woman*, ed. Cade (New York: Washington Square Press, 1970), 123–135.

53. Manning Marable, *How Capitalism Underdeveloped Black America* (1983; reprint, Cambridge, MA: South End Press, 2000), 84.

54. Constance M. Carroll, "Three's a Crowd: The Dilemma of the Black Woman in Higher Education," in *But Some of Us Are Brave*, ed. Gloria T. Hull, Patricia Bell Scott, and Barbara Smith (New York: Feminist Press at the City University of New York, 1982), 116.

55. Ibid., 117, 118.

56. Ibid., 117.

57. Mary Jane Hewitt, interview by Elston L. Carr, July 8, 1997, transcript, 76, UCLA Oral History Program, Center for African American Studies Library, UCLA.

58. Carroll, "Three's a Crowd," 115, 119.

59. Lillian Anthony, quoted in transcript of the "Black Studies Directors' Seminar: Panel Presentations, 7, 8, 9, November 1969," Institute of the Black World, Atlanta, Georgia, IBW Papers, Box: Black Studies Directors' Seminar, Schomburg Center.

60. Gloria T. Hull, Patricia Bell Scott, and Barbara Smith, eds. *But Some of Us Are Brave* (New York: Feminist Press at the City University of New York, 1982), 376.

61. "Petition Circulated by the Black Women's Research Committee," n.d. [most likely 1973], Center for African American Studies Papers, Box 17, University Archives, University of California at Los Angeles.

62. Flyer, IBW Papers, "Conferences" Box, Women's Conference Folder, Schomburg Center.

63. Gloria T. Hull and Barbara Smith, "The Politics of Black Woman's Studies," in *But Some of Us Are Brave*, ed. Gloria T. Hull, Patricia Bell Scott, and Barbara Smith (New York: Feminist Press at the City University of New York, 1982), xxi.

64. Sharon Harley, "The Politics of Memory and Place," in *Living Histories: Black Women Historians in the Ivory Tower*, ed. Deborah Gray White (Chapel Hill: University of North Carolina Press, 2008), 104; Marable, *How Capitalism Underdeveloped Black America*, 97.

65. Harley, "The Politics of Memory and Place," 103–104.

66. Ibid., 107–108.

67. Rosalyn Terborg-Penn, "Being and Thinking Outside of the Box: A Black Woman's Experience in Academia," in *Living Histories: Black Women Historians in the Ivory Tower*, ed. Deborah Gray White (Chapel Hill: University of North Carolina Press, 2008), 76–83.

68. Deborah Gray White, "My History in History," in *Living Histories: Black Women Historians in the Ivory Tower*, ed. White (Chapel Hill: University of North Carolina Press, 2008), 94–96.

69. John H. Bracey Jr., "Afro-American Women: A Brief Guide to Writing from Historical and Feminist Perspectives," *Contributions in Black Studies* 8, no. 1 (1996): 106. Available at http://scholarworks.umass.edu/cbs/vol8/iss1/9.

70. Manning Marable, "Groundings with My Sisters: Patriarchy and the Exploitation of Black Women," in *How Capitalism Underdeveloped Black America* (1983; reprint, Cambridge, MA: South End Press, 2000), 70.

71. See ibid., 71, 82.

72. Jones, "Black Studies Failures and 'First Negroes.'"

73. Colon, "A Critical Review of Black Studies Programs," 167–168.

74. Ibid., 146–147.

75. Robert G. O'Meally and Valerie Smith, "Evaluation of Ford-Funded African American Studies Departments, Centers and Institutes" (1994), in *Inclusive Scholarship: Developing Black Studies in the United States; A 25th Anniversary Retrospective of Ford Foundation Grant Making, 1982–2007* (New York: Ford Foundation, 2007), 140.

76. Evelyn Hu-DeHart, "The Undermining of Ethnic Studies," *Chronicle of Higher Education*, October 20, 1995.

77. See for example the European-based Collegium for African American Research.

CONCLUSION

1. See Penny M. Von Eschen, *Race against Empire: Black Americans and Anticolonialism, 1935–1957* (Ithaca, NY: Cornell University Press, 1997).

2. La TaSha Levy, "Remembering Sixth-PAC: Interviews with Sylvia Hill and Judy Claude," *Black Scholar* 37 (2008); Francis Nesbitt, *Race for Sanctions: The Movement against Apartheid, 1946–1994* (Bloomington: Indiana University Press, 2004); Ronald W. Walters, *Pan Africanism in the African Diaspora:*

An Analysis of Modern Afrocentric Political Movements (Detroit: Wayne State University Press, 1993).

3. Martha Biondi, "Student Protest, 'Law and Order' and the Rise of African American Studies in California," *Contested Democracy: Freedom, Race and Power in American History,* ed. Manisha Sinha and Penny M. Von Eschen (New York: Columbia University Press, 2007).

4. San Francisco State awarded Glover a Presidential Medal in 1999 at a ceremony honoring the thirtieth anniversary of the Educational Opportunity Program, www.sfsu.edu/~news/prsrelea/fy98/069.htm.

5. "Returning to City College to Revisit a 1969 Struggle," *New York Times,* October 29, 1999.

6. The *Hilltop* (Howard University), March 28, 1969, microfilm, HUL.

7. Ramona Tascoe, telephone interview by author, December 3, 2009.

8. The literature here is voluminous. See for example Stephen Steinberg, *Turning Back: The Retreat from Racial Justice* (Boston: Beacon Press, 1995).

Selected Bibliography

ARCHIVAL COLLECTIONS

Lyndon Baines Johnson Presidential Library, Austin, Texas; Records of the National Commission on the Causes and Prevention of Violence

San Francisco State University, San Francisco; Strike Collection; San Francisco Bay Area Television Archive; www.library.sfsu.edu/about/collections/sfbatv/index.php

University of California, Berkeley; Social Protest Collection

University of California, Los Angeles; Center for African American Studies, Oral History Collection

Northwestern University, Evanston, Illinois; University Archives

Brooklyn College, Brooklyn, New York; University Archives

City College, New York; Legacy of Struggle Collection; Five Demands Collection

Howard University, Washington, DC; Moorland-Spingarn Library; Ralph Bunche Civil Rights Documentation Project, Moorland-Spingarn Collection

National Archives, College Park, MD, Robert Finch Papers, in the Richard Nixon Papers, White House Central Files, Subject Files, Human Rights

New York University; University Archives, Institute of African-American Affairs Papers

Schomburg Center for Research in Black Culture, New York Public Library
    Ewart Guinier Papers
    St. Clair Drake Papers
    John Henrik Clarke Papers
    Black Academy of Arts and Letters Collection
    Institute of the Black World Papers
    Black Economic Research Center Collection
    National Council of Black Studies Papers

National Association for the Advancement of Colored People Papers, microfilm
Ford Foundation, New York; Ford Foundation Papers

JOURNALS

Black Issues in Higher Education
Black Scholar
Black World
Integrated Education
Journal of African American History (formerly *Journal of Negro History*)
Journal of Blacks in Higher Education
Journal of Black Studies
Journal of Negro Education
Negro Digest

NEWSPAPERS

Chicago Defender
Chicago Tribune
Daily Northwestern
Hilltop
Muhammad Speaks
New York Amsterdam News
New York Times
Sun-Reporter

GROUP PUBLIC REMEMBRANCES

"Columbia: 1968 + 40," April 25, 2008, Columbia 1968 Web site, www.colum
bia1968.com/conference.
"1968 + 40: The Black Student Movement and Its Legacy," November 1, 2008,
Center for African American History, Northwestern University, Evanston, IL.

PUBLICATIONS

Ahmad, Muhammad. *We Will Return in the Whirlwind: Black Radical Organi-
zations, 1960–1975.* Chicago: Charles H. Kerr, 2007.
Aldridge, Dolores P., and E. Lincoln James, eds. *Africana Studies: Philosophical
Perspectives and Theoretical Paradigms.* Pullman: Washington State Univer-
sity Press, 2007.
Anderson, James D. *The Education of Blacks in the South: 1860–1935.* Chapel
Hill: University of North Carolina Press, 1988.
Ballard, Allen B. *Breaking Jericho's Walls.* Albany: State University of New
York Press, 2011.
———. *The Education of Black Folk: The Afro-American Struggle for Knowl-
edge in White America.* New York: Harper and Row, 1973.

Barlow, William, and Peter Shapiro. *An End to Silence: The San Francisco State College Student Movement in the '60s.* New York: Pegasus, 1971.

Bass, Jack, and Jack Nelson. *The Orangeburg Massacre.* Macon, GA: Mercer University Press, 1970.

Bermanzohn, Sally Avery. *Through Survivors' Eyes: From the Sixties to the Greensboro Massacre.* Nashville, TN: Vanderbilt University Press, 2003.

Blassingame, John, ed. *New Perspectives on Black Studies.* Urbana: University of Illinois Press, 1971.

Bradley, Stefan. *Harlem vs. Columbia University: Black Student Power in the Late 1960s.* Urbana: University of Illinois Press, 2009.

Brown, Elaine. *A Taste of Power: A Black Woman's Story.* New York: Pantheon Books, 1993.

Brown, Scot. *Fighting for Us: Maulana Karenga, the US Organization and Black Cultural Nationalism.* New York: New York University Press, 2003.

Carmichael, Stokely, with Ekwueme Michael Thelwell. *Ready for Revolution: The Life and Struggles of Stokely Carmichael (Kwame Ture).* New York: Scribner, 2003.

Chafe, William H. *Civilities and Civil Rights: Greensboro, North Carolina, and the Black Struggle for Freedom.* New York: Oxford University Press, 1981.

Corson, William R. *Promise or Peril: The Black College Student in America.* New York: Norton, 1970.

Countryman, Matthew. *Up South: Civil Rights and Black Power in Philadelphia.* Philadelphia: University of Pennsylvania Press, 2006.

Edwards, Harry. *The Revolt of the Black Athlete.* New York: Macmillan, 1969.

Estes, Steve. *I am a Man! Race, Manhood and the Civil Rights Movement.* Chapel Hill: University of North Carolina Press, 2005.

Fergus, Devin. *Liberalism, Black Power and the Making of American Politics, 1965–1980.* Athens: University of Georgia Press, 2009.

Ford, Nick Aaron. *Black Studies: Threat or Challenge?* Port Washington, NY: Kennikat Press, 1973.

Foster, Julian, and Durward Long, eds. *Protest! Student Activism in America.* New York: William Morrow, 1969.

Glasker, Wayne. *Black Students in the Ivory Tower: African American Student Activism at the University of Pennsylvania, 1967–1990.* Amherst: University of Massachusetts Press, 2002.

Gordon, Lewis R., and Jane Anna Gordon, eds. *A Companion to African American Studies.* Malden, MA: Blackwell, 2006.

Graham, Gael. *Young Activists: American High School Students in the Age of Protest.* DeKalb: Northern Illinois University Press, 2006.

Green, Adam. *Selling the Race: Culture, Community, and Black Chicago, 1940–1955.* Chicago: University of Chicago Press, 2009.

Haas, Jeffrey. *The Assassination of Fred Hampton: How the FBI and Chicago Police Murdered a Black Panther.* Chicago: Lawrence Hill Books, 2009.

Hall, Stephen G. *A Faithful Account of the Race: African American Historical Writing in Nineteenth Century America.* Chapel Hill: University of North Carolina Press, 2009.

Hayes, Floyd, ed. *Turbulent Voyage: Readings in African American Studies*. San Diego: Collegiate Press, 2000.

Henderson, George. *Race and the University: A Memoir*. Norman: University of Oklahoma Press, 2010.

Hentoff, Nat, ed. *Black Anti-Semitism and Jewish Racism*. New York: Richard Baron, 1969.

Horne, Gerald. *Fire This Time: The Watts Uprising and the 1960s*. Cambridge, MA: Da Capo Press, 1997.

Hull, Gloria T., Patricia Bell Scott, and Barbara Smith, eds. *But Some of Us Are Brave: All the Women Are White, All the Blacks Are Men: Black Women's Studies*. New York: Feminist Press at the City University of New York, 1982.

Joseph, Peniel. *Waiting till the Midnight Hour: A Narrative History of Black Power in America*. New York: Henry Holt, 2007.

Joyce, Joyce A. *Black Studies as Human Studies: Critical Essays and Interviews*. Albany: State University of New York Press, 2005.

Justice, Blair. *Violence in the City*. Fort Worth: Texas Christian University Press, 1969.

Karaguezian, Dikran. *Blow It Up! The Black Student Revolt at San Francisco State and the Emergence of Dr. Hayakawa*. Boston: Gambit, 1971.

Keita, Maghan. *Race and the Writing of History: Riddling the Sphinx*. New York: Oxford University Press, 2000.

Kotlowski, Dean. *Nixon's Civil Rights: Politics, Principle and Policy*. Cambridge, MA: Harvard University Press, 2001.

Lavin, David E., ed. *Right Versus Privilege: The Open Admissions Experiment at the City University of New York*. New York: Free Press, 1981.

Lewis, George E. *A Power Stronger Than Itself: The AACM and American Experimental Music*. Chicago: University of Chicago Press, 2008.

Marable, Manning. *Blackwater: Historical Studies in Race, Class Consciousness and Revolution*. Boulder: University Press of Colorado, 1993.

———, ed. *Dispatches from the Ivory Tower*. New York: Columbia University Press, 2000.

———. *How Capitalism Underdeveloped Black America*. 1983. Reprint, Cambridge, MA: South End Press, 2000.

McEvoy, James, and Abraham Miller, eds. *Black Power and Student Rebellion*. Belmont, CA: Wadsworth, 1969.

Murch, Donna. *Living for the City: Migration, Education and the Rise of the Black Panther Party in Oakland, CA*. Chapel Hill: University of North Carolina Press, 2010.

Norment, Nathaniel, ed. *The African American Studies Reader*. Durham, NC: Carolina Academic Press, 2001.

Ogbar, Jeffrey O.G. *Black Power: Radical Politics and African American Identity*. Baltimore, MD: Johns Hopkins University Press, 2004.

Orrick, William H., Jr. *Shut It Down! A College in Crisis: San Francisco State College, October 1968–April 1969*. Washington, DC: National Commission on the Causes and Prevention of Violence, 1969.

Perlstein, Daniel H. *Justice, Justice: School Politics and the Eclipse of Liberalism*. New York: Peter Lang, 2004.

Roebuck, Julian B., and Komanduri S. Murty. *Historically Black Colleges and Universities: Their Place in American Higher Education*. Westport, CT: Praeger, 1993.

Rojas, Fabio. *From Black Power to Black Studies: How a Radical Social Movement Became an Academic Discipline*. Baltimore, MD: Johns Hopkins University Press, 2007.

Rooks, Noliwe. *White Money/Black Power: The Surprising History of African American Studies*. Boston: Beacon Press, 2006.

Rosser, James M., and Jacob U. Gordon, eds. *The Black Studies Debate*. Lawrence: University of Kansas, Division of Continuing Education, 1974.

Self, Robert. *American Babylon: Race and the Struggle for Postwar Oakland*. Princeton, NJ: Princeton University Press, 2004.

Sellers, Cleveland. *The River of No Return: The Autobiography of a Black Militant and the Life and Death of SNCC*. New York: William Morrow, 1973.

Sitkoff, Harvard. *The Struggle for Black Equality: 1954–1992*. New York: Hill and Wang, 1993.

Smith, Robert, Richard Axen, and Devere Pentony. *By Any Means Necessary: The Revolutionary Struggle at San Francisco State*. San Francisco: Jossey-Bass, 1970.

Summerskill, John. *President Seven*. New York: World Publishing, 1971.

Swearingen, M. Wesley. *FBI Secrets*. Boston: South End Press, 1995.

Taber, Robert. *The War of the Flea: A Study of Guerrilla Warfare Theory and Practice*. New York: L. Stuart, 1965.

Tyson, Timothy. *Radio Free Dixie: Robert F. Williams and the Roots of Black Power*. Chapel Hill: University of North Carolina Press, 1999.

Van Deburg, William. *New Day in Babylon: The Black Power Movement and American Culture*. Chicago: University of Chicago Press, 1992.

Von Eschen, Penny M. *Race against Empire: Black Americans and Anticolonialism, 1935–1957*. Ithaca, NY: Cornell University Press, 1997.

Waller, Signe. *Love and Revolution: A Political Memoir: People's History of the Greensboro Massacre, Its Setting and Aftermath*. Lanham, MD: Rowman and Littlefield, 2002.

Walters, Ronald. *Pan-Africanism in the African Diaspora: An Analysis of Modern Afrocentric Political Movements*. Detroit: Wayne State University Press, 1997.

White, Deborah Gray, ed. *Living Histories: Black Women Historians in the Ivory Tower*. Chapel Hill: University of North Carolina Press, 2008.

Williamson, Joy Ann. *Black Power on Campus: University of Illinois, 1965–1975*. Urbana: University of Illinois Press, 2003.

Acknowledgments

Like many revolutions, *The Black Revolution on Campus* took a long time to gestate before it finally burst on the scene. I have so many people to thank, more than I will likely remember, so please forgive me if I fail to include your name. Being part of a profession that you are writing about means that you are influenced by dinner party conversations, hallway conversations, conference conversations, and even chance encounters in the archive. I have learned to always have a pen handy. I have been more enriched and moved by this journey than I can adequately convey. I am honored to be part of such a challenging, engaging, and vital intellectual tradition and a brilliant community of scholars.

I am indebted first of all to the scholars and former student activists who shared their memories with me. From San Francisco to New York, their lives and struggles, and then, crucially, their willingness to share them, made this book possible. I am forever thankful. I also thank the many archivists and librarians who assisted me in locating materials, especially at City College, Northwestern, San Francisco State, and Howard. The staff at the Schomburg Center for Research in Black Culture in Harlem, a division of the New York Public Library, always deserves special thanks. I first imagined this book many, many years ago after the late Andre Elizee introduced me to the papers of Ewart Guinier. Howard Dodson, the retired chief of the Schomburg, offered support and encouragement, in addition to great stories. Sharon Howard always pointed me in the right direction.

When Charles Hamilton handed me a plain brown envelope, I had no idea that it contained his unpublished manuscript on Black students from 1969. His on-the-ground interviews from decades ago, and then his extraordinary generosity in sharing them with me, greatly enhanced chapter 1. Michael Martin was enormously helpful and generous in sharing not only his recollections but also his many journals and other printed material from the early 1970s. John Bracey was likewise extremely generous in sharing both his memories and his personal archive. His contributions and support made this a much stronger book. Sterling Stuckey and Lerone Bennett also offered documents from their personal collections in addition to their recollections, and I am very grateful. Sterling spent considerable time and energy gathering material and sharing his reflections, and I am ever so thankful. I am indebted to Stan Willis, who opened his files to me, affording me a rich window on Chicago activism in the late 1960s. Eric Foner, as always, was very generous with his memories and sage advice. Fred Prejean graciously shared documents and difficult memories. Thanks to Myles Link, who very generously shared memories and materials from his student days at Harvard. I am grateful to Lani Guinier for putting me in touch with many people from Harvard. The participation of veterans of the San Francisco State strike was indispensable to this project. I cannot thank Hari Dillon enough. Because the photo archive at San Francisco State had closed, he worked very, very hard to track down photographs and photographers. Moreover, he was generous and gracious in sharing many memories and insights.

A fellowship from the Dorothy and Lewis B. Cullman Center for Scholars and Writers at the New York Public Library enabled me to accomplish a great deal of research and writing. I am particularly thankful to fellow fellows Hilary Ballon and Elizabeth Kendall. I am also indebted to the Northwestern University Weinberg College of Arts and Sciences, especially former Dean Aldon Morris, for affording me the time to complete the manuscript. Additionally, the Alice Berline Kaplan Institute for the Humanities at Northwestern awarded me a course reduction that helped make *The Black Revolution* possible. The American Bar Foundation provided the space and collegiality for a very productive year of writing. I am grateful in particular to Robert Nelson, Christopher Schmidt, Dylan Penningroth, Bernadette Atuahene, and Susan Shapiro.

Thanks to a stimulating writing group at the University of Chicago with Cathy Cohen, Michael Dawson, Celeste Watkins-Hayes, and Mario Smalls, whose comments and camaraderie were very helpful at an important juncture.

I was fortunate to organize a fortieth anniversary conference commemorating the Black student movement at Northwestern, thanks to the generous support of many, especially the Center for African American History and the always supportive and savvy Darlene Clark Hine. I thank Victor Goode for being persistent in his belief that it should happen. His support and leadership were instrumental to the event and my understanding of the dynamics of 1968. Thank you, Victor! The returning alumni offered deeply affecting commentary about their experiences in 1968, and the conference contributed immensely to this book.

I thank my wonderful literary agent, Jill Marr, of the Sandra Dykstra Agency, and a big thank-you to my outstanding editor, Niels Hooper. I likewise thank all the wonderful people at the University of California Press, especially Kim Hogeland, Suzanne Knott, and everyone else who participated in the production of this book; Bonita Hurd for her splendid and careful copyediting; and Barbara Roos for her expert index. I am enormously grateful. I offer a special note of gratitude to two anonymous reviewers whose comments were astute, comprehensive, and extraordinarily helpful.

I am grateful for the support and encouragement of all my wonderful colleagues in the Department of African American Studies at Northwestern, especially Darlene Clark Hine, who was so generous in sharing materials and memories, and Sandra Richards, Mary Pattillo, Celeste Watkins-Hayes, E. Patrick Johnson, Dwight McBride, Michelle Wright, Tracy Vaughn, and Nitasha Sharma for important feedback and suggestions along the way. Nancy MacLean, we miss you in Evanston. Thanks for your great sense of humor and sharp thinking over the years. Thanks to Erik Gellman, whose insistence kept Roosevelt in the book, if only briefly! Thanks to all of my students, especially La TaSha Levy, Keeanga Taylor, D'Weston Haywood, Tera Agyepong, Andrew Baer, and Dwayne Nash, for keeping my brain running and inspiring me with your brilliance and passion for learning. Thanks to all the undergraduate students who read the manuscript in seminar and offered sharp and very helpful comments. Thanks as well to all the students in the Living Wage Campaign at Northwestern, especially Adam, Vicky, Kellyn, Chenault, Will, Jordan, Maggie, and Mike (and so many others) for inspiring me with your dedication and commitment.

I am sustained by the love and support, not to mention incisive political analysis, of my Chicago people: Lynette Jackson, Barbara Ransby, Adam Green, Alice Kim, Peter Sporn, Tessie Liu, Bernardine Dohrn, Bill Ayers, Harishi Patel, Prexy Nesbitt, Lisa Lee, and the "chief ideologist," James Thindwa. Thank you for your brilliant suggestions and sage advice through this long process! Thanks to everyone in ARC '09 and Ellas's Daughters, and to my many friends and allies in the wider social justice movement in Chicago, whose work I admire enormously and whose thinking has shaped me. Thanks to Elaine Charnov and Bruce Stutz for being my New York family. I send big hugs and appreciation to my parents, Ann Matteis and James Biondi, for their love, support, and encouragement. And love and thanks as well to my entire family, from Albuquerque to Malawi.

Finally, I am very fortunate to share my life with James Thindwa. As Bill Moyers knows, James is a dedicated and brilliant organizer. His solidarity, sharp thinking, great record collection, delicious cooking, and steadfast love enrich my life. And he was very tolerant as the guts of my book spread around the house. Thank you! It's done.

Photo Credits

Figures 1, 3, 8, 11, 13, and 16 are from the Archives of the *Chicago Defender*.
Figures 2, 14, and 15 are from Archives, The City College of New York, CUNY.
Figure 4 is by Gerald Grow, Courtesy Labor Archives and Research Center, San Francisco State University Press.
Figure 5 is reproduced by permission of Tony Rogers, photographer. Digital copy courtesy of Chris Carlsson.
Figure 6 is reproduced by permission of Terry Schmitt, photographer. Digital copy courtesy of Chris Carlsson.
Figures 7, 9, and 10 are from the James S. Sweet Collection, Northwestern University Archives.
Figures 12 and 17 are from the Ewart Guinier Photograph Collection, Photographs and Prints Division, Schomburg Center for Research in Black Culture, New York Public Library, Astor, Lenox and Tilden Foundations.
Figure 18 is reproduced by permission of Anthony Barboza, photographer.
Figures 19 and 20 are from the Institute of the Black World Photograph Collection, Photographs and Prints Division, Schomburg Center for Research in Black Culture, New York Public Library, Astor, Lenox and Tilden Foundations.

Index

A&T State University, North Carolina, 30, 33, 157–60, 192, 234, 273
AASU (Afro-American Student Union), Northwestern, 83, 84, 89–91
activism, 236–39; students across U.S., 2–3, 6, 151. *See also* Black Power; Black student activism; civil rights movement; internationalism; militancy; sit-ins; strikes; Third Worldism
Adams, Carol, 107, 113
Adams, Russell, 153
Adams v. Richardson, 143
admissions criteria, 51–52, 114, 116, 269, 277–78; CUNY, 114–17, 124, 125, 133–40, 200, 269; Harvard, 196–97; Malcolm X College, 109; SFSC, 43, 48, 51–52, 56, 72; standardized tests, 140. *See also* affirmative action; Black student enrollment; tests
affirmative action, 3, 51–52, 73, 170, 269; Harvard, 196; Northwestern, 80; opposition to, 78, 115, 196, 272, 277; "professionalization" of, 75; SEEK, 115–16, 124–29, 134, 139, 140; UCLA, 258; for women, 259
Affro-Arts Theater, Chicago, 104–5
Africa: ASA, 254; Black Power and, 4; Black studies, 244, 245, 246, 247, 251; Carmichael, 22, 146, 237–38; Communi-

versity studies, 112; enslavement, 245, 246; Marxism, 237; Sadauki's trip to, 236; socialism, 236–37. *See also* African diaspora; African liberation struggles; Afrocentricism; colonialism in Africa; Ghana; Pan-Africanism; South Africa
African American studies. *See* Black studies
African American Women and the Struggle for the Vote, 1850–1920 (Terborg-Penn), 263
Africana Studies and Research Center, Cornell, 110, 186, 188, 203, 275, 276
African diaspora, 10, 250; Black studies, 10–11, 101, 178, 230, 244, 249, 251–56, 264, 271; SOBU and solidarity efforts in, 235. *See also* Africa; Pan-Africanism
African Heritage Ensemble, 109
African Heritage Studies Association (AHSA), 205, 254–55, 275
"Africanization," of Blacks, 236
African Liberation Day, 235, 250
African liberation struggles, 235–38, 251, 271; African Liberation Support Committee, 233, 237, 238, 250–51; Black nationalism and, 249, 251, 255; Black studies and, 255; Cuban support, 23; new nation-states, 10, 249, 255, 276; Pan-Africanism, 235, 237, 238, 250

Black communities *(continued)*
103, 211; Black studies movement and,
47, 49, 100, 119, 211, 228, 275–76,
277; Black university and, 22, 144;
Chicago, 83, 104, 109, 111; emphasis
on higher education, 14; Greensboro,
157, 234–35; Harvard, 198; Houston,
31; Howard, 34, 151, 153; institution
building, 112, 207–40; integrationist old
guard, 133; Kawaida worldview, 247;
Los Angeles, 68–70; Nairobi Schools,
225; New York City, 114, 119, 122, 124,
125, 127–28, 130, 133–34; Northwestern, 100; SFSC strike, 56, 57, 65–66, 67,
72; Voorhees, 155. *See also* Black arts
movement; NAACP
Black Economic Research Center, Harlem,
148
"Black Excellence Unlimited," 109
"The Black Experience at Harvard"
(Kilson), 198
Black faculty: Black student demand for, 3,
48, 186–92; cohort fighting for Black
studies, 209–10; departments other than
Black studies, 277; hiring issues, 74,
186–93, 199, 276; predominantly white
universities, 277
Black female leadership: Crane/Malcolm X
College, 102, 108; CUNY, 117, 125–26;
FMO, 83; heads of families, 26; IBW,
229; NCBS, 208; Ohio State, 217;
sexism by Black men toward, 27, 46,
58–59, 256–57; SFSC, 18, 46; SOBU/
YOBU, 238; University of Chicago, 111;
Vassar, 22. *See also* Black women and
Black male leadership; feminism
Black Fire, BSU, 75
Black Heritage: A History of Afro-Americans,
10, 25, 211, 212–16, 227, 231
Black history, 180, 244; BAAL and, 218;
*Black Heritage: A History of Afro-
Americans,* 10, 25, 211, 212–16, 227,
231; Clarke, 10, 17, 211–12, 212*fig,*
214, 244; Columbia study groups, 19;
Harding, 10, 178, 211–13, 231; HBCUs
turning away from, 30–31; internation-
alist, 251; Merritt College, 41; SFSC,
48; UCLA, 191; women and, 26,
257–64; written and taught by Blacks,
10, 17, 178
Black History Week, 218
*The Black Image in the White Mind: The
Debate on Afro-American Character
and Destiny* (Frederickson), 83

Black institution building, 112, 207–40
"Black Institutions and Black Students"
(Cheek), 163
Black intelligentsia: Black studies employ-
ment, 227; Black university and, 35;
Caribbean, 127, 229–30; Du Bois, 218;
IBW and, 227, 231; and Marxism,
229–30; threatened by student demands
of Black faculty, 186; women, 127,
258–59, 261–63, 264. *See also* Black
faculty
*The Black Jacobins: Toussaint L'Ouverture
and the San Domingo Revolution*
(James), 94, 219
Black lesbians, 260
*Black Liberation: A Comparative History
of Black Ideologies in the United States
and South Africa* (Frederickson), 83
Black liberation movement: BAAL and,
219–20; Brooklyn College, 123;
catalyzing activity against various facets
of oppression, 264–65; Crane, 102;
decline, 275; gender and, 26, 125, 257;
government repression, 232; historians,
211; after King's assassination, 268;
lesbians, 260; Pan-Africanism and, 235,
237. *See also* African liberation
struggles; Black student activism
Black male leadership: AHSA, 255; *Black
Heritage* lecturers, 216; IBW, 229, 260;
NCBS conference, 208, 263; student,
26–28, 46, 58–59, 102, 115, 117–18,
125, 257. *See also* Black women and
Black male leadership; patriarchy
Black men: Black studies dominated by,
258; images, 26, 103; one hundred
leading Black Americans, 258;
University of Pittsburgh associate and
full professor positions, 258; with white
women, 81, 187, 236. *See also* Black
male leadership
Black Metropolis (Drake and Cayton), 112
Black Muslim, 27
Black nationalism, 34, 115, 233, 271–72;
and African liberation struggles, 249,
251, 255; Black-brown alliances, 27,
115, 123; Black communities and, 103,
211; *Black Heritage* and, 215, 216;
Black studies, 16–17, 46–47, 48, 95,
174–75, 189, 205–6, 243, 244, 246,
252, 255, 276; BPP, 44; CCNY, 129;
Chinese communists supporting, 236;
Crane, 103, 107; gender issues, 26, 46,
83, 226, 262–63; Hare, 48; Howard

Black women and Black male leadership, 26–27; Crane, 102; CUNY, 115, 117; IBW, 129; sexism by men, 27, 46, 58–59, 256–57, 261, 262–63

Black Women in White America, 262

Black Women's Conference, IBW, 260

Black World, 249. *See also* African diaspora; Institute of the Black World (IBW); Pan-Africanism

Black World (previously *Negro Digest*), 34

Blassingame, John, 186, 187, 191, 199, 249

Bok, Derek, 199

Bond, Horace Mann, 213

Bontemps, Arna, 217

Boston University, 40, 252

Bowker, Albert H., 139

Boyd, Melba, 246

BPP. *See* Black Panther Party (BPP)

Bracey, John: Amistad Society, 98; hired as Black studies faculty, 188, 189, 275, 276; Northwestern, 81–85, 89, 94, 98, 188

Bracey, John Jr., 264

Brimmer, Andrew, 199

Bronx: Bronx Community College, 217; Fordham University, 190–91; Lehman College, 187, 250; Morgan-Cato, 251

Brooklyn, Uhuru Sasa School, 226

Brooklyn College, 8, 114–23, 128; admissions programs, 116–17, 137, 138, 139, 269; arrests, 121–23, 130–31; "BC 19," 123; Black student leadership, 117; Askia Davis, 117–18, 120, 121, 123, 130–31, 137, 138, 275; demands by Black students, 118–20, 123; Jewish faculty and students, 124; *Kingsman,* 122–23; Midwood, 138; Pile, 117, 118, 119, 121, 137; Puerto Rican Alliance, 117, 120; School for Contemporary Studies (SCS), 119, 137–38; SDS, 117, 119–22; white percentage, 116

Brooks, Gwendolyn, 105, 193, 220

Brossard, Carlos, 185, 205

Brousard, Stephen, 86*fig*

Brown, Claude, 26

Brown, Ewart, 37, 149, 150, 151, 152–53

Brown, Frank London, 80

Brown, Leonard D., 163–64, 167–72, 273

Brown, Oscar Brown Jr., 95

Brown, Roscoe, 202, 204–5, 217, 253

Brown, Sterling, 34, 36, 98

Brown, Willie, 54, 58, 65, 75

Browne, Robert S., 10, 148, 213, 217

Brown University, Black studies, 248, 253, 256

Brown v. Board of Education, 2, 14, 38, 117, 270

BSU (Black Student Union), SFSC, 7, 43, 45–66, 50*fig*, 61*fig*, 71–76; admissions programs, 52, 56, 72; Alexis, 74; "autonomy" quest, 48; Black Arts and Culture series, 47; *Black Fire,* 75; Black high school graduates, 48; Black studies department, 48–49, 56–57, 73, 75–77; Dillon, 46, 53; Garrett, 47, 48, 52, 54; gender roles, 58–59; Glover, 52, 74; Hare and, 48, 50*fig*, 54, 76; march across campus, 56; Murray, 52, 55–57, 67, 71, 73; Ben Stewart, 45–46, 52, 57; Tascoe, 18, 47, 55, 58–59, 66, 72; Thomas, 52, 67, 75; twelve-member central committee, 58; and TWLF, 59–61, 72–73; Varnado, 45, 52, 56–57, 59. *See also* SFSC strike

Bunche, Ralph, 30, 276

Bundy, McGeorge, 201

Bunzel, John, 49

Burns, Haywood, 169, 170

Burroughs, Charles, 112

Burroughs, Margaret, 98, 112

But Some of Us Are Brave: All the Women Are White, All the Blacks Are Men: Black Women's Studies (Hull, Scott, and Smith), 260

Cabral, Amilcar, 83, 236–37

Cade, Toni, 125–27, 213, 216, 256, 257–58

California: Black student activism, 41, 55, 78; Black studies (early 1970s), 206; Claremont Colleges, 222; Department of Education, 224; ethnic studies, 265; Governor Reagan, 7, 43, 55, 62, 67, 73, 132; Master Plan for Education, 51; Nairobi Schools, 10, 220–26; TWLF, 59. *See also* Bay Area; Los Angeles; University of California

California State University, Long Beach, 71

Calvin, Willie, 106

Cambodia, U.S. invasion, 160

Cannon, Alfred, 69

capitalism, Black, 109

Carew, Jan, 100–101

Caribbean: Black newspaper coverage, 251; Black studies, 251, 252–53; communities in Canada, 230; intellectuals, 127, 229–30; Arthur Lewis, 201. *See also* Cuba; Haiti

Goodlett, Carleton, 64, 65, 72, 78, 274
Goodwin, Leroy, 72–73
Graham Du Bois, Shirley, 219
Grant, Joanne, 216
grassroots organizing, 271; admissions
    programs, 52; Black Power social
    movement, 2, 157; Black studies
    program, 47–48; civil rights movement,
    129, 157; Greensboro Black community,
    234–35; Nairobi Schools, 10
Gray, Hanna, 100
Gray, James, 173
Green, Adam, 112
Greensboro, 157–58, 160, 234–35, 273;
    Beloved Community Center, 240;
    Greensboro Massacre, 160, 239; Ku Klux
    Klan, 239; Malcolm X Liberation
    University, 235; North Carolina A&T
    State University, 30, 33, 157–60, 192,
    234, 273; Trouble in Greensboro, 160;
    Truth and Reconciliation Commission,
    239
Gregg, Lucius, 87–89, 93
Gregory, Dick, 104, 109
Griffin, Farah, 201
Griffin, Skip, 184
Grimes, Willie, 158–59, 160
"Groundings with My Sisters: Patriarchy
    and the Exploitation of Black Women"
    (Marable), 264
guerilla tactics, SFSC strike and, 57
Guinea, Carmichael moving to, 146
Guinea-Bissau: anticolonial struggles, 235,
    250; socialism, 236–37
Guinier, Ewart, 178, 193–96, 194fig, 199,
    276–77
Guyanese, 100, 229, 244

"H2o Gate Blues" (Scott-Heron), 172
Haiti: earthquake relief, 275; Revolution,
    94, 219
Haley, Alex, 217, 225
Hall, Perry, 247
Hamilton, Charles, 23, 25; Black faculty
    hiring, 188, 190; Black Power: The
    Politics of Liberation (with Carmichael),
    20–21, 21fig, 22, 125, 271; Black
    scholarship vs. militancy, 204; Black
    students' gender roles, 27, 28; Black
    students' religion, 29; Black students'
    scholarships, 29; Black students in
    South, 30; Black university, 21fig,
    34–35; Guinier seeking help from, 193;
    Malcolm X College, 108; Merritt

College, 41; "The Place of the Black
    College in the Human Rights Struggle,"
    34; Roosevelt University, 80, 81
Hammond, Samuel, 32
Hampton, Francis, 109
Hampton, Fred, 106, 109
Handbook of Black Studies (Karenga and
    Asante), 245
Handy, John, 75
Hansberry, Lorraine, 276
Hansberry, William, 244
Harbert, Hattie, 31
Harding, Vincent, 188, 249; Aspen
    conference, 201–2, 203; Black Heritage,
    10, 25, 211, 212–14, 227; Black history,
    10, 178, 211–13, 231; on Blackness,
    177; Black university, 144–45; Commis-
    sion for Black Education, 192; IBW,
    212, 227–28, 229, 229fig, 230–31,
    232–33; Spelman College, 144, 188,
    211, 227; "Statement of the Black
    Members of the Advisory Committee
    of Black Heritage" (with Clarke and
    Strickland), 214
Hare, Nathan, 23; Black Anglo-Saxons, 125;
    The Black Scholar, 75, 205; on Black
    studies programs, 77, 201, 206; Howard,
    34, 35, 38, 48, 146, 206; SFSC, 35,
    48–49, 50fig, 54, 56, 73, 76, 206, 273
Harlem: Black Economic Research Center,
    148; CCNY's location in, 8, 13, 114,
    123–25, 130, 130fig; Clarke as historian
    of, 17, 212, 212fig; Columbia police
    violence and, 131; "University of
    Harlem," 123, 125, 130fig
Harley, Sharon, 261–62, 263
Harris, Abram, 276
Harris, Jocklyn, 86fig
Harris, Leslie, 82
Harris, Michael, 36
Harris, Patricia Roberts, 150
Harris, Robert L., 249, 251–52
Harris Bank, Chicago, 93
Harvard Bulletin, 197
Harvard University, 114, 124, 193–200;
    Association of African and Afro-
    American Students at Harvard and
    Radcliffe (AFRO), 181–84; Black studies,
    9–10, 174, 181–84, 185, 188, 191,
    193–200, 203, 208, 234, 242, 252,
    276–77; Crimson, 183–84; discrimina-
    tion vs. Black students, 18–19; Du Bois
    as first Black recipient of PhD from,
    218; Guinier, 178, 193–96, 194fig, 199,

Journal of Negro History, 209, 218
Joyce, Joyce A., 246
Julian, Percy, 38
junior colleges. *See* community colleges
Justice Department, vs. Shirley Graham Du
 Bois visa, 219

Kamen, Jeff, 87
Karenga, Maulana/Ron: Black studies, 201,
 243, 245; *Handbook of Black Studies*
 (with Asante), 245; vs. interracial dating/
 marriage, 187; *Introduction to Black
 Studies,* 243; Kawaida worldview, 243,
 247; TABU, 146; US, 68, 69, 70–71
Kawaida worldview, 243, 247
Kelsey, George, 203
Kemet, Afrocentricity and Knowledge
 (Asante), 246
Kempton, Murray, 134
Kennedy-King College, 112
Kent State, Ohio, 157, 161, 171–72
Kerner commission, 92, 157, 214
Killens, John Oliver, 98, 145, 217
Kilson, Martin, 184, 194–201, 217, 242
King, Barbara Lewis, 107, 108
King, Coretta Scott, 227
King, Martin Luther Jr.: vs. Black Power,
 231; Harding close with, 211;
 nonviolence, 24, 40, 162; Rustin, 133.
 See also King's assassination
King, Martin Luther Jr. family: and IBW,
 230–31; wife, 227
King Memorial Center, 227–28, 231
King Memorial Foundation Board, 230–31
King's assassination: Atlanta community
 and, 227; Black faculty demand after,
 188; Black liberation movement after,
 268; Black student activism after, 2, 7,
 14, 40, 81, 83–84, 123; Black student
 unrest prior to, 39; Black studies and,
 181, 206; Crane memorial, 106; EOP
 quota after, 52; Ohio State and, 160
Kirby, Larry, 158–59
Kirkpatrick, Thelma Wheaton, 227
Knight, Franklin, 220
Kofsky, Frank, 75
Kotlowski, Dean, 163
KQED, 63
Kreml, Franklin, 87–89
Ku Klux Klan: bombings of Black homes,
 15; CCNY activism and, 132; Nation of
 Islam and, 52; Robert F. Williams vs.,
 23; vs. WVO, 239
Kwanzaa, 71, 223, 247

Labor Department, U.S., 26
labor unions: Chicago, 104; Coalition of
 Black Trade Unionists, 111; International Longshore and Warehouse Union,
 67; Transport Workers Union, 67; WVO,
 239–40
LaBrie, Aubrey, 47
Ladner, Joyce, 229, 249
Latinos: Black activists inspiring, 2, 264,
 265, 269; Black alliances with, 27, 115,
 123; San Francisco, 53. *See also*
 Mexican Americans; Puerto Ricans
lawyers, civil rights, 273–74
Lawyers Committee for Human Rights, 274
leadership: Black activist (non-student), 26,
 108, 226–27. *See also* Black female
 leadership; Black male leadership; Black
 student leadership; civil rights
 movement
Leahy, Margaret, 61
Lee, Carol, 220
leftism. *See* communists; Marxism; New
 Left; socialism
Lehman College, Bronx, 187, 250
Leninism, Marxist-Leninism, 233, 237
Lerner, Gerda, 262
lesbians. *See* gays and lesbians
Leslie, Joshua, 97, 98–99, 100
Lester, Julius, 129
Levin, John, 60, 61, 62, 74
Lewin, Arthur, 242
Lewis, Arthur, 201
Lewis, John, 169
liberalism: *Black Heritage* and, 215; Black
 Power as critique of, 37; cold war, 16,
 145; elite private historically white
 universities, 7; Sen. Hayakawa vs., 77;
 Northwestern, 82; postwar, 14; SFSC,
 43, 45, 51
liberation movements. *See* African liberation
 struggles; Black liberation movement;
 feminism
"liberation school," Watts, 44
Lincoln, Abby, 147
Lincoln, Abraham, 228
Lincoln, C. Eric, 213, 217
Lincoln University, Pennsylvania, 252
Lindsay, Clyde, 183
Lindsay, John, 130, 131
Locke, Alain, 30, 207
Logan, Rayford, 30
Lorraine Motel, Memphis, 274
Los Angeles: BPP, 68, 69, 70–71, 190; US,
 68, 70–71, 245. *See also* UCLA; Watts

Orangeburg Massacre, South Carolina State
University, 6, 32–33, 272; armed
self-defense and, 153, 154; Crane and,
104; Greensboro funeral procession,
158; Howard and, 36, 39; Sellers, 32,
157, 234, 273; Southern University and,
171
Organization of American Historians, 262
Organization of Black American Culture,
105, 227
organizations. See Black student organizations; fraternities; professional
organizations; sororities; individual
organizations

Paige, Miles, 37–38
Palmer, Edward L. "Buzz," 104
Pan-Africanism, 4, 271; and African
liberation struggles, 235, 237, 238, 250;
Al-Wadi, 46; Black studies, 215, 242,
243, 249, 250, 254–55, 275; feminism
vs., 238; Fuller, 28; independent Black
institutions, 10, 225; Sixth Pan-African
Congress in Tanzania, 250; SOBU and,
235, 237, 238. See also African diaspora
Panthers. See Black Panther Party (BPP)
parents, Black student: college-educated, 4,
28–29; Howard, 37; Northwestern,
86–87, 88; SFSC, 43; Tascoe, 58. See
also Black student backgrounds
Parker, Elizabeth, 262
Parks, Gordon, 217
Parks, Rosa, 223
Paster, George, 133
Paterson, Basil A., 274
Paterson, Eva Jefferson, 86–87, 88fig, 274
patriarchy, 176; Black feminism and, 11,
257–58, 264; Black nationalist, 26, 226,
263; Black Power, 26–28; Marable's
"Groundings with My Sisters: Patriarchy
and the Exploitation of Black Women,"
264. See also Black male leadership;
Black men; Black nationalism
Patterson, Orlando, 196
Peck, George A., 116–17, 120–21
Peebles, Tim, 66
Pennsylvania: Black studies, 242, 252;
Cheyney State College, 40; Diopian
Institute for Scholarly Advancement in
Philadelphia, 245; Lincoln University,
252
People's College, 243
Perkins, Eric, 83, 85
Perry, Matthew, 156

perspective. See Black perspective
Peters, Erskine, 246
PhDs: Black, 64, 188, 201, 203, 218, 245;
Black studies, 275
Phoenix, Crane, 103, 104
Phylon, 209
Pile, Blanche, 121
Pile, Orlando, 117, 118, 119, 121, 137
"The Pill: Genocide or Liberation?" (Cade),
257–58
Pitts, James, 83, 190
Pittsburgh Courier, 251
Pitzer, 222
pluralism: Black perspective, 176; Black
Power, 4; Black studies, 248; educational
system, 143; Harvard Blacks, 198
Poitier, Sidney, 217
police, 233, 272; Affro-Arts Theater, 105;
vs. arsonists, 106; Brooklyn College,
120, 121–23; CCNY, 130, 131–32;
Greensboro, 158–60, 239; Hampton,
106; Northwestern and, 7, 85, 87–88,
92; SFSC, 7, 13, 52–53, 54, 58, 61–64,
64fig, 66, 71–72, 73; Southern
University, 165–67; UCLA, 190. See also
arrests/trials/sentences/imprisonment;
police violence
police violence, 160–72, 240, 272, 273;
Augusta, Georgia, 161; BPP and, 4–5,
161, 162; Brooklyn College, 121–23;
Columbia University, 7, 81, 87, 131;
Edwin Edwards on, 168; "genocide,"
161–62; Greensboro, 158–60; HBCUs,
3, 6, 9, 31–32, 38–40, 142–43, 153–73,
272, 273; Jackson State, 157, 161, 171,
172; Kent State, 157, 161, 171–72; Ohio
State, 160–61; Poor People's Campaign's
encampment (Resurrection City), 36;
SFSC, 7, 13, 52–53, 54, 62–64, 64fig,
71–72; torture ring in Chicago, 274;
urban unrest, 32. See also Orangeburg
Massacre
"Politics of the Attack on Black Studies"
(Allen), 200
Pontecorvo, Gillo, 23; Battle of Algiers,
23, 56, 84–85
Poor People's Campaign's encampment
(Resurrection City), 36
Porter, John, 105
Portuguese colonies, 235, 250
Potts, John, 154
Powell, Adam Clayton Jr., 125
Powell, Charles, 125
Powell, Charles M. Jr., 274

University of Bridgeport, 28
University of California: Educational
  Opportunity Program (EOP), 51–52;
  ethnic studies, 265; San Francisco
  School of Medicine, 274–75; Santa
  Barbara, 13, 55. *See also* Berkeley
  (University of California); UCLA
University of Chicago, 104, 109, 111,
  193, 227
University of Illinois: Chicago, 104, 106;
  Urbana, 204
University of Islam, Chicago, 103
University of Massachusetts: Amherst, 264,
  275, 276; Black studies, 181–82, 189,
  212, 219, 264, 275, 276; Du Bois
  papers, 189, 219; Shirley Graham Du
  Bois visit, 219
University of Michigan, Ann Arbor, 6,
  253–54
University of Mississippi, 16
University of North Carolina, Charlotte, 33
University of Oklahoma, 14, 23–24, 25
University of Pittsburgh, 205, 206, 258
University of the District of Columbia, 54
University of Wisconsin: Milwaukee, 263.
  See also Madison
Urbana, University of Illinois, 204
urban unrest, 22, 24, 82; admissions criteria
  and, 116; Black public affairs shows
  and, 214; Chicago, 83–84, 104;
  National Commission on the Causes
  and Prevention of Violence, 65, 157;
  police violence, 32; socioeconomic
  conditions and, 91; Watts rebellion,
  18, 32
US, 68, 69, 70–71, 245
Uzoigwe, Godfrey, 254

Vanderbilt, desegregation, 202
Vanguard Public Foundation, 273
Varnado, Jerry, at SFSC, 45; admissions
  programs, 52; arrested, 62, 66, 74;
  Experimental College, 47; strike, 45,
  56–57, 59, 66; and TWLF, 59; on
  women in BSU, 59
Vassar, Black female students, 22
Vazcko, Jim, 52
Venceremos, Redwood City, 224–25
Venceremos Brigade, Atlanta, 232
Vietnam war, 24, 57, 250, 271; Black
  nationalism and, 249, 271; BPP vs., 5;
  Murray and, 55; opposition to, 2–3, 35,
  46, 87, 148, 161, 182; SFSC strike and,
  60

violence, 24–25, 162; Brooklyn College
  students, 120; Carmichael on, 146;
  Howard, 37, 152; North Carolina A&T,
  158–59; SFSC strike students, 66,
  76–77; Southern University, 166; UCLA,
  68, 70–71; U.S. government as purveyor
  of, 24; by whites on nonviolent
  protesters in South, 13, 24. *See also*
  armed self-defense; assassinations;
  militancy; police violence; urban
  unrest
Voorhees College, Denmark, South
  Carolina, 153–57, 273
voting rights: Black women and, 262, 263;
  Du Bois and, 264; in U.S. Department of
  Education, 184

Waddell, Charles, 165
Wade, George, 122
Walker, Alice, 259–60
Waller, Jim, 239
Wallerstein, Immanuel, 254
Walls, Rufus "Chaka," 106
Wall Street Journal, 200
Walters, Ron, 195, 249
War of the Flea (Taber), 57
Washington, D.C.: Center for Black
  Education, 222, 235; Garrett, 54, 95,
  151; Poor People's Campaign's
  encampment (Resurrection City), 36;
  Revolutionary Workers League, 238;
  University of the District of Columbia,
  54, 95. *See also* Federal City College;
  Howard University
Washington, Booker T., 39, 108, 144
Washington, Harold, 80, 113
Washington, Mary Helen, 249
Washington Post, 200
Watson, Wayne, 85, 275
Watts: "liberation school," 44; rebellion,
  18, 32
Wayne, James, 170
Wayne State University, 205; Reginald
  Wilson speech, 204
WBBM, Chicago, 214
WCBS-TV, 25, 213, 214
Weaver, Fred, 220
Welker, Helen, 92
Wellesley College, 15, 17–18, 20, 40
Wells, Ida B., 276
Wesley, Charles, 217
Wesleyan, 17, 186
Western Addition Community Organiza-
  tion, 65

TEXT
10/13 Sabon

DISPLAY
Sabon

COMPOSITOR
Westchester Book Group

INDEXER
Barbara Roos

PRINTER AND BINDER
Maple-Vail Book Manufacturing Group